Disaster Dollars

Financial Preparation and Recovery for Towns, Businesses, Farms, and Individuals

JAMES L. JAFFE, J.D.

Copyright © 2015 James L. Jaffe, J.D.

All rights reserved. No part of this book may be reproduced, stored, or transmitted by any means—whether auditory, graphic, mechanical, or electronic—without written permission of both publisher and author, except in the case of brief excerpts used in critical articles and reviews. Unauthorized reproduction of any part of this work is illegal and is punishable by law. This material is not a substitute for financial, legal or other expert advice.

The author does not approve or endorse any particular agency, organization, program, individual or practice listed in this Manual. The purpose of this publication is to offer knowledge amassed from a range of sources which provide financial information on disasters. This knowledge may be especially helpful to individuals and organizations that develop financial aspects of a disaster plan and respond to the financial needs of disaster victims. The author did his best to verify the accuracy of all information at the time of printing; however, some data may have changed since then. Any omissions or oversights are unintentional and inadvertent.

ISBN: 978-1-4834-2833-8 (sc)
ISBN: 978-1-4834-2832-1 (e)

Library of Congress Control Number: 2015904296

Because of the dynamic nature of the Internet, any web addresses or links contained in this book may have changed since publication and may no longer be valid. The views expressed in this work are solely those of the author and do not necessarily reflect the views of the publisher, and the publisher hereby disclaims any responsibility for them.

Any people depicted in stock imagery provided by Thinkstock are models,
and such images are being used for illustrative purposes only.
Certain stock imagery © Thinkstock.

Cover pictures are from FEMA News Photos.

The 2003 Jefferson nickel is a United States Mint image.

Cover by Anne Beekman, F.M.A.

Lulu Publishing Services rev. date: 4/10/2015

Remember Every Nickel Counts

Acknowledgments

This Disaster Dollars Manual compiles materials garnered (i.e.: copied) from many federal government and other sources. Without the means to cut and paste material from the sources listed in this manual (thanks to whoever put that option in the "Word" software) this Disaster Dollars Manual might not have come into existence. This Disasters Dollars Manual does contain original research regarding present federal program mandates. It is important to thank the individuals and organizations who have contributed to this Disaster Dollars Manual.

Individuals, businesses, farms/ranches and communities are strongly encouraged to "localize" the content of this publication as appropriate so that the information better meets the specific needs of the affected population.

In emergency planning one size does not fit all do keep in mind during the preliminary stages of a project your goal. Rank predictions by occurrence, cost, and disruptive ability. First and foremost, PRIORITIZE: rank risks using tiered mitigation, in essence ask yourself if you take care of a big risk will that automatically take care of small risks, or are the risks independent of each other.

Note: Portions of the Disaster Dollars Manual will change with each disaster so update the contents. In particular, all cited legal authorities and web sites should be reviewed for revisions.

Contact the author with requests, comments or suggestions at Disasterdollars@gmail.com

Contents

Introduction 1

Before The Incident 3
    Individual/Family 3
        Cash 3
        Salaries and Wages 3
        Credit, Debit, and "Preloaded" Cards 4
            Credit Cards 4
            ATM and Debit Cards 4
        Insurance 5
        Deductibles and Exclusions 5
        Actual Cash Value and Replacement Cost Coverage 6
        Types of Insurance Policies for Homeowners, Renters and Condo Owners ... 6
        There are some special requirements regarding flood insurance 8
        Increased Cost of Compliance (ICC) Program 9
        Mortgage Payments and Condo Fees 10
        Recordkeeping 10

    Farm/Ranch Agriculture 12
        Farm/Ranch 12
        Cash 12
        Insurance 12
        Federal Crop Insurance 12
        Risk Management Agency (RMA) Insurance 13
        Actual Production History (APH) 14
        Actual Revenue History (ARH) 14
        Adjusted Gross Revenue (AGR) 14
        Area Risk Protection Insurance (ARPI) 14
        Commodity Exchange Price Provisions (CEPP) 14
        Group Risk Plan (GRP) 14
        Group Risk Income Protection (GRIP) 15

- Group Risk Income Protection - Harvest Revenue Option (GRIP-HRO) 15
- Rainfall Index (RI) 15
- Revenue Protection With Harvest Price Exclusion 16
- Vegetation Index (VI) 16
- Yield Protection 16
- Catastrophic Risk Protection Endorsement (CAT Coverage) 16
- High-Risk Alternate Coverage Endorsement (HR-ACE) 16
- Crop Hail Insurance 18
- Basic Hail Insurance Policy 18
- Crop Hail Endorsements 19
- Barn Endorsements (BE) 19
- Companion Hail (CP) 19
- Cotton Wind (CW) 19
- Oklahoma Added Perils (OW) 19
- Reject Coverage (RC) 19
- Sugar Beet Crusting, Freeze, and Wind Endorsement (SB) 20
- Tobacco Wind (with set up) (SU) 20
- Tobacco Theft (TT) 20
- Corn, Seed Corn, and Sweet Corn Wind Endorsement (WE) 20
- Cotton Escalator Buy-Out Option 20
- Replant Exclusion for Corn, Seed Corn, and/or Soybeans 20
- Seed Corn Endorsement 20
- Production Plan Hail Insurance (PP) 20
- Corn and Soybean Replant Endorsement (RG) 20

Noninsured Crop Disaster Assistance Program 21
- Eligible Producers 21
- Eligible Crops 21
- Eligible Causes of Loss 21
- Coverage Levels 22
- Applying for Coverage 22
- Service Fees and Premiums 22
- Coverage Period 23
- Information Required to Remain Eligible for NAP 23
- Reported Acreage and Production 24
- Providing Notice of Loss and Applying for Payment 24
- Defining a NAP Unit 25
- Information FSA Uses to Calculate Payment 25
- Payment Limitation 25
- 2008 Farm Act & the Agricultural Act of 2014 Changes 25
- Supplemental Agriculture Disaster Assistance Programs 25
- **Chart:** Program Summary 26

Record Keeping 27
- Production Records 27
- Financial Records 27

Ownership/Personal Records 28
National Animal Identification System (NAIS) 28

Small Businesses 29

Small Business 29
General Information on Likely Disasters 29
Cash 29
Salaries and Wages 30

Record Keeping 31
Paperless Recordkeeping 31
Check on Fiduciary Bonds 31
Update Emergency Plans 31
Insurance 31
Deductibles and Exclusions 32
Actual Cash Value and Replacement Cost Coverage 32
Special Requirements Regarding Flood Insurance 32
Voluntary Private Sector Preparedness Accreditation and Certification Program 33
Designation of Preparedness Standards 33
Other Business Preparedness Resources 34

Local Government 35

Local Government 35
Which Disaster to Plan For? 35
The Council for Excellence in Government has developed the following Emergency
  Management Financial Checklist for local governments 37
    1. Include Procurement and Financial Managers in Disaster Planning 37
    2. Relationships 37
    3. Memoranda of Understanding 37
    4. Collaboration - Government Must Work Across Organizational Boundaries 37
    5. Documentation of property and systems 37
    6. Practice, Practice, Practice 37
    7. Recovery 38
Pre Contract 38
Mutual Aid Agreements 38
    A. General 39
    B. Pre-Event Written Mutual Aid Agreements 39
    C. Post-Event Mutual Aid Agreements 40
Eligible Applicants 41
Cash on Hand 42

Insurance 43
National Flood Insurance Program (NFIP) 43
Hazard Mitigation 45
Flood Mitigation Assistance Program 46
Hazard Mitigation Grant Program 48

  Pre-Disaster Mitigation Grant Program (PDM) 48
  Repetitive Flood Claims Program (RFC) 50
  Severe Repetitive Loss Program (SRL) 51
  Increased Cost of Compliance Program (ICC) 52
  Chart: Hazard Mitigation Assistance (HMA) Program Eligible Projects 53
  Chart: Approved Mitigation Plan Requirement for Funding 53
  Chart: Percent of Federal/Non-Federal Share 54

After the Incident 55
Federal Emergency Management Agency (FEMA) 55
  Disclaimer 55
  Overview 55
  I. Declaration of a Disaster 56
    A. Local Disaster or State of Emergency 56
    B. Disaster Declaration Process for a Major Disaster 56
      1. State Action 56
      2. Federal Response 57
      3. Action by FEMA 57
    Presidential Declaration of Disaster 57
      1. Human Services (Individual Assistance) 57
      2. Infrastructure Assistance to State and Local Governments and Eligible Private Non-Profit Organizations (Public Assistance) 57
      3. Hazard Mitigation Grant Program for State and Local Governments and Eligible Private Non-Profit Organizations 57
    D. Deadlines for Individual Assistance Programs 57
    E. Denials and Appeals 58
    F. No Duplication of Benefits 58
    G. Sequence for Disaster Aid 58
    H. Cora Brown Fund 58
      1. Disaster Assistance 58
      2. Identification of Candidates for Assistance 59
  II. Who Can Get FEMA Assistance 59
    A. Eligibility for FEMA Assistance 59
    B. Aliens 60
    C. Red Cross or Voluntary Aid 60
  III. Deadlines For Applications 60
    A. FEMA Can Extend the Deadline 61
  IV. How Long Does It Take? 61
    A. To get help from FEMA 61
    B. After The Application is Submitted 61
  V. FEMA At Work 61
    A. Teleregistration and On-Line Registration 61
    B. FEMA Application Process 62
    C. Outreach Teams and Workshops 63

      D. DRCs -- Disaster Recovery Centers 63
      E. DRCs -- Crisis Counseling 63
      F. Individuals and Households Program (IHP) 63
      G. Voluntary Assistance Agencies (VOLAGs) at DRCs Including Legal Services 64
      H. The applicant does NOT have to own a business to apply for an SBA loan 64
      I. Removal of Debris 64
  VII. FEMA's Inspection, Verification, Recertification and Audit Process Consequences for Misuse 64
      A. Inspections 64
      B. Inspection Reports 65
      C. Audits 65
      D. Appeal Rights 65
      E. Right to an Authorized Representative 66
      F. Final Decision 66
      G. Recoupment 66
  Chart: Sequence of Delivery of Financial Assistance 67

Individual/Family 68
Individual/Family 68
  Chart: Application Deadlines for Individual Assistance Programs 68
Individuals and Households Program (IHP) 68
  Conditions & Limitations of FEMA IHP Assistance 70
      A. Non-discrimination 70
      B. Residency 70
      C. Supplemental Assistance 70
      D. Household Composition 70
      E. Type of Assistance 70
      F. Proper Use of Assistance 71
      G. Documentation 71
      H. Insurance 71
      I. Duration of Assistance 71
      J. Flood Insurance Requirements for Recipients of Federal Disaster Assistance 71
Initial Application To FEMA For an IHP Grant 72
  A. Application Information 72
  B. Application Deadline -- 60 Days 73
  C. Extenuating Circumstances 73
  D. Mandatory Application for All Available Assistance 73
  E. No Refusal of Other Assistance 73
  F. Only One Application Per Household 73
  G. Applicant Credit Requirements 73
  H. Applicant Collateral Requirement 74
  I. Term of Loan 74
  J. Denial of Benefits 74
  K. Appeal Rights 74

  1. Basic Reasons for an Appeal 74
  2. Inspection Reports 75
  3. Deadlines 75
  4. Right to an Authorized Representative 75
  5. Final Decision 76
  6. Recoupment 76

Types of Housing Assistance 76
 Information To Support An Application 77
  A. Home Owners 77
  B. Renters 77
  C. To receive money for repair or help with housing needs the applicant must first file a claim under any insurance policy they have 78
  D. If insurance settlement is insufficient to meet disaster-related damage or need 78
  E. Legal Presence Requirement for Disaster Housing Assistance (DHA) Eligibility 78

Temporary Housing (Homeowners and Renters) 78
 FEMA Housing Portal 78
 Transient Accommodations 79
 Residence in Unsafe Areas 79
 Deadline, Benefit Calculation and Duration 79
  Eligible Renters 79
  Homeowners 79
 Transient Accommodations 80
  A. Purpose 80
  B. Eligibility 80

Rental Assistance 80
 A. Initial and Continued Rental Assistance 80
  1. Initial Rental Assistance 80
  2. Continued Rental Assistance 80
 B. Eligibility 81
 C. Verification and Documentation 81
 D. Major Reasons for Denials 82
  1. Primary Residence 82
  2. Serious Disaster-Related 82
  3. Insurance Coverage 82
 E. Additional Benefits 83
  1. Security Deposits 83
  2. Essential Furniture 83

Home Repair Assistance (HRA) 83
 A. Eligibility for Home Repair Assistance 83
 B. Scope of Repairs 83
 C. Deadline, Amount of Grant, Duration 84
 D. Interrelationship with Existing Insurance 84
 E. Interaction With Other Disaster Programs 84
 F. Verification and Documentation 85

Mortgage Insurance for Homeowners who are Disaster Victims 85
Renters Personal Property Loans 86
    A. Eligibility 86
    B. Limitations and Conditions 86
Homeowner Assistance 87
    A. FEMA Outright Grants of Money 87
SBA Home Disaster Loans (HDL) 87
    A. Eligibility Requirements 87
    B. Amount of Loan 88
    C. Credit Requirements 88
    D. Collateral Requirement 88
    E Flood Insurance Requirement 88
    F. Moving and Storage 88
    G. Limitations on Use 89
    H. Waiting Period 89
    I. Home Loan Refinance by SBA 89
    J. Application Deadline 89
    K. Application Information 89
    L. Contractor's Estimates 90
    M. Insurance Settlement 90
    N. Relocation Allowance 90
    O. Interest Rate 90
    P. Insurance Requirements 91
    Q. Minimum Monthly Payment 91
    R. Refinancing 91
    S. Mitigation Measures 91
    T. Loan Modifications 92
    U. Additional Information 92
    V. Consequences for Misuse 92
    W. Reconsiderations and Appeals of Declined Applicants 92
    Chart: Home Repair and Replacement Grants and Loans 93
Other Needs Assistance (ONA) 94
    A. Personal Property (available to both tenants and homeowners) 94
    B. Transportation 94
    C. Medical and Dental Expenses 95
    D. Funeral and Burial Costs 95
    F. Cost Estimates and Other Necessary Expenses 95
    G. Limits on IHP Spending and Duplication of Benefits 96
    H. Calculation of Benefits 96
    I. Inspection Process 96
Other Housing Assistance 96
    A. United States Department of Agriculture: Rural Development Agency (RDA) 96
    B. Veterans Affairs 96

    C. Department of Housing and Urban Development 97
    D. Section 203(H) Mortgage Insurance for Homeowners... 97
    E. Aid to Families with Dependent Children (AFDC) 98
    F. Government Provided Temporary Housing 98
    G. Rural Development Agency 98
    Chart: Overview of FEMA Disaster Individual Assistance Programs Available for Renters
        and Homeowners 99

Insurance Payments to Homeowners and Condo Owners [Who gets to keep the money?] 101

Mortgage Payments During and After a Disaster 102
    Fannie Mae Disaster Assistance 103
        How to Respond in the Event of a Disaster 103
    Freddie Mac Disaster Assistance 104
        Some of the things Freddie Mac can do for disaster victims 104
        Freddie Mac Policies for Major Disaster Declarations 105
    Ginnie Mae Disaster Assistance 106
        Ginnie Mae Policies for Disaster Assistance.. 106
    FHA Mortgages 108
        Disaster Relief Options for FHA Homeowners 108
       If Your FHA Loan Was Current before the Disaster but Now You Can't Make
          Your Next Month's Payment.. 108
        FHA Mortgage Insurance for Disaster Victims Section 203(h) 109

National Student Loan Program (NSLP) 111
    1. Disaster Declared by The President 111
        Loans while in school 111
        Loans in "grace" 111
        If your loan is in an in-school or graduate fellowship deferment 111
        Loan in repayment 111
    2. Disaster Determined by the United States Department of Education 111
        If you are in school 112
        If your loan is in repayment 112
    3. Other Disasters 112
        If you are in school 112
        If your loan is in repayment 112
    4. For more information about these programs 112

Disaster Unemployment Assistance (DUA) 112
    In General.. 113
    A. Unemployed Workers 113
    B. Unemployed Self-Employed Individual 114
    C. Farm Workers 114
    D. Immigration Issues 114
    E. Injured Workers 114
        1. Disaster-Related Injuries 114
        2. Non disaster-Related Injuries.. 114
        3. Mental Stress 114

F. Deadlines, Benefit Period 115
G. Benefit Calculations and Amounts..115
    1. Employees...115
    2. Self-employed 115
    3. Calculating Benefits 115
H. Proof of Eligibility, Wages and Income 116
    a. Employees...116
    b. Self-Employed..116
I. DUA Limitations 117
J. Effect of Traditional Unemployment Insurance Disqualifications 117
    1. Able and Available for Work 117
    2. Voluntary Quit or Termination for Misconduct 117
K. Denials and Appeals..117
    1. Reasons for Denials..117
    2. Appeals Process..117
        a. First Stage...117
        b. Second Stage 118
L. Overpayments..118
Chart: Proof Requirements for the Recertification of Self-Employed Workers and
    Employees...118

Disaster Food Stamps 119
1. Disaster Food Stamp Benefits (D-SNAP) 119
Chart: Eligibility for SNAP & D-SNAP..119
    a. Eligibility.. 120
    b. Amount of Benefits 121
2. Replacement Food Stamps [To Replace Destroyed Food]... 121
    a. Eligibility.. 121
    b. Amount of Benefits 121
    c. Receipt of Food Stamps.. 122
3. Expedited Service Food Stamps 122
    a. In General.. 122
    b. Eligibility.. 122
        1. Income.. 122
        2. Families with High Housing Costs.. 122
        3. Families with Limited Funds 122
    c. Other Requirements... 123
        1. Identification/Application Requirements... 123
        2. Work Registration and Exemptions... 123
    d. Timeframe for Expedited Service Food Stamps 123
        1. Three-Day Processing Deadline.. 123
        2. Right To Apply at First Visit to the Welfare Office.. 123
Chart: Food Stamp Eligibility During a Disaster 124
Chart: Disaster Supplemental Nutrition Program Income Eligibility Standards and
    Allotments 125

  Chart: State Information/Hotline Numbers..126
Emergency Assistance to Needy Families with Children..**129**
 A. Kinds of emergencies covered 129
 B. Kinds of assistance provided to meet emergency situations 129
 C. Amount of assistance 129
 D. Kinds of services provided to meet the emergency situations 129
  Chart: Public Assistance and Disaster Assistance Programs for Disaster Victims 131
Supplemental Security Income **132**
 A. Eligibility...132
  1. In General..132
  2. Definition of Disability 133
  3. Income and Resources...133
 B. Program Benefit Levels...133
  SSI Emergency Advance Payments 133
  1. Emergency..133
  2. Application Must be on File with SSA 134
  3. SSI Immediate Payment Procedure 134
   a. Critical Payments..134
   b. Immediate Payment -- Same-Day Payments..134
   c. During Disasters 134
   d. Adverse Public Relations Problem 134
Rural Assistance **134**
 Section 502 Loans 135
 Section 504 Loans and Grants..136
  Chart: Summary of Differences Between Section 504 Loans and Grants.............................138

Farm/Ranch..140
Farm/Ranch..140
 Overview 140
 Types of Assistance...140
 Prerequisite to Assistance:...141
 Emergency Farm Loans 142
 Livestock Indemnity Program (LIP) Overview..143
 Livestock Forage Disaster Program (LFP)..149
 Chart: Livestock Payment Rates 152
 Emergency Assistance Program for Livestock, Honey Bees, and Farm-Raised Fish (ELAP)
  Overview 153
Livestock Feed Payment Calculations 156
 Orchard and Nursery Tree Assistance Program (TAP)..160
 Emergency Forest Restoration Practices 162
 Emergency Haying and Grazing...163
 Emergency Conservation Program (ECP)...164
 Be so costly to repair that Federal assistance is or will be required to return the land to
  productive agricultural use..165

Chart: Summary of Farm/Ranch Disaster Programs 167
Income Tax Treatment of Crop Insurance and Crop Disaster Payments 170
How To Postpone Reporting Of Crop Insurance Proceeds 171

Business 172
U.S. Small Business Administration Disaster Loan Program 172
Overview 172
Business Physical Disaster Loans 174
1. Eligibility 174
2. Verification and Documentation 174
3. Credit Requirements 174
4. Collateral Requirement 174
5. Term of Loan 175
Economic Injury Disaster Loans 175
1. Eligibility 175
2. Verification and Documentation 175
3. Credit Requirements 175
4. Collateral Requirement 175
5. Interest Rates 176
6. Immigration Status 176
7. Refinancing 176
Current Interest Rates 176
Military Reservist Economic Injury Disaster Loans 176
Disbursement of Funds 177
Essential Employee 177
Substantial Economic Injury 177
Small Business 177
Credit Requirements 177
Collateral Requirements 177
Interest Rate 177
Loan Term 177
Loan Amount Limit 177
Insurance Requirements 178
Filing Requirements 178
Contact 178
Fisheries Disaster Relief 178
Money 178
Objectives 178
Uses and Use Restrictions 179
How the Process Begins 179
Applicant Eligibility 179
Beneficiary Eligibility 179
Credentials/Documentation 179
Application Procedure 179

  Criteria for Selecting Proposals...180
  Only One Positive Determination per Disaster 180
  Award Procedure 180
  Deadlines 180
  Formula and Matching Requirements...180
  Length and Time Phasing of Assistance..180
  Reports...180
  Audits...181
  Records 181
  Regulations, Guidelines and Literature 181
  Range and Average of Financial Assistance 181
  NOAA Regional or Local Office Contacts 181
  NOAA Headquarters Office Contacts...181
How It all Really Works...181
  Initiating a request for a fishery resource disaster..181
  Necessary Information 182
  The Three Prong Test 183

Local Government...184
Government 184
  Cash 184
  First Thing to Do...184
  FEMA..184
  A. Public Assistance: Local, State, Tribal and Non-Profit..185
    Eligibility..186
    Eligible Applicants 186
    Eligible Facilities 187
    Restrictions 187
    Eligible Work 188
    Other federal agency (OFA) programs 188
    Negligence..188
    Special considerations requirements 188
    Categories of Work 188
    Emergency Work 188
    Category A: Debris Removal...188
    Category B: Emergency Protective Measures...188
    Permanent Work...188
    Category C: Roads and Bridges 188
    Category D: Water Control Facilities..188
    Category E: Buildings and Equipment..189
    Category F: Utilities..189
    Category G: Parks, Recreational Facilities, and Other Facilities 189
    Eligible Costs..189
    Reasonable costs can be established through...189

  Debris Removal 189
    Private Property Debris Removal 191
    FEMA Public Assistance Grant Funding for Debris Removal 191
    Costs Must Be Reasonable 191
    Applicant Resources 191
    Mutual Aid Agreements 192
    Documentation 192
    Duplication of Benefits 192
    Insurance Settlements 192
    Salvage Value 193
    Debris Monitoring Roles and Responsibilities 193
    Monitoring Contracts 197
    Reporting Requirements & Performance Measures 198
    Contract Procurement Requirements 199

Local Governments Reimbursement Program for Hazardous Substance Releases 199
USDA Emergency Watershed Protection Program 201
Emergency Watershed Protection Program - Floodplain Easement Option (EWP-FPE) 202
Environmental and Historic Preservation Special Considerations 204
  National Environmental Policy Act (NEPA) 204
  Clean Water Act 204
  Clean Air Act 204
  Coastal Barrier Resources Act 205
  Resource Conservation and Recovery Act 205
  Endangered Species Act 205
  National Historic Preservation Act 205
  Coastal Zone Management Act 205
  Fish and Wildlife Coordination Act 205
  Wild and Scenic Rivers Act 205
  Executive Orders 205

Record Keeping 205
  Government Officers Finance Association Recommendations 206
    1. Establish Formal Policies and Procedures for the documentation of disaster-related costs 206
    2. Ensure Adequate Detail to Support Claims 207
  Department of Homeland Security, Office of Inspector General Recommendations 207
  FEMA Forms Governmental Agencies and Non-Profits must utilize 208

Government Audits After the Grant Has Been Received (and most likely spent) 210
  A. Poor Project Accounting 210
  B. Unsupported Costs 210
  C. Duplication of Benefits 210
  D. Excessive Equipment Charges 210
  E. Excessive Labor and Fringe Benefit Charges 210
  F. Unrelated Project Charges 211
  G. Unapplied Credits 211

  H. Excessive Administrative Charges 211
  I. Poor Contracting Practices 211

Record Keeping, Audits & Income Tax Issues 212
Rules to live by 212
Stafford Act Requirements...212
  Stafford Act regulations relating to financial records... 212
    44 C.F.R. 206.4 State emergency plans 212
    Sec. 13.1 Purpose and scope of this part 213
    Sec. 13.20 Standards for financial management systems 213
    Sec. 13.41 Financial reporting 214
    Sec. 13.42 Retention and access requirements for records 216
    Sec. 13.21 Payment..218
    Sec. 13.22 Allowable costs 220
    Sec. 13.23 Period of availability of funds 220
    Sec. 13.24 Matching or cost sharing... 221
    Sec. 13.25 Program income... 223
    Sec. 13.26 Non-Federal audit... 225
    Sec. 13.30 Changes 225
    Sec. 13.35 Subawards to debarred and suspended parties 227
    Sec. 13.36 Procurement... 227
    Sec. 13.37 Subgrants 236
    Sec. 13.40 Monitoring and reporting program performance............................... 237
    Sec. 13.50 Closeout... 237
    44 C.F.R. § 206.14 Criminal and civil penalties 237
Single Audit Act [31 U.S.C. § 7502] 238
  Audit requirements 238
  Single Audit Act Regulations and Requirements imposed by the Director of OMB............ 239
  Chart: Overview of the Single Audit Process 240
Income Tax Issues 240
  Obtaining Copies of Income Tax Returns 240
  IRS publications and web sites regarding disasters 241
    For Individuals and Businesses..241
    For Tax Professionals 241
    Disaster Assistance Self-Study 241
    For Charitable Organizations..241
    For assistance and additional information, use these resources........................241
Income Tax Aspects of the Emergency Economic Stabilization Act of 2008....................242
  National Disaster Relief... 242
IRS answers to disaster income tax questions 242
  Are mitigation payments under Code Section 139 tax free?.. 242
  Do you have to subtract FEMA payments, such as the $10,000 and $5,200 payments, in arriving at the calculation for your net casualty loss? 242

How are FEMA "Individuals and Households Program" payments treated for income tax purposes? 243

An individual whose principal residence is damaged or destroyed by a disaster receives a FEMA IHP repair assistance or replacement assistance payment and/or insurance proceeds that exceed his or her adjusted tax basis in the damaged or destroyed principal residence. How is this treated for federal income tax purposes? 243

Record Reconstruction 244
Personal Residence/Real Property 244
Vehicles 245
Personal Property 246
Business Records 246
Locate Unknown Insurance Policies 247
Living Individual's Insurance 247
Deceased Person's Life Insurance 247

Credit Reports 248
a. Legal Authority 248
b. Incomplete or Inaccurate Information 248
c. Obtaining a Credit Report 249
d. Fraud Alert Messages 249
Consumer Credit Reporting Agencies 250
Experian 250
Equifax 250
TransUnion 251
Stolen Checks and Checks Using Your Identity 251
TeleCheck 251
Cetergy, Inc 252

Documents 252
Federal Documents 253
A. Federal Information Center 253
B. Social Security Cards 253
C. Medicare Cards 253
D. Veterans Administration 253
E. Citizenship and Immigration Services (USCIS) 253
Note on Replacing a "Green Card" 254
F. Passports and Department of State Documents 254
Other Records 254
A. Bank Accounts/ATM Cards 254
B. Credit Cards 254
C. Birth, Marriage and Death Certificates 254
D. Driver's License 254
E. Wills 254
F. Deeds 254
G. Court Records 255

    H. Food Stamp Identification, Medicaid Cards/Stickers 255
    I. Unemployment Insurance or State Disability 255

Handy Dandy FEMA, SBA & Farm Service Agency Disaster Forms 256
FEMA Disaster Assistance Forms 256
  Farm Services Agency Disaster Assistance Forms 256
  SBA Disaster Assistance Forms 257

Publications Regarding the Economic Aspects Of Disaster Planning, Response & Mitigation .. 259
Farmer/Rancher 259
  Farmers' Guide to Disaster Assistance (Sixth Edition, 2008) 259
USDA Farm Service Agency Emergency Conservation Program Manual 259
  Emergency Conservation Program Handbook 1-ECP (Revision) 259
    Emergency Forest Restoration Handbook 259
    Livestock Disaster Assistance Programs Handbook 259
    Tree Assistance Program Handbook 259
    Disaster Designations Handbook 260
    Program Appeals, Mediation, and Litigation Handbook 260
USDA Food & Nutrition Service 260
  Food Distribution Disaster Assistance 260
  EBT Disaster Plan Guide 260
USDA Rural Housing Service 260
  The "Handbook" {HB-1-3550) (called "The Field Office handbook") 260
FEMA 260
  Are You Ready 260
  Emergency Management Guide for Business and Industry 260
  FEMA 321 Public Assistance Policy Digest 260
  FEMA 322 Public Assistance Guide 260
  FEMA 323 Applicant Handbook 260
  FEMA 325 Debris Management Guide 261
  Hazard Mitigation Assistance Program Guidance Pre-Disaster Mitigation, Flood
    Mitigation Assistance, Repetitive Flood Claims, Severe Repetitive Loss 261
  Local Multi-Hazard Mitigation Planning Guidance, July 1, 2008 261
  Sample Local Mitigation Plan Scope of Work for Mitigation Grant Application 261
  National Flood Insurance Program Community Rating System Coordinator's Manual
    FIA-15/2006 261
  Applicant's Guide to the Individuals & Households Program 261
  FEMA 9500 Policy Publication 261
  HAZUS-MH [FEMA's Software Program for Estimating Potential Losses from Disasters] . 264
Small Business Administration 265
  Disaster Recovery Plan, 2012 265
Social Media sites that can be used before during and after a disaster 266

Miscellaneous **266**
    FEMA Hurricane Response web site 267
        Before a Hurricane 267
        During a Hurricane 267
        After a Hurricane 268
    FEMA Tornado Response and Recovery web site 269
        Before a Tornado 269
        During a Tornado 270
        After a Tornado 271
    FEMA Earthquake Response and Recovery web site 272
        Before an Earthquake 272
        During an Earthquake 273
        After an Earthquake 274
    FEMA Wildfire Response and Recovery web site 275
        Before a Wildfire 275
        During a Wildfire 276
        Surviving a Wildfire 277
        After a Wildfire 277

Introduction

Having watched the town I live in (Findlay, Ohio) struggle with the aftermath of a 100 year flood, and continue to struggle several years later, it is obvious that the financial aspects of emergency management demands greater emphasis when planning and responding to "incidents". Thus the concept for this material was born.

The goal of this material is to acquaint the reader with financial preplanning for incidents and disasters, and responding to the financial aftermath of these situations with the goal of lessening their financial impact. As to how much preplanning and response is sufficient, depends upon the individual situation as "one size fits all" does not apply in disaster planning and response.

As a friend once said, "Sufficient is like effective. You must first ask 'sufficient for what purpose'. That is, to be sufficient it must be suitable to the purpose, at the time, and under the circumstances since these all vary independently. A life ring may be sufficient for a swimming pool but most of us would expect a lifeboat on a cruise ship. On the other hand, if the ship is going down and I have no lifeboat then, I'll take the life ring!"

This material is divided into sections dealing with individuals, farms/ranches, businesses and local governments.

One thing became very clear in preparing this material and that is; when you have a disaster and are applying for disaster relief funds you must be very persistent and ready, willing and able to follow complex time consuming requirements. In essence you must play well with others while coping with the emotional aspects of a disaster and while involved in a bureaucratic setting.

One point consistently made by all who were involved in with dealing with FEMA during and after a disaster was the lack of continuity in the FEMA decision making process. One town mayor said he thought FEMA plays "good cop-bad cop". Early on in a disaster FEMA staff is supportive, and say "good job, that expense is covered". Then later, during the recovery/remediation period, FEMA staff then says "sorry that expense is not allowable". The upshot is that you must be very careful in fully documenting all that is done, and understand the FEMA process. So one thing you will probably end up doing is making checklists: checklists of things to do, checklists of forms, and checklists of documentation. Checklists, easy to say and often difficult to create. An excellent web site on how to make a checklist is found at: http://www.wmich.edu/evalctr/checklists/

James L. Jaffe, J.D.

In planning for the economic impact of a disaster[1], weigh the frequency of the loss against the severity of the loss to determine what steps, if any, to take to minimize the loss. There are three basic economic phases to disasters that we are concerned with in this manual. They are, planning for, response to, and rehabilitation from the economic impact of disasters.

---
[1] A disaster in terms of this manual means any economic loss caused by man-made or naturally occurring events that is not part of the "normal and usual" day-to-day risks we humans take. A disaster can be a loss to one person, a single business, an entire community or a region. "Disaster" is also a relative term, your neighbor's house burns down and that is "too bad", your house burns down and that is a disaster.

Before The Incident

Individual/Family

During our day-to-day lives individuals and families seldom, if at all, think about the financial aspects of a disaster. So let's look at these issues one at a time.

Cash

In a disaster electricity will probably be out, off, or shut down, which means that ATM machines will not work, and stores can't process debit, credit, and preloaded "money cards." Cash will be king!

In today's world we seldom pay cash for gas, food, or other purchases works as long as the person from whom we are buying the goods or services will accept our credit card. In a disaster when electric power is down or a computer system is not working, cash is king. Individuals and families should review their emergency needs for a week (including pets) and estimate how much cash is needed on hand to cover that period if forced to evacuate. Keeping that amount of cash in a "grab and go" box at home is a smart plan. Thus, should residents have to evacuate during an emergency, they don't have to worry about whether or not their credit cards are usable. Keeping money in small denominations, ones, fives and tens, is also a wise move. Sometimes emergencies happen when individuals are not home, so they may want to think about keeping some case in their wallet or on their person at all times as an emergency fund. Since public pay telephones are still around keep one or two rolls of quarters for their use is prudent.

Also, cell phones may not be rechargeable due to electrical outages, so keeping an extra cell phone charger in a vehicle is important.

Salaries and Wages

Most of us work for wages. In a disaster if you can't get to work, or your employer is shut down, what happens to our wages?

Governmental agencies and larger companies generally have written policies regarding when and how employees get paid during a disaster. If employees are on duty during a disaster their employer will pay them. If employees are on restricted stand-by duty, that is they have to remain ready to work and are not free to go about their personal business, their employer will generally pay for that time. If their employer restricts their freedom on stand-by duty during a disaster, and then refuses to pay for that time, they need to check with their state employment agency. But if employees are not on duty during a disaster, the question to ask is will their employer allow the use of vacation and sick time to stay on the payroll. Since there is no standard answer to this question employees need to find out their employer's policy on these matters.

James L. Jaffe, J.D.

If an employer does not allow employees to use vacation and sick time to stay on the payroll during a disaster, then employees need to save enough money to pay the bills during the time they expect to be out of work. [See page 112 for Disaster Unemployment Benefits]

Past experience of employees in your community, in your trade or profession, can be used as an indicator of how long they have to wait before being called back to work. Knowing this, employees can plan for the loss of income during a disaster. Saying that employees should have enough money in the bank for this eventuality is easy to say, but putting enough money in the bank to take care of loss of income during a disaster is almost impossible for most of us. Individuals and families should consider other sources of emergency money, credit cards, and short term loans. Whatever you do, planning ahead, especially when living in an area that is prone to hurricanes, floods, storms and other disasters that occur on a regular basis is a wise investment of time.

Credit, Debit, and "Preloaded" Cards

Credit Cards

In a disaster there is always the possibility that individuals will lose their wallet or purse along with their credit cards. The loss of a credit card is important and should be reported to the issuing institution as soon as discovered. Keeping a list of credit cards in a "grab and go" box, including the card number and the telephone number to report a missing or stolen card is the best proactive practice one can adopt.

Cardholders are contractually liable for debts incurred by the use of the credit card. Credit card users even if authorized to use the card, are not liable for such debts. A cardholder always has actual authority to use the card. As a general rule, a cardholder is not liable for unauthorized use of a credit card.

There is no liability for unauthorized use of a credit card, except where the card is an "accepted credit card," then liability is not in excess of $50. A cardholder is not liable for charges when another person forges the cardholder's name on a credit card application, and the cardholder knows nothing about the credit card until he or she receives the monthly statement.

If the cardholder reports that a card is lost before the credit cards are used, the card issuer cannot hold him or her responsible for any unauthorized charges.

If a thief uses a credit card before it is reported missing, the most a cardholder will owe for unauthorized charges is *$50 per card*.

If the loss involves a credit card number, but not the card itself, the cardholder has *no liability* for its unauthorized use.

ATM and Debit Cards

As with credit cards, keeping a list of ATM cards in a "grab and go" box, including the card number and the telephone number to report a missing or stolen card is the best proactive practice one can adopt.

Your liability under federal law for unauthorized use of your ATM or debit card depends on how quickly you report the loss.

IF a cardholder reports an ATM or debit card missing before it's used without their permission, the Electronic Funds Transfer Act says the card issuer cannot hold the cardholder responsible for any unauthorized transfers.

1. If unauthorized use occurs before the cardholder reports it liability under federal law depends on how quickly the loss is reported.

   For example,

   a. If cardholders *report the loss* within two business days after realizing the card is missing, they will not be responsible for more than *$50* for unauthorized use.

   b. If cardholders *don't report the loss* within two business days after discovering the loss, they can lose up to *$500* because of an unauthorized transfer.

   c. Cardholders risk unlimited loss if they fail to report an unauthorized transfer *within 60 days* after their bank statement containing unauthorized use is mailed to them; thus losing all the money in their bank account and the unused portion of their overdraft protection.

   d. For unauthorized transfers involving only the debit card number (not the loss of the card), cardholders are liable only for transfers that occur *after 60 days* following the mailing of their bank statement which contains the unauthorized use, and occurs before the loss is reported.

Insurance

Insurance is another way to protect yourself and your assets from loss. But remember insurance comes with a deductible, which is the amount of loss you are personally responsible for before insurance begins to pay.

Basically, insurance is akin to gambling. You are betting that you will have a loss, and the insurance company is betting that you won't. If the law, your mortgage holder or lender requires insurance then that's that. But otherwise you need to decide if you should have insurance for a particular risk, put money aside to cover the loss, or do nothing.

Often in a disaster, insurance company staff opens an emergency claims facility at a disaster location to promptly pay policyholders for disaster losses, so they are often the fastest means of obtaining payment for losses. However be cautious when accepting a quick insurance payment, an issue we will discuss in the section regarding insurance issues after a disaster.

One point to check regarding your homeowners insurance policy is whether or not it will pay for living expenses if you are forced out of your home due to a potential disaster, or a disaster declaration by the authorities or actual damage to your home or condo.

Always remember that if you just leave your home or condo because the authorities recommend it, your insurance probably will not cover the expenses associated with your temporary move. But, *if the authorities order you to evacuate* your residence due to an impending disaster such as flood or storm then your homeowners insurance may pay your living expenses for a limited time. Generally speaking, your homeowners policy will pay living expenses for different lengths of time depending upon if your residence is damaged/destroyed versus if you evacuate due to the authorities ordering an evacuation.

Deductibles and Exclusions

Two key items to take into account when discussing insurance policies are deductibles and exclusions. A deductible is the basic amount of a loss that insurance won't pay. For example, if you have earthquake insurance and your house is destroyed by an earthquake your policy may pay for the loss of your house except for the first 10% of the loss. You are responsible for that amount, which is called the deductible.

Exclusions, on the other hand, are those events or items that your insurance policy doesn't cover. So think about how you plan to cover the deductible and exclusions contained in your insurance policy. Do you put money aside on a regular basis to cover out of pocket costs of a loss, or just hope it doesn't happen? Or hope insurance covers enough of the loss that you can make up the difference with the money you have on hand when disaster strikes.

Actual Cash Value and Replacement Cost Coverage

A homeowner's and condo owner's insurance policy covers the cost of replacing items destroyed in one of two ways.

The more common way is by reimbursing the home/condo owner for *ACTUAL CASH VALUE* (ACV).

Actual cash value is the value of the insured item immediately before it is destroyed. If your TV cost $1,000.00 three years ago and now it's worth is $200.00, and the cost of a new replacement TV is $800.00, you will get $200.00 (less your deductible) as the actual cash value of the TV. On the other hand, if you have a *REPLACEMENT VALUE* insurance policy you will be paid the cost of a replacement TV which is $800.00 (less your deductible). But, in no event will insurance pay more than the policy limits.

Types of Insurance Policies for Homeowners, Renters and Condo Owners

A homeowner, renter, or condo owner should have a basic understand of the different types of insurance policies that are available. The following explanation of different types of homeowner, renter, and condo owner insurance policies which is from the Insurance Information Institute's web site http://www.iii.org/article/are-there-different-types-policies provides a basic description of standard homeowner and renter insurance policies, remember these are subject to change so talk to your insurance agent.

"If you own your home
If you own the home you live in, you have several policies to choose from. The most popular policy is the HO-3, which provides the broadest coverage. Owners of multi-family homes generally purchase an HO-3 with an endorsement to cover the risks associated with having renters live in their homes.

HO-1: Limited coverage policy
This "bare bones" policy covers you against the first 10 disasters. It's no longer available in most states.

HO-2: Basic policy
A basic policy provides protection against all 16 disasters. There is a version of HO-2 designed for mobile homes.

HO-3: The most popular policy
This "special" policy protects your home from all perils except those specifically excluded. (Click on the link below for a sample HO-3 form; you will need Acrobat which you can download, free of charge, from the Adobe Web site.

Paper: Homeowners 3 - Special Form (PDF)

HO-8: Older home
Designed for older homes, this policy usually reimburses you for damage on an actual cash value basis which means replacement cost less depreciation. Full replacement cost policies may not be available for some older homes.

If you rent your home

HO4-Renter
Created specifically for those who rent the home they live in, this policy protects your possessions and any parts of the apartment that you own, such as new kitchen cabinets you install, against all 16 disasters.

If you own a co-op or a condo

H0-6: condo/co-op
A policy for those who own a condo or co-op, it provides coverage for your belongings and the structural parts of the building that you own. It protects you against all 16 disasters.

Your level of coverage

Regardless of whether you are an owner or renter, you have the following three options:

Actual cash value.
This type of policy pays to replace your home or possessions minus a deduction for depreciation.

Replacement cost.
The policy pays the cost of rebuilding/repairing your home or replacing your possessions without a deduction for depreciation.

Guaranteed or extended replacement cost.
This policy offers the highest level of protection. A guaranteed replacement cost policy pays whatever it costs to rebuild your home as it was before the fire or other disaster–even if it exceeds the policy limit. This gives you protection against sudden increases in construction costs due to a shortage of building materials after a widespread disaster or other unexpected situations. It generally won't cover the cost of upgrading the house to comply with current building codes. You can, however, get an endorsement (or an addition to) your policy called Ordinance or Law to help pay for these additional costs. A guaranteed replacement cost policy may not be available if you own an older home.

Some insurance companies offer an extended, rather than a guaranteed replacement cost policy. An extended policy pays a certain percentage over the limit to rebuild your home. Generally, it is 20 to 25 percent more than the limit of the policy. For example, if you took out a policy for $100,000, you could get up to an extra $20,000 or $25,000 of coverage.

Even though a guaranteed/extended replacement cost policy may be a bit more expensive, it offers the best financial protection against disasters for your home. These coverages, however, may not be available in all states or from all companies."

The best internet site I have found for individuals and families' regarding disaster preparation and insurance issues is http://www.flash.org/

This site is maintained by "The non-profit Federal Alliance for Safe Homes (FLASH®) is the country's leading consumer advocate for strengthening homes and safeguarding families from natural and manmade disasters." This site specifically explains what is covered by different types of homeowner and renter insurance policies. The following link will take the reader to this list of insurance related topics which are listed below: http://homeownersinsuranceguide.flash.org/knowyourchoices.htm

A homeowner's guide to natural disasters.

Dear Homeowner
Courting Disaster: Perils Discussed in this Guide
Sources & Types of Homeowners Insurance: Know the Basics

Insurance Coverage: Know Your Choices
Ways You May Be Able to Affect Your Premium
Availability of Insurance
Reduce Potential Damages and Premiums
Preparing for a Flood
How Do I File a Homeowners Claim?
Record Keeping
Some Final Thoughts

Learning the Language: Glossary of Terms

An excellent series of questions that should be answered when preparing for a disaster can be found at The Backup Plan https://rnn10.wordpress.com/tag/how-much-money-do-i-need-in-a-disaster/

The suggested questions to ask yourself are:

1. If you needed to leave your area due to a disaster evacuation, could you still access your money in a different neighborhood? A different city? A different state?
2. Do you know how much money you can take out of your primary bank's ATM at one location? During one 24 hour period?
3. If you could only use the cash you have in your home for one to three weeks, how much cash would you and your family need?
4. Do you know how much credit you have available on your credit cards? Do you know if it's possible to get an emergency increase? If so, do you know how to get one?
5. If there was a disaster in your geographical area that affected your home as well as your workplace, would you still receive a paycheck from your company? Do you receive you check via direct deposit, via mail or do you physically pick it up?

There are some special requirements regarding flood insurance

The Flood Disaster Protection Act of 1973 (42 U.S.C. 400i *et seq.*) requires that Federal agencies and federally insured or regulated lenders require flood insurance on all grants and loans for acquisition or construction of buildings in designated Special Flood Hazard Areas (SFHAs) in communities that participate in the National Flood Insurance Program (NFIP). This requirement is referred to as the Mandatory Flood Insurance Purchase Requirement. Local governments will advise a building owner if flood insurance is required.

NOTE:

If you own your home outright this insurance is not mandatory, but it may be a good idea if you live in a flood prone area.

Any property owner of insurable property may purchase this flood insurance coverage, provided that the community in which the property is located is participating in the NFIP.

Flood insurance under the NFIP is sold through two mechanisms:

1. *through state-licensed property and casualty insurance agents and brokers who deal directly with FEMA; and*

2. *through private insurance companies with a program known as "Write Your Own" (WYO).*

The premium charged for NFIP flood coverage by a WYO Company is the same as that charged by the Federal Government through the direct program.

The Standard Flood Insurance Policy (SFIP) is issued on one of three available policy forms, depending on the occupancy of the building, to provide coverage for the peril of flood.

- The Dwelling Form is used to insure 1-4 family buildings & individual residential condominium units.

- The General Property Form covers residential buildings of more than 4 families as well as non-residential risks.

- The Residential Condominium Building Association Policy (RCBAP) Form insures associations under the condominium form of ownership.

Flood insurance is available to 1-4 family residential buildings, small businesses, and churches other residential properties, other business properties, agricultural properties, properties occupied by private nonprofit organizations, and properties owned by State or local governments.

Increased Cost of Compliance (ICC) Program[2]

Flood insurance policyholders in high-risk areas, also known as Special Flood Hazard Areas, can get up to $30,000 of ICC coverage to help pay the costs to bring their home or business into compliance with their community's floodplain ordinance.

There are four options you can take to comply with your community's floodplain management ordinance and help reduce your future flood damage.

1. Elevation. This raises your home or business to or above the flood elevation level adopted by your community.

2. Relocation. This moves your home or business out of harm's way.

3. Demolition. This tears down and removes flood-damaged buildings.

4. Floodproofing. This option is available primarily for nonresidential buildings. It involves making a building watertight through a combination of adjustments or additions of features to the building that reduces the potential for flood damage.

You can file a claim for Increased Cost of Compliance coverage in two instances:

1. If the municipality determines that the home or business is damaged by flood to the point that repairs will cost 50 percent or more of the building's pre-damage market value. This is called substantial damage.

2. If your community has a repetitive loss provision in its floodplain management ordinance and determines that your home or business was damaged by a flood two times in the past 10 years, where the cost of repairing the flood damage, on the average, equaled or exceeded 25 percent of its market value at the time of each flood. Additionally, there must have been flood insurance claim payments for each of the two flood losses. This is called repetitive damage.

The ICC claim is adjusted separately from the flood damage claim filed under the Standard Flood Insurance Policy.

How to Apply

A claim can only be filed if the municipality determines that the home or business has been substantially damaged or repetitively damaged by a flood. This determination is made when upon application for a building permit to begin repairing the home or business.

Once a determination has been made that the property qualifies for an ICC claim, contact the insurance company or agent who wrote the flood policy to file an ICC claim.

---

[2] http://www.fema.gov/national-flood-insurance-program-2/increased-cost-compliance-coverage

A partial payment will be made once the claims representative has a copy of the signed contract for the work, a permit from the municipality to do the work, and a signed ICC Proof of Loss. If the work is not completed, you must return any partial payment to the insurer.

Upon completion of the work certificate of occupancy or a confirmation letter must be submitted to the claims representative, then the insurer will pay the final installment in full.

Mortgage Payments and Condo Fees

Since 2002 homeownership as a percentage of total dwellings in the United States has remained in the 67%-68% range[3]. Since most of us own our home, along with the outfit holding the mortgage, we need to be aware of what the mortgage agreement says.

Generally speaking, unless you obtain a forbearance agreement from your lender, you must continue to pay your mortgage, regardless of whether your residence is destroyed or damaged. So you should think about mortgage insurance, or have enough money saved to continue to make payments during a disaster.

With regard to homeowners' association fees or insurance premiums, you should review the language of your association's by-laws. Generally, however, to the extent that you still have some property affected by the activities of the homeowners' association, it is likely in your best interests to pay the amounts owed during a disaster. Again you may want to look to insurance to cover that cost, or have money put aside.

Recordkeeping

For preplanning purposes keep a record, in your "grab and go" box, of your credit cards, ATM / Debit cards and insurance policies so you can obtain any replacement credit cards and notify your insurance company of any losses. Also include a record of all monthly payments you make, such as mortgage, car loans, insurance, bank loans, and credit cards. That way you can contact the lender when you are forced out of your home during a disaster. Of course, on-line or automatic payments and automatic payments can ease this burden. The problem with automatic payments is that you better have money in the bank to cover the payments, or have a credit line that the bank can use to cover the payments if there are insufficient funds in your account. If you have automatic payments and your income stops during a disaster, then you will want to notify your bank as soon as possible to halt the automatic pay provision.

Alex White of Virginia Cooperative Extension[4] suggests keeping a kit with all the necessary financial information. This "kit will contain a lot of personal information that should be "for your eyes only." Be sure to keep your Emergency Financial Kit in a safe, secure place at home to prevent it from falling into the wrong hands; however, be sure that you can get to your EFK in a hurry in the event of an emergency."

Suggested items to include in your Emergency Financial Kit are:

- Copy of your Power of Attorney
- Copy of your Advance Medical Directive (living will)
- Copy of your will
- Copy of your birth certificate
- Copy of your Social Security card

---

[3] http://www.census.gov/housing/hvs/

[4] Disaster Preparation From a Financial Standpoint, Farm Business Management Update, June 2002.

- Copies of deed and titles to property
- List of contacts (names, phone numbers, mailing addresses, e-mail addresses, policy numbers) for
    o All insurance products: homeowners/renters, health/medical, disability, life, flood, auto, etc.;
    o All financial accounts: checking, savings, investment accounts, retirement accounts, debts, etc.;
    o Other important contacts: family, friends, doctors, attorneys;
    o List of family medical conditions: pre-existing conditions, blood types, allergies, etc.; and
    o A modest amount of cash or a valid credit/debit card.

With regard to the contents of your home including personal items, the best course of action is to keep an inventory of what you own. Following is an excellent method for starting, updating, and using an alternate method for a homeowner contents inventory[5].

- *Inventory one room at a time. List every item in the room, its purchase price, the date of purchase (as close as you can remember), and where you purchased it (if you don't have an actual record of the purchase, the store might). Use any accounts of your expenditures on file (old checks, receipts, or similar records) to help refresh your memory. If the item isn't on that room's list, either write it in at the bottom or look through the other pages in the inventory until you find it.*

- *Use a camera or video camera to record what you own. Photograph your home systematically:*

    Start with one wall of a room and take as many pictures as necessary to record everything along that wall, overlapping slightly.

    Move around the room clockwise. Remember to open closets and drawers and photograph what's inside.

    Record the purchase prices and purchase dates of the items on the back of each photograph or on the forms in this book.

- *List all brand names, model numbers, and serial numbers for items that have them to help verify purchase dates and approximate replacement costs.*

- *If you use a personal computer, you might want to investigate the various software packages on the market for compiling a household inventory.*

    As you're doing your inventory, think about items you own that may be in a temporary residence (like a college dormitory) or in your vehicle. Do include these items in your inventory list — they are covered by your homeowners' insurance policy. Your personal property is covered anywhere in the world under your normal policy.

NOTE:

The IRS has a disaster loss workbook, Publication 584, which can help you compile a room-by-room list of belongings.

---

[5] Circular 1346: Holly Hunts, Extension specialist, consumer and family economics, and Brenda Cude, Extension specialist, consumer and family economics, Division of Agricultural and Consumer Economics, College of Agricultural, Consumer and Environmental Sciences, University of Illinois at Urbana-Champaign. Copyright © 1997 by University of Illinois Board of Trustees.

Farm/Ranch Agriculture

Farm/Ranch

Farming and ranching, while a business with daily expenses, have a very different income stream than a manufacturing or retail business. The expenses may accumulate daily, but the income is periodic, often coming only after the crop, or livestock is sold. And, if the crop or livestock is lost due to a disaster, a new crop or herd may take a year to replace with no income during that year. So insurance for crop or livestock protection is crucially important.

Cash

In an agricultural operation where the operator receives periodic, or in many cases annual, payments for crops or livestock operating with crop loans until harvest is the norm.

In a small operation cash is king, which means that cash flow is critical to the existence of the operation. A disaster tends to upset that nice steady flow of cash and can "tank" a small operation in no time flat. So the key in planning for a disaster is to determine if your cash flow will be interrupted by a disaster. And to what extent you can survive without a regular inflow of cash. How you receive your cash, and from where, are facts that will dictate how you deal with a disaster. Financially there are several things you can do in advance of a disaster to lessen the financial shock to your operation such as, set aside savings, have a line of credit, obtain a farm loan, and have insurance.

Insurance

Deductibles and Exclusions

Two key items to take into account when discussing insurance policies are deductibles and exclusions. A deductible is the basic amount of a loss that insurance won't pay. For example, if you have earthquake insurance and your house is destroyed by an earthquake your policy may pay for the loss of your house except for the first 10% of the loss. You are responsible for that amount, which is called the deductible.

Exclusions, on the other hand, are those events or items that your insurance policy doesn't cover. So think about how you plan to cover the deductible and exclusions contained in your insurance policy. Do you put money aside on a regular basis to cover out of pocket costs of a loss, or just hope it doesn't happen? Or hope insurance covers enough of the loss that you can make up the difference with the money you have on hand when disaster strikes.

Federal Crop Insurance[6]

Farmers and ranchers face many risks, including the loss of crops and livestock due to the vagaries of weather and disease. Once a risk assessment (also known as a threat and vulnerability assess-

---

[6] Introduction to federal crop insurance is from the *Farmers' Guide to Disaster Assistance (Sixth Edition, 2008); Farmers Legal Action Group, Inc.*}

ment) is completed, whether it is a momentary thought, or a well prepared review of the risks to the operation and the likelihood of their occurrence, crop/livestock insurance may be a prudent option. Of course, if you are in a federal farm program then federal Multiple-Peril Crop Insurance is mandatory.

The federal crop insurance programs are a mixture of private contracts and government regulations. In general, crop insurance coverage is obtained from private insurance providers. These providers, typically private insurance companies, must be approved by the Federal Crop Insurance Corporation (FCIC) to offer the federal insurance programs.

Federal crop insurance policies typically consist of the Common Crop Insurance Policy, the specific crop provisions, and policy endorsements and special provisions.

If crop insurance coverage is sufficiently available in an area through private insurance providers, FCIC is prohibited from directly providing insurance to the producers in that area. In the vast majority of cases, therefore, a producer buys crop insurance from a private insurance agent who works with an approved insurance provider.

If the producer bought crop insurance from a private insurance provider, the producer has a written contract with that provider. The private provider will have a reinsurance contract with FCIC, but the producer does not have a contract with FCIC. The producer's rights and responsibilities are based primarily on his or her contract with the insurance provider, and the insurance provider will be the decision maker on loss claims and other issues under the contract.

For example, for the Common Crop policy, the contract includes the accepted application, the Basic Provisions, the Crop Provisions, and the Special Provisions, actuarial documents for the insured agricultural commodity, the Catastrophic Risk Protection Endorsement (if applicable), and other applicable endorsements or options added, and applicable regulations.

Risk Management Agency (RMA) Insurance

The USDA-Risk Management Agency (RMA) administers numerous farm/ranch insurance policies that many companies sell. This federally administered insurance is sold through Authorized Insurance Providers (AIP) and not by the RMA or FSA. Additionally, private insurers sell hail insurance as a supplement to federal Multiple-Peril Crop Insurance or as a stand-alone insurance.

The RMA provides insurance plans for more than 100 crops. For the current crop list go to: http://www.rma.usda.gov/policies/2015policy.html

Multiple-peril crop insurance (MPCI) policies are available for most insured crops. Other plans may not be available for some insured crops in some areas. Some policies are not available nationwide; they are tested in pilot programs available in selected states and counties.

RMA provides policies for more than 100 crops. Policies typically consist of general crop insurance provisions, specific crop provisions, policy endorsements and special provisions. See RMA's county crop program listings for information about crop policies available in specific counties and states.

Policies are available for most commodities; however, some policies are being tested as pilots or have not been expanded nationwide so are not available in all areas.

Insurance Plans provide different types of insurance coverage to specific commodities:

- **Actual Production History (APH)** policies insure producers against yield losses due to natural causes such as drought, excessive moisture, hail, wind, frost, insects, and disease. The producer selects the amount of average yield to insure; from 50-75 percent (in some areas to 85 percent). The producer also selects the percent of the predicted price to insure; between 55 and 100 percent of the crop price established annually by RMA. If the harvested plus any appraised production is less than the yield insured, the producer is paid an indemnity based on the difference. Indemnities are calculated by multiplying this difference by the insured percentage of the price selected when crop insurance was purchased and by the insured share.

- **Actual Revenue History (ARH)** plan of insurance has many parallels to the APH plan of insurance, with the primary difference being that instead of insuring historical yields, the plan insures historical revenues. The policy is structured as an endorsement to the Common Crop Insurance Policy Basic Provisions. It restates many of the APH yield procedures to reflect a revenue product. Each crop insured under ARH has unique crop provisions. Like current revenue coverage plans, the ARH pilot program protects growers against losses from low yields, low prices, low quality, or any combination of these events.

- **Adjusted Gross Revenue (AGR)** and **AGR-Lite** policies insure revenue of the entire farm rather than an individual crop by guaranteeing a percentage of average gross farm revenue, including a small amount of livestock revenue. The policies use information from a producer's Schedule F tax forms, and current year expected farm revenue, to calculate policy revenue guarantee.

- **Area Risk Protection Insurance (ARPI)** is an insurance plan that provides coverage based on the experience of an entire area, generally a county. ARPI replaces the Group Risk Plan (GRP) and the Group Risk Income Protection Plan (GRIP).

- **Commodity Exchange Price Provisions (CEPP)**

- **Contract Price Addendum (CPA)**

- **Dollar Plan** policies provide protection against declining value due to damage that causes a yield shortfall. The amount of insurance is based on the cost of growing a crop in a specific area. A loss occurs when the annual crop value is less than the amount of insurance. The maximum dollar amount of insurance is stated on the actuarial document. The insured may select a percent of the maximum dollar amount equal to CAT (catastrophic level of coverage), or purchase additional coverage levels.

- **Group Risk Plan (GRP)** is designed as a risk management tool to insure against widespread loss of production of the insured crop in a county. GRP policies use a county yield index as the basis for determining a loss. When the estimated county yield for the insured crop, as determined by National Agricultural Statistics Service (NASS), falls below the trigger yield level chosen by the producer, an indemnity is paid. Payments are not based on an individual producer's crop yields. Coverage levels are available for up to 90 percent of the expected county yield. GRP involves less paperwork and costs less than plans of insurance against individual loss, as described above. Under GRP, insured acreage for an individual producer's crop may have low yields and not receive a payment if the county does not suffer a similar level of yield loss. This insurance is primarily intended for producers whose crop yields typically follow the average county yield.

- **Group Risk Income Protection (GRIP)** is designed as a risk management tool to insure against widespread loss of revenue from the insured crop in a county. GRIP policies use a county revenue index as the basis for determining a loss by using the estimated county yield for the insured crop, as determined by National Agricultural Statistics Service (NASS), multiplied by the harvest price. If the county revenue falls below the trigger revenue level chosen by the producer, an indemnity is paid. Unlike GRP, it is not necessary to have a decline in yield to be indemnified, as long as the combination of price and yield results in a county revenue that is less than the trigger revenue. Payments are not based on individual producer's crop yields and revenues. Coverage levels are available for up to 90 percent of the expected county revenue. GRIP involves less paperwork and costs less than plans of insurance against individual loss as described above. Under GRIP, an individual producer's crop may receive reduced revenue from the insured acreage and not receive a payment under this plan if the county does not suffer a similar level of revenue loss. This insurance is primarily intended for producers whose crop yields typically follow the average county yield and wish to insure that the combination of yield and price result in a particular level of revenue.

- **Group Risk Income Protection - Harvest Revenue Option (GRIP-HRO)** is a supplemental endorsement to the GRIP Basic Provisions. The Harvest Revenue Option changes the trigger revenue to be the result of multiplying the expected county yield by the greater of the expected price or the harvest price and by the producer chosen coverage level percentage. If the county revenue for the insured crop, type, and practice falls below the GRIP-HRO trigger revenue, an indemnity is paid.

- **Livestock policies** are designed to insure against declining market prices of livestock and not any other peril. Coverage is determined using futures and options prices from the Chicago Mercantile Exchange Group. Price insurance is available for swine, cattle, lambs and milk. Producers decide the number of head (cwt of milk) to insure and the length of the coverage period. There are two types of plans available: Livestock Risk Protection, provides coverage against market price decline, if the ending price is less than the producer determined beginning price and indemnity is due; and Livestock Gross Margin, provides coverage for the difference between the commodity and feeding costs. If the producer determined expected gross margin is greater than the actual gross margin, an indemnity is due.

- **Rainfall Index (RI)** is based on weather data collected and maintained by the National Oceanic and Atmospheric Administration›s Climate Prediction Center. The index reflects how much precipitation is received relative to the long-term average for a specified area and timeframe. The program divides the country into six regions due to different weather patterns, with pilots available in select counties.

- **Revenue Protection** policies insure producers against yield losses due to natural causes such as drought, excessive moisture, hail, wind, frost, insects, and disease, and revenue losses caused by a change in the harvest price from the projected price. The producer selects the amount of average yield he or she wishes to insure; from 50-75 percent (in some areas to 85 percent). The projected price and the harvest price are 100 percent of the amounts determined in accordance with the Commodity Exchange Price Provisions and are based on daily settlement prices for certain futures contracts. The amount of insurance protection is based on the greater of the projected price or the harvest price. If the harvested plus any appraised production multiplied by the harvest price is less than the amount of insurance protection, the producer is paid an indemnity based on the difference.

- **Revenue Protection With Harvest Price Exclusion** policies insure producers in the same manner as Revenue Protection polices, except the amount of insurance protection is based on the projected price only (the amount of insurance protection is not increased if the harvest price is greater than the projected price). If the harvested plus any appraised production multiplied by harvest price is less than the amount of insurance protection, the producer is paid an indemnity based on the difference.

- **Vegetation Index (VI)** is based on the U.S. Geological Survey›s Earth Resources Observation and Science (EROS) normalized difference vegetation index (NDVI) data derived from satellites observing long-term changes in greenness of vegetation of the earth since 1989. The program divides the country into six regions due to different weather patterns, with pilots available in select counties.

- **Yield Protection** policies insure producers in the same manner as APH polices, except a projected price is used to determine insurance coverage. The projected price is determined in accordance with the Commodity Exchange Price Provisions and is based on daily settlement prices for certain futures contracts. The producer selects the percent of the projected price he or she wants to insure, between 55 and 100 percent.

- **Policy Endorsements and Options** are available for some crop provisions that add supplemental coverage, exclude coverage or otherwise modify coverage. An endorsement or option generally must be applied for on or before the sales closing date.

- **Catastrophic Risk Protection Endorsement (CAT Coverage)** pays 55 percent of the price of the commodity established by RMA on crop losses in excess of 50 percent. The premium on CAT coverage is paid by the Federal Government; however, producers must pay a $300 administrative fee (as of the 2008 Farm Bill) for each crop insured in each county. Limited-resource producers may have this fee waived. CAT coverage is not available on all types of policies.

- **High-Risk Alternate Coverage Endorsement (HR-ACE)** is a privately developed product approved through the 508(h) process which allows a producer who farms both high-risk and non-high-risk land to insure the high-risk land at an additional coverage level which is lower than the coverage level on the non-high-risk land. Beginning with the 2013 crop year. The HR-ACE is available for corn, soybeans, wheat, and grain sorghum in certain counties as specified in the actuarial documents.

- See actuarial documents for other endorsements and options available to a specific commodity.

Producer Obligations - Producers must:

- Report acreage, and any required protection, accurately,
- Meet policy deadlines,
- Pay premiums when due, and
- Report losses immediately.

Note: Contact a crop insurance agent for information regarding your specific obligations.

Producer Expectations - Producers will receive:

- Accurate answers to questions on types of coverage,
- Prompt processing of their policy, and
- Timely payments for covered losses.

Important Deadlines:

- **Sales closing date** - last day to apply for coverage.

- **Final planting date** - last day to plant unless insured for late planting.

- **Acreage reporting date** - last day to report the acreage planted. If not reported, insurance will not be in effect.

- **Date to file notice of crop damage** - for a planted crop; notice must be provided within 72 hours of discovery of damage or loss of production (but not later than 15 days after the end of the insurance period). If there is no damage or loss of production and a revenue plan of insurance is in effect, notice must be given no later than 45 days after the latest date the harvest price is released. For crops that are prevented from being planted, notice must be provided within 72 hours after the final planting date or the time the producer determines it will not be possible to plant during any applicable late planting period.

- **End of insurance period** - latest date of insurance coverage.

- **Payment due date** - last day to pay the premium without being charged interest.

- **Cancellation date** - last day to request cancellation of policy for the next year.

- **Production reporting date** - last day to report production for APH, ARH, Revenue Protection, and Revenue Protection with harvest price exclusion option.

- **Debt termination date** - date the approved insurance provider will terminate a policy for nonpayment.

New Policies and Policy Expansion

If an established crop policy is not available in a particular state or county, producers may request that their RMA Regional Office expand the program to their county the next crop year. They may also request insurance coverage under a written agreement, a kind of individual policy which bases premium rates on data from other counties. Producers are required to have documented experience in growing the crop, or in growing an agronomically similar crop, to obtain the agreement and written agreements must be allowed by the applicable policy. See the RMA fact sheet Requesting Insurance Not Available in Your County.

Although RMA has streamlined the process of developing new policies, much must be done before a policy can be made available nationwide, especially if it is a new type of policy or a policy on a crop which is not similar to any crop already insured. Generally, the process takes several years.

Frequently Asked Questions provides information regarding new insurance policies developed under contract for RMA by private entities or privately developed 508(h) insurance products approved by the Federal Crop Insurance Corporation. Also see the Concept Proposals option for submitting proposals for 508(h). RMA has developed some training resources for pilot programs.

Contact

Risk Management Agency
USDA/RMA/Stop 0801
Room 3053-South
1400 Independence Ave., SW
Washington, DC 20250
Phone: (202) 690-2803; Fax: (202) 690-2818

James L. Jaffe, J.D.

E-mail: RMA_mail@wdc.usda.gov

The RMA also has 10 Regional Service Offices, in various locations across the country, which may be contacted for information specific to any area. Call (800) 205-9953 for the address of the nearest office.

Crop Hail Insurance

"Crop hail losses in recent years nationally are estimated at $1.3 billion annually, representing between 1 and 2 percent of the annual crop value. Hail losses vary considerably regionally, representing, for example, 1 to 2 percent of the crop value in the Midwest, 5 to 6 percent of the crops produced in the High Plains, and much less elsewhere in the nation." [7]

Thus hail insurance can be an important part of the financial aspect of disaster planning. Hail insurance can be used to defray the Multiple Peril Crop Insurance (MPCI) deductible, or as a stand-alone insurance policy. Hail insurance is not guaranteed by the USDA and is a private insurance product. Since it is a non-federal insurance policy, it is regulated by the insurance commissioner of each state and can vary from state to state. Essentially, the various hail insurance policies are similar in fashion. Most require you to purchase hail insurance at least 24 hours in advance of coverage. So long as you purchase it before noon, coverage begins mid-night the following day. But there is coverage that begins 6 hours after purchase, depending upon the policy and insurer.

Once you buy hail insurance, you have it for the season, not just for the duration of the storm you see on the horizon.

The loss from hail is measured by a 10 year actual production history (APH) for the farmer's last 10 years' crop production for the field that sustains the hail loss.

Here's an example of a typical hail scenario with a loss on two common types of policies:

Basic Hail Insurance Policy[8]

A farmer insures 300 acres of spring wheat at $100 per acre for a total liability limit of $30,000 in May. A storm occurs in mid-June which destroys 100% of about 50 acres of the field and about 60% on 100 acres and 30% on 150 acres.

Under this basic policy the loss scenario would work like this:

50 acres x $100 x 1.00 = $5,000 indemnity 100 acres x $100 x .60 = $6,000 indemnity 150 acres x $100 x .30 = $4,500 indemnity

Total indemnity: $15,500

Companion Hail Insurance Policy with Increasing Payment Factor 2.0:

A farmer insures 300 acres of spring wheat at $100 per acre for a total liability limit of $30,000 in May. A storm occurs in mid June which destroys 100% of about 50 acres of the field and about 60% on 100 acres and 30% on 150 acres.

Under this companion hail policy the loss scenario works like this:

50 acres x $100 x (1.00 - 0.05 = 0.95 x 2 = 1.90 > 1.00 = 1.00) = $5,000 indemnity

---

[7] Trends in Hail in the United States: Stanley Changnon, Chief Emeritus & Principal Scientist Illinois State Water Survey, Mahomet, IL http://sciencepolicy.colorado.edu/socasp/weather1/changnon.html

[8] Andrew R. Brekke
Erickson Insurance Group
First Street West
Havre, MT 59501
http://www.ericksoninsurancegroup.com/index.html

100 acres x $100 x (0.60 - 0.05 = 0.55 x 2 = 1.10 > 1.00 = 1.00) = $10,000 indemnity

150 acres x $100 x (0.30 - 0.05 = 0.25 x 2 = 0.50 < 1.00 = 0.50) = $7,500 indemnity

Total indemnity: $22,500

Under these scenarios the companion plan, even though the insured purchased the same amount of insurance, paid more due to the way the policy works. The difference is $7,000 which undoubtedly will pay for the increased premium which runs approximately $2400 for the basic and maybe $3600 for the companion. The reason for the difference though has to do with the insurance concept.

Under basic insurance the idea is to allow the farmer to purchase exactly the amount of coverage he wants to protect against any particular loss, dollar to dollar, regardless of other coverage available on the same acreage such as federal multi-peril crop insurance.

The companion plan; however, assumes you have underlying multi-peril coverage and does not reinsure the bottom half of the coverage again (meaning small losses 20-30% which is the deductible under federal crop) but rather compensates you for larger losses over 55% hence the 100% payout under the 60% loss.

Crop Hail Endorsements[9]

Farmers can purchase various "endorsements" (actually additions) to a Crop Hail insurance policy that will offer additional protection. Some of these endorsements are:

---

[9] Availability and coverage is subject to change. These endorsements are provided by Rain and Hail L.L.C.
Rain and Hail, L.L.C.
9200 Northpark Drive, Suite 300
Johnston, IA 50131.

Barn Endorsements (BE)

These endorsements cover the tobacco curing barns against damage due to fire. It does not cover any damage to the tobacco by fire.

Companion Hail (CP)

Designed to cover, on an acre basis, the portion of the crop not insured under an MPCI policy identified as the difference between the potential yield and the yield guaranteed by the MPCI coverage. An underlying MPCI policy is required.

Cotton Wind (CW)

Provides coverage against direct loss to cotton caused by wind. Wind loss is defined as the removal of unharvested cotton in open bolls from the plant by wind, hail and/or rain in excess of the applicable deductible.

Oklahoma Added Perils (OW)

Provides coverage against direct loss to crops in Oklahoma caused by wind if accompanied by hail damage of 5% or more. Coverage is also provided against falling aircraft. This endorsement also increases the amount of insurance up to twice the amount shown on the Schedule of Insurance for any loss caused by fire and lightning before harvest and while the crop is still in the harvester.

Reject Coverage (RC)

Provides coverage against direct loss due to hail which causes the crop to be rejected by the processor or buyer. The underlying Crop-Hail policy will cover the direct damage caused by hail and this endorsement will cover the additional loss in value from rejection of the crop.

Sugar Beet Crusting, Freeze, and Wind Endorsement (SB)

Provides coverage to sugar beets against crusting, freeze or wind. The policy liability is limited by stage and the growing season is broken into five stages: Stage 1 = 33%, Stage 2 = 66%, Stage 3 = 100%, Stage 4 = 66%, and Stage 5 = 33%. Coverage is provided for the actual costs of replanting the sugar beets as well as direct damage to the original sugar beet crop. The direct damage accounts for the reduction in quantity and quality of the replanted sugar beets.

Tobacco Wind (with set up) (SU)

Provides coverage against wind damage which causes the breaking off of stalks or destruction and/or removal of leaves from the plant. Coverage options available vary by state. This endorsement also provides for the cost of labor to set-up tobacco blown over by wind up to a maximum limitation as specified in the endorsement. The set-up provision only applies if 10% or more of the tobacco plants have been blown over by wind.

Tobacco Theft (TT)

Provides coverage against direct loss to tobacco caused by theft and vandalism. A $100 deductible will apply for each occurrence of loss. Can also be attached to the barn fire policy.

Corn, Seed Corn, and Sweet Corn Wind Endorsement (WE)

Provides coverage against direct loss to corn, seed corn and sweet corn by wind. Wind loss includes damage which flattens, bend or breaks the stalk, causing the ear to be unrecoverable by mechanical harvesting equipment.

Cotton Escalator Buy-Out Option

Removes the cotton escalator provision and provides the producer 100% of the limit of insurance at the time coverage incepts.

Replant Exclusion for Corn, Seed Corn, and/or Soybeans

Excludes replanting coverage from the underlying Crop-Hail policy for a reduction in the premium rate. The crop(s) insured under must also be insured under a policy reinsured or approved by the Federal Crop Insurance Corporation (FCIC). Hail and fire coverage cannot be excluded from the policy reinsured or approved by the FCIC for the crop(s) insured under this endorsement (except for seed corn).

Seed Corn Endorsement

Provides coverage against lack of pollination due to direct loss from hail. It also covers direct loss to the ears and indirect loss to leaves, stalks or tassels from hail which affects the production of commercially acceptable seed corn. This endorsement pays an additional eight tenths of a percent of loss for each percent of loss in excess of 30%.

Production Plan Hail Insurance (PP)

Covers, on a unit basis, the portion of the crop not insured under your Multiple Peril Crop Insurance (MPCI), Crop Revenue Coverage (CRC) or Revenue Assurance (RA) policy. An underlying MPCI, CRC, or RA policy is required.

Corn and Soybean Replant Endorsement (RG)

Coverage is provided for causes of loss other than hail that damages the corn or soybeans to the extent that they need to be replanted. An underlying GRP or GRIP policy is required.

Noninsured Crop Disaster Assistance Program[10]

"The purpose of the Noninsured Crop Disaster Assistance Program (NAP) is to help manage and reduce production risks faced by producers of eligible commercial crops or other agricultural commodities during a coverage period." 7 U.S.C. § 1347.1 (a)

Overview

The Noninsured Crop Disaster Assistance Program (NAP), reauthorized by the 2014 Farm Bill and administered by the U.S. Department of Agriculture (USDA) Farm Service Agency (FSA), provides financial assistance to producers of noninsurable crops to protect against natural disasters that result in lower yields or crop losses, or prevents crop planting.

Eligible Producers

An eligible producer is a landowner, tenant or sharecropper who shares in the risk of producing an eligible crop and is entitled to an ownership share of that crop. The 2014 Farm Bill specifies that an individual or entity's average adjusted gross income (AGI) cannot exceed $900,000 to be eligible for NAP payments.

Eligible Crops

Eligible crops must be commercially produced agricultural commodities for which crop insurance is not available and be any of the following:

- Crops grown for food;
- Crops planted and grown for livestock consumption, such as grain and forage crops, including native forage;
- Crops grown for fiber, such as cotton and flax (except trees);
- Crops grown in a controlled environment, such as mushrooms and floriculture;
- Specialty crops, such as honey and maple sap;
- Sea oats and sea grass;
- Sweet sorghum and biomass sorghum;
- Industrial crops, including crops used in manufacturing or grown as a feedstock for renewable biofuel, renewable electricity, or biobased products;
- Value loss crops, such as aquaculture, Christmas trees, ginseng, ornamental nursery, and turfgrass sod; and
- Seed crops where the propagation stock is produced for sale as seed stock for other eligible NAP crop production.

Producers should contact a crop insurance agent for questions regarding insurability of a crop in their county. For further information on whether a crop is eligible for NAP coverage, producers should contact the FSA county office where their farm records are maintained.

Eligible Causes of Loss

Eligible causes of loss include the following natural disasters:

- Damaging weather, such as drought, freeze, hail, excessive moisture, excessive wind or hurricanes;
- Adverse natural occurrences, such as earthquake or flood; and
- Conditions related to damaging weather or adverse natural occurrences, such as excessive heat, plant disease, volcanic smog (VOG) or insect infestation.

---

[10] http://fsa.usda.gov/FSA/newsReleases?area=newsroom&subject=landing&topic=pfs&newstype=prfactsheet&type=detail&item=pf_20141212_distr_en_nonins_cr.html

James L. Jaffe, J.D.

The natural disaster must occur during the coverage period, before or during harvest, and must directly affect the eligible crop.

Coverage Levels

NAP provides catastrophic level (CAT) coverage based on the amount of loss that exceeds 50 percent of expected production at 55 percent of the average market price for the crop.

The 2014 Farm Bill authorizes additional coverage levels ranging from 50 to 65 percent of production, in 5 percent increments, at 100 percent of the average market price. Additional coverage must be elected by a producer by the application closing date. Producers who elect additional coverage must pay a premium in addition to the service fee. Crops intended for grazing are not eligible for additional coverage.

Applying for Coverage

Eligible producers must apply for coverage using form CCC-471, "Application for Coverage," and pay the applicable service fee at the FSA office where their farm records are maintained. The application and service fee must be filed by the application closing date. Application closing dates vary by crop and are established by the FSA State Committee.

Producers who apply for NAP coverage acknowledge that they have received the NAP Basic Provisions, available at FSA county offices and at http://www.fsa.usda.gov/nap.

Service Fees and Premiums

For all coverage levels, the NAP service fee is the lesser of $250 per crop or $750 per producer per administrative county, not to exceed a total of $1,875 for a producer with farming interests in multiple counties.

Producers who elect additional coverage must also pay a premium equal to:

- The producer's share of the crop; times
- The number of eligible acres devoted to the crop; times
- The approved yield per acre; times
- The coverage level; times
- The average market price; times
- A 5.25 percent premium fee.

For value loss crops, premiums will be calculated using the maximum dollar value selected by the producer on form CCC-471, "Application for Coverage."

The maximum premium for a producer is $6,562.50 (the maximum payment limitation times a 5.25 percent premium fee).

Beginning, limited resource, and traditionally underserved farmers are eligible for a waiver of the service fee and a 50 percent premium reduction when they file form CCC-860, "Socially Disadvantaged, Limited Resource and Beginning Farmer or Rancher Certification." To be eligible for a service fee waiver or premium reduction, producers must qualify as one of the following:

Beginning farmer – a person who:

- Has not operated a farm or ranch for more than 10 years, and
- Materially and substantially participates in the operation.

For legal entities to be considered a beginning farmer, all members must be related by blood or marriage and must be beginning farmers.

Limited resource farmer – a person or legal entity that:

- Earns no more than $176,800 in each of the two calendar years that precede the complete

taxable year before the program year, to be adjusted upwards in later years for inflation; and
- Has a total household income at or below the national poverty level for a family of four, or less than 50 percent of county median household income for both of the previous two years.

Limited resource producer status may be determined using the USDA Limited Resource Farmer and Rancher Online Self Determination Tool located at http://www.lrftool.sc.egov.usda.gov. The automated system calculates and displays adjusted gross farm sales per year and the higher of the national poverty level or county median household income.

Socially disadvantaged farmer – these traditionally underserved farmers are a member of a group whose members have been subject to racial, ethnic, or gender prejudice because of their identity as members of a group without regard to their individual qualities. Groups include:

- American Indians or Alaskan Natives;
- Asians or Asian Americans;
- Blacks or African Americans;
- Native Hawaiians or other Pacific Islanders;
- Hispanics; and
- Women.

For legal entities to be considered socially disadvantaged, the majority interest must be held by socially disadvantaged individuals.

Coverage Period

The coverage period for NAP varies depending on the crop.

The coverage period for an annual crop begins the later of:

- 30 days after application for coverage and the applicable service fees have been paid, or
- The date the crop is planted (cannot exceed the final planting date).

The coverage period for an annual crop ends the earlier of the:

- Date the crop harvest is completed,
- Normal harvest date for the crop,
- Date the crop is abandoned, or
- Date the entire crop acreage is destroyed.

The coverage period for a perennial crop, other than a crop intended for forage, begins 30 calendar days after the application closing date and ends the earlier of:

- 10 months from the application closing date;
- The date the crop harvest is completed;
- The normal harvest date for the crop;
- The date the crop is abandoned; or
- The date the entire crop acreage is destroyed.

Contact a local FSA office for information on the coverage periods for perennial forage crops, controlled-environment crops, specialty crops, and value loss crops.

Information Required to Remain Eligible for NAP

To be eligible for NAP assistance, the following crop acreage information must be reported:

- Name of the crop (lettuce, clover, etc.);
- Type and variety (head lettuce, red clover, etc.);
- Location and acreage of the crop (field, subfield, etc.);
- Share of the crop and the names of other producers with an interest in the crop;
- Type of practice used to grow the crop (irrigated or non-irrigated);

- Date the crop was planted in each field; and
- Intended use of the commodity (fresh, processed, etc.).

Producers should report crop acreage shortly after planting (early in the risk period) to ensure reporting deadlines are not missed and coverage is not lost.

In addition, producers with NAP coverage must provide the following production information:

- The quantity of all harvested production of the crop in which the producer held an interest during the crop year;
- The disposition of the harvested crop, such as whether it is marketable, unmarketable, salvaged or used differently than intended; and
- Verifiable or reliable crop production records (when required by FSA).

When those records are required, producers must provide them in a manner that can be easily understood by the FSA county committee. Producers should contact the FSA office where their farm records are maintained for questions regarding acceptable production records.

Failure to report acreage and production information for NAP-covered crops may result in reduced or zero NAP assistance. Be aware that acreage reporting and final planting dates vary by crop and by region. Producers should contact the FSA office where their farm records are maintained for questions regarding local acreage reporting and final planting dates.

For aquaculture, floriculture and ornamental nursery operations, producers must maintain records according to industry standards, including daily crop inventories. Unique reporting requirements apply to beekeepers and producers of Christmas trees, turf-grass sod, maple sap, mushrooms, ginseng, and commercial seed or forage crops. Producers should contact the FSA office where their farm records are maintained regarding these requirements.

Reported Acreage and Production

FSA uses acreage reports to verify the existence of the crop and to record the number of acres covered by the application. The acreage and the production reports are used to calculate the approved yield (expected production for a crop year). The approved yield is an average of a producer's actual production history (APH) for a minimum of four to a maximum of 10 crop years (five years for apples and peaches). To calculate APH, FSA divides a producer's total production by the producer's crop acreage.

A producer's approved yield may be calculated using substantially reduced yield data if the producer does not report production for a crop with NAP coverage, or reports fewer than four years of crop production.

Beginning with the 2015 crop year, FSA has changed the production reporting requirements to avoid penalizing producers for years when they do not participate in NAP and do not report their production. Those producers will no longer receive an assigned yield or zero-credited yield in their actual production history (APH) for that year. Producers may also request replacement of assigned yields and zero-credited yields in their APH for the 1995 through 2014 crop years with the higher of 65 percent of the current crop year T-yield or the missing crop year's actual yield.

Providing Notice of Loss and Applying for Payment

When a crop or planting is affected by a natural disaster, producers with NAP coverage must notify the FSA office where their farm records are maintained and complete Part B (the Notice of

Loss portion) of form CCC-576, "Notice of Loss and Application for Payment." This must be completed within 15 calendar days of the earlier of:

- A natural disaster occurrence;
- The final planting date if planting is prevented by a natural disaster;
- The date that damage to the crop or loss of production becomes apparent; or
- The normal harvest date.

Producers of hand-harvested crops and certain perishable crops must notify FSA within 72 hours of when a loss becomes apparent. The crops subject to this requirement will be listed in the NAP Basic Provisions.

To receive NAP benefits, producers must complete form CCC-576, "Notice of Loss and Application for Payment," Parts D, E, F, and G, as applicable, within 60 days of the last day of coverage for the crop year for any NAP covered crop in the unit. The CCC-576 requires acceptable appraisal information. Producers must provide evidence of production and note whether the crop was marketable, unmarketable, salvaged, or used differently than intended.

Defining a NAP Unit

The NAP unit includes all the eligible crop acreage in the county where the producer has a unique crop interest. A unique crop interest is either:

- 100 percent interest, or
- A shared interest with another producer.

Information FSA Uses to Calculate Payment

The NAP payment is calculated by unit using:

- Crop acreage;
- Approved yield;
- Net production;
- Coverage level elected by the producer;
- An average market price for the commodity established by the FSA state committee; and
- A payment factor reflecting the decreased cost incurred in the production cycle for a crop that is not harvested or prevented from being planted.

For value loss crops with additional coverage, payments will be calculated using the lesser of the field market value of the crop before the disaster or the maximum dollar value for which the producer requested coverage at the time of application.

Payment Limitation

NAP payments received, directly or indirectly, will be attributed to the applicable individual or entity and limited to $125,000 per crop year, per individual or entity.

2008 Farm Act & the Agricultural Act of 2014 Changes[11]

The 2008 Farm Act created the Agricultural Disaster Relief Trust Fund, with 3.08 % of receipts attributable to duties collected on articles entered, or withdrawn from warehouse, for consumption under the Harmonized Tariff Schedule to fund Supplemental Agricultural Disaster Assistance (SADA).

Supplemental Agriculture Disaster Assistance Programs

Emergency Assistance for Livestock, Honey Bees, and Farm-Raised Fish (ELAP) {Renewed by the Agricultural Act of 2014}

---

[11] http://www.usda.gov/wps/portal/usda/farmbill2008?navid=FARMBILL2008

Livestock Forage Disaster Program (LFP) {Renewed by the Agricultural Act of 2014}

Livestock Indemnity Program (LIP) {Renewed by the Agricultural Act of 2014}

Tree Assistance Program (TAP) {Renewed by the Agricultural Act of 2014}

Noninsured Crop Disaster Assistance Program (NAP) {Renewed by the Agricultural Act of 2014}

Apply for these programs at the administrative county FSA office in which the loss occurs. These office locations can be found at: http://www.fsa.usda.gov/FSA/stateOffices?area=about&subject=landing&topic=sao-do-so

The payment limit is $125,000.00 per year per eligible producer.

For USDA Farm/Ranch Post Disaster Relief Programs see Page 140 and following

Program Summary

Program	Eligibility	Disaster Declaration	NAP/CI Required	Payment	Payment Limitation
LFP	U.S. Drought Monitor Severity D2, D3, D4	No	No	60% of monthly feed cost x dm factor (50% for fire on public lands)	$125,000.00 Combined
LIP	Livestock death in excess of normal mortality	No	No	75% payment rate for eligible losses	$125,000.00 Combined
ELAP	As determined by the Secretary of USDA	No	No	As determined by the Secretary of USDA	$125,000.00 Combined
TAP	Tree, vine, bush losses in excess of 15%	No	No	Reimbursement: 75% for replanting and 50% for removal, salvage and land preparation	$125,000.00
NAP	A natural disaster must have: Reduced the expected unit production of the crop by more than 50 % or; Prevented the producer from planting more than 35 percent of the intended crop acreage.	No	No	NAP covers the amount of loss greater than 50 percent of the expected production based on the approved yield and reported acreage.	$125,000.00

Record Keeping

Record keeping is a necessity in our modern way of life, and farming/ranching is no exception. A farmer/rancher is burdened with two sets of records that must be maintained in anticipation of a loss of income or assets. For crop loss insurance, it is necessary to keep production records for the previous 10 years. Additionally, records of equipment and structures must also be maintained so that the cost basis of any loss can be documented. In addition to the profit and loss records these records are required for income tax purposes.

As for business records, Internal Revenue Service Publication 225 establish which records farmers should maintain for income tax purposes. These same records can be used to record and track purchases of equipment and structures related to farming/ranching for purposes of establishing the cost basis of disaster losses. Keep a copy of your records at a secondary location so if your original records are lost or destroyed there are back up copies.

To computerize farm records, The Ohio State University Extension Bulletin 931 *Computerized Farm Record Keeping with Quicken® 2007* describes how to maintain farm records using a personal computer with Quicken® software. Bulletin 931 can be found at: http://ohioline.osu.edu/b931/index.html.

Oklahoma State University Agricultural Economics Extension also has an excellent online manual with step-by-step instructions for using *Quicken for Farms and Ranches* which can be found at: http://www.agecon.okstate.edu/quicken/download_manual.asp

Dr. Laurence M. Crane, Director of Education and Training, National Crop Insurance Services, Inc. in his paper *Record-Keeping: Essential to Risk Management*[12] lists the following production, financial and ownership records that farmers/ranchers may want to maintain:

Production Records

Enterprise Budgets* (Crop Budgets): Projects costs and returns over a production period including direct costs (seed, chemicals, fertilizer, crop insurance, fuel, repairs, hired labor, irrigation, etc.), indirect costs (marketing overhead, depreciation, investment and land taxes), returns to management and labor; and yield records including both quantity and quality.

*An enterprise budget is a projection of costs and returns based on projected yields and prices, whereas, an enterprise account is a historic summary based on actual yields and prices.

Resources Flow Budgets: Similar to cash flow in concept, each limiting resource should have a flow budget that reflects sources and uses over time. Examples of limited resources include labor, machinery (by function—seeding, cultivating harvesting, etc.).

Financial Records

Income Statement: Reports the amount of profit the business generates on an annual basis. An accrual statement provides a better measure of the firm's performance because it considers changes in inventories, rather than cash transactions.

Balance Sheet: Summarizes the values of the firm's owned assets and liabilities. The difference between the two totals is the owner's equity (net worth).

---

[12] Reprinted with permission from *Record-Keeping: Essential to Risk Management* by Dr. Laurence M. Crane, Crop Insurance and Risk Management Primer, February 2004, Page 31, Copyright 2004 by National Crop Insurance Services, Inc.

Cash Flow Budget: Reports the sources and uses of the business' cash resources reflecting both the change in cash, and the timing of when the cash was spent or received.

"Sweet Sixteen" Measures: Liquidity (current ratio, working capital) Solvency (debt/asset ratio, equity/asset ratio, leverage ratio) Profitability (rate of return on farm assets, rate of return on farm equity, net farm income) Financial Efficiency (asset turnover ratio, operating profit margin, operating expense ratio, depreciation expense ratio, interest expense ratio, net farm income from operations ratio) Repayment Capacity (term debt and capital lease coverage ratio, capital replacement and term debt repayment margin).

Family Living: A complete listing of family living expenses to include sources of off-farm income and cash withdrawals from the farm to meet living expenses. In-kind contributions from the farm operation to the family should be included.

Ownership/Personal Records

Asset Inventory: A complete listing of all assets controlled by the business including ownership type and/or control arrangements including leases and terms of agreement. For each asset an estimation of its productive capacity, and its opportunity cost.

Ownership Arrangements: Listing of all partnership, landlord/tenant, resource sharing (machinery, labor, etc.) agreements explaining how each owner/party is compensated and what the responsibilities and authorities of each are.

National Animal Identification System (NAIS)[13]

One problem is how to identify the animals, poultry, or fish that were lost due to a disaster. One way to track this loss is by using the NAIS to keep count of the animals, poultry, or fish that is on the farm or ranch.

On January 9, 2013, the U.S. Department of Agriculture (USDA) published a final rule establishing general regulations for improving the traceability of U.S. livestock moving interstate. The rule became effective on March 11, 2013.

"The United States now has a flexible, effective animal disease traceability system for livestock moving interstate, without undue burdens for ranchers and U.S. livestock businesses," said Agriculture Secretary Tom Vilsack. "The final rule meets the diverse needs of the countryside where states and tribes can develop systems for tracking animals that work best for them and their producers, while addressing gaps in our overall disease response efforts. Over the past several years, USDA has listened carefully to America's farmers and ranchers, working collaboratively to establish a system of tools and safeguards that will help us target when and where animal diseases occur, and help us respond quickly."

Under the final rule, unless specifically exempted, livestock moved interstate would have to be officially identified and accompanied by an interstate certificate of veterinary inspection or other documentation, such as owner-shipper statements or brand certificates.

---

[13] http://www.aphis.usda.gov/newsroom/2012/12/pdf/traceability_final_rule.pdf

Small Businesses

Small Business

"In sum, the duty to undertake emergency preparedness is consistent with the basic principles of negligence law and constitutes a significant exposure for the corporation."[14]

General Information on Likely Disasters

A good general website for homeowners and small businesses on how to plan for disasters that are most likely to occur in a specific area (by zip code): http://www.disastersafety.org/

Cash

In a small business cash is king, which means that cash flow is critical to the existence of the business. A disaster tends to upset that nice steady flow of cash and can "tank" a small business in no time flat. So the key in planning for a disaster is to determine if cash flow will be interrupted by a disaster, be it an office fire or a situation that forces evacuation. Determine to what extent the business can survive without a regular inflow of cash. Does it depend upon walk-in customers, or does it send out monthly bills to customers? How money is received, and from where, will dictate how a business deals with a disaster. Financially there are several things a business can do in advance of a disaster to lessen the financial shock.

First, and easiest to say, but oftentimes impossible to accomplish, is keeping enough cash on hand (in the bank) to pay for any immediate needs. In this writer's business our expenses often exceeded $200,000.00 per month, and there was no way we were going to keep that amount of cash sitting around unused. So we went to our banker, hat in hand, and opened a line of credit to cover expenses when the bank account was a little shy of cash. A line of credit, if used properly, can get a small business over a rocky period created by a disaster. It gives the business that steady inflow of cash to pay operating expenses.

Many small businesses perform a service and bill monthly, if this is the case, the most important thing the business sends to its customer is the monthly bill. To overcome the financial aspects of a disaster, figure out an alternative way to prepare and send out customers' bills. After all, no money comes in if the bills don't go out. And plan for an alternate location for the receipt of payments. With personal computers it may be to a business's advantage to set up a system for receiving money and paying bills via the internet.

If there is insurance to cover a loss in business due to a disaster, arrange with the insurance carrier to have insurance payments made directly to

---

[14] The Legal Obligation for Corporate Preparedness: Bill Raisch, M.B.A. – Director & Matt Statler, Ph.D. – Associate Director New York University International Center for Enterprise Preparedness: Denis Binder, S.J.D., Professor of Law Chapman University; October 16, 2006, Subject to Ongoing Revision

James L. Jaffe, J.D.

the business bank account, thus avoiding having to obtain a "hard copy" of a check. Understand what the business has to do in order to quickly receive insurance payments. And, make absolutely certain to understand what the insurance policy covers *and does not* cover.

If a disaster requires an evacuation make sure to move business checkbooks and credit cards to a safe location. If appropriate, also take along customer, supplier and creditors lists with contact numbers and e-mail addresses. Thus contact with people essential to the businesses economic survival can be maintained.

When considering suppliers find out how willing they are to "work" with the business in the event of a disaster. Additionally, consider what would happen if a supplier or large customer has a disaster. Can the business work with suppliers caught up in a disaster? Disaster preparedness is a two way street so a business must consider how to cooperate with suppliers caught in a disaster.

Salaries and Wages

In a disaster if employees can't get to work, or the business is shut down, what is the policy regarding employee's wages? How will employees be paid for wages earned before the disaster that they have yet to receive? Are employees going to be asked to work during the disaster, and if so, how are they going to get paid? Will employees be on restricted stand-by duty, and if so, how will they be paid for that time? Will employees that lose a day or two of work due to a disaster be paid for the time lost?

For wages employees earned prior to the onset of a disaster the employer has a duty to see to it that payment is made on a timely basis. A payroll service that has several locations in different geographical areas may be the best answer to this concern. If this is the solution, make certain they can transfer data from one payroll center to another. If employees are asked to during a disaster, then determine, in advance how they will be paid. Again a payroll service may be the best answer to this issue. On the other hand, if the business has several locations, then sharing data and service among the locations may be the solution. If employees are on stand-by duty during a disaster, then the business must decide if they will be paid for this duty. Are the employees having to restrict their freedom of movement while on stand-by, or not? If so, then they are paid for the stand-by time. Also, the business should decide whether or not to pay employees if they can't come to work during a disaster. This is not as easy a question to answer as you may first think.

If you are the victim of a short term disaster that prevents your employees from working for a day or two, should you pay them for the time off? In answering this question consider the effect upon employee morale and productivity. Paying workers for this time lost shows that the employer is considerate of employees and value them and their effort. The cost of paying employees for a short period of lost work may be more than compensated by increased worker morale and productivity. But what to do if your employees are out for more than a day or two?

If the disaster prevents employees from working for more than a day or two, what does the employer do? The first question to answer is, does the business have enough money, or will have money coming in to meet a payroll? If that question is answered in the affirmative, then the issue becomes allowing employees to utilize vacation time and sick time to stay on the payroll. Allowing the use of vacation time, and perhaps sick time, to remain on the payroll again is a morale issue that the employer must answer. If there is no money to cover the payroll, then the answer is simple, unpleasant, but simple. In any event, this is an issue that businesses need to think about and prepare for.

But whatever decisions the business makes regarding employees, plan ahead, especially if the business is in an area that is prone to hurricanes and other disasters that occur on a regular basis.

Record Keeping

In advance of a disaster the IRS recommends that a business undertake the following activities

Paperless Recordkeeping

Many people now receive bank statements and documents by e-mail or over the Web. Paper records such as W-2s, tax returns and other documents can be scanned and saved electronically.

With documents in electronic form, taxpayers can copy them onto a USB drive as a backup, which can be sent to a relative in another city for safe-keeping in case the taxpayer's computer and paper files are destroyed.

Other options include copying files onto a CD or DVD. Many retail stores also sell computer software packages that can be used for recordkeeping.

Check on Fiduciary Bonds

Employers who use payroll service providers should ask the provider if they have a fiduciary bond in place. The bond could protect the employer in the event of default by the payroll service provider.

Update Emergency Plans

Review your emergency plan annually. Personal and business situations change over time as do preparedness needs. Individual taxpayers should make sure they are saving documents such as W-2s, home closing statements and insurance records. When employers hire new employees or when a company or organization changes functions, plans should be updated accordingly and employees should be informed of the changes.

Insurance

Insurance is another way to protect a business and assets from loss. The balance to achieve is having enough insurance, both in coverage and amount, to protect the business from reasonably anticipated losses. But remember insurance comes with a deductible, which is the amount of loss the business is personally responsible for before insurance begins to pay for the loss, or incurred expense.

Basically, insurance is akin to gambling. The insured is betting on having a loss, and the insurance company is betting that the insured won't have a loss. If the law, customer or lender requires insurance then that's that. But otherwise the business should decide if it is wise to have insurance for a particular risk, put money aside to cover the loss, or do nothing and take the risk.

Let's say the risk of loss is 10% in any given year, and the amount of loss will be $1,000.00, then the business may decide to accept the risk. Or it may decide to put $100.00 into savings each year to pay for the possibility of the loss, hoping it won't happen for at least 10 years. Or it may decide to buy insurance to cover the loss in the event it happens. Whatever decision is made, it is based upon a risk/benefit analysis regardless of whether the decision is made in a split second or after much thought and analysis.

Often in a disaster, insurance company's staffs open an emergency claims facility at a disaster location to promptly pay policyholders for losses incurred as a result of the disaster, so they are often the fastest means of obtaining payment for losses. However one must be cautious when accepting a quick insurance payment, an issue discussed in the section regarding insurance issues after a disaster.

Always remember that if a business is evacuated because the authorities recommend it, insurance probably will not cover the expenses associated with this temporary move. But, *if the authorities order an evacuation* of the business due to an impending disaster such as flood or storm then insurance may the dislocation costs. The key is to read the insurance policy and understand what is and is not covered by the policy.

Deductibles and Exclusions

Two key items to take into account when discussing insurance policies are deductibles and exclusions. A deductible is the basic amount of a loss that insurance won't pay. For example, if the business has earthquake insurance with a 10% deductible on its office building which is destroyed by an earthquake the policy may pay for the loss except for the first 10%. The insured is responsible for that amount, which is called the deductible.

Exclusions, on the other hand, are those events or items that the insurance policy doesn't cover.

So determine the deductibles and exclusions that the business can "live with" and plan how to cover those deductible and exclusions contained in the insurance policy. Business's have a choice of putting money aside on a regular basis to cover out of pocket costs of a loss, or hope nothing happens, or decide that insurance covers enough of the loss that the business will have enough money on hand to cover the exclusions and deductibles when disaster strikes.

Actual Cash Value and Replacement Cost Coverage

An insurance policy covers the cost of replacing items covered that are destroyed in one of two ways. The more common way is by reimbursing the owner for ACTUAL CASH VALUE (ACV). Actual cash value is the value of the insured item immediately before it is destroyed. If a computer cost $3,000.00 five years ago and now it's worth is $200.00, and the cost of a new replacement computer is $2,000.00, the insured will get $200.00 (less the deductible) as the actual cash value of the computer.

On the other hand, if the insurance policy is for REPLACEMENT VALUE the insured will be paid the cost of a replacement computer which is $2,000.00 (less the deductible). But, in no event will insurance pay more than the policy limits.

Special Requirements Regarding Flood Insurance

The Flood Disaster Protection Act of 1973 (42 U.S.C. 400i *et seq.*) requires that Federal agencies and federally insured or regulated lenders require flood insurance on all grants and loans for acquisition or construction of buildings in designated Special Flood Hazard Areas (SFHAs) in communities that participate in the National Flood Insurance Program (NFIP). This requirement is referred to as the Mandatory Flood Insurance Purchase Requirement. Local governments will advise a building owner if flood insurance is required.

NOTE:

This insurance is not mandatory if there is no mortgage, but it may be a good idea if the building is in a flood prone area.

Any property owner of insurable property may purchase this flood insurance coverage, provided that the community in which the property is located is participating in the NFIP.

Flood insurance under the NFIP is sold through two mechanisms:

1. *through state-licensed property and casualty insurance agents and brokers who deal directly with FEMA; and*

2. *through private insurance companies with a program known as "Write Your Own" (WYO).*

The premium charged for NFIP flood coverage by a WYO Company is the same as that charged by the Federal Government through the direct program.

The Standard Flood Insurance Policy (SFIP) is issued on one of three available policy forms, one of which applies to business structures, to provide coverage for the peril of flood.

- The General Property Form covers residential buildings of more than 4 families as well as non-residential risks.

Flood insurance is available to 1-4 family residential buildings, small businesses, and churches other residential properties, other business properties, agricultural properties, properties occupied by private nonprofit organizations, and properties owned by State or local governments.

Voluntary Private Sector Preparedness Accreditation and Certification Program[15]

Congress directed the Department of Homeland Security (DHS) to develop and implement a voluntary program of accreditation and certification of private entities using standards adopted by DHS that promote private sector preparedness, including disaster management, emergency management and business continuity programs.

This program called "The Voluntary Private Sector Preparedness Accreditation and Certification Program (PSPrep)" is mandated by Title IX of the *Implementing Recommendations of the 9/11 Commission Act of 2007 (the Act).*

The purpose of the PS-Prep Program is to enhance nationwide resilience in an all-hazards environment by encouraging private sector preparedness. The program provides a mechanism by which a private sector entity-a company, facility, not-for-profit corporation, hospital, stadium, university, etc.-may be certified by an accredited third party establishing that the private sector entity conforms to one or more preparedness standards adopted by DHS.

Voluntary Program

Participation in the PS-Prep program is completely voluntary. No private sector entity will be required by DHS to comply with any standard adopted under the program. However, DHS encourages all private sector entities to seriously consider seeking certification on one or more standards that will be adopted by DHS.

Designation of Preparedness Standards

Congress directed DHS to designate one or more standards for assessing private sector preparedness. The standards will be used by accredited certifying entities to evaluate and certify compliance by private sector entities with the standards adopted by DHS.

Following a series of regional public meetings and the incorporation of public comments, the three standards were approved in June 2010:

- ASIS International SPC.1-2009 *Organizational Resilience: Security Preparedness, and Continuity Management System – Requirements with Guidance for use (2009 Edition).* Available at no cost.

- British Standards Institution 25999 *(2007 Edition) - Business Continuity Management.(BS 25999:2006-1 Code of practice for business continuity management and BS 25999: 2007-2 Specification for business continuity management)* The British Standards Institution is making

---

[15] http://www.fema.gov/privatesector/preparedness/

both parts available for a reduced fee of $19.99 each.

- National Fire Protection Association 1600- *Standard on Disaster / Emergency Management and Business Continuity Programs, 2007 and 2010 editions.* Available at no cost.

Small businesses are treated differently in the PS-Prep program than large businesses. The December 24, 2008, Federal Register Notice (73 FR 79140) contained an extensive discussion of DHS' approaches to best reflect the interests of small businesses and the purpose of the PS-Prep Program.

"Under an agreement with the Department of Homeland Security, ANAB has developed a program to oversee the certification process, manage accreditation, and accredit qualified third parties to carry out certifications of private sector entities for disaster preparedness, emergency management, and business continuity. Certification bodies can be accredited for any or all of the designated PS-Prep standards: ASIS SPC.1, BS 25999-2, and NFPA 1600." http://www.anab.org/accreditation/preparedness.aspx Accessed April 17, 2011. The NFPA 1600, 2010 Edition[16] can be found at: http://www.nfpa.org/assets/files/PDF/NFPA16002010.pdf

Other Business Preparedness Resources

A good web site for small businesses along with downloadable short manuals on topics of interest for small businesses: http://www.ready.gov/business

If you need more help getting a business or organization prepared, please use http://www.ready.gov/business-continuity-planning-suite developed by DHS' National Protection and Programs Directorate and FEMA.

This software was created for any business with the need to create, improve, or update its business continuity plan. The Suite is scalable for optimal use by organizations of any size and consists of a business continuity plan (BCP) training, automated BCP and disaster recovery plan (DRP) generators, and a self-directed exercise for testing an implemented BCP. Businesses can utilize this solution to maintain normal operations and provide resilience during a disruption.

---

[16] "In November of 2009, NFPA 1600 received designation and certification as anti-terrorism technology under the SAFETY Act. the technical committee extends its appreciation to the U.S. Department of Homeland Security for authorizing the use of the SAFETY Act Certified™ seal on the cover of the 2010 edition." This Designation and Certification will expire on October 31, 2013.

Local Government

Local Government

Which Disaster to Plan For?

"Historically, when disaster strikes, all levels of government do what is necessary and worry about paying for it later. Many, but not all, local and state governments have contingency or rainy day funds for disaster response. Once these emergency funds are exhausted, most governors have to call a special session of the legislature to seek additional appropriations. Local governments have assumed, at least since the New Deal, that if it gets bad enough, Congress will bail them out."[17]

Residents count on their local governments to be prepared for and respond to disasters, regardless of the nature and scope of the disaster.[18]

Residents have come to rely upon the local fire, police, and EMS departments for local single incident emergencies. While a disaster may be significantly larger, more complex, and devastating, residents still rely upon the local government to rise to the occasion and respond effectively. Therefore, it is critical for local governments to be prepared for disasters. The question for local government then becomes how to plan for the economic cost of disasters.

The United States General Accounting Office reviewed six past disasters from 1989 to 2005 and arrived at these four insights[19]:

1. Create a clear, implementable, and timely recovery plan.

2. Build state and local capacity for recovery... including having sufficient financial resources.

3. Implement strategies for businesses recovery... Small businesses can be especially vulnerable to major disasters because they often lack resources to sustain financial losses.

4. Adopt a comprehensive approach toward combating fraud, waste, and abuse.

---

[17] Page 1, Budgeting for disasters: Part I.: James F. Smith; The Public Manager; Spring 2006,

[18] "During the last year [2007-2008] the Council [for Excellence in Government], J.P. Morgan and Visa hosted a national series of panel discussions focused on financial management preparation surrounding emergency situations. More than 200 local, county, state, and federal financial managers and experts met in Boston, San Francisco and Washington, D.C to discuss best practices and gaps in current plans to prepare, respond and recover financially during a major emergency. *According to research conducted during the program, less than 50 percent of responding jurisdictions reported having established financial plans for emergency preparedness and a mere 20 percent reported having the pre-existing relationships with organizations to enable the distribution and accountability of funds for aid.*" http://www.jpmorgan.com/tss/General/Best_Practices_in_Emergency_Financial_Management_Offered_to_Public_Sector/1159367462441

[19] Recovering from Hurricanes Ike and Gustav and Other Recent Natural Disasters, September 2008, GAO-08-1120

Pre planning, of course, requires that one first analyze the scope and extent of reasonably anticipated disasters. Following the preparation of a *Threat and Vulnerability Analysis* which *identifies* potential catastrophic hazards and their operational impacts, an economic analysis can be performed.

An excellent tool for preplanning is **HAZUS-MH** (**See page 264**) http://www.fema.gov/hazus

Potential loss estimates analyzed in HAZUS-MH include:

- **Physical damage** to residential and commercial buildings, schools, critical facilities, and infrastructure;

- **Economic loss**, including lost jobs, business interruptions, repair and reconstruction costs; and

- **Social impacts**, including estimates of shelter requirements, displaced households, and population exposed to scenario floods, earthquakes and hurricanes.

In performing this economic analysis one must keep in mind "that the distribution of disaster losses exhibits "fat tails" – losses experienced in the worst disasters are many times worse than those experienced in the second worst – implying that the most serious events may be expected to be extraordinarily costly".[20]

By its very nature a disaster stretches and sometimes breaks the budget. The goal then is to put the reasonably anticipated cost of a disaster into the budget in a way that allows the community to pay, in advance, for the cost of a disaster they hope will never happen. The conflict is between emotions (the hope the disaster will never happen) and reasonably anticipated facts (disasters have happened in the past, and will most likely happen in the future).

Thus the first decision to be made regarding how much economic disaster pre-planning a community can afford. If an area is prone to flooding, should the community plan for a 100 year flood or a 500 year flood? The answer to this question is one of policy and politics. The best plan estimates the economic cost of the maximum event shown in the *Threat and Vulnerability Analysis* as a reasonably anticipated disaster, although the analysis may show that several different types of events are reasonably anticipated. In essence, prepare a budget for each type of disaster based upon a *Threat and Vulnerability Analysis*.

If the *Threat and Vulnerability Assessment* concludes, for example, that a 100 year flood is a reasonably anticipated event then the community must determine what that event will cost. The easiest way to prepare a budget for a disaster is to look at the costs associated with previous similar disasters. This assumes that the costs will be readily apparent, which will probably not be the case. Thus cost will have to be estimated using the best tools readily available for the job. For example, the use of police during a disaster will necessitate determining the total cost of police for the length of the disaster, and then backing out the "normal" cost for police services to arrive at the disaster costs for police services. The same will have to be performed for all public services, since routine services are not considered part of disaster costs. The most difficult aspect of this task will most likely be determining all the parts of a disaster response.

When preparing the budget for a disaster therefore, the first step is to identify all the parts of a

---

[20] Page 2, IFIR WORKING PAPER SERIES: On the Optimal Design of Disaster Insurance in a Federation; Timothy J. Goodspeed & Andrew Haughwout; IFIR Working Paper No. 2006-14; This Draft: November 3, 2006 quoting from Zeckhauser, Richard, 2006. "Floods, Fires, Earthquakes and Pine Beetles: JARring Actions and Fat Tails," presentation at Berkeley Symposium on Real Estate, Catastrophic Risk and Public Policy

full response and recovery operation for a particular disaster. Then determine the cost of each part of the operation. Finally, the community must decide if they are willing to pay the anticipate cost of an event, or several different events, that may, or may not, actually occur.

NOTE

The goal is to have an emergency process in place with the municipal council or board of supervisors giving one person emergency powers to move forward quickly, and that includes the ability to contract and spend monies.

The Council for Excellence in Government has developed the following Emergency Management Financial Checklist for local governments[21]

1. Include Procurement and Financial Managers in Disaster Planning

Financial and Procurement Managers are often left out of preparedness strategy discussions; this is a fundamental flaw in disaster planning. There is a direct link from the resources required to react in an emergency and the financial managers responsible for acquiring and accounting for those resources. The key financial officials must be prepared with a plan for loss of revenue - payroll back-up pay to pay accounts payable. Purchase cards (EBT) are a critical tool to ease the disbursement of benefits quickly; flexibility in EBT cards for citizens is difficult while keeping the accountability.

2. Relationships

Relationships with peers and vendors must be in place before an emergency occurs. These relationships must be proactive and include pre-set arrangements for vendors to facilitate a smooth procurement process. Examples include pre-established vendors, EBT (Electronic Benefits Transfer) Cards and pre-existing MOUs (Memorandum of Understanding). These relationships must also be effectively communicated.

3. Memoranda of Understanding

Pre-established partnerships with financial institutions are also important; including collaboration among banks and credit card companies before the emergency. MOUs for office space, computer capacity, infrastructure, web-based agreements, etc., must also be taken into consideration.

4. Collaboration - Government Must Work Across Organizational Boundaries

=It is evident that in emergency situations, success comes from collaboration – with the private sector, and non-profit organizations. Innovative collaborations have included counties working across state-lines to develop agreements in the case of emergencies.

5. Documentation of property and systems

It is vital to have one source for documentation and that keeping good records that are accessible and well-communicated in an emergency is crucial to a sustainable system. The Massachusetts Emergency Management Agency was recognized as a best practice because it has standardized forms with a common format that increases the fluidity of reporting across localities, through the state and federal levels, all of which are available online.

6. Practice, Practice, Practice

Emergency Managers dedicate tremendous time and resources to training for emergency preparedness and response. Financial and procurement

---

[21] The council for Excellence in Government ceased in 2009

managers are too often left out of emergency preparedness drills and activities. To address that issue, financial managers must also make a solid commitment of time, education, and exercise around preparation and recovery.

7. Recovery

Recovery takes just as much, if not more collaboration and support than the response stage; too often, everyone focuses on the short-term response, and lack long-term strategy for true recovery.

Pre Contract

Once a decision has been made as to which disasters a community will pre plan for from an economic standpoint, then they should decide how to pay for that disaster: by insurance, a sinking fund, or monies available at that time. In advance, pre contact for goods and services necessary for disaster response to get the best possible price at pre-disaster rates.

Create agreements with private sector companies that may be called upon to support your operations. If during a mass casualty event there are insufficient means of transporting the injured, an agreement with the private ambulance companies can fill the gap, or if a large area needs to be evacuated quickly, an arrangement with private bus companies can help speed the process.

Establish agreements with national suppliers like the Graingers, Home Depots, and Wal-Marts of the world. These companies have established distribution systems and access to large inventories of critical supplies such as water, cots, and blankets, and of lumber, saws, and other basic supplies that both responders and victims may need. Advance agreements with each vendor allows you to establish pricing upfront so you are not overcharged after the act. It also gives you the ability to predefine their response times and other critical protocols. Establish multiple agreements so you are not reliant on any one vendor.

Understand the capabilities and expectations of support agencies like the Salvation Army and Red Cross. Can they provide cots and foods to an entire region affected by an ice storm or floods, or are there limits? Can the responders being deployed to a disaster several states away stop at designated locations the Salvation Army or Red Cross has established along the route? Putting agreements or even plans in place that define the thresholds or reimbursement terms for providing such support is another critical proactive solution to consider.

Participate in or establish private sector industry segment consortium groups. Building managers and owners, utility and other infrastructure companies, healthcare organizations, hotels, as well as universities and colleges, can play an important role in disaster management. Having previously established relationships, contacts, and agreements with these industry segments can make life a lot easier during a disaster.[22]

Mutual Aid Agreements

<u>Mutual aid agreements must be in place to obtain any FEMA reimbursement for any disaster assistance from other agency staff and equipment.</u>

Mutual Aid Agreements for Public Assistance and Fire Management Assistance[23]

Many State, Tribal, and local governments and private nonprofit organizations enter into mutual aid agreements to provide emergency assistance to each other in the event of disasters or emergencies. These agreements often are written, but occasionally are arranged verbally after a disaster or emergency occurs. This policy addresses both written and verbal mutual aid agreements and the

---

[22] <u>Being prepared for disaster: strategies and tactics for finance managers.</u> Wilson, Vicki; 01 December 2007; Government Finance Review: Volume 23; Issue 6, Page 24-25; Copyright 2007 Gale Group Inc.

[23] ***Disaster Assistance Policy 9523.6*** http://www.fema.gov/pdf/government/grant/pa/9523_6.pdf

eligibility of costs under the Emergency Management Assistance Compact (EMAC).

The National Incident Management System (NIMS) maintains that states should participate in these agreements and should look to establish intrastate agreements that encompass all local jurisdictions. The Incident Management Systems Division will be responsible for developing a national system of standards and guidelines as described in the NIMS as well as the preparation of guidance to assist agencies in implementing the system. This policy supports the NIMS by establishing standard criteria for determining the eligibility of costs incurred through mutual aid agreements.

This policy specifies criteria by which the Federal Emergency Management Agency (FEMA) will recognize the eligibility of costs under the Public Assistance (PA) Program and the Fire Management Assistance Grant (FMAG) Program incurred through mutual aid agreements between applicants and other entities.

This policy applies to emergency work authorized under Sections 403, 407, 420, and 502, of the Robert T. Stafford Disaster Relief and Emergency Assistance Act (Stafford Act), 42 U.S.C. 5121-5206, and the implementing regulations of 44 CFR § 204 and § 206.

There are two types of mutual aid work eligible for FEMA assistance: Emergency Work and Grant Management Work. Both are subject to the eligibility requirements of the respective PA and FMAG programs:

A. General

1. To be eligible for reimbursement by FEMA, the mutual aid assistance should have been requested by a Requesting Entity or Incident Commander; be directly related to a Presidentially-declared emergency or major disaster, or a declared fire; used in the performance of eligible work; and the costs must be reasonable.

2. FEMA will not reimburse costs incurred by entities that "self-deploy" (deploy without a request for mutual aid assistance by a Requesting Entity) except to the extent those resources are subsequently used in the performance of eligible work at the request of the Requesting Entity or Incident Commander.

3. The reimbursement provisions of a mutual aid agreement must not be contingent on a declaration of an emergency, major disaster, or fire by the Federal government.

4. This policy is applicable to all forms of mutual aid assistance, including agreements between Requesting and Providing Entities, statewide mutual aid agreements, and the mutual aid services provided under the EMAC.

B. Pre-Event Written Mutual Aid Agreements

FEMA recognizes mutual aid agreements between Requesting and Providing Entities, and statewide mutual aid agreements wherein the State is responsible for administering the claims for reimbursement of Providing Entities. In addition, FEMA recognizes the standard EMAC agreement as a valid form of mutual aid agreement between member states.

1. FEMA encourages parties to have written mutual aid agreements in place prior to a declared fire, emergency, or major disaster.

    a. When a pre-event written agreement exists between a Requesting Entity and a Providing Entity, the Providing Entity may be reimbursed through the Requesting Entity. In these circumstances, the Requesting Entity should claim the eligible costs of the Providing Entity, pursuant to the terms and conditions of the mutual aid agreement and the requirements of this policy, on its subgrant application, and agree to disburse the Federal share of funds to the Providing Entity.

b. When a statewide pre-event mutual aid agreement exists that designates the State responsible for administering the reimbursement of mutual aid costs, a Providing Entity may apply, with the prior consent of the Requesting Entity, for reimbursement directly to the Grantee, in accordance with applicable State law and procedure. In such cases, the Providing Entity should obtain from the Requesting Entity the certification required in section H. (3) of this policy and provide it to the State as part of its reimbursement request.

2. FEMA encourages parties to address the subject of reimbursement in their written mutual aid agreements. FEMA will honor the reimbursement provisions in a pre-event agreement to the extent they meet the requirements of this policy.

   a. When a pre-event agreement provides for reimbursement, but also provides for an initial period of unpaid assistance, FEMA will pay the eligible costs of assistance after such initial unpaid period.

   b. When a pre-event agreement specifies that no reimbursement will be provided for mutual aid assistance, FEMA will not pay for the costs of assistance.

C. Post-Event Mutual Aid Agreements

   a. When the parties do not have a pre-event written mutual aid agreement, or where a written pre-event agreement is silent on reimbursement, the Requesting and Providing Entities may verbally agree on the type and extent of mutual aid resources to be provided in the current event, and on the terms, conditions, and costs of such assistance.

   b. Post-event verbal agreements must be documented in writing and executed by an official of each entity with authority to request and provide assistance, and provided to FEMA as a condition of receiving reimbursement. The agreement should be consistent with past practices for mutual-aid between the parties. A written post-event agreement should be submitted within 30 days of the Requesting Entity's Applicant's Briefing.

1. *Emergency Work.* Mutual aid work provided in the performance of emergency work necessary to meet immediate threats to life, public safety, and improved property, including firefighting activities under the FMAG program, is eligible.

   a. Examples of eligible emergency work include:

      i. Search and rescue, sandbagging, emergency medical care, debris removal;

      ii. Reasonable supervision and administration in the receiving State that is directly related to eligible emergency work;

      iii. The cost of transporting equipment and personnel by the Providing Entity to the incident site, subject to the requirements of paragraphs B(1), (2) and (3) of this policy;

iv. Costs incurred in the operation of the Incident Command System (ICS), such as operations, planning, logistics and administration, provided such costs are directly related to the performance of eligible work on the disaster or fire to which such resources are assigned;

v. State Emergency Operations Center or Joint Field Office assistance in the receiving State to support emergency assistance;

vi. Assistance at the National Response Coordination Center (NRCC), and Regional Response Coordination Center (RRCC), if requested by FEMA (labor, per diem and transportation);

vii. Dispatch operations in the receiving State;

viii. Donations warehousing and management (eligible only upon approval of the Assistant Administrator of the Disaster Assistance Directorate);

ix. Firefighting activities; and,

x. Dissemination of public information authorized under Section 403 of the Act.

b. Examples of mutual aid work that are not eligible, include:

i. Permanent recovery work;

ii. Training, exercises, on-the-job training;

iii. Long-term recovery and mitigation consultation;

2. Costs outside the receiving State that are associated with the operations of the EMAC system (except for FEMA facilities noted in paragraph F.(1)(a)(v) and (vi) above);

3. Costs for staff performing work that is not eligible under the PA or the FMAG programs;

4. Costs of preparing to deploy or "standing-by" [except to the extent allowed in the FMAG program pursuant to 44 CFR § 204.42(e)];

5. Dispatch operations outside the receiving State;

6. Tracking of EMAC and U.S. Forest Service Incident Cost Accounting and Reporting System (ICARS) resources; and

7. Situation reporting not associated with ICS operations under VII(F)(iv) of this policy.

Eligible Applicants

1. Only Requesting Entities are eligible applicants for FEMA assistance. With the exception of.(2), below, a Providing Entity must submit its claim for reimbursement to a Requesting Entity.

2. States may be eligible applicants when statewide mutual aid agreements or compacts authorize the State to administer the costs of mutual aid assistance on behalf of local jurisdictions.

Reimbursement of Mutual Aid Costs

1. Requesting and Providing Entities must keep detailed records of the services requested and received, and provide those records as part of the supporting documentation for a reimbursement request.

2. A request for reimbursement of mutual aid costs must include a copy of the mutual aid agreement - whether pre- or post-event - between the Requesting and Providing Entities.

3. A request for reimbursement of mutual aid costs should include a written and signed certification by the Requesting Entity certifying:

   a. The types and extent of mutual aid assistance requested and received in the performance of eligible emergency work; and

   b. The labor and equipment rates used to determine the mutual aid cost reimbursement request.

4. FEMA will not reimburse the value of volunteer labor or the value of paid labor that is provided at no cost to the applicant. However:

   a. To the extent the Providing Entity is staffed with volunteer labor, the value of the volunteer labor may be credited to the non-Federal cost share of the Requesting Entity's emergency work in accordance with the provisions of Disaster Assistance Policy #9525.2, Donated Resources.

   b. If a mutual aid agreement provides for an initial period of unpaid assistance or provides for assistance at no cost to the Requesting Entity, the value of the assistance provided at no cost to the Requesting Entity may be credited to the non-Federal cost share of the Requesting Entity's emergency work under the provisions of Disaster Assistance Policy #9525.2. Donated Resources.

5. Reimbursement for work beyond emergency assistance, such as permanent repairs, is not eligible for mutual aid assistance

Cash on Hand

In a disaster one major concern of local government is how to pay its employees and for the goods and services it will need. A local or county governmental body should have a reserve of one or two months' cash on hand at any given time, or five to fifteen percent (5-15%) of the government's revenue base. This budgetary reserve can be used to pay salaries and expenses for emergency response needs during the early days of a disaster. Another way to look at this is to have 6 month cash flow that can be reasonably anticipated as not being disrupted as the result of a disaster.

To have a good bond rating, a municipality should have 25% of its annual budget in cash. Most communities can't afford this, but if they can then they probably have the requisite amount of cash on hand to, pardon the pun, weather the storm.

Although a sinking fund, or "rainy day" fund, may be a good idea, there are problems associated with a municipal or county government keeping a large "rainy day fund" on hand.

First, A "rainy day" means different things to different people. An emergency to one person might just be a normal event to another. Therefore, when will the fund be utilized is a threshold question that must be answered. So if there is a "rainy day" fund there must be an agreement as to what constitutes a "rainy day".

Second, having a significant fund in the bank gathering interest may be used as justification for demands in pay and benefits by employees, when in fact it was created only for emergency use.

Third, the taxpayers who are paying for this fund may look at it as a reason to request a reduction in taxes they pay to the municipality or county. "If you guys have all this money in the bank, why am I paying such high taxes?"

Fourth, having a "rainy day" fund means you are in good financial shape which tends to allow a local government to postpone making cuts that should be made.

Thus, a "rainy day" fund may not be politically feasible, a good idea with no "traction" as they say in political circles.

Most local governments will not have sufficient cash on hand to pay for the aftermath of a disaster. If they do, then well and good. The most likely option is to borrow money for the initial emergency response. Generally speaking, as one mayor said, "you do what you have to do." If the local government is in good financial shape, then borrowing money is a viable option. A short-term loan can pay for a response until FEMA reimbursement is received. If FEMA monies are not forthcoming, then the debt becomes long-term and is paid for with municipal bonds or some other long-term obligation. A prudent local government will sit down with their lenders and work out the terms of a loan for disaster recovery before the disaster strikes.

NOTE:

For a variety of reasons, a big deal is quickly getting rid of disaster debris, and a municipality will most likely have to contract with outside companies for this service, so you will need "quick money" to pay for this.

Insurance

National Flood Insurance Program (NFIP)[24]

If a community is located in a Flood Hazard Area the local government must have flood insurance itself. FEMA WILL NOT reimburse the municipality for any loss that would have been covered by flood insurance, if it had had flood insurance. So get flood insurance for municipal buildings located within a Flood Hazard Area or you are out of luck.

NOTE: *Flooding due to the back up of storm drains is not covered by flood insurance.*

The National Flood Insurance Program (NFIP) is a Federal program enabling property owners in participating communities to purchase insurance as a protection against flood losses in exchange for State and community floodplain management regulations that reduce future flood damages. It applies to land within the floodplain of a community subject to a 1 percent or greater chance of flooding in any given year, commonly referred to as the 100-year flood. *IT IS A VOLUNTARY PROGRAM*

This insurance is designed to provide an insurance alternative to disaster assistance to reduce the escalating costs of repairing damage to buildings and their contents caused by floods.

However, FEMA is prohibited from providing flood insurance to property owners *unless the community adopts and enforces floodplain management criteria* established under the authority of National Flood Insurance Act of 1968, as amended (42 U.S.C. 4001 *et seq.*)

Participation in the NFIP is based on an agreement between communities and the Federal Government. If a community adopts and enforces a floodplain management ordinance to reduce future flood risk to new construction in floodplains, the Federal Government will make flood insurance available within the community as a financial protection against flood losses.

Where a State requires that communities adopt more restrictive requirements than the NFIP minimum requirements, the State requirements take precedence over the NFIP minimum.

---

[24] The National Flood Insurance Program http://www.fema.gov/business/nfip/index.shtm

To join the (NFIP) the local governments agree to regulate new development in their floodplains in accordance with NFIP minimum criteria

The Community Rating System (CRS) is a part of the NFIP. The CRS reduces flood insurance premiums to reflect what a community does above and beyond the NFIP's minimum criteria for floodplain development. The objective of the CRS is to reward communities for what they are doing, as well as to provide an incentive to undertake new flood protection activities.

The Community Rating System (CRS) provides a flood insurance premium discount in participating communities that implement floodplain management activities above and beyond the minimum criteria of the National Flood Insurance Program (NFIP). Policy holders receive 5 to 45% discounts on their annual premiums, depending on their flood zone and the community's CRS classification.

Community participation in the CRS is VOLUNTARY.

If a community wants to participate, it submits an application to FEMA. During a "verification visit," the community's programs are reviewed and scored according to the formulas in the *CRS Coordinator's Manual* (found at http://training.fema.gov/EMIWeb/CRS).

The total score determines the community's CRS classification. Classes are from 10 (no discount) to 1 (45% discount) with a 5% flood insurance premium rate discount for each class. Properties outside the "Special Flood Hazard Area" shown on FEMA's Flood Insurance Rate Maps receive a 5% or 10% discount, depending on the community's class. ***Policies on non-compliant structures and "preferred risk" policies do not receive a discount.***

There are some special requirements regarding flood insurance.

The Flood Disaster Protection Act of 1973 (42 U.S.C. 400i *et seq.*) requires that Federal agencies and federally insured or regulated lenders require flood insurance on all grants and loans for acquisition or construction of buildings in designated Special Flood Hazard Areas (SFHAs) in communities that participate in the National Flood Insurance Program (NFIP). This requirement is referred to as the Mandatory Flood Insurance Purchase Requirement. Local governments will advise a building owner if flood insurance is required.

NOTE

Flood insurance is available for properties owned by State or local governments. Flood insurance under the NFIP is sold through two mechanisms:

1. through state-licensed property and casualty insurance agents and brokers who deal directly with FEMA; and
2. through private insurance companies with a program known as "Write Your Own" (WYO).

The premium charged for NFIP flood coverage by a WYO Company is the same as that charged by the Federal Government through the direct program. The Standard Flood Insurance Policy (SFIP) is issued to provide coverage for the peril of flood.

The General Property Form covers residential buildings of more than 4 families as well as non-residential risks.

Flood insurance is available to 1-4 family residential buildings, small businesses, and churches other residential properties, other business properties, agricultural properties, properties occupied by private nonprofit organizations, and properties owned by State or local governments.

Hazard Mitigation[25]

Congress has created a variety of funding sources to help repetitive loss property owners—through their community, state, or tribal government—use long-term mitigation measures to reduce their exposure to flood damage.

In addition to Increased Cost of Compliance (ICC) insurance coverage, the Federal Emergency Management Agency (FEMA) now has a number of grant programs for this purpose.

FEMA requires a FEMA approved Hazard Mitigation Plan as a prerequisite for the following FEMA sources of funding:

Hazard Mitigation Grant Program (HMGP),

Pre-Disaster Mitigation Program (PDM),

Public Assistance (PA),

Flood Mitigation Assistance (FMA),

Repetitive Flood Claims (RFC), and

Severe Repetitive Loss (SRL).

The requirements for the Hazard Mitigation Plan are found at 44 C.F.R. Part 201.

Regional Directors may grant an exception to the plan requirement in extraordinary circumstances, such as in a small and impoverished community, when justification is provided. In these cases, a plan will be completed within 12 months of the award of the project grant. {44 C.F.R.§ 201.6 (a)(3)}

The Plan *must include* a special emphasis on the extent to which benefits are maximized according to *a cost benefit review* of the proposed projects and their associated costs. {44 C.F.R.§ 201.6 (c)(3)(iii)}

The programs have different funding periods and eligibility requirements. Most of the FEMA grants provide 75% of the cost of a project. The owner is expected to fund the other 25%, although in some cases the state or local government may contribute to the non-FEMA share.

They are:

Flood Mitigation Assistance (FMA) — provides funds every year to states and communities for projects that reduce or eliminate the long-term risk of flood damage to buildings, homes, and other structures that are insured under the NFIP. (http://www.fema.gov/government/grant/fma/index.shtm)

Hazard Mitigation Grant Program (HMGP) — provides funds to states and communities after a disaster declaration to protect public or private property through various mitigation measures. (http://www.fema.gov/government/grant/hmgp/index.shtm)

Pre-Disaster Mitigation Grant Program (PDM) — a nationally competitive program that provides funds each year to states and communities, including tribal governments, to help with hazard mitigation planning and mitigation projects before a disaster occurs. (http://www.fema.gov/government/grant/pdm/index.shtm)

Repetitive Flood Claims (RFC) — a nationally competitive program that funds mitigation projects for certain repetitive loss properties in communities or states that cannot participate in the FMA program because they do not have funds for the non-federal match or lack the capacity to manage FMA grant activities. (http://www.fema.gov/government/grant/rfc/index.shtm)

---

[25] Hazard Mitigation Assistance (HMA) Unified Guidance introduces the HMA programs. This document is found at: http://www.fema.gov/library/viewRecord.do?id=4225

Severe Repetitive Loss (SRL) — a grant that is reserved for "severe" repetitive loss properties, i.e., residential properties with a high frequency of losses or a high value of claims. (http://www.fema.gov/government/grant/srl/index.shtm)

Increased Cost of Compliance (ICC) — an extra flood insurance claim payment that can be made if an insured building was flooded and then declared substantially damaged by the local permit office. ICC pays 100% (up to $30,000) of the cost of bringing the damaged building up to the local ordinance's flood protection standards. (http://www.fema.gov/library/viewRecord.do?id=3010)

Public Assistance: Local, State, Tribal and Non-Profit

— FEMA grants to assist state and local governments and certain private nonprofit entities with the response to and recovery from disasters, specifically, the program provides assistance for debris removal, emergency protective measures, and permanent restoration of infrastructure. The eligible share cannot be less than 75% of eligible costs.

FEMA's Emergency Management Institute (EMI) conducts courses on floodplain management and CRS-related topics. These are oriented to local building, zoning, planning, and engineering officials. Tuition for these courses is free for state and local government officials and travel stipends are available. For more information, contact the training office of your state emergency management agency, visit http://training.fema.gov/EMICourses/or call EMI at (301) 447-1000.

NOTE: Duplication of Benefits

FEMA will not provide assistance under HMA programs for activities that duplicate benefits received by or available to Applicants, subapplicants, and other project participants from insurance, other assistance programs, legal awards, or any other source to address the same purpose. Such individuals or entities must notify the Grantee and FEMA of all benefits that they receive or anticipate from other sources for the same purpose, and must seek all such benefits available to them. FEMA will reduce the grant by the amounts available for the same purpose from another source.

The absolute best manual on this subject is the <u>Hazard Mitigation Assistance Program Guidance Pre-Disaster Mitigation, Flood Mitigation Assistance, Repetitive Flood Claims, Severe Repetitive Loss</u>; dated June 19, 2008, published by FEMA which can be found at: http://www.fema.gov/library/viewRecord.do?id=3309

Sample Local Mitigation Plan Scope of Work for Mitigation Grant Application (www.fema.gov/library/viewRecord.do?id=1858).

Flood Mitigation Assistance Program[26]

The Flood Mitigation Assistance (FMA) program administered by FEMA provides funding to assist States and communities to accomplish flood mitigation planning and implement measures to reduce future flood damages to structures.

This program is authorized under the National Flood Insurance Reform Act (NFIRA) of 1994 *(42 U.S.C. §4001).*

These funds can be used before disaster strikes.

The FMA program provides funding up to $20 million a year with a *75/25* cost share. Only projects for mitigation activities specified in an approved Flood Mitigation.

The total amount of FMA grant funds provided during any 5-year period will not exceed

---

[26] http://www.fema.gov/government/grant/fma/index.shtm

$10,000,000 to any State agency or $3,300,000 to any community.

The total amount of FMA grant funds provided to any State, including all communities located in the State, will not exceed $20,000,000 during any 5-year period.

The Administrator of the Homeland Security Agency may waive these limits for any 5-year period when a major disaster or emergency is declared pursuant to the Robert T. Stafford Disaster Relief and Emergency Assistance Act for flood conditions.

Each State, Territory, or Tribal government shall designate one agency to serve as the Applicant for this program as the eligible applicant for this program. Then state-level agencies and local communities that are participating in the NFIP become "eligible subapplicants".

The purpose of FMA project grants is to assist States and communities in implementing flood mitigation projects to reduce the risk of flood damage to NFIP-insurable structures. Examples of eligible types of projects include:

- Elevation of NFIP-insured residential structures and elevation or dry-floodproofing of non-residential structures in accordance with 44 CFR §60.3.

- Acquisition of NFIP-insured structures and underlying real property.

- Relocation of NFIP-insured structures from acquired or restricted real property to sites not prone to flood hazards.

- Demolition of NFIP-insured structures on acquired or restricted real property.

- Beach nourishment activities that focus on facilitating natural dune replenishment through the planting of native dune vegetation and/or the installation of sand fencing. Placement of sand on beach is not eligible.

- Minor physical flood control projects that do not duplicate the flood-prevention activities of other Federal agencies that address localized flood problem areas such as stabilization of stream banks, modification of existing culverts, creation of small stormwater retention basins. Major structural flood control structures, such as levees, dams, and seawalls are not eligible.

To be eligible for funding, a project must be:

- Cost-effective;
- Be technically feasible;
- Conform with the Flood Mitigation Plan; and applicable Federal and State regulations and executive orders; and
- Be located physically in a participating NFIP community that is not on probation.

For projects that directly affect individual structures, such as elevation, acquisition, or relocation, each structure must have a flood insurance policy in force.

FMA will be available to States and communities for mitigation activities that may benefit insurable properties not insured under the NFIP.

For minor structural flood control projects, the effectiveness of the project can be based on benefits provided to insurable structures not insured under the NFIP.

Cost Share

FEMA may contribute up to *75 percent* Federal funding for the amount approved under the grant award to implement approved activities. An increased Federal cost share of up to **90 percent** is available for the mitigation of severe repetitive loss properties for any State or federally recognized Indian Tribal government acting as an Applicant that has taken actions to reduce the number of repetitive loss properties, including severe repetitive loss properties, and has a FEMA-approved State or Tribal Mitigation Plan that specifies how it has reduced, and how it intends to reduce, the number of such repetitive loss properties.

Hazard Mitigation Grant Program[27]

The Hazard Mitigation Grant Program (HMGP) was created in 1988 by Section 404 of the Robert T. Stafford Disaster Relief and Emergency Assistance Act, as amended (*42 U.S.C. § 5121-5207*)

The HMGP assists States and communities in implementing long-term hazard mitigation measures for all hazard types *following a major disaster declaration*. A key purpose of the HMGP is to ensure that the opportunity to take critical mitigation measures to protect life and property from future disasters is not lost during recovery and reconstruction process following a disaster.

HMGP funds are made available based on 15% of the estimated Federal funds to be spent on the Public and Individual Assistance programs (minus administrative expenses) for each disaster. States whose mitigation planning process meets enhanced criteria will be able to receive 20% funding under the regulations implementing the Disaster Mitigation Act of 2000 (42 U.S.C. §5133 et seq.).

Eligible mitigation measures under the HMGP include acquisition or relocation of flood-prone structures, elevation of flood-prone structures, seismic rehabilitation of existing structures, and strengthening of existing structures against wildfire. Additionally, *up to seven percent* of the HMGP funds may be used to develop State and/or local mitigation plans.

The State, as grantee, is responsible for administering the HMGP. Communities develop HMGP project applications and apply for funds through the State. The State notifies potential applicants of the availability of funding, defines a project selection process, ranks and prioritizes projects for funding, and forwards projects to FEMA for approval. The applicant, or subgrantee, carries out approved projects.

Cost Share

The State or local government must provide a *25 percent match*, which can be from a combination of cash and in-kind sources.

Funding is allocated using a "sliding scale" formula based on the percentage of the funds spent on Public and Individual Assistance pro-grams for each Presidentially-declared disaster. For States with a Standard State Mitigation Plan, the formula provides 15 percent of the first $2 billion of estimated aggregate amounts of disaster assistance; 10 percent for the next portion of amounts between $2 billion and $10 billion; and 7.5 percent for the next portion of amounts between $10 billion and $35.333 billion.

FEMA has published the **Hazard Mitigation Grant Program Brochure-Desk Reference** a 252 page reference manual on how to comply with this program. The FEMA publication number for this manual is, FEMA 345.

Pre-Disaster Mitigation Grant Program (PDM)

The Disaster Mitigation Act (DMA) of 2000 (42 U.S.C. §5133 et seq.) authorizes the creation of a *pre-disaster mitigation* program to make grants

---

[27] http://www.fema.gov/government/grant/hmgp/index.shtm

to State, local and tribal governments. It also includes a provision that defines mitigation planning requirements for State, local and tribal governments. The purpose is to reduce or eliminate the long-term risk of flood damage to repetitive loss structures insured under the NFIP.

The DMA authorizes up to *7 percent* of the HMGP funds available to a State to be used for development of State, local and tribal mitigation plans; and provides for States to receive an increased percentage of HMGP funds from *15 percent to 20 percent* if, at the time of the disaster declaration, the State has in effect a FEMA approved State Mitigation Plan that meets the criteria established in regulations.

Each State, Territory, or Tribal government shall designate one agency to serve as the Applicant for this program as the eligible applicant for this program. Then state-level agencies and local communities that are participating in the NFIP become "eligible subapplicants".

PDM grants are awarded on a competitive basis. Eligible subapplications will compete nationally for PDM grant funds. The primary applicant is the state with local governments as "subapplicants".

- The total State cap on Federal share is 15 percent of the total appropriation in any year;
- Mitigation projects: $3 million cap on Federal share;
- New Mitigation plans: $800,000 cap on Federal Share for new plans;
- Updating Mitigation plans: $400,000 cap on Federal share for update of plans; and information dissemination activities: not to exceed 10 percent, must directly relate to a planning or project subapplication.

Certain non-participating political subdivisions (e.g., Councils of Governments, Regional Planning Commissions, or County governments) may apply and act as subgrantee on behalf of the NFIP-participating community in areas where the political subdivision provides zoning and building code enforcement, or planning and community development professional services for that community.

Only those NFIP-participating communities or federally recognized Indian Tribal governments that are not suspended or withdrawn from the NFIP are eligible to receive HMA grant funds.

All Applicants must have a FEMA-approved State Mitigation Plan (Standard or Enhanced) or Tribal Mitigation Plan by the application deadline to be eligible to apply for and receive HMA grant funding. 44 C.F.R. Part 201

All subapplicants must be participating in the NFIP to be eligible to apply for HMA grant funds and to act as subgrantee.

Certain non-participating political subdivisions (i.e., Councils of Governments, Regional Planning Commissions, or County governments) may apply and act as subgrantee on behalf of the NFIP-participating community in areas where the political subdivision provides zoning and building code enforcement or planning and community development professional services for that community.

There are two exceptions for PDM only:

- Applicants/subapplicants that have not been identified or issued a Flood Hazard Boundary Map (FHBM) or FIRM are eligible for the PDM program; and

- Federally recognized Indian Tribal governments may be eligible to receive PDM planning grants even if they have been issued a FHBM or FIRM and are not participating in the NFIP. Tribal governments will not be eligible for PDM project grants, however, until they are participating in the NFIP.

Cost Share

The federal share of the cost of this grant can be up to *75 percent*. Small and impoverished communities may be eligible for up to a *90 percent* Federal cost share.

Repetitive Flood Claims Program (RFC)[28]

The Repetitive Flood Claims (RFC) grant program provides funding to *reduce or eliminate the long-term risk* of flood damage to structures insured under the NFIP that have had one or more claim payments for flood damages.

RFC funds may only mitigate structures that are located within a State or community that cannot meet the cost share or management capacity requirements of the FMA program.

Funding is restricted to a maximum of *$1 million* for minor localized flood reduction projects.

All currently NFIP-insured residential or non-residential (commercial) properties with one or more claims to the NFIP are eligible to apply for RFC funds.

At least 50 percent of the structures directly benefiting from the mitigation activity must be properties that are both NFIP-insured and have one or more claims to the NFIP.

The Repetitive Flood Claims Grant Program is a nationally competitive program and is not based on target allocations.

Each State, Territory, or Tribal government shall designate one agency to serve as the Applicant for this program who shall act as the program applicant.

State-level agencies and local communities that are participating in the NFIP are subapplicants.

Private nonprofit (PNP) organizations and individuals are not eligible subapplicants; however, a relevant State agency or local community in which the PNP or individual resides may act as the subapplicant and apply to the Applicant for assistance to mitigate a private or PNP property.

Property owners who participate in the RFC program must have a flood insurance policy on the structure to be mitigated that is current at the time of application and maintained through award, or until the property transfer is complete.

- All Applicants must have a FEMA-approved State Mitigation Plan (Standard or Enhanced) or Tribal Mitigation Plan by the application deadline to be eligible to receive project grant funding under the RFC program, in accordance with 44 CFR Part 201; and
- If any plan is due to lapse soon after application, the project award may be held pending approval of a new or updated plan.

RFC funds are available for mitigation projects involving:

- Acquisition and demolition or relocation of structures, with conversion of the underlying property to deed-restricted open space;
- Elevation of existing structures to at least the BFE or an ABFE or higher;
- Dry floodproofing of non-residential structures; and
- Minor localized flood reduction projects (funding limited to $1 million per project).

---

[28] http://www.fema.gov/government/grant/rfc/index.shtm

A separate management cost subapplication must be submitted for Applicant management costs.

Applicants may include a maximum of 10 percent of the total funds requested in their RFC grant application budget (Federal and non-Federal shares) to *residential structures* insured under the NFIP support the project subapplications.

Subapplicants may include a maximum of 5 percent of the total funds requested in their project subapplication for management costs to support the project subapplication.

Cost Share

All RFC grants are eligible for up to *100 percent* Federal assistance

Severe Repetitive Loss Program (SRL)[29]

The Severe Repetitive Loss (SRL) Pilot Program, hereafter referred to as the SRL program, provides funding to *reduce or eliminate the long-term* risk of flood damage to severe repetitive loss.

Each State, Territory, or Tribal government shall designate one agency to serve as the Applicant for this program who shall act as the program applicant.

State-level agencies and local communities that are participating in the NFIP are subapplicants.

Private nonprofit (PNP) organizations and individuals are not eligible subapplicants; however, a relevant State agency or local community in which the PNP or individual resides may act as the subapplicant and apply to the Applicant for assistance to mitigate a private or PNP property.

All Applicants must have a FEMA-approved State Mitigation Plan (Standard or Enhanced) or Tribal Mitigation Plan by the application deadline to be eligible to receive project grant funding under the SRL program, in accordance with 44 CFR Part 201.

All subapplicants must have a FEMA-approved mitigation plan by the application deadline to be eligible to receive project grant funding under the SRL program.

Eligible projects include:

- Acquisition and demolition or relocation of structures, with conversion of the underlying property to deed-restricted open space;
- Elevation of existing structures to at least the BFE or an ABFE or higher. Mitigation reconstruction is permitted when traditional elevation cannot be implemented;
- Minor physical localized flood reduction projects; and
- Dry floodproofing (historic properties only).

Eligible management costs include:

A separate management cost subapplication must be submitted for Applicant management costs. Applicants may include a maximum of 10 percent of the total funds requested in their SRL grant application budget (Federal and non-Federal shares) to support the project subapplications.

Subapplicants may include a maximum of 5 percent of the total funds requested in their project subapplication for management costs to support the project.

SRL property owners who decline a formal offer of mitigation under the SRL program will be subject to an increase in their insurance premium rates under the NFIP.

---

[29] http://www.fema.gov/government/grant/srl/index.shtm

Cost Share

Funding is restricted to a maximum Federal cost share of *$150,000* for Mitigation Reconstruction projects.

FEMA may contribute up to *75 percent* Federal funding for the amount approved under the grant award to implement approved activities.

An increased Federal cost share of up to *90 percent* is available for any State or federally recognized Indian Tribal government acting as an Applicant that has taken actions to reduce the number of repetitive loss properties, including severe repetitive loss properties, and has a FEMA-approved State or Tribal Mitigation Plan that specifies how it has reduced, and how it intends to reduce, the number of such repetitive loss properties.

Increased Cost of Compliance Program (ICC)[30]

Flood insurance policyholders in high-risk areas, also known as Special Flood Hazard Areas, can get up to $30,000 of ICC coverage to help pay the costs to bring their home or business into compliance with their community's floodplain ordinance.

There are four options you can take to comply with your community's floodplain management ordinance and help reduce your future flood damage.

1. Elevation. This raises your home or business to or above the flood elevation level adopted by your community.
2. Relocation. This moves your home or business out of harm's way.
3. Demolition. This tears down and removes flood-damaged buildings.
4. Floodproofing. This option is available primarily for nonresidential buildings. It involves making a building watertight through a combination of adjustments or additions of features to the building that reduces the potential for flood damage.

You can file a claim for Increased Cost of Compliance coverage in two instances:

1. If the municipality determines that the home or business is damaged by flood to the point that repairs will cost 50 percent or more of the building's predamage market value. This is called substantial damage.

2. If your community has a repetitive loss provision in its floodplain management ordinance and determines that your home or business was damaged by a flood two times in the past 10 years, where the cost of repairing the flood damage, on the average, equaled or exceeded 25 percent of its market value at the time of each flood. Additionally, there must have been flood insurance claim payments for each of the two flood losses. This is called repetitive damage.

The ICC claim is adjusted separately from the flood damage claim filed under the Standard Flood Insurance Policy.

How to Apply

A claim can only be filed if the municipality determines that the home or business has been substantially or repetitively damaged by a flood. This determination is made when upon application for a building permit to begin repairing the home or business.

Once a determination has been made that the property qualifies for an ICC claim, contact the insurance company or agent who wrote the flood policy to file an ICC claim.

---

[30] http://www.fema.gov/plan/prevent/floodplain/ICC.shtm

A partial payment will be made once the claims representative has a copy of the signed contract for the work, a permit from the municipality to do the work, and a signed ICC Proof of Loss. If the work is not completed, you must return any partial payment to the insurer.

Upon completion of the work certificate of occupancy or a confirmation letter must be submitted to the claims representative, then the insurer will pay the final installment in full.

Hazard Mitigation Assistance (HMA) Program Eligible Projects

Mitigation Project	PDM	FMA	RFC	SRL
Property Acquisition & Demolition or Relocation	Yes	Yes	Yes	Yes
Property Elevation	Yes	Yes	Yes	Yes
Mitigation Reconstruction[1]				Yes
Localized Minor Flood Reduction Projects	Yes	Yes	Yes	Yes
Dry Flood proofing of Residential Property[2]		Yes		Yes
Dry Flood proofing of non-Residential Structures		Yes	Yes	
Stormwater Management	Yes	Yes		
Infrastructure Protection Measures	Yes			
Vegetative Protection Measures	Yes			
Retrofitting Bldgs and Facilities (Wind/Earthquake)	Yes			
Safe Room Construction	Yes			
All Hazard/Flood Mitigation Planning	Yes	Yes		

1. The Severe Repetitive Loss (SRL) Program allows mitigation reconstruction projects located OUTSIDE the regulatory floodway or Zone V as identified on the effective Flood Insurance Rate Map (FIRM), or the mapped limit of the 1.5-foot breaking wave zone. Mitigation reconstruction is only permitted if traditional elevation cannot be implemented.

2. The residential structure must meet the definition of "Historic Structure" in 44 C.F.R. § 59.1

Approved Mitigation Plan Requirement for Funding

Plan Requirement	PDM		FMA		RFC	SRL
	Funding Activity Project Planning		Funding Activity Project Planning		Funding Activity Project	Funding Activity Project
State or Tribal Mitigation Plan	Yes	No	Yes	No	Yes	Yes
Local Mitigation Plan	Yes	---	Yes	---	---	Yes
Repetitive Loss Strategy (to be eligible for 90%/10% cost share)	---	---	Yes	---	---	Yes

Percent of Federal/Non-Federal Share

Program	Project Grant Grantee	Planning Grant Subgrantee	Management Cost-Grantee amount in ()	Management Cost-Subgrantee amount in ()
PDM-Regular	75/25	75/25	75/25 (10)*	75/25 (5)*
PDM-Small & Impoverished	90/10	90/10	75/25 (10)*	90/10 (5)*
FMA-Regular	75/25	75/25	75/25 (10)*	75/25 (10)*
RFC	100/0	---	100/0 (10)*	100/0 (5)*
SLR-Regular	75/25	---	75/25 (10)*	75/25 (5)*
SLR-with Repetitive Loss Strategy	90/10	---	90/10 (10)*	90/10 (5)*

After the Incident

"It's true that a certain amount of waste and fraud is inevitable in the early stages of a catastrophic event ..., in some cases, the benefits of cutting deals quickly and expediently exceed the few rotten apples that are bound to surface."[31]

Federal Emergency Management Agency (FEMA)[32]

Generally speaking, the Federal Emergency Management Agency (FEMA) coordinates federal post disaster relief for individuals, farmers, businesses and local governments. For this reason, an understanding of how FEMA operates is critical for post disaster financial aid and reimbursement.

NOTE:

FEMA does not coordinate all disaster relief that is available through the federal government. Other agencies such as the Department of Agriculture and Department of Education have their own programs that they administer.

Disclaimer

FEMA disaster assistance programs are flexible and discretionary in nature. Accordingly, it is strongly recommended that users of this Manual verify the following information with FEMA following a particular disaster declaration.

Overview

The Federal Emergency Management Agency (FEMA) provides disaster victims with assistance under several programs. The eligibility rules for each program differ -- an applicant who does not qualify for one program, may qualify for another.

FEMA is also responsible for emergency planning, preparedness, mitigation, response and recovery through administration of the Robert T. Stafford Disaster Relief and Emergency Assistance Act (Stafford Act)[33]. FEMA provides assistance to both public entities and individuals. This section will focus only on the programs which assist individuals and families. For an overview of disaster individual assistance programs available for renters and homeowners, see the chart at the end of this section.

FEMA provides tax-free grants to households that have been displaced from their primary residence as the result of a federally declared disaster through its Rental Assistance program. The Rental Assistance program provides need-based grants to enable homeowners and renters who

---

[31] Mark Lacter; 26 September 2005; Los Angeles Business Journal

[32] *The United States government has a web portal for disaster information and disaster relief applications. http://www.disasterassistance.gov/daip_en.portal*

[33] Public Law 93-288 as amended, 42 U.S.C. § 5121 et seq.

are victims of disaster-related dislocation to obtain temporary replacement housing.

The Individuals and Households Program-Other Needs Assistance (IHP-ONA) program is administered by states to cover necessary expenses and serious needs that cannot be met through other forms of disaster assistance. This assistance may cover repairing/rebuilding real or personal property, transportation, medical, dental and funeral expenses incurred by disaster victims.

The maximum amount of the total IHP grant is adjusted each fiscal year and for the year ending September 30, 2015, the amount is set at $32,900

In most states the state Emergency Management Agency (EMA) has the responsibility for administering the following disaster assistance programs:

- FEMA Individuals and Households Program (IHP)
- FEMA Public Assistance Program
- State Individual Assistance Program
- State Disaster Relief Program

The Cora Brown Fund which is administered by FEMA. This fund is used for disaster victims who have exhausted all other avenues of assistance but still have unmet needs.

Disaster Unemployment Assistance (DUA) provides help for workers and those who are self-employed if they become unemployed as a direct result of the effects of a disaster. DUA is funded 100 % by FEMA but is administered by the Department of Labor through the state unemployment agency. Benefits can extend up to 26 weeks after the date of the declaration of disaster or until the applicant is reemployed, whichever is earlier.

FEMA provides grant funds to state or local mental health agencies to help relieve grief, stress or other mental health problems associated with the disaster. The program is funded by FEMA but administered by the U.S. Department of Health and Human Services.

FEMA, through a program with the American Bar Association's Young Lawyers Section, coordinates free disaster legal services to victims of major disasters. These services include assistance with insurance claims (life, medical, and property), landlord-tenant problems, consumer protection, and wills and estates.

I. Declaration of a Disaster

A. Local Disaster or State of Emergency

When a natural or manmade disaster arises, the local community -- both governmental and volunteer --responds. The local Red Cross, Salvation Army, or other private relief agencies usually initiate assistance to victims of a local disaster such as a fire or flood. In some cases, the degree of the disaster exceeds local resources. When local resources are insufficient to meet the needs of the crisis, the county or city government requests the state's governor to proclaim a state of emergency. This releases state funds for reimbursement of local costs.

It is a prerequisite for requesting federal recovery assistance.

B. Disaster Declaration Process for a Major Disaster

1. State Action

If the damage exceeds state, local and private relief resources, the governor submits a letter to the FEMA Regional Director[34] requesting Federal Government assistance.

---

[34] FEMA Regional offices are found at: http://www.fema.gov/about/regions/index.shtm

2. Federal Response

The Regional Director investigates and makes a recommendation to the Director of FEMA in Washington, D.C. The Director of FEMA recommends to the President whether or not a federal disaster should be declared.

3. Action by FEMA

Once the President makes a Federal disaster declaration, the Director of FEMA appoints a Federal Coordinating Officer (FCO) to coordinate the administration of local disaster assistance programs. The FEMA Regional Director may designate a Disaster Recovery Manager (DRM), but often the FCO and DRM is the same person. The Associate Director of FEMA designates the types of available assistance to disaster victims and the eligible program assistance areas.

Also, the State Governor appoints a State Coordinating Officer (SCO) to coordinate state and local disaster assistance efforts with FEMA. A Disaster Field Office (DFO) is established in or near the affected area. The DFO houses federal and state staff responding to the disaster.

Presidential Declaration of Disaster

The date that the President makes a Declaration of a Major Disaster (or Emergency) is the key to releasing funds for three major types of federal disaster assistance, if requested and designated.

1. Human Services (Individual Assistance)

a. Disaster Housing Assistance
b. Small Business Administration loans to individuals and businesses
c. Farm Service Agency
   Emergency loans to farmers and ranchers
d. Individual and Households Program
e. Emergency Food Stamps [now called "Supplemental Nutrition Assistance Program (SNAP)]
f. Crisis Counseling
g. Disaster Unemployment Assistance {different than regular UA}
h. Disaster Legal Services {via Volunteer Attorneys}

2. Infrastructure Assistance to State and Local Governments and Eligible Private Non-Profit Organizations (Public Assistance)

a. Debris clearance;
b. Repair of public roads, streets, bridges, buildings;
c. Emergency protective measures, search and rescue, demolition of unsafe structures; and
d. Repair/replacement of water control facilities (dikes and levees).

3. Hazard Mitigation Grant Program for State and Local Governments and Eligible Private Non-Profit Organizations

Provides financial assistance for approved mitigation measures which are cost effective and substantially reduce the risk of future damage from a major disaster.

D. Deadlines for Individual Assistance Programs

The declaration date is an important date because it is the basis for all disaster assistance deadlines. The Incident Period which is the time interval during which the disaster-causing incident occurred is also important because the damages or hardship claimed must have resulted from the disaster-causing incident during that period or in anticipation of that incident. A chart listing the number of days or months after the disaster declaration date within which an applicant may submit a timely application can be found at the end of this section.

E. Denials and Appeals

Individuals who miss deadlines, are found ineligible for assistance, or receive an inadequate amount of assistance may appeal the decision. In addition, individuals whose applications are withdrawn or whose applications are refused because of late filing may appeal. All FEMA appeals must be filed within 60 days of the date of the notice of decision. The agency must review the appeal and make a final decision within 90 days.

Every program and agency has a separate appeals program. An applicant must file a separate appeal for each denial.

F. No Duplication of Benefits

Individuals and families may receive assistance from various sources: private insurance, FEMA, traditional government benefits, Small Business Administration loans, etc. However, the rule is that FEMA may not provide benefits duplicated through insurance or other governmental assistance programs. FEMA can provide assistance that may ultimately be paid for by insurance, for example, subject to a repayment requirement (see below).

G. Sequence for Disaster Aid

The FEMA delivery sequence for disaster assistance is the following:

- Emergency assistance provided by voluntary agencies
- Insurance
- Disaster Housing Assistance
- SBA loans
- Individual and Household Program (IHP)-Other Needs Assistance (ONA) Additional assistance
- The Cora Brown Fund

Assistance only duplicates other aid which is higher on the list. Duplication of benefits exists when a family receives disaster assistance funds for the same need more than once.

For example, a family may receive money for home repairs from both the Individual and Households Program (IHP) (#5 in the sequence) and from insurance (#2 in the sequence) for the same repairs. Since IHP is #5, the family will probably have to pay IHP back since it comes later in the sequence. However, if they can show that the cost for eligible repairs exceeded the money received or the IHP award covered their insurance deductible, they may not have to repay the award.

H. Cora Brown Fund[35]

The Cora Brown Fund ("Fund") which is administered by FEMA provides special disaster assistance awards which are made possible by a bequest of funds from the late Cora C. Brown of Kansas City, Missouri. The fund is used for extraordinary circumstances involving serious, unmet disaster-related needs of individuals.

1. Disaster Assistance

Fund awards are to be used to provide for disaster-related needs that have not been or will not be met by governmental departments and agencies, or any other organizations which have programs to address such needs. It is not intended to replace or supersede these programs or to duplicate assistance for which a person is eligible from other sources. General categories of assistance include:

---

[35] "The Congressional Digest estimates that the annual obligations for the entire program are typically less than $225,000." McMahon, P., FEMA's Cora Brown Fund, Institute for Crisis, Disaster, and Risk Management Crisis and Emergency Management Newsletter Website, March 2006, Vol. 10-No.2.

a. Disaster-related home repair and rebuilding assistance;
b. Costs associated with temporary housing or permanent rehousing;
c. Disaster-related unmet needs; and
d. Other services which alleviate human suffering and promote the well-being of disaster victims.

2. Identification of Candidates for Assistance

Assistance is not available to disaster victims in non-declared disasters or in non-declared counties. Because the Fund is not automatically available, disaster victims do not apply for such assistance. Candidates who may be in need of this assistance may be identified by the Regional Director through contacts with other departments or agencies, or by local governments, the American Red Cross, and other volunteer agencies active in disasters. A panel consisting of agency representatives, meeting as an unmet needs committee, may be established to facilitate identification of disaster victims who may benefit from the Fund. An award may be provided to the disaster victim or jointly to him/her and to the State, a local agency or volunteer organization to assist in providing the approved assistance. Assistance may be awarded to provide authorized services which benefit a group of disaster victims.

<u>Contact FEMA for more information on the operation of the fund.</u>

II. Who Can Get FEMA Assistance

A. Eligibility for FEMA Assistance

If an individual, business, local government, or non-profit has experienced a loss as a result of a federally declared disaster, they may be eligible for assistance through FEMA.

Register with FEMA as quickly as possible. *(The victim does not necessarily have to live in the declared disaster area to be eligible for FEMA's programs, but the loss must have been caused by devastation from the disaster)*

FEMA does not accept paper applications. You cannot print out the online application and mail it to FEMA.

The easiest way to register with FEMA is to call **(800) 621-FEMA (3362)** Monday – Friday between 8 a.m. to 6 p.m. For the speech- or hearing-impaired, call **TTY: (800) 462-7585**. Be prepared to give the FEMA representative the following information:

1. your name;
2. your Social Security number;
3. any applicable insurance information;
4. a description of your losses;
5. directions to your damaged property; and
6. a phone number where you can be reached.

A disaster victim can also register at FEMA's website: *http://www.fema.gov* by clicking on the "register for assistance" link. A disaster victim may also check on the status of their application online. A disaster victim can also register at one of FEMA's local assistance centers or disaster recovery centers.

You will need the following information to complete the registration:

Social Security Number

You will be asked to provide your social security number; if you are registering for a business, your tax ID number should be provided.

If you do not have a social security number, your household may still be able to receive assistance if there is a minor child in the household who is a U.S. Citizen, Non-Citizen National, or Qualified Alien with a social security number.

NOTE:

If you, your spouse or a minor child in the household who is a U.S. Citizen, Non-Citizen National, or a Qualified Alien does not have a social security number, FEMA will not be able to complete a registration.

The *Social Security number is required for Identity Verification purposes.*

Insurance information

You will be asked to identify the type(s) of insurance coverage you have.

Financial information

You will be asked to enter your family's gross total household income at the time of the disaster.

Contact information

Along with the address and phone number where the damages occurred, you will be asked for information on how FEMA can contact you. It is very important that you provide FEMA with your current mailing address and phone numbers where you can be contacted.

Electronic Funds Transfer (EFT) Direct Deposit Information (optional)

If you are determined to be eligible for assistance and would prefer that funds be transferred to your account, you will be asked for your banking information, which includes; the institution name, type of account, routing and account number.

The various programs that FEMA coordinates have different eligibility criteria, and usually the victim only can receive assistance under one housing program at a time. FEMA will determine eligibility for the various programs after the disaster victim registers.

B. Aliens

To be qualified for cash assistance from FEMA the applicant must be a U.S. citizen or a qualified alien. A qualified alien generally includes persons who are lawful permanent residents (possessing an alien registration card) or those with legal status due to asylum, refugee, or parole.

C. Red Cross or Voluntary Aid

Disaster assistance available from FEMA is different than the emergency clothing, food and shelter administered by the Red Cross and other voluntary relief agencies.

If a disaster victim received assistance from the Red Cross or other agency, he/she still must register with FEMA to receive federal disaster assistance.

III. Deadlines For Applications

There will be important application deadlines that must be meet (unless specifically extended by FEMA), each of which is calculated from the date of the disaster declaration.

Application Deadlines for Individual Assistance Programs	
Individual Assistance Programs	Application Deadline
Rental Assistance	60 days after disaster *
Mortgage Assistance	6 months after disaster*

Application Deadlines for Individual Assistance Programs	
Individual Assistance Programs	Application Deadline
Home Repair Assistance	60 days after disaster*
Individual & Households Program (IHP)	60 days after disaster*
Disaster Unemployment Assistance	30 days after disaster*
SBA Loans for damage or loss to real and personal property	60 days after disaster*
SBA Loans for economic injury to small businesses	9 months after disaster*
Emergency Food Stamps [now called Supplemental Nutrition Assistance Program (SNAP)]	10 days after disaster*

* The date that the President makes a Declaration of a Major Disaster (or Emergency) is the date used for the running of the above statute of limitations.

The standard deadline for registration for individual disaster assistance is within 60 days following the date the President declares the disaster unless another date is specified.

A. FEMA Can Extend the Deadline

FEMA is authorized to accept late registrations for an additional 60 days beyond the standard registration period. However, FEMA rules require suitable documentation of the reasons for the delay.

IV. How Long Does It Take?

A. To get help from FEMA

If a disaster victim has damage to his/her home or its contents and is uninsured, or have suffered damage due to a flood, a FEMA inspector should contact the victim within 14 days of applying, to set up an appointment to assess the damage. Typically, within about 10 days after the inspection, if FEMA determines that the victim is qualified for help, a direct deposit to the victim's bank account will be made, or a check will be sent in the mail. The amount of the deposit or check will only be for the amount determined by FEMA, not necessarily the amount of the total loss.

B. After The Application is Submitted

If an applicant has questions call the FEMA Disaster Helpline at 1-800-621-FEMA (hearing/speech impaired only: 1-800-462-7585).

If it has been more than 12 days since the FEMA inspector's visit and there has been no word from FEMA, call the FEMA Disaster Helpline at 1-800-621-FEMA (hearing/speech impaired only: 1-800-462-7585) to ask about your application. If there is a Disaster Recovery Center (DRC) in the applicant's area, he or she also may inquire there about their application.

V. FEMA At Work

Each applicant must register for assistance (either by telephone or, if provided for, in-person). A FEMA screener registers each person and completes a one-page computerized application form. A control number appears on the top of each application for identification purposes.

A. Teleregistration and On-Line Registration

After the President makes a Declaration of Disaster, call toll-free 1-800-621-3362,

TDD 1-800-462-7585 and register for disaster assistance, or register on-line at www.fema.gov/assistance/register.shtm .

AT&T and FEMA may provide interpreter services for non-English speakers. Procedures for in-person registration are decided on a disaster-by-disaster basis and will generally not be implemented except as a last resort when teleregistration is impossible or impractical.

Applicants will need to have the following information available when they teleregister or register on-line:

a. Social security number;
b. Physical and mailing address of the damaged property;
c. Insurance information;
d. Phone number where they can be reached; and
e. A description of their losses.

An applicant's response to the questions on the FEMA registration/application form the basis for consideration for programs administered by FEMA, as well as referral by FEMA to disaster assistance programs such as SBA and IHP which are administered by other agencies.

B. FEMA Application Process

At the time of registration, the FEMA representative will give the applicant a **control (application) number**. This number is very important for referencing the applicant's case, so please keep it handy. In the event the applicant did not register online, it is also a good idea to keep the name of the person who took the registration information, in case any problems arise regarding the paperwork.

FEMA may then refer the applicant to the Small Business Administration (SBA), which offers special loans to disaster victims. (It does not matter whether the applicant owns a small business or not.)

Review, Verification and Recertification

The NPSC is responsible for processing the disaster assistance registrations. The processing is centralized in order to provide consistent, efficient, orderly, and responsive service. The NPSC's duties include gathering and reviewing information and making eligibility determinations on FEMA DHA applications; maintaining records; and responding to applicant questions, concerns and issues.

The NPSC reviews the inspection data and the application information and makes the decision to grant or deny assistance or to request additional information and/or verification of eligibility criteria and may request for example records of home ownership or tenancy, copies of insurance documents, estimates of repairs, pay stubs, etc. FEMA notifies the applicant by mail of the decision to grant or deny assistance. The assistance, if any, is generally provided in the form of a check issued by the United States Treasury Department to the applicant and mailed separately from the notice.

If additional assistance is requested, FEMA may request additional verifications after the initial grant. Some programs, such as rental assistance or mortgage and rental assistance may be provided for an initial one-, two-, or three-month period and require recertification if assistance is needed for a longer period of time. An applicant must submit additional information/documentation on his or her housing and/or financial status depending on the type of assistance requested to obtain recertification. Receipts documenting how the initial grant was spent must also be provided.

NOTE:

If the applicant is referred to the SBA, the applicant must complete and send in the SBA loan

application; even if the applicant does not think he/she will qualify for a loan.

The SBA serves as a gatekeeper to other government-run programs. Unless the victim sends in the application and fails to qualify for an SBA loan (or a large enough loan to meet the needs), the application will not be passed on to the Other Needs Assistance (ONA) Programs, and the applicant may not be eligible for additional assistance from other federal disaster programs.

C. Outreach Teams and Workshops

In addition to using the media, FEMA and the State EMA conduct workshops at outreach locations to inform local government, non-profit agencies and disaster victims about the available disaster programs, as well as the most current state/federal regulations. FEMA uses the outreach teams and workshops as a means to inform persons throughout a widespread disaster area about the disaster relief effort and to encourage individuals to apply for benefits.

D. DRCs -- Disaster Recovery Centers

Disaster Recovery Centers (DRCs) are temporary facilities that may be established in disaster areas to provide assistance information to disaster victims. FEMA in coordination with the State EMA decides whether to, and for how long to, establish DRCs after each disaster. Geography and the extent of damage are major factors in considering whether to open DRCs and their locations. Each DRC is managed and staffed by both FEMA and EMA personnel. DRCs may include representatives from various federal, state, local government and volunteer agencies. They may provide information and assistance in areas such as legal services, individual loans, financial grants, tax advice, consumer concerns, public benefits, unemployment insurance, agricultural assistance, medical services, veteran's services and volunteer services. FEMA may use mobile DRCs to reach homebound victims or isolated communities as necessary.

E. DRCs -- Crisis Counseling

- Disaster victims are eligible for crisis counseling if they were residents of the designated major disaster area or located in the area at the time of the disaster event. They must have a mental health problem which was caused or aggravated by the disaster or its aftermath or benefit from preventive care techniques. Crisis counseling is available not only for victims but also for emergency workers who may become overwhelmed during disaster work. Disaster crisis counseling services are not limited to the DRCs.

- Administered through the State Mental Health Agency in cooperation with the Center for Mental Health Services (CMHS).

- Provided as immediate services during the first 60 days following a declaration, and must be supplied within 14 days of the disaster declaration.

- The regular program provides up to 9 months of CC services and must be applied for separately by the Governor within 60 days of the declaration.

Outreach services include public information, community networking, and education services.

F. Individuals and Households Program (IHP)

The purpose of the FEMA Individuals and Households Program (IHP) is to help individuals and households be safely housed and to cover necessary expenses and serious needs following the effects of a disaster. Housing Assistance (includes Temporary Housing, Repair, Replacement, and

Permanent Housing Construction); and Other Needs Assistance (includes personal property, medical, dental, funeral, and other items).

To be initially considered for any type of FEMA IHP assistance, the affected home must be an individual's primary residence located in the declared disaster area, and necessary expense or serious need must have occurred in the declared disaster area, and the individual (or an adult household member) must be a United States citizen, a non-citizen national, or a qualified alien.

G. Voluntary Assistance Agencies (VOLAGs) at DRCs Including Legal Services

Each community also has many voluntary agencies including, but not limited to, the American Red Cross, Salvation Army, Economic Opportunity Councils, food banks, agencies on aging, independent living centers, local legal services providers and bar associations. Each of these agencies may provide information or persons who can assist survivors with community resources. Not all DRCs will have representatives from the same entities and participation varies from disaster to disaster.

H. The applicant does NOT have to own a business to apply for an SBA loan

The SBA's low-interest loan program is one of the primary sources of federal assistance for long-term recovery for homeowners as well as business owners. For more information call the SBA at (800) 659-2955 [TTY: (704) 344-6640] or visit the SBA website at *http://www.sba.gov/disaster*.

I. Removal of Debris

Contact the local or state government, but not FEMA since FEMA does not cover these costs, But, if the applicant obtains an SBA loan it may be used for debris removal.

VII. FEMA's Inspection, Verification, Recertification and Audit Process Consequences for Misuse

The penalty for misusing disaster funds is immediate repayment of one-and-a-half times the original amount of the loan.

A. Inspections

If the disaster victim has requested help from FEMA because of damage to his/her home, FEMA will send an inspector to look at the damage. These inspectors are not FEMA employees but are contractors. Nevertheless, the FEMA inspection is FREE. *Do not let anyone charge you for an "inspection service."* Request identification from the inspector, and request a copy of his or her inspection report. FEMA inspectors file a report but do not determine eligibility.

The inspection information gathered will be used for eligibility determinations for DHA and for IHP home repair and personal property damage assistance.

The victim does not need to wait until the inspection to begin cleaning and repairing the property, but should document the damage by taking pictures. (Video is a good record, too!) If possible, save damaged items.

Be prepared to meet with the inspector on short notice. If the disaster victim is not available for the inspection, your application may be withdrawn. The disaster victim must be prepared to supply the inspector with several pieces of information:

1. valid identification;
2. proof of home ownership or tenancy;
3. proof of damages to your primary residence;

4. receipts for expenses you have incurred; and
5. photos of your property before you began repairs.

The disaster victim will also need to sign the disaster application and a declaration that he/she is a citizen, a national, a resident alien, or otherwise lawfully present in the U.S. *See* Appendix A of this Handbook for information regarding immigration issues.

The FEMA inspector will complete a report and transmit it to FEMA's National Processing Servicing Center (NPSC). The NPSC will review the information and decide whether the disaster victim qualifies for assistance. (In the interim, the NPSC may ask for additional records, such as insurance papers, a copy of title, pay stubs, or repair estimates.) FEMA will mail a notice of its decision to the disaster victim. Thus the disaster victim needs a viable mailing address at this time.

Applicants must be available for inspections on short notice or their application may be withdrawn. They do not need to wait until the FEMA inspector comes to their home in order to start cleaning up.

B. Inspection Reports

Applicants may obtain a copy of FEMA's records regarding a challenged decision. By examining the records, an applicant can determine its accuracy in describing property damage, and regarding insurance coverage or eligibility information. The documents on which FEMA based its decision can help the applicant to frame his or her appeal. A written request for copies of documents should be made to the address provided for that purpose on the FEMA notice of decision.

Applicants may elect to both appeal and make a request for documents and/or inspection reports. These are, however, separate and distinct processes and must be sent to the appropriate FEMA address.

C. Audits

FEMA audits a random sampling of all persons granted assistance for verification of lawful presence status. Other individuals may be audited for assistance eligibility, fraud or documentation on how they spent the money in accordance with their award. For example, housing assistance cannot be used for food or to replace personal property; money for repairs cannot be used for mortgage or rent payments. Those found ineligible or who have misspent FEMA grants may have to repay the money they received. All households that receive FEMA grants should keep copies of all receipts and documents in case of an audit.

D. Appeal Rights

An appeal may be denied if the applicant fails to provide new additional information or documentation supporting a change in the initial decision.

All appeals must be postmarked no later than **60 days after the date of the FEMA notice of decision.** FEMA does not accept appeals if the postmark is after the deadline date. FEMA generally acknowledges receipt of appeals within 15 days. If an applicant does not receive an acknowledgment within that time period, s/he should contact the FEMA Information Helpline.

The appeal and supporting documentation should be sent to the address provided on the FEMA notice of decision. If more time is needed in order to submit additional supporting information and/or documentation to FEMA, this should be noted in a timely appeal.

FEMA Appeals web site is:
https://www.fema.gov/appeals

Mail your appeal letter and/or appeal form to: FEMA – Individuals & Households Program National Processing Service Center P.O. Box 10055

James L. Jaffe, J.D.

Hyattsville, MD 20782-7055

OR

Fax your appeal letter and/or appeal form to: (800) 827-8112
Attention: FEMA – Individuals & Households Program

For a form letter to use go to http://www.disasterlegalaid.org/femaappeals/

If you need information about your case, you or someone from your household may request a copy of the information by writing to:

FEMA - Records Management
National Processing Service Center
P.O. Box 10055
Hyattsville, MD 20782-7055

If someone outside of your household is submitting the request for you, then the request also must contain a statement signed by you giving that person your authorization to request this information

E. Right to an Authorized Representative

Applicants can file an appeal directly. However, each applicant is entitled to have his/her authorized representative, such as a Legal Aid or volunteer attorney, or a family member or friend file the appeal and represent the applicant.

FEMA must have a written authorization from the applicant in order for anyone else to act on an applicant's behalf or request copies of records.

F. Final Decision

FEMA issues a final written decision **within 90 calendar days** of the date it receives the appeal. There is no right to a hearing except for applicants living in FEMA-leased housing.

G. Recoupment

Some applicants receive assistance and later, FEMA finds them to be ineligible. Some applicants receive duplicate funds for the housing or property for which FEMA paid. Others unwittingly spend checks that FEMA issues in error. Still others spend money from one program, such as Rental Assistance, to replace personal property or for food. FEMA may initiate recoupment procedures against these persons when it discovers the error. An applicant can resolve the situation by showing that an error was made in determining the applicant was not entitled to the funds. If an applicant cannot resolve the situation, FEMA will collect the debt. Although FEMA contends that lack of fault is not a defense to recoupment, there are exceptions and circumstances that may excuse or reduce the obligation to repay.

Advocates can assist applicants in finding an exception to recoupment or in establishing a reasonable repayment schedule.

Sequence of Delivery of Financial Assistance

Local/Voluntary, FEMA's Individuals and Households Program (IHP) and SBA

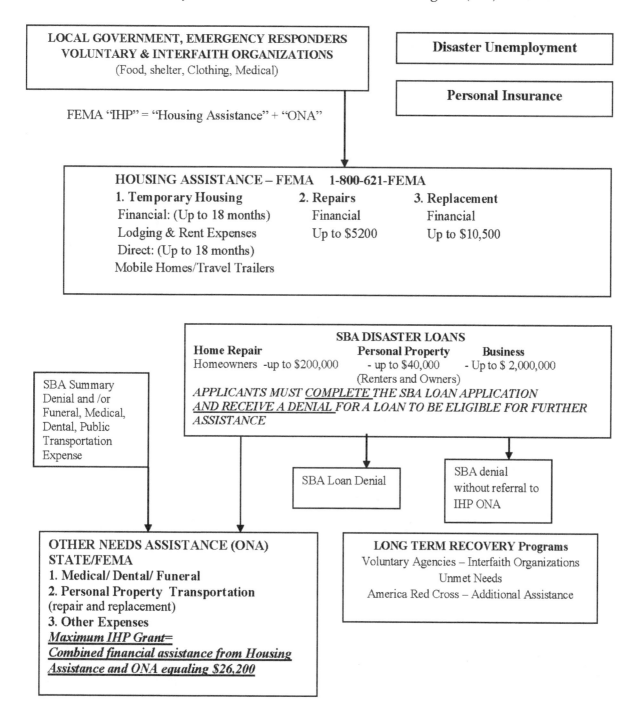

Individual/Family

Individual/Family

FEMA Assistance

As stated above in the FEMA overview, individuals and families are eligible to apply for FEMA assistance.

Before we begin the discussion of post disaster activities, let us understand that there are significant federal programs available to the individual/family for disaster relief. But, and there is always a but, these programs have application deadlines that must be met. The following chart lists the programs and application deadlines.

Application Deadlines for Individual Assistance Programs

Individual Assistance Programs	Application Deadline
Rental Assistance	60 days after disaster *
Mortgage Assistance	6 months after disaster*
Home Repair Assistance	60 days after disaster*
Individual & Households Program (IHP)	60 days after disaster*
Disaster Unemployment Assistance	30 days after disaster*
SBA Loans for damage or loss to real and personal property	60 days after disaster*
SBA Loans for economic injury to small businesses	9 months after disaster*
Emergency Food Stamps	10 days after disaster*

* The date that the President makes a Declaration of a Major Disaster (or Emergency) is the date used for the running of the above statute of limitations.

Individuals and Households Program (IHP)[36]

The purpose of the FEMA Individuals and Households Program (IHP) is to help individuals and households be safely housed and to cover uninsured necessary expenses and serious needs following the effects of a disaster. Housing Assistance (includes Temporary Housing, Repair, Replacement, and Permanent Housing Construction); and Other Needs Assistance (includes personal property, medical, dental, funeral, and other items).

IHP is made available following a presidential disaster declaration. Following a disaster, damage assessment is conducted in the affected areas to

---

[36] Applicant's Guide to the Individuals & Households Program FEMA 545 / July 2008. http://www.fema.gov/pdf/assistance/process/help_after_disaster_english.pdf

determine the need for Individual Assistance (IA) programs such as the FEMA Disaster Housing (DH) Program, the Small Business Administration (SBA) Home/Personal Property disaster loan Program and the FEMA IHP Program.

The state Governor must specifically request supplemental federal disaster assistance and specifically include FEMA DH and IHP Programs; SBA is automatically triggered if the two FEMA IA Programs are made available.

After the President declares a major disaster area and the declaration includes the IHP Program, the state Emergency Management Agency (EMA) administers the IHP program. Although IHP is interrelated with the two federal agencies, FEMA and SBA, it is a separate program.

Under the FEMA/SBA umbrella of Individual Assistance (IA) programs there are:

1. FEMA Disaster Housing (DH) Program,
2. Small Business Administration (SBA) Home/Personal Property disaster loan Program, and
3. FEMA IHP Program.

The assistance limit under the FEMA DH/IHP program is $28,200.00[37] per individual/family, and under the SBA loan program the assistance limit is $40,000.00 for personal property and $200,000.00 for home repair/replacement.

Within these programs an individual/family is eligible for:

1. Temporary Housing
2. Homeowner Repair
3. Home Replacement
4. Permanent Housing Construction
5. Other Needs Assistance (ONA) this includes:
    a. Personal Property
    b. Transportation
    c. Medical and Dental expenses
    d. Funeral and Burial costs
    e. Other Items:
        i. Fuel (fuel, chain saw, firewood)
        ii. Moving and storage expenses related to the disaster
        iii. Other necessary expenses or serious needs (e.g., towing, or setup or connecting essential utilities for a housing unit not provided by FEMA)
        iv. The cost of a National Flood Insurance Program Group Flood Insurance Policy

NOTE:

You must apply for an SBA disaster loan for personal property before being considered for ONA

While these programs seem, and are, complex, the individual/family seeking assistance makes one initial application with FEMA. Depending upon the needs, there may be an additional application with SBA.

To be initially considered for any type of FEMA IHP assistance, the affected home must be your primary residence, the home must be located in the declared disaster area, your ***necessary expense or serious need*** must have occurred in the declared disaster area.

FEMA defines a necessary expense as the cost of a serious need which the disaster directly caused. A serious need is "an item or service essential to an individual or family to prevent, mitigate, or overcome a disaster-related hardship, injury, or adverse condition." And you (or an adult household member) must be a United States citizen, a non-citizen national, or a qualified alien.

---

[37] The maximum amount of Individual Assistance available to an individual or household is determined annually by the Consumer Price Index with the 2012-13 limit being $31.900, and of that, the maximum amount available for repairs is $5,600. The amount is subject to change based on the federal fiscal year.

Because processing times vary, households may receive grants from insurance, charitable organizations or other governmental programs at different times. They must reimburse IHP when they receive the duplicate payment. For example, IHP pays for new household furniture. Later a welfare program or insurance policy pays for the identical replacement furniture. The household must repay the amount of the IHP grant.

IHP assists survivors primarily with the repair or replacement of eligible personal property, moving and storage costs, tools, transportation-related costs, medical/dental expenses and eligible housing repairs over $10,000. IHP is a program of last resort available when disaster survivors do not qualify for other assistance programs.

The application process for the FEMA DH, SBA and the IHP Programs is initiated by the

applicant calling the FEMA teleregistration number and speaking with a registrar or registering on-line at http://www.disasterassistance.gov/ . The information is collected and disseminated to the applicable Programs. If there is a need for an inspection of the damaged property for the FEMA DH and/or IHP Program, FEMA contracted habitability inspectors will be assigned to do so.

Conditions & Limitations of FEMA IHP Assistance

A. Non-discrimination

All forms of FEMA disaster assistance are available to any affected household that meets the conditions of eligibility. No Federal entity or official (or their agent) may discriminate against any individual on the basis of race, color, religion, sex, age, national origin, disability, or economic status.

B. Residency

To be considered for disaster assistance, the individual or an adult household member must provide proof of identity and sign a declaration stating that you/they are a United States citizen, a non-citizen national, or a qualified alien.

C. Supplemental Assistance

Disaster assistance is not intended to substitute for private recovery efforts, but to complement those efforts when needed. FEMA expects minor housing damage or the need for short-term shelter to be addressed by homeowners or tenants. Furthermore, IHP is not a loss indemnification program and does not ensure that applicants are returned to their pre-disaster living conditions.

D. Household Composition

People living together in one residence before the disaster are expected to continue to live together after the disaster. Generally, assistance is provided to the pre-disaster household as a unit. If, however, the assistance provided to the household is not shared, or if the new residence is too small or causes the individual undue hardship, the individual may request assistance separate from their pre-disaster household.

E. Type of Assistance

Generally, more than one type of IHP assistance may be provided to the household. Only FEMA has the authority to determine which type of assistance is most appropriate for the household and the period of assistance to be covered.

- Housing Assistance (includes Temporary Housing, Repair, Replacement, and Permanent Housing Construction); and

- Other Needs Assistance (includes personal property, medical, dental, funeral, and other items).

F. Proper Use of Assistance

All financial assistance provided by FEMA should be used as specified in writing: to rent another place to live, to make the home repairs identified by FEMA, or to prevent eviction or foreclosure. Failure to use the money as specified may make the individual ineligible for additional assistance. All money provided by FEMA is tax-free.

G. Documentation

It is the individual's responsibility to provide all documentation necessary for FEMA to evaluate their eligibility. The individual may need to provide proof of occupancy, ownership, income loss, and/or information concerning their housing situation prior to the disaster. The individual should keep all receipts and records for any housing expenses incurred as a result of the disaster. This includes receipts for repair supplies and labor, and rent payments.

H. Insurance

If the individual has insurance, any assistance provided by FEMA should be considered an advance and must be repaid to FEMA when they receive their insurance settlement payment. If their settlement is less than FEMA's estimated cost to make their home habitable, the individual may qualify for funds to supplement their insurance settlement, but only for repairs relating to the home's habitability. FEMA does not provide replacement value amounts or assistance with non-essential items.

I. Duration of Assistance

Repair Assistance is provided as a one-time payment. Temporary Housing Assistance (or a mobile home/travel trailer) is provided for an initial period of 1, 2, or 3 months. To be considered for additional assistance, the individual must demonstrate that they have used any previous assistance from FEMA as instructed, and they must demonstrate their efforts to re-establish permanent housing. Additional assistance is generally provided for 1, 2, or 3 months at a time. The maximum period for IHP assistance is 18 months.

J. Flood Insurance Requirements for Recipients of Federal Disaster Assistance

If you are a homeowner and receive Federal financial assistance, flood insurance coverage must be maintained at the address of your home even if the damaged building is replaced by a new one.

If you sell your home, you are required to inform the new owner that they must maintain flood insurance coverage on the building.

If you are a renter and receive Federal financial assistance, flood insurance coverage must be maintained on the contents for as long as you live at the flood-damaged rental property. The requirement for flood insurance is lifted once you move from the building.

If you receive a Certificate of Flood Insurance from FEMA, flood insurance has been provided under a Group Flood Insurance Policy following a Presidential disaster declaration.

This policy provides minimum building and/or contents coverage in exchange for a small premium.

Group Policies have a term of 3 years, after which you will be required to purchase and maintain a Standard Flood Insurance Policy through the National Flood Insurance Program (NFIP) until you are no longer the homeowner or renter at that location. In order to avoid any lapse in coverage, it is important to apply for your new coverage at least 30 days before the expiration of the Group Policy. You may cancel your participation in the Group Policy at any time during its policy term, provided that you have purchased your own NFIP flood insurance coverage.

Initial Application To FEMA For an IHP Grant

In order to be eligible for an IHP grant, applicants must complete the FEMA application process:

Saving original documents is important for assistance and recertification.

A. Application Information

When registering, applicants will need to provide the following information:

- Name and Social Security number
- Address of the damaged property
- Current address and telephone number
- Insurance information
- Total household annual income
- A bank routing and account number for direct deposit
- A description of your losses caused by the disaster

Many forms of assistance require copies of your income tax returns, you can request copies of your tax returns, and all attachments (including Form W-2), from the IRS by using Form 4506, Request for Copy of Tax Return. An information return or transcript can be ordered by calling 1-800-829-1040 or using Form 4506-T, Request for Transcript of Tax Return. There is no fee for a transcript. Transcripts are available for the current year and returns processed in the three prior years.

There are separate agencies with different application forms that may need to be completed. Sometimes the applicant completes the form (e.g. SBA), and in other instances, applications (e.g. FEMA) are completed by a staff person or volunteer who asks the applicant questions. The applicant should receive and keep a copy of all applications

Once the registration is complete, a copy of the registration/application will be sent to the applicant and if a need is identified, an inspector will be assigned to view the damaged property.

In order to be eligible for an IHP grant, applicants must complete the FEMA application process, which may include a referral to the Small Business Administration. If an applicant receives an SBA application, it must be completed.

If it is not completed, the applicant will not be eligible for an IHP grant for real property, personal property, tools or transportation. However, IHP eligibility for medical/dental, funeral, and moving/storage disaster-related expenses are processed without a SBA application because SBA does not cover or include these costs.

Applications that SBA either rejects or grants in part are forwarded to FEMA and if FEMA determines that there are FEMA-eligible damages not covered by SBA, FEMA will refer the case to IHP. This is a summary denial procedure from the SBA program so applications of low income people should be expeditiously forwarded from SBA to FEMA and IHP.

Applicants receiving public benefits or persons fearful about obtaining public benefits should be advised that IHP is not a welfare program and does not affect eligibility for public benefits such as Aid to Families with Dependent Children (AFDC), Supplemental Security Income (SSI), or Food Stamps.

B. Application Deadline -- 60 Days

The basic deadline for application is 60 days from the date that the President issues the disaster declaration. However, because this is a program of last resort there are two other ways to get FEMA to accept an application:

C. Extenuating Circumstances

Late applicants must show that they were not able to apply because of circumstances beyond their control. FEMA defines extenuating circumstances to include hospitalization, illness or inaccessibility of application centers. If late applicants can prove extenuating circumstances, then they have **an additional 30 days** to apply.

[**Note that SBA loans for economic injury have a nine month application deadline, which is much longer than the SBA home and business loan application deadlines.**]

Applicants should be strongly encouraged to submit a SBA application, even if the deadline has passed. Applicants who cannot afford to repay a loan are eventually forwarded to IHP. If SBA accepts a late application because of "substantial causes essentially beyond the control of the applicant," then refers the application to the IHP, then IHP must accept the late application as well.

D. Mandatory Application for All Available Assistance

Applicants must apply for all other forms of assistance that can cover these expenses. This includes obtaining assistance from voluntary agencies for replacement of personal property and clothing and applying for insurance to cover expenses. Applicants must apply for SBA loans for home repairs even if they feel that they will be rejected because of inability to repay a loan.

E. No Refusal of Other Assistance

Applicants who receive money, loans or in-kind contributions from other programs, insurance companies or charitable organizations may not refuse them. Applicants must be found ineligible for SBA loans. Applicants must accept SBA loans if they qualify.

F. Only One Application Per Household

A family living in one household may make only one application. FEMA defines a family as legally married individuals, a couple living together as if they were married, a single person with dependents, two or more persons who own a home together and their dependents. However, besides the aforementioned categories, unrelated adults who live together should submit separate applications.

In order for an applicant to be eligible, his/her primary residence must have one of the following conditions:

1. Destroyed or damaged home (damages which are in excess of the maximum home repair award, or which make the home unlivable);
2. Utilities cut off;
3. Serious health and safety hazard;
4. Inaccessible residence; or
5. Other disaster-related circumstances which prevent occupancy.

All damage must be to the renter's or homeowner's primary residence.

G. Applicant Credit Requirements

a. SBA's disaster assistance is in the form of low-interest loans. Applicants must show a reasonable assurance of their ability to repay all loans and must demonstrate a reasonable assurance that they will comply with the terms of a loan agreement, based upon their credit history (as reported by a credit bureau).

b. Applicants must not be delinquent on a federal debt obligation or child support payments.

H. Applicant Collateral Requirement

Collateral is required for all physical loss loans over $10,000. SBA takes real estate as collateral where it is available. Applicants do not need to have full collateral; SBA will take what is available to secure each loan. However, if a borrower refuses to pledge collateral, SBA may decline a disaster loan for that reason.

I. Term of Loan

The law authorizes loan terms of up to a maximum of 30 years. SBA determines the term of each loan in accordance with the borrower's ability to repay the loan. Based on the financial circumstances of each borrower, SBA determines an appropriate installment payment amount which, in turn, determines the actual term of the loan. Generally, the first payment on disaster loans is not due until five months after the date of the loan.

J. Denial of Benefits

Those denied assistance or who disagree with the amount granted must file an appeal with the resource agency within **60 days**.

K. Appeal Rights [44 C.F.R. § 206.101(m)]

Applicants have distinct appeal rights for each of the agencies to which they apply.

Applicants have *60 days* to appeal decisions from FEMA and IHP after denial.

Applicants have *30 days* to appeal SBA decisions, after denial of a reconsideration is denied.

Application deadlines are rigid, so applicants should consider writing an appeal letter as soon as possible and should keep a photocopy of it. Even a simple initial letter is adequate, because the agencies accept revisions. Applicants who believe that the denial is based on an inadequate inspection should request a reinspection rather than appeal.

Applicants should tell the FEMA application registrar all of their disaster-related damage and to make sure that the registrar writes everything down by asking the registrar to read the list back.

Rent receipts, leases, all correspondence with FEMA, SBA or IHP, verification of disaster-related medical or mental health treatment and all correspondence with insurance carriers. It is also important to save damaged personal property until the inspector sees the property.

FEMA Helpline

The FEMA Helpline provides information about the status of applications.
1-800- 621-3362 (TDD: 1-800-462-7585)

1. Basic Reasons for an Appeal

Applicants may file an appeal for many reasons. The major ones include:

a. Applicant eligibility;
b. Grant of less than the amount requested;
c. Withdrawal of the applicant's application;
d. Cancellation of an application "for cause";
e. Denial because insurance is available;
f. Denial of continued assistance; and
g. Denial for late filing for a program.

Persons filing an appeal should have a clear understanding of FEMA's decision in their cases. If the

FEMA decision is not specific, applicants can call the FEMA Information Helpline at 1-800- 621-3362 (TDD: 1-800-462-7585) for clarification. Applicants must also determine the specific documentation required for each program and provide supporting documentation showing why the decision was wrong and why they are entitled to assistance. When warranted, an appeal may result in a reinspection of the damaged property.

An appeal may be denied if the applicant fails to provide new additional information or documentation supporting a change in the initial decision.

2. Inspection Reports

Applicants may obtain a copy of FEMA's records regarding a challenged decision. By examining the records, an applicant can determine its accuracy in describing property damage, and regarding insurance coverage or eligibility information. The documents on which FEMA based its decision can help the applicant to frame his or her appeal. A written request for copies of documents should be made to the address provided for that purpose on the FEMA notice of decision.

Applicants may elect to both appeal and make a request for documents and/or inspection reports. These are, however, separate and distinct processes and must be sent to the appropriate FEMA address.

3. Deadlines

All appeals must be postmarked no later than **60 days after the date of the FEMA notice of decision.**

FEMA does not accept appeals if the postmark is after the deadline date. The Regional Director shall reconsider the original decision **within 15 calendar days** after its receipt. If an applicant does not receive an acknowledgment within that time period, s/he should contact the FEMA Information Helpline. If the reconsideration does not result in a reversal of the original decision, then the appeal process is triggered.

The appeal and supporting documentation should be sent to the address provided on the FEMA notice of decision. If more time is needed in order to submit additional supporting information and/or documentation to FEMA, this should be noted in a timely appeal.

If a hearing pursuant to paragraph 44 CFR. § 206.101 (m)(2)(ii) has not been requested, the occupant has waived the right to a hearing. The appropriate program official shall deliver or mail a written response to the occupant **within 5 business days** after the receipt of the appeal.

If the occupant requests a hearing pursuant to 44 CFR. § 206.101 (m)(2)(ii) of this section, FEMA shall **schedule a hearing date within 10 business days** from the receipt of the appeal, at a time and place reasonably convenient to the occupant, who shall be notified promptly thereof in writing. The notice of hearing shall specify the procedure governing the hearing.

The occupant shall be afforded a fair hearing and provided the basic safeguards of due process, including cross-examination of the responsible official(s), access to the documents on which FEMA is relying, the right to counsel, the right to present evidence, and the right to a written decision. 44 CFR. § 206.101 (m)(2)(ii)(E)(2)

At the hearing, the occupant must first attempt to establish that continued assistance is appropriate; thereafter, FEMA must sustain the burden of proof in justifying that termination of assistance is appropriate. 44 CFR. § 206.101 (m)(2)(ii)(E)(4)

4. Right to an Authorized Representative

Applicants can file an appeal directly. However, each applicant is entitled to have his/her authorized representative, such as a Legal Aid or volunteer attorney, or a family member or friend file the appeal and represent the applicant.

FEMA must have a written authorization from the applicant in order for anyone else to act on an applicant's behalf or request copies of records.

5. Final Decision

The Hearing Officer shall issues a final written decision within 5 business after the hearing. 44 CFR. § 206.101 (m)(2)(ii)(F)

6. Recoupment

Some applicants receive assistance and later, FEMA finds them to be ineligible. Some applicants receive duplicate funds for the housing or property for which FEMA paid. Others unwittingly spend checks that FEMA issues in error. Still others spend money from one program, such as Rental Assistance, to replace personal property or for food. FEMA may initiate recoupment procedures against these persons when it discovers the error. An applicant can resolve the situation by showing that an error was made in determining the applicant was not entitled to the funds. If an applicant cannot resolve the situation, FEMA will collect the debt. Although FEMA contends that lack of fault is not a defense to recoupment, there are exceptions and circumstances that may excuse or reduce the obligation to repay.

Advocates can assist applicants in finding an exception to recoupment or in establishing a reasonable repayment schedule.

Types of Housing Assistance [38]

The purpose of the FEMA Disaster Housing Assistance is to provide assistance to enable households to address their disaster-related housing needs. It is not intended to alleviate chronic housing issues or problems existing prior to the disaster. The assistance is generally provided in the form of a check to the applicant. It is a grant, not a loan, and is not income based although eligibility for some forms of assistance may require an analysis of one's' financial condition. It is not considered as income or as a resource for determining eligibility for federally- funded income assistance or resource-tested benefit programs. It is tax free, exempt from garnishment or levy and cannot be assigned or transferred.

Non-emergency disaster assistance for all FEMA DHA Programs is limited to persons lawfully present in the United States. But, all persons, regardless of their immigration status, are eligible for short-term, in-kind, non-cash disaster assistance. Moreover, the U.S. Attorney General has the authority to designate certain government-funded community programs or services or assistance necessary for the protection of life and safety for which all persons will be eligible, regardless of immigration status.

All applicants applying for FEMA DHA will be requested to sign a self-certifying declaration that they are a United States Citizen or National, Lawful Permanent Resident, or are otherwise lawfully present within the United States.

FEMA must inform applicants of the types of disaster housing assistance available for the particular disaster.

(1) Temporary Housing (Rent and Lodging Expense): Money to rent a different place to live or a temporary housing unit, when rental properties are not available

(2) Repair: Money for homeowners to repair damage from the disaster that is not covered by insurance. The goal is to repair the home to a safe and

---

[38] Housing Assistance http://www.fema.gov/assistance/process/assistance.shtm

sanitary living or functioning condition. FEMA may provide up to $5,000; then the homeowner must apply for a U.S. Small Business Administration (SBA) disaster loan for additional repair assistance. Sadly, many eligible individuals will "walk away" from an SBA loan because they can't afford the loan, and this means in some cases they abandon their homes.

(3) Replacement: Money to replace a disaster-damaged home, under rare conditions, if this can be done with limited funds. If the home is located in a Special Flood Hazard Area, the homeowner must comply with flood insurance purchase requirements and local flood codes and requirements.

FEMA will not pay to return a home to its condition before the disaster. Flood insurance may be required if the home is in a Special Flood Hazard Area. Repair and replacement items include:

- Structural parts of a home (foundation, outside walls, roof)
- Windows, doors, floors, walls, ceilings, cabinetry
- Septic or sewage system
- Well or other water system
- Heating, ventilating, and air conditioning system
- Utilities (electrical, plumbing, and gas systems)
- Entrance and exit ways from the home, including privately owned access roads
- Blocking, leveling and anchoring of a mobile home and reconnecting or resetting its sewer, water, electrical and fuel lines and tanks

(4) Permanent Housing Construction: Direct assistance or money for the construction of a home. This type of assistance occurs only in very unusual situations, in remote locations specified by FEMA where no other type of housing assistance is possible. Construction shall follow current minimal local building codes and standards where they exist, or minimal acceptable construction industry standards in the area. Construction will aim toward average quality, size, and capacity, taking into consideration the needs of the occupant. If the home is located in a Special Flood Hazard Area, the homeowner must comply with flood insurance purchase requirements and local floodplain management codes and requirements.

Information To Support An Application

A. Home Owners

A few types of documents that may be provided to prove ownership are:

1. Deed or official record may be the original deed or deed of trust to the property listing the disaster victim as the legal owner. Or, the land sales contract.

2. Title number which lists the disaster victim on the actual escrow or title document for the purchase of the dwelling.

3. Mortgage payment book or other mortgage documents (*i.e.*, late payment notice, foreclosure notice) may be used to verify the ownership when the disaster victim's name is listed along with the damaged dwelling address.

4. Real property insurance must be for the damaged dwelling the applicant is occupying with his or her name listed as the insured.

5. Tax receipts or a property tax bill showing the damaged dwelling and listing the applicant as the responsible party to the assessments.

B. Renters

A few types of documents that may be provided to prove where the applicant lived are:

1. Utility Bill sent to the damaged dwelling the applicant is occupying with his or her name

(or name of co-applicant). The utility bill should be for one of the major utilities, such as electricity, gas, or water.

2. Merchant's Statement sent to the damaged dwelling the applicant is occupying with his or her name (or name of co-applicant). Merchant statements include credit card bills, delivery notices, or other first class mail addressed to the applicant and showing the damaged dwelling address.

3. Employer's Statement sent to the damaged dwelling the applicant is occupying with his or her name (or name of co-applicant). An employer's statement refers to pay stubs and similar documents sent to the applicant and showing the damaged welling address.

4. Current Driver's License showing the address of the damaged dwelling.

C. To receive money for repair or help with housing needs the applicant must first file a claim under any insurance policy they have

In order to receive money or help with housing needs the applicant must have filed for insurance benefits (if there is insurance) and the damage to the applicant's property must not be covered by insurance.

D. If insurance settlement is insufficient to meet disaster-related damage or need

An eligible applicant will need to write a letter to FEMA indicating the amount of the unmet need. The applicant will need to present adequate documentation from his or her insurance company for FEMA's review.

E. Legal Presence Requirement for Disaster Housing Assistance (DHA) Eligibility

All applicants applying for FEMA DHA will be requested to sign a self-certifying declaration that they are a United States Citizen or National, Lawful Permanent Resident, or are otherwise lawfully present within the United States.

Section 401 of The Personal Responsibility and Work Opportunity Reconciliation Act, specified that all persons, regardless of their immigration status, are eligible for short-term, inkind, non-cash disaster assistance. Moreover, the Attorney General of the United States has the authority to designate certain government-funded community programs or services or assistance necessary for the protection of life and safety for which all persons will be eligible, regardless of immigration status.

Temporary Housing (Homeowners and Renters)[39]

FEMA provides tax-free grants to households that have been displaced from their primary residence as the result of a federally declared disaster through its Rental Assistance program. The Rental Assistance (RA) program provides need-based grants to enable homeowners and renters who are victims of disaster-related dislocation to obtain temporary replacement housing.

FEMA Housing Portal

http://asd.fema.gov/inter/hportal/home.htm

The FEMA Housing Portal is intended to help individuals and families, who have been displaced by a disaster, find a place to live. The portal consolidates rental resources identified and provided by federal agencies, such as the U.S. Department

---

[39] http://www.benefits.gov/benefits/benefit-details/813

of Housing and Urban Development (HUD), U.S. Department of Agriculture (USDA), U.S. Veterans Administration (VA), private organizations, and the public, to help individuals and families find available rental units in their area. FEMA recommends to those who use this portal, that they contact the number on the listing prior to traveling to the location of the property to make sure the property is still available. This site is updated regularly, and we encourage those who use the portal to check back often for the most current information. Other helpful housing resources may be available on commercial websites.

NOTE:

To find a hotel participating in the Transitional Shelter Assistance (TSA) Program go to http://www.femaevachotels.com/

Transient Accommodations (reimbursement for lodging) is provided for up to 30 days and Rental Assistance (RA) for up to 90 days. If assistance is needed for longer than 90 days, stringent certification procedures must be met. Rent receipts are required in order to be eligible for assistance beyond 90 days. (Both programs are available for renters and homeowners.)

The purpose of the Transient Accommodation program is to reimburse disaster victims for the cost of short term housing incurred as a result of damage to the disaster victim's home or an enforced evacuation. Note that food, transportation, telephone charges, and other separately billed services are not eligible for reimbursement from this program.

FEMA will pay rent or mortgage payments for tenants or homeowners who are subject to immediate eviction or foreclosure due to disaster-related "financial hardship". Hardship could be the loss of a job, or a business for people who are self-employed.. Applicants should tell the FEMA registrar if they have been approved for DUA when they are applying for MRA since this should prove that they are unemployed as a result of the disaster.

Finally, if FEMA determines that there is no rental housing available in the local

community due to the disaster, it may provide temporary housing to disaster victims by entering into leases or providing mobile homes, travel trailers or other housing. Call the FEMA Hotline and keep in close contact with volunteer organizations to learn about these options.

Residence in Unsafe Areas

Even if the disaster victim's home was not destroyed, he/she may still be eligible for Rental Assistance if he/she cannot reach it because of the damage caused by the disaster, such as the destruction of roads and bridges, or curfews or other restrictions put into place by government officials due to continued health and safety problems.

Deadline, Benefit Calculation and Duration

The application deadline is *60 days after the disaster declaration.* FEMA calculates benefits on the Fair Market Rent (FMR) for the area and bedroom size appropriate for the size of the family. FEMA grants initial Rental Assistance as follows, depending on individual household need:

Eligible Renters normally receive at least one month's FMR. Thereafter, if they cannot find alternate housing, they must document the need for additional funds for additional months and go through recertification.

Homeowners with damaged homes may receive up to three months initial rental assistance before going through a formal recertification process.

If a household receives initial rental assistance but does not move from the damaged residence or use the funds for other disaster-related housing needs, they may be required to return the funds.

<u>*Renters generally receive rental assistance for a shorter time period than homeowners*</u> under the premise that a renter will normally require less time to find alternate affordable housing than a homeowner will in order to complete major repairs to his/her home. Renters or homeowners who require additional assistance can request recertification.

Transient Accommodations

A. Purpose

The purpose of Transient Accommodations is to reimburse a disaster victim for the cost of *short-term lodging up to 30 days*, such as hotel rooms, that was incurred because of damage to the home or an official evacuation announcement. Expenditures for food, transportation, telephone, separately billed utilities, and other services are not eligible for reimbursement.

B. Eligibility

The applicant's home must have sustained disaster damage. Paid receipts for transient accommodation expenses must be provided.

Rental Assistance

There are two programs, one is for rental assistance where the disaster victim's primary housing is no longer habitable as a result of the disaster, that program is called Rental Assistance (RA). The second program, called Mortgage and Rental Assistance (MRA) is to help homeowners or renters whose pre-disaster primary residence is habitable but who may lose them due to financial hardships resulting from the disaster.

A. Initial and Continued Rental Assistance

1. Initial Rental Assistance

Rental Assistance (RA) is a grant in the form of a check to enable victims, both homeowners and renters, to rent temporary replacement housing. RA is a tax-free grants program which seeks to shelter victims in the fastest, most economic way possible. It must be used only for disaster related housing purposes. These include short-term lodging, rent or housing payments. *This is for rent only, not mortgage payments.*

Eligible homeowners include those whose homes are destroyed or uninhabitable and need repairs which cannot be done in a short period of time and the amount of damages is in excess of an amount established for the particular disaster. For these homeowners the fastest most economical way to put a roof over their heads is to provide them with money that will enable them to rent another place rather than to provide them with money to do the repairs.

Renters and homeowners may be eligible for rental assistance if they suffer disaster-related displacement from their primary residences. Eligible renters include those who have lost their rental and need time to find new housing. Eligible homeowners may also receive assistance based on the Fair Market Rental value calculated for the area.

Initial rental assistance, with minimal certification requirements, is available to renters and homeowners for one to three months to enable them to find alternate housing.

2. Continued Rental Assistance

For continued assistance, FEMA requires a second stringent verification process. Applicants must request recertification for continued assistance.

They must be able to show they have used their initial assistance for appropriate disaster housing related needs and are making reasonable efforts to establish a permanent housing plan.

B. Eligibility

To be eligible for Rental Assistance, the disaster victim or someone who lives with the disaster victim must be a citizen of the United States, a non-citizen national, or a qualified alien, the disaster victim must not have other, adequate rent-free housing that can be used (for example, a vacation residence or unoccupied rental property), and *the disaster victim must be affected by one or more of the following conditions:*

- the primary residence is destroyed or unlivable;
- there is no utility service at the primary residence;
- the primary residence is a serious health or safety hazard;
- the primary residence is not accessible; or
- other disaster related circumstances prevent the disaster victim from occupying the primary residence.

In addition, homeowners may be required to show that they have attempted to obtain reimbursement for temporary housing from their insurance companies, and must agree to repay FEMA if they are later reimbursed.

Only one application will be taken from each household, which FEMA generally considers to be all people living in one apartment or house.

Rental assistance is usually available to eligible renters and homeowners for at least one month's rent. Thereafter, if they cannot find alternate housing, they must apply for additional funds.

For assistance for more than three months, a household must go through a recertification process. FEMA will grant continued rental assistance **only if**:

- Verified receipts show that the initial Rental Assistance grant was spent properly;
- The household has made reasonable efforts to find housing *and* provides a housing plan for obtaining permanent housing;
- For renters, no affordable housing exists; *and*
- A renter who was displaced and suffered a disaster-related reduction of income continues to be unable to pay for rent.

Continued rental assistance may be provided in one to three month increments for up to 18 months.

If the disaster victim applies for and receive funds from FEMA's rental assistance program he/she **must** follow the program rules and procedures in the letter that you receive from FEMA. This includes obtaining and saving receipts for rental payments. **Obtain and save all receipts**, otherwise FEMA may refuse to provide additional assistance and may require that the recipient refund any monies received.

C. Verification and Documentation

FEMA is very strict about accurate documents and verifications accompanying applications. Meeting FEMA's complex documentation requirement may be a problem for some applicants. If their primary residence was destroyed, applicants may no longer have records. Renters may have problems because their prior landlords may refuse to provide verification of residence. Where multiple families lived together, the names of additional occupants may not appear on a lease. However, applicants should not hesitate to register or apply for assistance if they think they may be eligible.

D. Major Reasons for Denials

There are several major reasons FEMA denies RA grants: failure to establish that home was the pre-disaster primary residence; insufficient damage; lack of proof that the disaster caused serious damage to essential living areas; and lack of proof that insurance did not cover the cost.

1. Primary Residence

The damaged home must be the applicant's residence at the time of the disaster. It includes recently purchased homes or rental units obtained and moved into shortly before the disaster.

Proof of Primary Residence: utility bills with applicant's name and address, or other verifiable documents showing primary address. Secondary documentation includes verifiable documentation from landlords who can verify the applicant's address.

2. Serious Disaster-Related

Damage to Residence

A FEMA inspector will conduct an on-site inspection of the primary residence with the applicant to assess disaster-related damages. Applicants can point out why their primary residence cannot be lived in safely. They can point out serious damage to the physical structure of the house.

Serious damage to plumbing, wiring, heating/cooling, and gas, water or sewage disposal must be visible to a FEMA inspector or in a report by a contractor.

[Basements and garages are not considered essential living areas and consequently are not included in eligibility determinations.]

Although, many persons may be living in illegal units that are converted garages or basements, if it is their primary residence, they should not hesitate to register or apply for assistance.

Inspectors may miss water damage such as wet wall board, carpeting or concrete which may not appear serious until it begins to mold and mildew.

[Applicants should contact FEMA immediately if they become aware of new or additional damage.]

3. Insurance Coverage

Homeowners may be required to show that they made every attempt to get reimbursement for temporary housing from their insurance companies. There have been many problems with insurance coverage during disasters. Some companies refuse to provide coverage for alternate living expenses (ALE).

Some insurance companies are non-admitted (out of-state or offshore) carriers who are undercapitalized or who simply refuse to pay benefits. In past disasters, FEMA denied assistance to an insured homeowner or renter until it had been determined how much (if any) coverage their insurance company would provide.

Depending on the applicant's situation, FEMA may grant assistance subject to recoupment (e.g. proceeds from insurance company will be delayed).

Proof of Insurance coverage: Copy of policy and coverage, letter denying coverage for housing and relocation costs, letter denying coverage for relatives or renters at the same address, letter confirming delay of benefits, insurance settlement breakdown.

E. Additional Benefits

1. Security Deposits

FEMA issues RA checks directly to renters or homeowners, not to landlords. In most instances, households may not use the RA program to pay for security deposits or replacement of personal property.

Security deposits are normally the responsibility of the applicant. However the Regional Director or official designee may authorize such payments when the applicant is unable to obtain the funds to the pay the deposit, and the Red Cross or other agencies also sometimes provide this assistance. When FEMA approves RA for security deposits necessary for obtaining replacement housing, the applicant must repay the money to FEMA when the applicant's rental assistance ends.

2. Essential Furniture

Furniture assistance may be provided under Disaster Housing Assistance. It must be specifically requested and a need for furniture demonstrated. This assistance is not be construed as a means to replace damaged furniture, it is solely intended to make the applicant's temporary or permanent residence livable until the applicant's furniture can be replaced through another form of disaster assistance. The grant is generally based on the cost of renting furniture although *the funds may be used as a down payment for furniture*. This assistance is not considered a duplication of benefits with respect to any subsequent SBA or IHP award for furniture replacement.

Home Repair Assistance (HRA)[40]

Note: This program only applies to homeowners who cannot return to their houses due to the fact that the home is not safe, sanitary or functional.

---
[40] Applicant's Guide to the Individuals & Households Program FEMA 545 / July 2008 http://www.fema.gov/pdf/assistance/process/help_after_disaster_english.pdf

Disaster survivors obtain cash assistance for home repairs through the Home Repair Assistance Program (HRA). This cash grant program is available if the repairs will:

1. *return the home to livable condition;*
2. *reestablish access to the home;*
3. *be completed within 30 days.*

A. Eligibility for Home Repair Assistance

Applicants must be owner-occupants.

Applicants must have the legal responsibility for making the repairs to their primary residence. They must need to make repairs to essential living areas which include:

1. Living room
2. Dining room
3. Kitchen
4. One bathroom
5. Bedrooms of residents
6. Windows and doors.

It would not include nonessential areas such as guest bedrooms, additional bathrooms, swimming pool and landscaping. Generally, the repairs must be able to be *completed within 30 days*. The cost of the repairs must come within a maximum amount which FEMA establishes for each disaster site. The owner must show that insurance will not cover the repairs.

B. Scope of Repairs

The regulations are quite specific. FEMA limits the type of work for which it will pay with these funds.

Repairs include those for:

1. Plumbing, electrical systems, heating systems, fuel systems for cooking, septic sys-

tems water wells, windows, doors, roofs, interior floors;
2. Blocking, leveling and anchoring mobile homes;
3. Stoves and refrigerators, when feasible;
4. Emergency access repairs
5. And: Elimination of health and safety hazards.

While FEMA will not pay for cosmetic repairs to a structure in and of themselves, it may provide assistance for paint and sheetrock if repairs are required to eligible underlying structural items. FEMA does not provide assistance for repairs to non-essential living areas, such as garages or basements, unless hazards exist in these areas impacting the safety of the essential living area. The grant will not be provided if the damage is a result of deferred maintenance. The funds may not be used to replace personal property.

The funds may not generally add previously unavailable utilities to a home; however, FEMA has permitted use of assistance for repairs to bring the damaged elements of a home up to building code standards.

C. Deadline, Amount of Grant, Duration

Owner-occupiers must file an application within **60 days from the date of the disaster declaration**. FEMA bases each grant on the amount of damage verified through a FEMA inspection. It sets cost limits for each item based on the reasonable costs for repair and replacement in the locality. FEMA generally makes only a **one-time payment** for repairs.

D. Interrelationship with Existing Insurance

Many homeowners have fire, flood, earthquake or other specialized insurance that may cover repairs. FEMA may find these applicants ineligible for assistance on the basis that their insurance will cover eligible expenses. However, FEMA regulations provide that insured applicants may be provided with assistance when benefits are significantly delayed, exhausted or insufficient to cover the actual damage. In past disasters involving unique circumstances, FEMA has allowed grants to be used to cover insurance deductibles necessary to complete repairs. Homeowners must agree to repay FEMA if they later obtain duplicate insurance benefits.

E. Interaction With Other Disaster Programs

Home repair grants under the Home Repair Assistance Program for essential repairs differ from assistance available from the Individual and Household Program (IHP) or the Small Business Administration (SBA) loans for more extensive repairs.

A homeowner may be eligible for a Home Repair Assistance grant to cover eligible emergency essential repairs and eligible for a SBA loan to cover more extensive damage.

A homeowner whose home has been destroyed, or whose scope of home repairs are too great for FEMA home repair assistance may be eligible for FEMA rental assistance and may be referred to other assistance programs for unmet needs.

FEMA, not the applicant, determines what type of FEMA assistance, if any, is available. Generally only one type of FEMA assistance is available. The purpose of FEMA's DHA programs is to put a roof over the applicant's head in the fastest and most economical way. If an applicant's home has been destroyed and it will take a long time to repair or if the amount exceeds the limits established for the program, then the fastest and most economical way to house the applicant may be to provide Rental Assistance rather than

Home Repair Assistance. In such an instance, the applicant should apply for a SBA loan to cover the repairs. If SBA declines to cover all or part of the repairs, then the applicant may be eligible for IHP assistance for the repairs. Duplicate payments from insurance or other repair programs may result in recoupment procedures.

F. Verification and Documentation

FEMA may require receipts for repair work performed such as in the case of a special Home Repair Assistance program. Otherwise receipts are generally not required unless the applicant is being audited; is requesting assistance for eligible repair items which were not funded; or must otherwise demonstrate exhaustion of benefits.

Households may not receive a grant under this program if they fail to provide essential documentation about insurance coverage; to provide proof that their insurance carrier will not cover the loss claimed or to document that the homeowner has been unable to get payments.

The extent of repairs may require funds from a program with greater resources because needed repairs exceed the HR limits.

Supporting documents include, but are not limited to:

1. Receipts for repair work already performed;
2. Reports by structural engineers;
3. Estimates on the essential repair work;
4. Insurance reports, letters of delays, denials ;
5. Photographs or videos of actual damage; and
6. Denials of assistance from other Programs.

Mortgage Insurance for Homeowners who are Disaster Victims

Anyone whose home has been destroyed or severely damaged in a presidentially declared disaster area is eligible to apply for mortgage insurance. The idea is that by having mortgage insurance, a lender is more likely to provide qualifying homeowners with a mortgage to replace or repair their homes.[41]

This program applies to an owner-occupied primary residence only.

No refinances allowed; only purchases are eligible.

The borrower is eligible for mortgage insurance equal to 100 percent of the appraised value.

Insured mortgages may be used to finance the purchase or reconstruction of a one-family home that will be the principal residence of the homeowner.

Individuals are eligible for this program if their homes are located in an area that was designated by the President as a disaster area and if their homes were destroyed or damaged to such an extent that reconstruction or replacement is necessary.

This program provides mortgage insurance to protect lenders against the risk of default on mortgages to qualified disaster victims. FHA-approved lending institutions, such as banks, mortgage companies, and savings and loan associations, are eligible for Section 203(h) insurance.

A down payment of at least 3.5% is required. Closing costs and prepaid expenses must be paid by the

---

[41] The Section 203(h) program allows the Federal Housing Administration (FHA) to insure mortgages made by qualified lenders to victims of a major disaster who have lost their homes and are in the process of rebuilding or buying another home. Thus making it easier for them to get mortgages and become homeowners or re-establish themselves as homeowners. This program is authorized under Section 203, National Housing Act (12 U.S.C. 1709, 1715(b)). Program regulations can be found at 24 CFR Part 203. http://portal.hud.gov/hudportal/HUD?src=/program_offices/housing/sfh/ins/203h-dft

borrower in cash or paid through premium pricing or by the seller, subject to a 6 percent limitation on seller concessions.

FHA mortgage insurance is not free. Mortgagees collect from the borrowers an up-front insurance premium (which may be financed) at the time of purchase, as well as monthly premiums that are not financed, but instead are added to the regular mortgage payment.

Some fees are limited. FHA rules impose limits on some of the fees that lenders may charge in making a mortgage. For example, the lenders mortgage origination charge for the administrative cost of processing the mortgage may not exceed one "point" that is, one percent of the amount of the mortgage excluding any financed up front mortgage insurance premium. In addition, property appraisal and inspection fees are set by FHA.

FHA sets limits on the dollar value of the mortgage. (see https://entp.hud.gov/idapp/html/hicostlook.cfm to determine your mortgage limit). These figures vary over time and by place, depending on the cost of living and other factors (higher limits also exist for two- to four-family properties).

The borrower's application for mortgage insurance must be submitted to the lender within one year of the President's declaration of the disaster. Applications are made through an FHA-approved lending institution, which make their requests through a provision known as "Direct Endorsement" which authorizes them to consider applications without submitting paperwork to HUD.

Mortgage insurance processing and administration for this and other FHA single-family mortgage insurance products are handled through HUD's Homeownership Centers.

This program is administered by the Office of Single-Family Housing Programs in HUD's Office of Housing-Federal Housing Administration.

Renters Personal Property Loans [42]

Renters are eligible for personal property loans of up to $40,000 to replace personal property such as furniture, household items, personal items and automobiles. If SBA analyzes the income and debts of the renter and determines that the disaster victim cannot afford an SBA disaster loan, SBA will automatically refer the applicant to the Individuals and Households Program.

A. Eligibility

1. Applicants must have owned the damaged property at the time of the disaster and
2. All physical losses or damages to real or personal property must have been as a direct result of the disaster.

B. Limitations and Conditions

These loans may not be used to:

a. Repair or replace secondary residences or vacation properties;
b. Repair or replace recreational vehicles, luxury items, etc.; or
c. Upgrade or make additions to the home, unless required by building codes.

SBA requires that borrowers maintain receipts and records of all loan expenditures for three years.

If SBA determines that the loan has been misused, borrowers must repay one and a half times the original amount of the loan.

---

[42] Homeowners, Renters Can Qualify For SBA Loans. FEMA Release No.: 1933-019

Homeowner Assistance

A. FEMA Outright Grants of Money

Through its Home Repair Assistance program, FEMA provides grants to homeowners whose primary residences require relatively little repair to essential living areas in order to become livable or accessible. (Repairs to nonessential living areas, such as guest rooms or an additional bathroom, as well as cosmetic repairs, are not eligible for funding under the program.) The repairs must be able to be completed *within 30 days* of the start of work, cannot exceed a maximum repair amount set by FEMA, and must be necessary as a result of damage from the disaster. Deferred maintenance is not covered by the program.

These grants are available only to owner-occupants for their primary residence. Examples of proof of primary residence include mortgage statements, leases, and utility bills with names and address of occupants, driver's license with primary address, declarations from neighbors or the post office. Mobile homes and travel trailers are included if they are the primary residence.

When the disaster victim applies for Home Repair Assistance, FEMA will inspect the home and base the amount of its grant on the reasonable cost of repair to the damaged property. Repairs covered by Home Repair Assistance may include:

1. repairs to plumbing, electrical systems, heating systems, fuel systems for cooking, septic systems, and water wells;
2. repairs to windows, doors, roof, and floor;
3. repairs to stoves and refrigerators;
4. repairs necessary to provide access to a residence;
5. repairs necessary to eliminate health and safety hazards.

If a mobile home and it is the disaster victim's primary residence, Home Repair Assistance will cover repair costs related to blocking, leveling and anchoring the mobile home. If the disaster victim's home needs more extensive repairs than allowed under the FEMA program, then the SBA may be of help.

FEMA inspectors make initial damage estimates. FEMA issues checks for real property damage not exceeding $10,000. If the damage exceeds $10,000, then the applicant will be referred to IHP for a real property grant award (if the applicant does not qualify for an SBA loan). The limit for repairs is $5,600.

SBA Home Disaster Loans (HDL)[43]

SBA disaster loans are available to homeowners to repair or replace disaster damages not fully covered by insurance to real estate and personal property owned by the victim.

The application deadline for home disaster loans is 60 days from the disaster declaration date.

The SBA provides low-interest, long-term loans to repair or replace a primary residence owned by a disaster victim-applicant in a federally declared disaster area.

A. Eligibility Requirements

To be considered for housing assistance, the affected home must be the individual's primary residence and it must be located in the disaster area designated for Individual Assistance.

1. Applicants must have owned the damaged property at the time of the disaster and
2. All physical losses or damages to real or personal property must have been as a direct result of the disaster.

---

[43] Fact Sheet for Homeowners and Renters http://www.sba.gov/content/fact-sheet-homeowners-and-renters

To be considered for assistance for necessary expenses or serious needs, the loss must have occurred in the disaster area designated for Individual Assistance.

An individual or a pre-disaster member of the household must be a United States citizen, a non-citizen national or a qualified alien.

SBA does not require proof of immigration status. Please note, however, that *Social Security numbers are required for SBA disaster loans.*

B. Amount of Loan

SBA disaster loans of up to $200,000 are available to homeowners for real estate repairs to their primary residence to return the property to its pre-disaster condition, and up to $40,000 to replace personal property such as furniture, household items, personal items and automobiles. Subject to the maximums, loan amounts cannot exceed the verified uninsured disaster loss.

As a rule of thumb, personal property is anything that is not considered real estate or a part of the actual structure. This loan may not be used to replace extraordinarily expensive or irreplaceable items, such as antiques, collections, pleasure boats, recreational vehicles, fur coats, etc.

The amount of money that SBA can loan depends on the actual cost of repairing or replacing the damage, less insurance recovery, grants, etc. If SBA analyzes the income and debts of the homeowner and determines that the disaster victim cannot afford an SBA disaster loan, *SBA will automatically refer the applicant to the Individuals and Households Program.*

C. Credit Requirements

SBA's disaster assistance is in the form of low-interest loans. Applicants must show a reasonable assurance of their ability to repay all loans and must demonstrate a reasonable assurance that they will comply with the terms of a loan agreement, based upon their credit history (as reported by a credit bureau).

Applicants must not be delinquent on a federal debt obligation or child support payments.

D. Collateral Requirement

Collateral is required for all physical loss loans over $10,000.

SBA takes real estate as collateral where it is available. Applicants do not need to have full collateral; SBA will take what is available to secure each loan. However, if a borrower refuses to pledge collateral, SBA may decline a disaster loan for that reason.

E Flood Insurance Requirement

Applicants who live in a flood plain who wish to replace or repair damaged homes must purchase and maintain flood insurance. If a disaster destroys or damages their home a second time and they have not paid for flood insurance, FEMA will find them ineligible for IHP funding.

For homeowners in a flood area, IHP will pay the first year's premium of flood insurance through the National Flood Insurance Program (NFIP). Owners must purchase and maintain the insurance in order to qualify for IHP in the event of destruction or damage in another disaster.

For information about the NFIP, call 1-888-379-9531, for the hearing impaired call TTY 1-800-427-5593.

F. Moving and Storage

This category includes expenses to move personal property out of a damaged home that is uninhabitable. It includes the cost of up to two months of storage during the repair period. Estimates or receipts are essential to obtain this benefit. IHP covers only the actual cost up to a maximum as provided in the IHP pricing guidelines. New pricing guidelines are published annually, as a part of the State plan.

G. Limitations on Use

The disaster loan is to help the disaster victim return their property to the same condition it was in before the disaster. The loan is for specific designated purposes. The SBA requires receipts and records of all loan expenditures to restore damaged property, and receipts and records be kept for three years.

The loan may not be used to upgrade the home or make additions to it. If, however, city or county building codes require structural improvements, the loan may be used to meet these requirements. Loans to repair or replace real property may be increased by as much as 20% for mitigation measures to protect the property from possible future disasters of the same kind.

These loans may not be used to:

a. Repair or replace secondary residences or vacation properties;
b. Repair or replace recreational vehicles, luxury items, etc.; or
c. Upgrade or make additions to the home, unless required by building codes.

The applicant's own labor and that of family members cannot be included. Amounts paid to others and any equipment rental can be listed as part of repairs to real estate.

NOTE:

If SBA determines that the loan has been misused, borrowers must repay one and a half times the original amount of the loan.

H. Waiting Period

The SBA's goal is to decide on each application within 21 days from the date it receives a complete application (missing information is the biggest cause of delay). The SBA processes applications in the order received, so submit a complete application as soon as possible. To make a loan, the SBA must estimate the cost of repairing the damage, be satisfied that the business or individual can repay the loan, and take reasonable safeguards to help ensure that the loan is repaid.

I. Home Loan Refinance by SBA

The SBA can refinance all or part of prior mortgages, evidenced by a recorded lien, if the application

1. does not have credit available elsewhere;
2. has suffered substantial uncompensated disaster damage (40% or more of the value of the property); and
3. intends to repair the damage.

J. Application Deadline

The deadline to file an application for a HDL is *60 days* after the Presidential declaration of a disaster.

K. Application Information

The necessary information is specified in the loan application. In all cases, it includes an itemized list of losses with an estimate of the repair or replacement cost of each item. It also includes permission for the IRS to give the SBA information from the last two federal income tax returns. If pictures of the damaged property are available, include them as well.

Applicants must provide the following information with the loan application, or after the application has been approved:

a. Social Security number;
b. Deed for homeowners or title if the home is a manufactured home;
c. Rental or lease agreement for renters;
d. Internal Revenue Service Form 8821 (authorization for SBA to obtain Federal Tax Returns);
e. Itemized list of personal property loss with estimates of repair or replacement costs;
f. Copy of insurance settlement or denial, adjuster's proof of loss or schedule of coverage if claim has not been settled;
g. Vehicle registration, if applicable; and
h. Current pay stub if employment changed within the past two years.

After an applicant submits a loan application, an SBA loss verifier will inspect the property to determine the cost of repairs. SBA loan amounts are based on this inspection.

The time frame between submission of loan application and inspection will vary, depending on the size of the disaster. Generally, for small disasters, the inspector will come within a few days. The time frame will be significantly longer for large disasters.

L. Contractor's Estimates

Do not wait to obtain a contractor's estimate to file an application, submit an application to the SBA as soon as possible. If the applicant has received a contractor's estimate, include it with the application; otherwise, include the applicant's estimate. The SBA will verify the damage estimate in the application.

M. Insurance Settlement

Do not wait to obtain an insurance settlement to file an application. Final insurance information can be added when a settlement is made.

SBA can lend them the full amount of their damages (up to the lending limit) even before they receive their insurance recovery. SBA can use the insurance funds to reduce the balance of their disaster loan.

Insurance proceeds that are required to be applied against outstanding mortgages may be included in disaster loan eligibility.

Insurance proceeds that are voluntarily applied against outstanding mortgages by the owner may not be included in disaster loan eligibility.

N. Relocation Allowance

If the applicant is unable to obtain a building permit to rebuild or replace his/her home at its original site, the cost of relocating the home might be included in the loan amount. If the applicant decides to relocate the home without being required to do so, the HDL will be only for the exact amount of the damage.

O. Interest Rate

SBA determines the term of each loan in accordance with the borrower's ability to repay the loan. Based on the financial circumstances of each borrower, SBA determines an appropriate installment payment amount which, in turn, determines the actual term of the loan.

Generally, the *first payment* on disaster loans is *not due until five months after the date of the loan.* If the applicant does not have credit available elsewhere, the maximum annual interest rate for an HDL will not exceed 4%. If the applicant has credit available elsewhere, the maximum annual interest rate will not exceed 8%.

Interest rates are determined by formulas set by law, and may vary over time with market conditions.

The laws requires the SBA to determine whether credit is available elsewhere to all disaster loan recipients from non-government sources in the amount needed to effect full repairs, without creating an undue financial hardship. Accordingly, the availability of sufficient credit (based on cash flow and available assets of the applicant) from non government sources on reasonable terms and conditions is determined through a comprehensive analysis of all the financial information submitted for consideration.

This test is uniformly applied to all disaster loan recipients.

As of April 18, 2014, the applicable interest rates are:

	No Credit Available	Credit Available
Home Loans	2.188%	4.375%
Business Loans	4.000%	6.000%
Non-Profits	2.625%	2.625%
Economic Injury Loan	4.000%	n/a
Economic Injury Loan (For Non-profits)	2.625	n/a

Call SBA at 1-800-695-2955 to inquire about current interest rates.

P. Insurance Requirements

The SBA requires borrowers to obtain and maintain insurance if the property is in a special flood hazard area. The SBA will not disburse a loan until the applicant has obtained flood insurance.

Applicants who did not comply with the terms of previous loans or who did not maintain required flood insurance for the insurable value of the property are ineligible for an SBA loan.

Borrowers are required to maintain appropriate insurance coverage for the life of the loan.

Q. Minimum Monthly Payment

The SBA does not have a minimum monthly payment. Payments vary depending upon income and expenses, size of family and other circumstances that may affect repayment ability. Generally, the first payment is not due until five months after the date of the loan.

The term of the loan will be determined by the SBA based on your needs and your ability to repay the loan. *The maximum term is 30 years.*

SBA requires that borrowers maintain receipts and records of all loan expenditures for three years.

R. Refinancing

SBA can refinance all or part of prior mortgages, evidenced by a recorded lien, when the applicant:

1. Does not have credit available elsewhere;
2. Has suffered substantial damage (40% or more of the value of the predisaster fair market value of the property); and
3. Intends to repair the damage.

Refinancing of prior debts improves the victim's ability to afford the SBA disaster loan.

S. Mitigation Measures

SBA can provide additional low-interest loan funds to homeowners and business owners to assist with the cost of constructing preventive measures. These funds may be available in addition to the amount loaned to repair damages caused by this disaster. *The maximum additional loan amount is limited to 20 % of the loan amount for damages.*

T. Loan Modifications

Loans can be modified if the borrower can substantiate in writing a change of circumstances which affects ability to repay, or justify a change in the purpose of the loan.

U. Additional Information

For more information call the SBA at (800) 659-2955 [TTY: (704) 344-6640] or visit the SBA website at *http://www.sba.gov/disaster*

V. Consequences for Misuse

The penalty for misusing disaster funds is immediate repayment of one-and-a-half times the original amount of the loan.

W. Reconsiderations and Appeals of Declined Applicants

Applicants who are denied an SBA loan can request reconsideration in writing within *six months* of the decision denying the loan.

The request must explain why the decision is wrong and include any new information which supports the request.

For example, the applicant may have increased his/her ability to repay the loan. Perhaps the applicant's income rose or the applicant refinanced his/her home. The notification letter will provide instructions on who to send the request to and where to send it.

If the request for reconsideration is denied, a written appeal may be filed within 30 days. The appeal should address the reasons for denial, listed in the denial letter. After the appeal is submitted, it may be amended with further information. The appeal should be sent to:

U.S. Small Business Administration Disaster Office
Disaster Assistance Processing & Disbursement Center
14925 Kingsport Road; Fort Worth, Texas 76155

Tele: (Toll Free) (800) 366-6303: or (817) 868-2300
(TTY) (817) 267-4688
(Fax) (817) 684-5616

Hours of Operation: am - Pam: Monday thru Friday

The decision on the appeal is final.

Home Repair and Replacement Grants and Loans

	FEMA GRANT (Home Repair Assistance)	**SBA LOAN**	**FHA MORTGAGE GUARANTEE** (Section 203(h))
Program	**Home Repair Assistance** *This program only applies to homeowners who cannot return to their houses due to the fact that the home is not safe, sanitary or functional.*		This program applies to an owner-occupied primary residence only.
Eligibility	Must be the primary residence. The applicants must be the <u>owner-occupants</u> and must have the <u>legal responsibility</u> for making the repairs to their primary residence. They must need to make repairs to <u>essential living areas</u> to: 1. *return the home to livable condition;* 2. *reestablish access to the home;* 3. *be completed within 30 days.*	**Must be primary residence**	**Must be primary residence**
Application Deadline	**60 days from the date of the disaster declaration**.		
Application Process	File an application with FEMA		
Maximum Amount	$32,900 (adjusted annually)		
Interest Rate	This grant is not paid back.		
How Paid to Applicant	FEMA generally only makes a **one-time payment** for repairs.		
Relationship with other Programs	A homeowner may be eligible for a Home Repair Assistance grant to cover eligible emergency essential repairs and also eligible for a SBA loan to cover more extensive damage.		
Interaction with Insurance	Insured applicants may be provided with assistance when insurance benefits are significantly delayed, exhausted, or insufficient to cover the actual damage.		
Repayment	Homeowners must agree to repay FEMA if they later obtain duplicate insurance benefits.		
Record Keeping	FEMA may require receipts for repair work performed		

James L. Jaffe, J.D.

Other Needs Assistance (ONA)[44]

(A Provision of the Individuals and Households Program)

A. Personal Property (available to both tenants and homeowners)

Money to repair or replace damaged and destroyed personal property as a result of the disaster that is not covered by insurance. The goal is help with the cost for the necessary expenses and serious needs. All applicants must apply for an SBA disaster loan for personal property before being considered for ONA.

FEMA will not pay for all damaged or destroyed personal property. Flood insurance may be required if the home is in a Special Flood Hazard Area. The program covers only *essential personal property* such as clothing, household furnishings, appliances, school books and supplies. Dishes are considered "essential personal property", but crystal is not. Similarly, a winter coat is essential, but a fur coat is not. Items which the disaster victim considers essential may not be so defined by IHP.

Repair and replacement of personal property include:

- Clothing
- Household items (room furnishings, appliances)
- Specialized tools or protective clothing and equipment required for your job
- Necessary educational materials (computers, school books, supplies)
- Clean-up items (wet/dry vacuum, air purifier, dehumidifier)

The disaster must damage or destroy property which has been designated "necessary." The amount of the grant depends on:

1. Extent of the loss or damage;
2. If repair or replacement is necessary; and
3. The price range the state agency has allocated.

IHP requires no proof of ownership for personal property. However, verification of disaster related damage is required.

Tool replacement is available only for employed persons who must provide essential tools or work clothing as a condition of employment. An employer must provide a declaration stating that the tools and clothing were mandatory for employment. Households receive only the amounts that the state has allocated to each item.

This program is not available to self-employed individuals.

B. Transportation

This money is intended to pay for the repair and/or replacement of an individual's primary means of transportation that is no longer usable because of disaster-related damage or for the increased cost of using public transportation.

IHP provides funds to replace or repair cars, trucks, motorcycles, bicycles, etc. It covers only a vehicle which serves as a disaster survivor's sole means of transportation. In some communities, IHP will provide funds for public transportation for an extended period of time. IHP may pay for towing vehicles to repair shops if the repair damages prove to be program-eligible. IHP will pay for repairs to only *one car*. However, families may demonstrate special needs including employment, medical reasons or lack of alternative pub-

---

[44] Disaster Assistance Available from FEMA http://www.fema.gov/assistance/process/assistance.shtm#1

lic transportation that necessitate repair of a second car or truck.

Applicants must provide:

a. Proof of ownership, including registration with the Department of Motor Vehicles current at the time of the disaster;
b. One official repair estimate or receipt, or, for a total loss, the salvage value; and
c. Proof of insurance or lack of replacement coverage.

C. Medical and Dental Expenses

This money is intended for an individual's medical and/or dental treatment costs or the purchase of medical equipment required because of physical injuries received as a result of the disaster. IHP covers certain injuries or illness resulting from a disaster that is not covered in other programs -- e.g., Red Cross, VA, health insurance, or county mental health.

Awards can cover medical and dental treatment including surgery, hospitalization, medication and psychiatric services. However, psychiatric services are usually covered through county services. They also cover durable goods such as wheelchairs, prostheses, eye glasses, dentures and prescription drugs.

Note that IHP will only cover medical/dental needs that arose directly from the disaster. The Program will not cover pre-existing needs.

Proof of expense includes receipts or written estimates of cost of treatment, statements from insurance companies showing amount of coverage or lack of coverage, and statements from physicians, psychiatrists or dentists documenting disaster-related injury or need for treatment.

Recipients are specifically precluded from receiving any medical or dental benefits from IHP. The assumption is that they can obtain free care from a county facility.

D. Funeral and Burial Costs

This money is intended for the individual to pay for funeral services, burial or cremation, and other funeral expenses related to a death caused by the disaster.

E. Other Items

This money is intended for specific disaster-related costs that FEMA approves that are not listed above, and generally will include:

- Fuel (fuel, chain saw, firewood)
- Moving and storage expenses related to the disaster
- Other necessary expenses or serious needs (e.g., towing, or setup or connecting essential utilities for a housing unit not provided by FEMA)
- The cost of a National Flood Insurance Program Group Flood Insurance Policy

NOTE:

Not included in IHP are business losses, improvements and additions to property, landscaping, recreational property, luxury and decorative items and debts owed prior to the disaster.

F. Cost Estimates and Other Necessary Expenses

In some cases, IHP funds are available to pay for estimates from doctors, dentists, funeral directors and vehicle repair shops (with appropriate documentation) for damage necessary to determine eligibility. Estimates for appeal purposes are excluded. Any necessary expense not included in another category is included under "other." Applicants must prove both the necessity for, and the cost of, the expenditure.

G. Limits on IHP Spending and Duplication of Benefits

Households must spend IHP funds only on the category for which FEMA designates them. If a household spends the money on other needs, it must refund any part of the grant improperly spent. For example, a household receives IHP funds for home repairs and spends the money on mortgage payments. FEMA will require the household to repay the grant.

In addition, households that receive payment from other sources after having spent IHP funds must repay the portion of the IHP grant that covered the same category of need. For example, IHP provides money to replace essential clothing. Later, insurance also pays for clothing replacement. The household may have to repay FEMA/IHP. However, if the total IHP-eligible expenses exceed the IHP grant and the insurance payment, then the household need not repay.

Any household that receives benefits should keep all receipts and records for at least three years.

H. Calculation of Benefits

The state agency annually establishes a pricing guide for necessary items. The amount of the grant depends on the extent of damage or loss, whether items can be repaired or must be replaced. States often requires written receipts or estimates. IHP grants have a fixed maximum for any category, regardless of the actual loss. Each state annually submits a state plan containing pricing guidelines to FEMA for approval.

I. Inspection Process

FEMA conducts inspections for IHP, as well as for the FEMA housing assistance programs. There may also be separate inspectors from the IHP. A FEMA inspector makes the initial assessment about damage to the home and/or to personal property. The inspection report establishes the basis for eligibility and the amount of the grant. It is important for applicants to review the report for accuracy. IHP may perform a re-inspection if it appears as if the initial inspection reported insufficient information.

Those denied assistance or who disagree with the amount granted must file an appeal with the resource agency within **60 days**.

Other Housing Assistance

A. United States Department of Agriculture: Rural Development Agency (RDA)

The United States Department of Agriculture (USDA) Rural Development (RDA), administers the Rural Housing Service (RHS). As one of three distinct services of RD, RHS operates a wide range of programs designed to increase rural housing opportunities and improve residential conditions for low-income rural renters and homeowners through loans and grants for rental assistance, housing construction, rehabilitation and home ownership, as well as the development of essential public service, safety and health care facilities. RHS also assists farmers to build, buy, or repair farm labor housing. These are on-going programs, not specifically for disaster victims, but may be useful after a disaster.

B. Veterans Affairs

If a disaster victim has a home loan through the United States Department of Veterans Affairs (VA), s/he may be able to have the loan adjusted. Exact terms are determined on a case-by-case basis. Call the VA regional office where the property is located. The proper regional office should be on the loan papers; if not available, call the VA at 800-

827-1000 [TDD 1-800-829-4833] for the number of the correct regional office.

C. Department of Housing and Urban Development

The Department of Housing and Urban Development (HUD) may offer Section 8 rental assistance and relocation plans for tenants in subsidized public housing, depending on the disaster.

Also, HUD provides Section 203(h) single family mortgage insurance for borrowers (homeowners or renters) to reconstruct or replace their principal residence that was damaged or destroyed by a disaster. *The application deadline is one year from the disaster declaration date.* This mortgage insurance program is administered by the Federal Housing Administration (FHA), a branch of HUD. For more information about either type of assistance, contact a local HUD office.

If you have an FHA mortgage and cannot pay your mortgage, you can call HUD's National Servicing Center at 1-888-297-8685 to ask about foreclosure relief.

If the disaster victim has a Section 8 voucher from a disaster affected area or was a resident of public housing, contact the local HUD office or housing authority where the disaster victim is currently located, or call:

1-800-FED-INFO (1-800-333-4636) the TDD/TTY number is: 1-800-483-2209

HUD can assist the disaster victim in finding a public housing unit or obtaining a Section 8 voucher. The disaster victim will be required to prove that he/she were participating in either HUD's public housing program or its voucher program prior to the disaster. Additionally, the disaster victim will also be asked to show some form of photo identification. If the disaster victim does not have any identification, then the victim will be asked for his/her name and the social security number of the head of household in the victim's family.

D. Section 203(H) Mortgage Insurance for Homeowners

Anyone who owns a home that has been destroyed or severely damaged in a Presidentially declared disaster area is eligible to apply for mortgage insurance under this program.

The Section 203(h) program allows the Federal Housing Administration (FHA) to insure mortgages made by qualified lenders to victims of a major disaster who have lost their homes and are in the process of rebuilding or buying another home.

The borrower's application for mortgage insurance must be submitted to the lender within one year of the President's declaration of the disaster.

This program provides mortgage insurance to protect lenders against the risk of default on mortgages to qualified disaster victims. Individuals are eligible for this program if their homes are located in an area that was designated by the President as a disaster area and if their homes were destroyed or damaged to such an extent that reconstruction or replacement is necessary. Insured mortgages may be used to finance the purchase or reconstruction of a one-family home that will be the principal residence of the homeowner.

No down payment is required. The borrower is eligible for 100 percent financing. Closing costs and prepaid expenses must be paid by the borrower in cash or paid through premium pricing or by the seller, subject to a 6 percent limitation on seller concessions.

FHA mortgage insurance is not free. Mortgagees collect from the borrowers an up-front insurance premium (which may be financed) at the time of purchase, as well as monthly premiums that are not financed, but instead are added to the regular mortgage payment.

Some fees are limited. FHA rules impose limits on some of the fees that lenders may charge in making a mortgage. For example, the lender's mortgage origination charge for the administrative cost of processing the mortgage may not exceed one "point"—that is, one percent of the amount of the mortgage excluding any financed upfront mortgage insurance premium. In addition, property appraisal and inspection fees are set by FHA.

HUD sets limits on the amount that may be insured. To make sure that its programs serve low- and moderate-income people, FHA sets limits on the dollar value of the mortgage. To find the current FHA mortgage limit go to https://entp.hud.gov/idapp/html/hicostlook.cfm These figures vary over time and by place, depending on the cost of living and other factors (higher limits also exist for two- to four-family properties).

Applications are made through an FHA-approved lending institution, which make their requests through a provision known as "Direct Endorsement," which authorizes them to consider applications without submitting paperwork to HUD. Mortgage insurance processing and administration for this and other FHA single-family mortgage insurance products are handled through HUD's Homeowenership Centers which can be found at https://entp.hud.gov/clas/info2.cfm

For More Information contact the FHA Resource Center at http://portal.hud.gov/hudportal/HUD?src=/program_offices/housing/sfh/fharesourcectr or the toll-free FHA Mortgage Hotline, 1-800-483-7342.

E. Aid to Families with Dependent Children (AFDC)

Aid to Families with Dependent Children (AFDC) may provide Non-Recurring Special Needs (NRSN) grants to eligible recipients to pay for interim shelter or temporary housing, to make essential repairs to a damaged home owned by an AFDC family, and to more and store personal property. AFDC also administers the Homeless Assistance Program (HAP) which provides temporary and permanent housing assistance to homeless families.

F. Government Provided Temporary Housing

If FEMA determines that rental housing is unavailable in the local community because of widespread destruction or danger, it may provide government owned or leased temporary housing in lieu of monetary grant awards for rent or home repairs. FEMA is reluctant to do this, but during particularly destructive hurricanes, earthquakes or floods, it has provided government housing, when determined appropriate because adequate rental resources were not available. FEMA may enter into leases when existing rental resources are unavailable or it may provide mobile homes or other manufactured housing.

G. Rural Development Agency

If the disaster victim was living in a Rural Development-financed apartment and been displaced, the disaster victim is likely to be qualified to receive priority admission to any Section 515 rural rental housing property or Section 514/516 labor housing property in the United States. Contact the USDA Rural Development Agency at (800) 414-1226 for a list of apartment complexes and more information.

Overview of FEMA Disaster Individual Assistance Programs Available for Renters and Homeowners

Individual Assistance Programs	Renter/Tenant	Homeowner

1. Housing Programs
 	
a. Rental Assistance (RA) (apply up to 60 days after disaster)
   (1) Initial
   (2) Continuing
 	
b. Mortgage and Rental Assistance (MRA) (apply up to six months after disaster)
   (1) Initial
   (2) Continuing
 	
c. Home Repair Assistance (HRA) (apply up to six months after disaster)
 	
d. Transient Accommodations (reimbursement for lodging for 30 days)
 	
e. Government Temporary Housing (e.g. temporary mobile homes)
	a. (1) Residence is damaged or uninhabitable because of the disaster (includes utility cut-off).
	   (2) Requires recertification
	
	b. Renter must receive an eviction notice from the landlord to qualify.
	   (1) Initial certification
	   (2) Requires recertification
	
	c. Not available
	
	d. Residence is damaged and paid receipts are required.
	
	e. Disaster specific
		a. (1) Residence is destroyed or is uninhabitable because of the disaster and cannot be repaired within 30 days (includes utility cut offs).
		   (2) Requires recertification
		
		b. Homeowner must receive a notice of foreclosure from lender.
		   (1) Initial Certification
		   (2) Requires recertification
		
		c. Homeowners are eligible for repairs which can be made within 30 days.
		
		d. Residence is damaged and paid receipts are required.
		
		e. Disaster specific

2. Individual and Households Program (IHP) (apply up to 60 days after disaster) a. Housing Repairs b. Personal Property c. Automobile transportation d. Medical/Dental e. Flood Insurance f. Funeral Expense g. moving Expense	 a. Not available b. Yes c. Yes d. Yes e. Limited coverage f. Yes g. Yes	 a. Yes b. Yes c. Yes d. Yes e. Yes f. Yes g. Yes
3. Disaster Unemployment Assistance (DUA) (apply up to 30 days after disaster) a. Self-employed b. Unemployed because of disaster	 a. Yes b. Yes	 a. Yes b. Yes

Individual Assistance Programs	Renter/Tenant	Homeowner
4. Crisis Counseling/Stress Management	Yes	Yes
5. Legal Services	Yes	Yes
6. Cora Brown Fund	Yes, If need is not met by another program such as IHP	Yes, If need is not met by another program such as IHP
Individual Assistance Programs	**Renter/Tenant**	**Homeowner**
1. American Red Cross	Emergency Shelter and Food	Emergency Shelter and Food
2. Department of Agriculture (USDA) a. Emergency Food Stamps) apply up to 10 days after the disaster b. Farm Service Agency (FSA) Emergency Loans c. Rural housing Service (RHS) (assistance provided is not disaster specific)	a. Yes b. Farm owners eligible for loans to cover production and physical losses c. Rental assistance to low-income rural families for rent and utilities	a. Yes b. Farm owners eligible for loans to cover production and physical losses c. Loans and grants to low-income homeowners to purchase, construct, improve, repair or relocate residence
3. Department of Housing and Urban Development (HUD)	Section 8 rental assistance; relocation plan for renters in already subsidized or public housing; Section 203(h) mortgage insurance	Section 203(h) single family mortgage insurance to reconstruct or replace principal residence that was damaged or destroyed by disaster
4. Small Business Administration (SBA) Loans a. Physical Disaster loans (apply up to 60 days after disaster) (1). Home repair (2). Personal property b. Physical disaster loans for businesses (apply up to 60 days after disaster) c. Economic injury to businesses (apply up to 9 months after disaster)	(1) No, unless lease makes tenant responsible for repairs (2) Yes b. Yes c. Yes	(1) Yes (2) Yes b. Yes c. Yes, if small business

Individual Assistance Programs	Renter/Tenant	Homeowner
5. Department of Veterans Affairs	Information about benefits, pensions and insurance settlements	Information about benefits, pensions and insurance settlements: adjustment for VA-insured home mortgage
6. Aid To Families with Dependent Children	Homeless Assistance Program (HAP) grants to AFDC recipients for temporary and permanent housing assistance or Non-Recurring Special Needs (NRSN) grant for temporary housing and personal property loss	Homeless Assistance Program (HAP) grants to AFDC recipients for temporary and permanent housing assistance or Non-Recurring Special Needs (NRSN) grant for temporary housing, essential home repairs and personal property loss
7. Supplemental Security Income (SSI)	Emergency Advance Payments (EAP) for applicants who are proven eligible or presumptively eligible for SSI	Emergency Advance Payments (EAP) for applicants who are proven eligible or presumptively eligible for SSI
8. Food Stamps	Disaster, Replacement, and Expedited Food Stamps	Disaster, Replacement, and Expedited Food Stamps

Insurance Payments to Homeowners and Condo Owners [Who gets to keep the money?]

This gets a little complicated and requires a multi-step analysis. Most individuals who own a home or condo have a mortgage, and the mortgage agreement requires that the individual carry insurance to cover damage or loss to the home or condo. The usual mortgage agreement requires the insurance policy obtained by the homeowner, or condo owner, to pay both the mortgage holder (called mortgagee) and the homeowner (called mortgagor). Generally with both parties named as "loss payees" on the insurance policy, the insurance company puts both names on the payment check.

So, when a home or condo is damaged in a disaster and the insurance company "pays up", who gets the money?

Let's use an example:

The insured's home is worth.................. $100,000
The mortgage is for $40,000
Damage caused by the disaster $20,000
Insurance Payment $15,000

The question is who gets the $15,000?

First, you have to look to the mortgage agreement between the homeowner and the mortgage holder.

Presently most, if not all, mortgages contain standard language similar to this:

Borrower further authorizes Lender to apply the balance of such proceeds to the payment of the sums secured by this Instrument, whether or not then due, http://www.mortgage-investments.com/resources/free-sample-forms/

This allows the lender to keep any insurance proceeds and apply it to the "back end" of the mortgage which has the effect of not reducing the monthly payment, to say nothing of the fact that the home owner, or condo owner, does not have the insurance proceeds to make repairs.

State laws differ on this issue, some states do not allow the lender to keep the money and some do. So check your state laws on this issue before you receive any insurance proceeds.

As a result of the August 2007 flood in Findlay, Ohio, lenders created different policies with regard to insurance proceeds. One bank allowed the homeowner to keep the first $25,000.00 and applied the remainder to the loan principal. Another bank allowed the homeowner to keep the first $10,000.00 and applied the remainder to the loan principal, while another bank just kept it all. *Make certain you negotiate a "deal" with the lender before receiving any insurance proceeds to make sure the proceeds are used for repairs, and not to pay down the mortgage.*

Mortgage Payments During and After a Disaster

As the result of a disaster a person may be out of work, or for some other reason caused by a disaster can't make the mortgage payments, so what must a person do? Since a mortgage payment is due every month, no exceptions. An individual needs to contact the lender or whoever gets the mortgage payments to and work something out. Don't quit making the mortgage payments and not contacting the lender. But, if the mortgage is held by one of two agencies created by Congress, or backed by a third or fourth agency created by Congress, there may be relief from mortgage payments during the disaster recovery period.

The agencies are;

Fannie Mae (Federal National Mortgage Association),
Freddie Mac (Federal home Loan Mortgage Corporation),
Ginnie Mae (Government National Mortgage Association), and
FHA (Federal Housing Administration).

Over half of all new mortgages in the United States are held by two agencies created by Congress to oversee home loans. Most people deal with their bank or Mortgage Company who follows the rules set by Freddie Mac or Fannie Mae depending upon who holds the mortgage.

Freddie Mac (Federal home Loan Mortgage Corporation) and Fannie Mae (Federal National Mortgage Association) purchase or guarantee 65% of new mortgages in the United States. Borrowers don't work directly with these agencies, but go through their bank or mortgage company who then work with Freddie Mac or Fannie Mae. If homeowners have a problem with paying their mortgage as a result of a disaster the lender follows the policies of Freddie Mac or Fannie Mae depending on whoever holds the mortgage. Knowing what Freddie Mac and Fannie Mae say about aiding borrowers hurt by a disaster is very helpful and pro-active.

A third way the federal government is involved with mortgages is through an Agency called Ginnie Mae (Government National Mortgage Association). Ginnie Mae guarantees securities backed by single-family and multifamily loans insured by government agencies allowing lenders to create a mortgage backed security that they sell to investors. The federal government guarantees the monthly payment to the investors. The program is based upon the fact that homeowner's will make their monthly payments so the lender can pay the investor who bought the lender's mortgage-backed security. In times of a disaster, the federal government can and does guarantee the monthly payments to the investors so the mortgage holder does not have to force homeowners to make monthly payment when, due to a disaster they cannot be made.

A fourth way the federal government is involved with mortgages is through FHA (Federal Housing Administration) FHA-insured mortgages.

All these agencies have assistance available to homeowners who are disaster victims.

Fannie Mae Disaster Assistance[45]

Lenders can accommodate borrowers who have been impacted by a disaster, including flexibilities to standard limited cash-out refinance policies on a borrower's principal residence that:

- Permit a refinance to consolidate non-purchase money subordinate mortgage loans that had been obtained to finance disaster-related property repairs; and

- Provide for a higher cash-out amount to reimburse borrowers for documented out-of-pocket expenses related to disaster-related repairs.

In addition, borrowers may use lump-sum disaster-relief grants or loans to satisfy Fannie Mae's minimum borrower contribution requirement.

Fannie Mae has the following policy with regard to homeowners who are affected by disasters:

We are committed to working with our lender customers to provide mortgage relief to homeowners whose lives have been disrupted by disasters, terrorist attacks, or other natural or man-made catastrophes not caused by the borrower. To help communities recover, we provide detailed policies in our Single-Family Selling and Servicing Guides. Should a disaster be significant, we may amend these policies to expand the relief available to homeowners.

Following a disaster, we rely on our customers to implement our disaster relief policies and assist impacted homeowners. We require servicers to assess property damage and the needs of homeowners in order to provide appropriate relief. In addition, our Customer Account Teams work closely with our customers to determine physical and operational impacts to their business operations and their ability to service mortgages owned or guaranteed by Fannie Mae.

- Selling and Servicing Guides

News and Announcements

News items will be added as appropriate.

How to Respond in the Event of a Disaster

Determine if the locality is designated in a Major Disaster Declaration

The Servicing Guide requires servicers to focus relief efforts on borrowers with properties located within federally defined disaster areas. To find a list of recent emergency and disaster declarations and locations, visit the Federal Emergency Management Agency's (FEMA) web site.

Look for Fannie Mae Announcements

When a significant disaster occurs that adversely affects either the value or habitability of mortgaged properties or borrower's ability to make further payments or payments in full on mortgage loans, we may issue special announcements such as press releases, Guide Announcements,

---

[45] https://www.efanniemae.com/sf/guides/ssg/hurrelief/index.jsp

Lender Letters, or Notices with updates or temporary relief policies.

- Single-Family Updates, Alerts, and Newsletters
- Selling and Servicing Guides

Refer to the Servicing Guide, Guide Announcements/Lender Letters, and the Selling Guide

Our policies related to disasters are included the Servicing Guide and may be amended by Servicing Guide Announcements. We also provide relief in the Selling Guide by providing lenders with mortgage loan flexibilities for borrowers seeking a mortgage following a disaster.

Summary of Servicing Guide Requirements for Disaster Relief

Our servicing policy covering disasters can be found in the Servicing Guide in Part III, Chapter 11: Assistance in Natural Disasters and Part VII, Chapter 4: Special Relief Measures. To protect the financial stability of those affected by a disaster, servicers must follow the disaster relief requirements outlined in the Guide, which include:

- determining whether the property is adequately insured against the damage;
- counseling the borrower on the availability of appropriate relief provisions;
- assessing property damage and impact to properties for loans in process at a time a disaster strikes;
- waiving any late payment charges that result from the disaster's impact;
- ensuring that insurance claims are filed and settled promptly and that properties are fully repaired; and
- determining the facts and circumstances related to a borrower and the mortgaged property to determine if a foreclosure prevention alternative is appropriate even though the borrower's mortgage loan is current, based on the servicer's determination that a payment default is reasonably foreseeable.

Selling and Servicing Guides

Summary of Selling Guide Requirements for Disaster Relief

Our selling policy covering disasters can be found in the Selling Guide in B5-4-07, Disaster-Related Limited Cash-Out Refinance Flexibilities and B3-4.3-07, Disaster Relief Grants or Loans. The Selling Guide outlines steps lenders can take to accommodate borrowers who have been impacted by a disaster, including flexibilities to standard limited cash-out refinance policies on a borrower's principal residence that:

- Permit a refinance to consolidate non-purchase money subordinate mortgage loans that had been obtained to finance disaster-related property repairs; and
- Provide for a higher cash-out amount to reimburse borrowers for documented out-of-pocket expenses related to disaster-related repairs.

In addition, borrowers may use lump-sum disaster-relief grants or loans to satisfy Fannie Mae's minimum borrower contribution requirement. Our Guides can be accessed from eFannieMae.com either by downloading a PDF version or through the AllRegs® Online portal link on the Selling and Servicing Guides.

Freddie Mac Disaster Assistance[46]

Some of the things Freddie Mac can do for disaster victims

- reduce or suspend mortgage payments for up to 12 months

---

[46] http://www.freddiemac.com/singlefamily/news/2013/0815_disaster_relief_options_and_requirements.html

- Suspend foreclosure or evictions for up to 12 months
- Waive penalties and late fees for homeowners with disaster-damaged homes
- Not report delinquencies or forbearances to credit bureaus

Freddie Mac has the following policy with regard to homeowners who are affected by disasters:

At Freddie Mac, we are committed to seeking ways to provide assistance to borrowers – especially when their homes have been impacted by disaster-related events. We are prepared to quickly respond with effective relief measures and guidance to help borrowers, Sellers, and Servicers through the aftermath of a disaster.

In the event a disaster strikes, borrowers whose homes have been damaged may experience disruptions in their ability to make on-time mortgage payments. Therefore, we ask Freddie Mac Sellers and Servicers to be responsive to any requests for assistance from affected borrowers using options available through our *Single-Family Seller/Servicer Guide* (Guide).

In addition to assisting borrowers who are disaster victims, Servicers must begin ascertaining the disaster's impact on homeowners with Freddie Mac-owned mortgages. Sellers should review the Guide and their procedures for inspecting and recertifying a mortgaged property's value, condition, and marketability when a major disaster occurs. Most importantly, we rely on both Sellers and Servicers to determine the number of impacted properties and the extent of damage to each.

Freddie Mac Policies for Major Disaster Declarations

When disaster strikes and causes extensive damage, the President of the United States may issue a Major Disaster Declaration for certain localities and authorize federal Individual Assistance programs for affected individuals and households. In the event a declaration is made, Sellers and Servicers should follow these steps:

Identify the localities designated in the Major Disaster Declaration

To find a list of eligible counties, parishes, and municipalities, visit the Federal Emergency Management Agency's (FEMA) Web site.

Look for Special Freddie Mac Announcements

Freddie Mac may make special announcements through press releases, Industry Letters, Guide Bulletins, and *Single-Family Advisory* e-mails.

Consult Guide Chapter 68 for Disaster Policies

In the interest of protecting credit ratings and financial interests of borrowers with Freddie Mac-owned mortgages who reside in the designated areas, Servicers must immediately begin following the disaster relief requirements outlined in Guide Chapter 68, which include:

- Short-term suspension of collection and foreclosure proceedings for up to 12 months from the date a disaster strikes, based on the relative merits of each case.
- Not assessing late charges or reporting to credit repositories for borrowers on a forbearance plan or paying as agreed on a repayment plan.
- Providing help with options for local, state, or federal disaster assistance.
- Monitoring and coordinating the insurance claim process.
- **Refer to Guide Exhibit 52 for Assistance Programs**
- Exhibit 52 in the Guide details information regarding FEMA, Small Business Administra-

tion (SBA), and Federal Housing Administration (FHA) assistance programs for residents of areas designated in a Major Disaster Declaration. These assistance programs are designed to supplement state or local aid that may be offered.

- **Review the Guide for Seller Responsibilities**
- Sellers should be prepared to address property damage as a result of a disaster, per Guide Section 44.2(c). Sellers should also review Guide Section 22.20 about circumstances that adversely affect the value of a mortgage, including condemnation. Sellers should also review Guide Section 44.2(a), which requires Sellers to warrant that improvements must be undamaged by fire, windstorm, and other perils.

Ginnie Mae Disaster Assistance[47]

Often times your mortgage is used by a lender to create a mortgage backed security that they sell to investors. The whole thing is based upon the fact that you will make your monthly payment so the lender can pay the investor who bought the lender's mortgage backed security. The federal government guarantees the monthly payment to the investor with a program called Ginnie Mae (Government National Mortgage Association).

Ginnie Mae guarantees only securities backed by single-family and multifamily loans insured by government agencies, including the FHA, Department of Veterans Affairs, the Department of Housing and Urban Development's Office of Public and Indian Housing and the Department of Agriculture's Rural Development.

What this all means is that your mortgage may have been used to guarantee a security sold to some investor. So that investor expects to get paid regardless of the fact that you can't make your payment due to a disaster. This means that your mortgage holder wants and needs the monthly payment no matter what. So to keep the holder of your mortgage from putting the arm on you to make your payment when a disaster prevents you from doing so, Ginne Mae offers the mortgage holder some relief so they don't have to go after you to make your monthly payment.

Ginnie Mae encourages all single-family, manufactured housing and multifamily Ginnie Mae issuers to provide forbearance to mortgagors in areas declared a disaster by the President. Ginnie Mae realizes that with the massive destruction of property and the temporary loss of jobs, many individuals will experience severe economic and personal hardships.

Ginnie Mae is prepared to assist issuers holding mortgage loans in the affected areas in making their Ginnie Mae pass-through payments.

Ginnie Mae Policies for Disaster Assistance

Ginnie Mae MBS Guide Chapter 34-Special Assistance Programs:

When the President declares a disaster, Issuers may contact the Federal Emergency Management Agency (FEMA) to obtain information on the related counties and their corresponding declaration dates. Eligible locations are those specified in the disaster areas declared by the President. Locations outside those areas may also be eligible if the disaster has directly and significantly reduced homeowners' employment opportunities and incomes.

Ginnie Mae will assist Issuers with pass-through payments to investors if the Issuer has more than five percent (5%) of its Ginnie Mae loan portfolio in the affected areas. Those Issuers who have large numbers of mortgagors unable to make loan pay-

---

[47] http://www.ginniemae.gov/doing_business_with_ginniemae/issuer_resources/MBSGuideLib/Chapter_34.pdf

ments because of the disaster and who, as Issuers, are unable to obtain private market financing to cover the delinquencies, may be eligible for Ginnie Mae assistance. Such requests for assistance shall only be made by an Issuer as a "last resort". Issuers must request assistance within one year of the date of the disaster declaration, and such disaster relief, if granted by Ginnie Mae, shall only be available for a period not to exceed 90 calendar days.

1. Request Procedures

    The Issuer must request assistance in accordance with the following procedures:

    a. For each eligible month for which assistance is requested, the Issuer will sign and submit, at least three business days prior to that month's remittance date or ACH date, the following:

        i. a single copy of a Request for Disaster Assistance (Appendix XI-1) (a request);
        ii. two copies of a Supervisory Agreement (Appendix XI-2), properly executed by an authorized corporate official; and
        iii. a single copy of Wire Instructions to Transmit Funds to Issuer from Ginnie Mae (Appendix XI-3).

    The Issuer must send these documents by express mail to the Senior Vice President of the Office of Mortgage Backed Securities, Attention: Declared Disaster (see Addresses). These documents are applicable under both the Ginnie Mae I MBS Program and the Ginnie Mae II MBS Program.

    b. If Ginnie Mae approves the Request, it will execute the Supervisory Agreements and return one copy to the Issuer. Ginnie Mae will wire the requested advances directly into the Issuer's P&I custodial accounts at times that will enable the Issuer to make payments to security holders at the times specified in Chapter 15.

2. Computation of Advances

    The Issuer will compute the amount of the advance required from Ginnie Mae for each eligible month as follows:

    a. Determine the total amount of advances that the Issuer made with respect to the eligible loans in the month (the base month) immediately prior to the initial month in which assistance is made available in a disaster APM. This sum is considered unrelated to the disaster and therefore not eligible for assistance under this Chapter 34. It is treated as the "base month amount" of advances.

    b. Estimate the advances that will be required for the eligible loans in the eligible month that is the subject of the request.

    c. Subtract (2) from (3). The balance is the amount of Ginnie Mae advance assistance (eligible assistance) that the Issuer will be eligible for in the eligible month that is the subject of the request. An Issuer that receives an eligible advance from Ginnie Mae will be obligated to repay it to Ginnie Mae within 90 days after Ginnie Mae wires the funds into the Issuer's P&I custodial accounts, with interest computed at the applicable interest rate, which will be set forth in the applicable Supervisory Agreement.

The applicable interest rate is the rate that Ginnie Mae pays for its monthly borrowing from the Treasury Department during the month of the related eligible advance. Issuers should use Instructions to Remit Funds to Ginnie Mae Via Electronic Funds Transfer (Appendix XI-4) to make the required repayments. Although the specified repayment dates and the associated Supervisory Agreements are not expected to be extended, they may be extended in the sole discretion of the President of Ginnie Mae.

FHA Mortgages

Disaster Relief Options for FHA Homeowners[48]

Was your home or your ability to make your mortgage payments harmed by an event that the President declared a disaster? You may qualify for relief to help you keep your home. Much of the mortgage industry and The United States Department of Housing and Urban Development is committed to assisting borrowers whose lives and livelihoods are thrown into turmoil by a disaster.

If you can't pay your mortgage because of what happened, your lender may be able to help you. If you are at risk of losing your home because of the disaster, your lender may stop or delay initiation of foreclosure for 90 days.

Lenders may also waive late fees for borrowers who may become delinquent on their loans. Just follow the four steps below to see if help may be available to you. You are strongly encouraged to contact your lender for further information, and to see if you are eligible for relief.

Step One - Answer Four Basic Questions

1. Did my expenses rise or income fall?
2. Were these changes in my finances caused directly or substantially by the disaster?
3. Have I missed any mortgage payments?
4. Am I without other resources, such as insurance settlements, to catch up?

If you answered "yes" to all of these questions, and you have a conventional or VA mortgage, contact your lender. If you have an FHA-insured mortgage, please continue reading.

Step Two - See If and How You Can Participate in FHA Disaster Relief

The next step is to determine if you are one of the affected borrowers as described below. You must be in one of three basic groups in order to qualify for a moratorium on foreclosure:

1. You or your family live within the geographic boundaries of a Presidentially declared disaster area, you are automatically covered by a 90-day foreclosure moratorium.
2. You are a household member of someone who is deceased, missing or injured directly due to the disaster, you qualify for a moratorium.
3. Your financial ability to pay your mortgage debt was directly or substantially affected by a disaster, you qualify for a moratorium.

If Your FHA Loan Was Current before the Disaster but Now You Can't Make Your Next Month's Payment

This special program is designed to help borrowers who are at risk of imminent foreclosure, so a moratorium won't apply to your situation. However, if your inability to pay your loan resulted from the disaster, your lender may waive any late fees normally charged and let you know about other options. Also, if you foresee ongoing problems in making your mortgage payments resulting from changes in your financial status, you should contact your lender immediately.

How Can This FHA Disaster Relief Help Me?

HUD has instructed FHA lenders to use reasonable judgment in determining who is an "affected borrower." Lenders are required to reevaluate

---

[48] http://portal.hud.gov/hudportal/HUD?src=/program_offices/housing/sfh/nsc/qaho0121

each delinquent loan until reinstatement or foreclosure and to identify the cause of default. Contact your lender to let them know about your situation. Some of the actions that your lender may take are:

- During the term of a moratorium, your loan may not be referred to foreclosure if you were affected by a disaster.
- Your lender will evaluate you for any available loss mitigation assistance to help you retain your home.
- Your lender may enter into a special forbearance plan, or execute a loan modification or a partial claim, if these actions are likely to help reinstate your loan.
- If saving your home is not feasible, lenders have some flexibility in using the preforeclosure sales program or may offer to accept a deed-in-lieu of foreclosure.

Step Three - Take Action to Qualify for Foreclosure Relief

A foreclosure moratorium applies only to borrowers who are delinquent on their FHA loan. If you are current on your loan payments, then you should continue to make them. When contacting your lender for further instructions, please be prepared to provide them information about disability or other insurance that may be available to assist you in making your payments.

FHA lenders will automatically stop all foreclosure actions against families with delinquent loans on homes within the boundaries of a Presidentially declared disaster area.

If you were physically or financially impacted by the disasters and are in default or foreclosure, contact your lender immediately to request assistance. Borrowers who were injured or whose income relied on individuals who were injured or died in the disaster will be asked for documentation such as medical records or death certificates, if available. Your lender will ask you for financial information to help evaluate what assistance can be provided to you to reinstate your loan.

FHA Loans Already in Foreclosure

It is very important that you notify your lender to be sure that they realize you are an affected borrower. Your lender may request supporting documentation and use it to determine if you meet the relief criteria. Once identified as an affected borrower, foreclosure action may be stopped for the duration of the moratorium period.

Step Four - If Your Lender Is Unable to Assist You

HUD is confident that your mortgage lender will make every attempt possible to assist you. If you are not satisfied after discussing possible relief actions with your lender, please call a HUD-approved counseling agency toll free at (800) 569-4287 or contact HUD's National Servicing Center.

FHA Mortgage Insurance for Disaster Victims Section 203(h)[49]

Summary:

The Section 203(h) program allows the Federal Housing Administration (FHA) to insure mortgages made by qualified lenders to victims of a major disaster who have lost their homes and are in the process of rebuilding or buying another home.

Purpose:

Through Section 203(h), the Federal Government helps victims in Presidentially designated disaster

---

[49] http://portal.hud.gov/hudportal/HUD?src=/program_offices/housing/sfh/ins/203h-dft

areas recover by making it easier for them to get mortgages and become homeowners or re-establish themselves as homeowners.

Type of Assistance:

This program provides mortgage insurance to protect lenders against the risk of default on mortgages to qualified disaster victims. Individuals are eligible for this program if their homes are located in an area that was designated by the President as a disaster area and if their homes were destroyed or damaged to such an extent that reconstruction or replacement is necessary. Insured mortgages may be used to finance the purchase or reconstruction of a one-family home that will be the principal residence of the homeowner. Like the basic FHA mortgage insurance program it resembles (Section 203(b) Mortgage Insurance for One to Four Family Homes), Section 203(h) offers features that make recovery from a disaster easier for homeowners:

- No down payment is required. The borrower is eligible for 100 percent financing. Closing costs and prepaid expenses must be paid by the borrower in cash or paid through premium pricing or by the seller, subject to a 6 percent limitation on seller concessions.

- FHA mortgage insurance is not free. Mortgagees collect from the borrowers an up-front insurance premium (which may be financed) at the time of purchase, as well as monthly premiums that are not financed, but instead are added to the regular mortgage payment.

- HUD sets limits on the amount that may be insured. To make sure that its programs serve low and moderate income people, FHA sets limits on the dollar value of the mortgage. The current FHA mortgage limit can be viewed online (https://entp.hud.gov/idapp/html/hicostlook.cfm). These figures vary over time and by place, depending on the cost of living and other factors (higher limits also exist for two to four family properties).

Eligible Participants:

FHA approved lending institutions, such as banks, mortgage companies, and savings and loan associations, are eligible for Section 203(h) insurance.

Eligible Customers:

Anyone whose home has been destroyed or severely damaged in a Presidentially declared disaster area is eligible to apply for mortgage insurance under this program.

Application:

The borrower's application for mortgage insurance must be submitted to the lender within one year of the President's declaration of the disaster. Applications are made through an FHA approved lending institution, who make their requests through a provision known as "Direct Endorsement," which authorizes them to consider applications without submitting paperwork to HUD. Mortgage insurance processing and administration for this and other FHA single family mortgage insurance products are handled through HUD's Homeownership Centers.

Technical Guidance:

This program is authorized under Section 203, National Housing Act (12 U.S.C. 1709, 1715(b)). Program regulations are in 24 CFR Part 203. These regulations, as well as handbooks, notices, and letters relevant to this program, are available through HUDCLIPS. The program is administered by the Office of Single Family Housing Programs in HUD?s Office of Housing, Federal Housing Administration.

For More Information:

Contact the FHA Resource Center. Homeowners can also visit HUD's website for a searchable listing of approved FHA lenders nationwide. Homeowners are encouraged to also contact a HUD-approved housing counseling agency, for assistance with disaster related issues or call toll-free at: (800) 569-4287.

National Student Loan Program (NSLP)[50]

There are three different programs under the NSLP depending upon who declares the disaster. They are disasters declared by the President, disasters declared by the United States Department of Education, and other disasters.

1. Disaster Declared by The President

If you are the victim of a natural disaster or local or national emergency, you are considered affected if you live or work in an area declared a disaster in connection with a national emergency as declared by the president of the United States.

Loans while in school

Loans that are in an "in-school" status will remain in that status for up to three years during the time you don't attend school due to the disaster. The Department of Education (ED) will continue to pay the interest on your subsidized Stafford loans during this time. You must pay the interest on your unsubsidized Stafford loans.

Loans in "grace"

"Grace" is the six-month period after you're no longer enrolled at least half-time during which you don't have to make payments on your Stafford loans. If, during your grace period, you are affected for more than 30 days by a disaster due to a national emergency, you may qualify for an "excluded" period of grace for up to three years. If you return to school at least half-time at the end of this excluded period, you are entitled to a new grace period when you stop being enrolled at least half-time again.

If your loan is in an in-school or graduate fellowship deferment

Your loan will remain in deferred status during the time you are affected by the disaster for up to three years. This three year period includes the time necessary for you to return to school. ED will pay the interest on your subsidized Stafford loans during this period. You must pay the interest on your unsubsidized Stafford loans.

Loan in repayment

If you can't make payments on your student loan due to a disaster, you may qualify for an initial forbearance for up to one year with a three-month transition period following the forbearance (total of 15 months). The lender may grant the forbearance based on a request from you, a family member, or some other reliable source. You must provide your lender with documentation if you need to extend the forbearance beyond the initial period.

2. Disaster Determined by the United States Department of Education

You are considered affected if you live or work in an area declared a disaster in connection with a national emergency as declared by the United States Department of Education.

---

[50] http://federalstudentaid.ed.gov/disaster.html

If you are in school

Ask your school about its policies concerning the emergency or disaster.

If your loan is in repayment

If notified of the emergency or disaster by ED, the lender will forbear your loan for the period of time specified by ED, plus the following 30 days. ED or the guaranty agency will notify the lender when the forbearance period no longer applies.

3. Other Disasters

If you are in school

Ask your school about its policies concerning the emergency or disaster.

If your loan is in repayment

If your lender determines you have been affected by a natural disaster or a local or national emergency, the lender may grant a forbearance not to exceed three months. If you need to extend the forbearance period beyond the initial three months, your lender will need documentation and an agreement.

4. For more information about these programs, contact

NSLP Customer Service
P.O. Box 82507
Lincoln, NE 68501-2507
1300 O Street, Lincoln, NE 68508
Telephone: 800-735-8778, ext. 6300
Fax: 402-479-6658
E-mail: nslpcs@nslp.org www.nslp.org

Disaster Unemployment Assistance (DUA)[51]

This program applies to the self-employed as well as employees.

DUA provides funds to individuals who are ineligible for regular unemployment insurance. DUA is funded by FEMA. DUA is a special form of unemployment insurance for disaster victims. See 42 U.S.C. § 5177, 20 CFR Part 625.1 et seq.

Individuals apply for disaster relief in the same manner as they apply for regular Unemployment Insurance (UI), i.e., at their local unemployment office, or, where available, by telephone or electronically.

DUA is triggered when the President declares a disaster.

Disaster Unemployment Insurance is a federal program administered through the states. The federal Department of Labor (DoL) and the state Department of Labor administer the program.

In addition to unemployment insurance, disaster survivors are eligible for local employment services.

The federal regulations governing Disaster Unemployment Assistance are found at 20 CFR Part 625

Eligibility for Unemployment Compensation is broadened under the Disaster Unemployment Assistance program to include people, who as a result of the disaster:

---

[51] http://workforcesecurity.doleta.gov/unemploy/disaster.asp

1. no longer have a job; are unable to reach their place of employment;
2. were to have started new employment but cannot;
3. have become the major supporter for a household because the head of household died in the disaster; or cannot work because of injury.

Self-employed individuals and farmers who are not covered by unemployment insurance may also be eligible for Disaster Unemployment Assistance benefits.

Individuals who have exhausted unemployment eligibility may also qualify for these benefits.

Applications for these benefits are filed with the state unemployment benefits agency.

Applicants should be prepared to provide a Social Security number and driver's license or state ID number and the names, addresses and telephone numbers of all employers within the last 18 months.

Applicants must apply for DUA within 30 days of the announcement of the disaster declaration and of the availability of DUA.

In General

After the President declares a disaster, DUA becomes available to any unemployed worker or self-employed individual who lived, worked or was scheduled to work in the disaster area. *The unemployment must be a direct result of the disaster 42 U.S.C. §5177(a)*

Several categories of precondition qualify a worker. The worker:

1. No longer has a job or a place to work;
2. Cannot reach the place of work;
3. Cannot work due to damage to the place of work;
4. Cannot work because of injury caused by the disaster; or
5. The head of household died and another individual becomes the major support of the household and is seeking work.
20 CFR § 625.5

To qualify for DUA a claimant must not be entitled to any other UI, to waiting period credit for UI or to state disability insurance.

The claimant may not be under a disqualification from a previous application for UI benefits, unless the claimant has found intervening work and has lost his/her most recent job because of the disaster.

The claimant must accept suitable jobs offered and must conduct a job search while receiving DUA. 42 U.S.C. § 5177(a).

DUA is not based on need. This program provides a weekly income to individuals who are out of work through no fault of their own due to a disaster. 20 CFR. § 625.4

A. Unemployed Workers

Individuals who are unemployed as a direct result of the disaster are eligible for DUA if they are *not eligible for regular unemployment* **benefits** or other wage replacement payments. 42 U.S.C. § 5177(a)

Employees must have been employed or about to begin employment in the disaster area at the time of the disaster. The job must have been the primary source of income for the individual. 20 CFR § 625.2(s).

B. Unemployed Self-Employed Individual

DUA is available to any individual who is self-employed or about to be self-employed in the disaster area at the time of the disaster. Self-employed for DUA means that the individual's principal source of income was from the performance of services by the individual in the individual's own business or on the individual's own farm.
20 CFR § 625.2 (n)(t).

Individuals qualify if they are unable to work, unable to reach the work place 20 CFR § 625.5(a)(2) or cannot provide services because of a disaster-related injury. 20 CFR § 625.5(b)(4)

For the self-employed, the state agency uses net earnings, as well as any wages, to establish the DUA amount.

If the self-employed individual had **no net earnings or a net loss** from self-employment activities, the individual will be paid the minimum DUA weekly benefit.

Past income during the individual's base period determines benefits. *The greater one's income, the greater the DUA benefit.* 20 CFR § 625.6

C. Farm Workers

Disasters frequently prevent migrant farm workers from performing their customary agricultural work. When the workers are in one state, and disaster strikes in the state to which they are moving or plan to move, they may be eligible for UI benefits. Workers who obtain regular UI benefits are not eligible for DUA. However, some farm workers are not eligible for regular UI because, for example, they are:

1. Not covered by UI or
2. Not monetarily eligible for UI.

Both of these categories of farm workers may be eligible for DUA. They may file their claims on an interstate basis (i.e., in their home states).

D. Immigration Issues

Individuals who file claims for UI or DUA benefits must indicate their immigration status. The state will require proof of work authorization for the period during which the individual is collecting DUA and for the past "base period."

Persons who are undocumented and without work authorization are not able to obtain benefits.

E. Injured Workers

1. Disaster-Related Injuries

DUA, in contrast to regular UI, allows workers injured as a result of a disaster to collect benefits. 20 CFR § 625.5(a)(5) This includes injuries at the work place or anywhere else.

2. Non disaster-Related Injuries

Non disaster-related injuries may qualify an individual for state disability, workers' compensation or other insurance programs, but *not DUA*. State disability is for nonwork-related injuries, illnesses or medical procedures. Workers' Compensation is for work-related injuries that are a result of working conditions. *Just because the injury happened during the disaster period does not mean it was disaster-related.*

3. Mental Stress

Injuries include mental stress related to the disaster.

Claimants who claim injury based on mental stress must provide a doctor's verification of the condition *and* that the condition was caused by the disaster.

Persons who suffer from stress and do not have medical insurance to pay for treatment may get funds through the Individuals and Households Program (IHP). FEMA also provides on-site crisis counseling for mental health assistance at Disaster Application Centers and one-on-one counseling for seriously ill persons. 42 U.S.C. § 5183

F. Deadlines, Benefit Period

Applicants must apply for DUA within 30 days of the announcement of the disaster declaration and of the availability of DUA. 20 CFR § 625.8(a) (Usually this is computed from the date that the state sends out a press release announcing the availability of DUA.)

Applicants who have good cause can file late applications for DUA, although not after the Disaster Assistance Period has ended. 20 CFR § 625.8(a)

A worker whose disaster-related unemployment is delayed until more than 30 days after the disaster may have good cause for filing a late application for DUA. (For example, a farm worker who usually would not report to work to harvest corn until October may have good cause for filing a DUA application in October, even though the floods which destroyed the corn crop he would have harvested occurred in August and the 30-day deadline for DUA applications was therefore in September.)

DUA benefits are payable for 26 weeks. This is called the **Disaster Assistance Period.**

It begins with the first week following the date of the disaster and ends 26 weeks later. 42 U.S.C. § 5177(a) Individuals cannot apply for DUA after the end of the Disaster Assistance Period.

Both the regional DoL office and the state usually publish Fact Sheets for each disaster, listing the application deadlines, Disaster Assistance Period, etc. Information and copies can usually be obtained from the Unemployment Insurance Specialist, Employment and Training Administration (ETA), U.S. Department of Labor Regional Offices will usually provide copies of DoL Unemployment Insurance Program Letters, which clarify and interpret the DoL regulations.

G. Benefit Calculations and Amounts

DUA is paid just like unemployment insurance, with a weekly check. 20 CFR § 625.6(a)

For DUA, the base period is the individual's most recent tax year, 20 CFR § 625.2(a) which for most taxpayers will be the calendar year preceding the disaster.

1. Employees

For *employees*, DUA benefits are computed based on wages earned during the most recent tax year. 20 CFR § 625.6(a) (2)

2. Self-employed

For *self-employed* individuals, DUA benefits are computed on the basis of the net income from *services* reported on the individual's tax return for the most recent tax year. 20 CFR § 625.6(a) (2)

In the case of a *family business*, the net income is divided evenly among all the adult family members regularly working in the business, unless the family members submit documentation supporting a different allocation of income. 20 CFR § 625.6(a) (3)

3. Calculating Benefits

DUA benefit amounts are calculated using the same formula as for regular UI, based on the amount earned during the highest quarter of the DUA base year. However, no claimant will receive DUA benefits which are greater than the maximum regular UI benefit payable in the state. Nor will anyone who is eligible for DUA receive less than the minimum **DUA** benefit, which is 50% of the average weekly UI payment in the state.

The **minimum DUA benefit** is paid to individuals who provide documentation of eligibility for DUA, and to those who are eligible for DUA because they were prevented from future employment or self-employment because of the disaster but who have no earnings or income during the DUA base period. 20 CFR § 625.6(e)(3)

DUA benefits are reduced proportionately for employees or self-employed individuals who customarily or routinely worked less than full time prior to becoming unemployed due to the disaster. 20 CFR § 625.6(b)(1)

H. Proof of Eligibility, Wages and Income

The state makes an immediate determination of:

1. Eligibility for DUA and
2. Base period earnings or income when the individual applies for DUA.

This determination is made on the basis of documentation provided by the applicant and information in state records. If the individual has no documentation, the state makes an immediate determination based on the applicant's Statement of Employment or Self-Employment.

An individual who does not present documents at the time of application for DUA has *21 days* to provide such documentation. If the individual does not present documentation of eligibility during that time, s/he will be declared ineligible for DUA and an overpayment will be declared.
20 CFR. § 625.6(e)(2)

If the individual presents documentation of eligibility but not documentation of earnings or income, s/he will receive the minimum DUA benefit.

Individuals who do not present sufficient documentation *within 21 days* have until the end of the Disaster Assistance Period to submit documentation or additional documentation, at which time the state will redetermine their eligibility and award benefits retroactively, if appropriate. 20 CFR § 625.6(e)(1)(2)

Examples of documentation include:

a. Employees

Employees may prove their wages and/or eligibility with the following documents:

1. W-2 form;
2. Income tax return or preparer's copy of same;
3. Check stubs/pay slips;
4. Other documents (e.g., statement from employer with wage information or a computerized printout of employer's wage documents); or
5. Bank records.

b. Self-Employed

Persons who are self-employed may submit:

1. IRS Schedule C;
2. Business license;
3. Profit and loss statements;
4. Tax returns or preparer's copies;
5. Documents from accountants;
6. Work orders or receipts;
7. Form 1099;
8. Statement from bank verifying business account or payroll deposit account; or
9. Copy of deed or title to property.

I. DUA Limitations

Under the regulations, **weekly payments are reduced** if the claimant receives any of the following benefits: 20 CFR § 625.6(f)(1)(2)

A. Partial earnings from work;
B. Insurance payments due to illness or disability (this includes workers' compensation, disability insurance or lost wages covered under various insurance policies);
C. Benefits from a union or as the result of a union agreement; or
D. Private income protection insurance.

J. Effect of Traditional Unemployment Insurance Disqualifications

1. Able and Available for Work

Under traditional unemployment insurance, injured workers are not eligible for UI because they are not "able and available" for work. Injured workers usually receive workers' compensation or state disability benefits. *However, in case of a disaster, persons injured due to the disaster are eligible for UI benefits.* 20 CFR. § 625.5(a)(5)

If the injury is not disaster-related, the person remains ineligible.

A worker can also get DUA if s/he is unable to reach the work place because of the disaster. 20 CFR § 625.5

Traditionally, such a worker would be disqualified because the job still exists, or, in other words, the job is available. For example, if the disaster destroys a worker's car or if the disaster destroys an essential bridge to the work place, the worker is eligible. *However, the access problem must be caused by the disaster, not the employee's negligence.*

2. Voluntary Quit or Termination for Misconduct

If an employee was disqualified from UI benefits because s/he had voluntarily quit or was terminated for misconduct from her previous job during the base period, s/he may still be eligible for DUA if s/he obtained new employment and s/he lost this new job due to the disaster. This also applies if s/he was about to commence a new job when the disaster struck. 20 CFR 625.5(a)(3)

K. Denials and Appeals

1. Reasons for Denials

An applicant who is denied benefits has a right to appeal.

The major reasons for denials revolve around two types of problems.

First are traditional UI reasons for denials such as voluntary quits, able and available for work, termination from employment for misconduct, etc.

Second are procedural issues regarding the disaster such as timely filing for benefits, employment or self-employment status, earnings records and inadequate verification of job status or wages. An individual is not entitled to DUA if s/he is under a disqualification (unless the individual has obtained intervening employment which s/he has lost due to the disaster), has excessive disqualifying income, is employed and earning more than the weekly benefit amount, or is not able and available to work.

2. Appeals Process

a. First Stage

Appeals must be filed *within 21 days* of the date the notice of denial is issued or mailed.

b. Second Stage

To appeal the decision of the Director regarding DUA, appeals are made to the Review Commission *within 21 days* of the mailing of the notice of denial, and a hearing will be conducted before a Hearing Officer.

L. Overpayments

An overpayment occurs when a claimant receives DUA to which s/he is not entitled, or receives a greater DUA payment than s/he is entitled to receive.

A claimant is required to repay any DUA overpayments. 20 CFR § 625.14

In addition, a claimant is penalized if s/he makes a false statement for the purposes of obtaining DUA. 20 CFR. § 625.14(i)

The treatment of overpayments and the penalties for fraud are different for DUA than for traditional UI. Unlike traditional UI overpayments, DUA overpayments cannot be waived (i.e., forgiven) by the state, even if the claimant is without fault.

DUA overpayments are collected in the same manner as traditional UI overpayments, e.g., by withholding future DUA benefits or traditional UI benefits, by seizing the "overpaid" claimant's income tax refund, etc. 20 CFR § 625.15, 20 CFR § 625.14(h)(1)(i)

A claimant who makes a false statement in order to obtain DUA, i.e., regarding eligibility, is penalized by being declared ineligible for DUA for the rest of the Disaster Assistance Period.
20 CFR § 625.14(h)(1)(i)

A claimant who makes a false statement regarding a week of eligibility for DUA is penalized by being declared ineligible for DUA for that week and the next two weeks. 20 CFR §625.14(h)(2)(i)

Proof Requirements for the Recertification of Self-Employed Workers and Employees

Self-Employed	Employees
1. Proof of payment of rent or mortgage with MRA grant-landlord/lender certification	1. Proof of payment of rent or mortgage with MRA grant-landlord/lender certification
2. Most recent Income Tax Return	2. Most recent Income Tax Return
3. Proof of Insurance (if applicable)	3. Proof of Insurance (if applicable)
4. Complete financial disclosure for all household members	4. Complete financial disclosure for all household members
5. Any unemployment or unemployment disability payments or claims	5. Any unemployment or unemployment disability payments or claims
6. Business information- monthly profit/loss statements, quarterly tax returns, sales tax reports	6. Record of recent employment search
7. Copy of SBA EIDL application to reestablish business	

Disaster Food Stamps[52]

As of Oct. 1, 2008, Supplemental Nutrition Assistance Program (SNAP) became the new name for the federal Food Stamp Program. The program no longer gives out "food stamps" but rather an electronic card called an EBT card, which is similar to a debit card.

Caveat: Many non-citizen legal immigrants are not eligible to receive Food Stamps. However, certain legal immigrants will be able to receive Food Stamps:

1. Disaster Food Stamp Benefits (D-SNAP)

The application deadline for Emergency Food Stamps is 10 days from the disaster date.

The concept of disaster Food Stamps is to help people with their temporary emergency food needs which arise from the disaster. This includes people normally not eligible for regular Food Stamps who have lost their jobs, been forced from their homes, had their homes or belongings damaged, or lost food in the disaster.

[52] http://www.fns.usda.gov/disaster-assistance .pdf

D-SNAP provides temporary food assistance for households affected by a natural disaster. A D-SNAP provides one month of benefits to eligible disaster survivors and can facilitate the issuance of supplemental SNAP benefits for ongoing households. To be eligible for D-SNAP, a household must live in the identified disaster area, have been affected by the disaster, and meet certain D-SNAP eligibility criteria. An affected area must have received a Presidential declaration of "Major Disaster" with Individual Assistance in order to request a D-SNAP.

The State has the primary role for planning, requesting, and operating a D-SNAP. The Food and Nutrition Service of the United States Department of Agriculture approves a State's request to operate a D-SNAP and supports the State's D-SNAP efforts.

D-SNAP is an entirely different program from the regular Supplemental Nutrition Assistance Program (SNAP). The chart on the next page[53] compares the programs.

[53] Evaluating Food Aid Options http://www.fns.usda.gov/disaster/disaster-snap-guidance

Eligibility for SNAP & D-SNAP

Eligibility Element	SNAP	D-SNAP
Disaster Status	N/A	Experienced an adverse effect as a result of a disaster
Identity of Applicant	Verified	Verified
Residency	Residence in State or Project Area is Verified	Living in disaster area at the time of the disaster, State option to include those working in disaster area. Verified where possible
Household Composition	Individuals who purchase and prepare meals together	Persons living and eating together at the time of a disaster

Eligibility Element	SNAP	D-SNAP
Benefit amount	Varies depending on circumstances	Maximum allotment for household size
Restricted Eligibility Categories	Student, IPV, citizenship status, and work registration restrictions apply	Student, IPV, citizenship status, and work registration not applicable

IF	Then
• Commercial channels of food distribution are not yet available, **and** • Mass feeding alone cannot meet the food needs of affected populations	A household **commodity distribution** program may be used as an **interim measure** until commercial channels of food distribution are available and the D-SNAP is operational.
• There is a fairly small, isolated affected population, **and** • That population's food needs are not being met by mass feeding	A household **commodity distribution** program may be an option for a small, **isolated area**.
• Channels of food distribution are available, **and** • Mass feeding cannot meet the food needs of the affected population	A **D-SNAP** or **modified** Supplemental Nutrition Assistance Program (SNAP) should be operated.
• The disaster has affected both densely and sparsely populated areas, **and** • Commercial channels of food distribution are only partially available in urban areas, **and** • Mass feeding cannot meet the food needs of the affected populations	A **D-SNAP** could be operated in the **densely populated areas**, **and** a household food **distribution program** could be considered where commercial channels of food are not yet available. **Note**: Household commodity distribution and D-SNAP may operate in a given disaster area simultaneously. However, States must take measures to ensure that households do not participate in both programs.

During a disaster, processing individuals for public benefits becomes difficult because of the nature of the disaster and the volume of applicants with need and limited documentation.

7 U.S.C. § 2014(h)(1) revises eligibility guidelines to provide Food Stamps to survivors of a disaster who would otherwise be ineligible for Food Stamps.

This has long been in the statute at 7 U.S.C. § 2014(h)(1),(2) and in the regulations at 7 CFR § 280.1. This authority is typically used to dispense with normal income or resource criteria or to allow flat minimum allotments to be issued without the usual complex benefit calculations.

a. Eligibility

The Secretary of Agriculture has broad discretion and can waive normal income and resource and other eligibility criteria. The most obvious groups who should be helped are those who might have a business, income or resources over the Food

Stamp limits, but whose homes, businesses or property were damaged in the disaster.

Among those groups that are most likely to be ineligible for Food Stamps under the regular program, and hence in need of section 2014(h)(1) emergency Food Stamps, are:

a. People who have already received Food Stamps for the month (and are therefore ineligible for another regular issuance) and whose food has been consumed or destroyed;

b. People whose incomes are too high although their jobs have been lost or interrupted;

c. People with incomes too high to get Food Stamps, or too high to get more than a few Food Stamps, with high disaster-related expenses (i.e., people who would be eligible if they were allowed to deduct these expenses from their incomes);

d. People over the resource limit for the regular Food Stamp program because of resources no longer accessible to them; and

e. Undocumented or otherwise ineligible aliens.

b. Amount of Benefits

The amount of benefits depends on the nature of the disaster and the state's request. The Secretary of Agriculture has broad discretion. In many areas (Florida, the Midwest, South Carolina, for example), individuals may be given a full month's benefit equal to the maximum allotment for a family of that size.

2. Replacement Food Stamps [To Replace Destroyed Food]

7 U.S.C. § 2014(h)(3) provides for Food Stamps to replace food that was destroyed in a disaster for households eligible for Food Stamps under regular Food Stamp eligibility criteria. An argument can also be made that those temporarily eligible under (h)(1) are also eligible for replacements as well.

The authority to issue replacements has long been in the regulations and it was expanded and inserted into the Food Stamp Act by the 1990 amendments at 7 U.S.C. § 2014(h)(3). The regulations at 7 CFR § 280.1 require that replacement stamps be issued after a disaster.

Replacing food lost by disaster victims who were eligible for Food Stamps (note they need not have been actually receiving Food Stamps prior to the disaster) should be somewhat more automatic than the (h)(1) program.

a. Eligibility

For many families receiving Food Stamps, a disaster may destroy their food supply through damage, spoilage due to cut-off electricity, or simply the loss of their home.

These individuals are normally eligible for regular Food Stamps. During a disaster they are eligible for replacement stamps. These could be families already receiving Food Stamps, or individuals who meet the normal resource and income criteria but had not yet applied. An argument can also be made that those temporarily eligible for (h)(1) benefit are also eligible for replacements.

b. Amount of Benefits

A family should receive stamps equal to the value of the food they lost. The Secretary can set a maximum amount up to the value of one month's allotment for a family of the same size.

Presumably, families could get this replacement only once in a disaster; however, the statute is silent about such a limit.

c. Receipt of Food Stamps

Once a household has been approved for Food Stamp benefits, the EBT Card will be sent to the recipient in the mail. It works like a debit/credit card. The recipient's name will be embossed on the card to help prevent theft, and they will have to call and choose a 4-digit PIN number to use as a password every time they use their card.

Benefits are automatically deposited onto the card **on the same day every month** and will decrease as money is spent at a store.

3. Expedited Service Food Stamps

a. In General

After the initial disaster period, temporary emergency Food Stamp programs end. However, families may still be in need. These persons may wish to apply for Expedited Service Food Stamps. People who are destitute and appear to be eligible for Food Stamps should get their entire monthly Food Stamp benefits within three days of applying. They should ask for "Expedited Service Food Stamps." The Food Stamps will be pro-rated over the month, so anyone applying after the first day of the month will get less than a full month's allotment. Food Stamp benefits vary depending on family size, income and housing costs.

b. Eligibility

1. Income

A household's countable assets, including checking and saving accounts, cannot exceed $2,000, [$3,000 if the applicant's are 60 years of age or older] or disabled. Resources of an SSI or OWF household member(s) are excluded.

Gross monthly income is a household's total income. It is everything the household receives that has value, including employment, SSI, Retirement Benefits, OWF, child support, etc. Gross monthly income cannot be above 130% of the poverty line unless someone in your household is aged or disabled.

The Food Stamp Program allows seniors who are disabled and who cannot prepare their own meals, living alone or with another person, to have a higher gross monthly income based on the income of the person with whom they live.

2. Families with High Housing Costs

Families and individual applicants without enough money for rent, mortgage and utilities are eligible for expedited service.

Households whose combined monthly gross income and liquid resources (cash) are less than the household's monthly rent or mortgage, and utilities, as appropriate, shall be eligible for expedited service.

3. Families with Limited Funds

Households with very limited funds, less than $100 in cash or in the bank and less than $150 gross income in the calendar month, are eligible for Expedited Service Food Stamps.

The county welfare office will look at:

a. Income already received in the month and
b. Income that the household is "reasonably certain" of getting before the end of the month.

Recipients should not list any income in the second category unless they are absolutely certain they will get the money. Also, if it is near the end of the month, and the recipient has already received income over $150, and no Food Stamp application has been filed yet, s/he should be advised to apply on the first day of the following month. This way s/he can get a full month's worth of Expedited Service Food Stamps in three days, rather than waiting 30 days for the normal application to be processed.

c. Other Requirements

1. Identification/Application Requirements

All an individual needs to do to start the process is submit an application with his/her name, address and signature on it to the welfare office. To get the stamps, however, individuals must verify their identity.

The regulations are very flexible, allowing verification with a driver's license, birth certificate, Social Security card, wage stubs *or through someone in the community who knows the client and will write a note or talk to welfare on the phone (known as a "collateral contact")*. No particular form of ID can be required, as long as the applicant has one of the above. The Expedited Service Food Stamps ID requirements are often much more flexible than those for the county general assistance program.

If you have an individual receiving General Assistance (GA) with an ID problem, don't forget to check eligibility for Expedited Service Food Stamps .

There is no requirement to furnish a Social Security number before getting Expedited Service Food Stamps.

2. Work Registration and Exemptions

Applicants must register for work unless exempted. However, the Expedited Service Food Stamps cannot be delayed because of lack of verification of the work exemption.

d. Timeframe for Expedited Service Food Stamps

1. Three-Day Processing Deadline

The county is required to provide benefits or deny an application for Expedited Service Food Stamps within three calendar days of the application. The weekend counts as one day. If the third day falls on a weekend or holiday, the county has to provide the stamps before the third day.

Individuals must be given an application the day they go into the welfare office.

2. Right To Apply at First Visit to the Welfare Office

Sometimes applicants are screened out or told to return in several days (or weeks) for an appointment. The law is clear that individuals must be given an application the day they come in, even if it is Friday at 4:30 p.m.

See Chart on Next page for Food Stamp Eligibility During a Disaster

James L. Jaffe, J.D.

Food Stamp Eligibility During a Disaster

Supplemental Nutrition Assistance Program (SNAP)			
		Food Destroyed or Spoiled	**EBT Card Lost or Damaged**
Currently On Food Stamps		Disaster Food Stamps. Expedited Service Food Stamps.	Replacement Food Stamps. Disaster Food Stamps. Disaster Replacement Food Stamps.
New Applicant	Must meet household gross income and assets test. Different tests for persons: able bodied, disabled, and over 60 years old. Contact County Welfare Department	Regular Food Stamps. Disaster Food Stamps. Expedited Service Food Stamps.	
		Personal Resources unavailable to applicant due to disaster	
New Applicant		Disaster Temporary Emergency Food Stamps does not require income and asset tests. Application deadline is 10 days from declaration of disaster.	

Disaster Dollars

Disaster Supplemental Nutrition Program Income Eligibility Standards and Allotments

October 1, 2014 – September 30, 2015 http://www.fns.usda.gov/sites/default/files/FY2015-income_standards.pdf

For complete information, visit http://www.fns.usda.gov/disaster/disaster-snap-guidance

Continental States, DC, Household Size	Disaster Gross Income Limit	Maximum Allotment
1	$1,618	$194
2	$1,956	$357
3	$2,295	$511
4	$2,643	$649
5	$3,009	$771
6	$3,376	$925
7	$3,714	$1,022
8	$4,052	$1,169
Each Additional member	+$339	+$146

Alaska Household Size	Disaster Gross Income Limit	Urban Maximum Allotment	Rural 1 Maximum Allotment	Rural 2 Maximum Allotment
1	$2,265	$227	$290	$353
2	$2,687	$417	$523	$648
3	$3,110	$598	$762	$928
4	$3,533	$759	$968	$1,178
5	$3,957	$902	$1,150	$1,359
6	$4,391	$1,082	$1,380	$1,679
7	$4,814	$1,196	$1,525	$1,856
8	$5,238	$1,367	$1,743	$2,121
Each Additional member	+$425	+$171	+$218	+$265

Hawaii Household Size	Disaster Gross Income Limit	Maximum Allotment
1	$1,998	$332
2	$2,387	$609
3	$2,776	$872
4	$3,165	$1,107
5	$3,557	$1,315
6	$3,980	$1,578

Hawaii Household Size	Disaster Gross Income Limit	Maximum Allotment
7	$4,369	$1,744
8	$4,758	$1994
Each Additional Member	+$390	+$249

Guam Household Size	Disaster Gross Income Limit	Maximum Allotment
1	$1,860	$287
2	$2,198	$526
3	$2,537	$753
4	$2,893	$957
5	$3,288	$1,136
6	$3,683	$1,364
7	$4,021	$1,507
8	$4,359	$1,723
Each Additional Member	+$339	+$215

State Information/Hotline Numbers

Use the following numbers to get information on SNAP benefit questions in the States and areas of States listed. Most are toll-free numbers. Some of the numbers that aren't toll free will accept collect calls. * Indicates numbers are for in-State and out-of-State calls. All other 800 numbers are for in-State calls only. ** Indicates numbers accept collect calls.

If you are having difficulties reaching your State's local office please contact your State's Ombudsman's phone number below. This information can be found at http://www.fns.usda.gov/snap/contact_info/hotlines.htm

State	Phone Number	Ombudsman	Notes
Alabama	334-242-1310 *		
Alaska	907-465-3347		
Arizona	1-800-352-8401 *		
Arkansas	1-800-482-8988 *	501-682-8269	#
California	1-877-847-FOOD (3663) *		
Colorado	1-800-536-5298		
Connecticut	1-866-974-SNAP		
Delaware	1-800-372-2022 *	302-255-9500	#
District of Columbia	202-671-4200*	202-724-7491; Toll free: 1-877-685-6391	#
Florida	1-866-762-2237 *		
Georgia	1-877-423-4746 *		

Disaster Dollars

State	Phone Number	Ombudsman	Notes
Guam	671-735-7245		
Hawaii	808-643-1643 *		
Idaho	1-877-456-1233 *		
Illinois	1-800-843-6154 * TTY 1-800-447-6404		
Indiana	1-800-403-0864 *	1-877-246-3243	#
Iowa	1-877-347-5678 *	1-888-426-6283	#
Kansas	1-888-369-4777		
Kentucky	1-800-372-2973 *		
Louisiana	1-888-524-3578 *		
Maine	1-800-442-6003 *		
Maryland	1-800-332-6347 *	410-767-7327	
Massachusetts	1-800-249-2007		
Michigan	1-855-275-6424 *	517-373-8230	#
Minnesota	1-888-711-1151 *		
Mississippi	1-800-948-3050		
Missouri	1-855-373-4636		
Montana	1-800-332-2272		
Nebraska	1-800-383-4278 *		
Nevada	1-800-992-0900 * or 775-684-0615* (ext. 40500)		
New Hampshire	1-603-271-9700 or 1-800-852-3345 Ext. 9700 (in-state only)	603-271-6941 local 1-800-852-3345 ext. 6941	#
New Jersey	1-800-687-9512	609-588-2197	#
New Mexico	1-800-432-6217 *	505-827-7783	#
New York	1-877-472-8411 / 718-557-1399 (NYC only)		
North Carolina	1-866-719-0141 *		
North Dakota	1-800-755-2716		
Ohio	1-866-244-0071 *		
Oklahoma	1-866-411-1877 or 405-521-3444 *	405-525-4850	#
Oregon	1-800-723-3638 or 503-945-5600		
Pennsylvania	1-800-692-7462 * TDD 1-800-451-5886	717-783-8975	#
Puerto Rico	877-991-0101 *	1-787-724-7373	#
Rhode Island	401-462-5300 *	401-785-3340	#
South Carolina	1-800-616-1309		

State	Phone Number	Ombudsman	Notes
South Dakota	1-877-999-5612 *	Toll free number: 1-866-854-5465	#
Tennessee	1-866-311-4287 *		
Texas	211 or 1-877-541-7905	1-877-787-8999	#
Utah	1-866-526-3663 *	1-800-371-7897 (all areas of Utah)	#
Vermont	1-800-479-6151 *		
Virgin Islands	1-340-774-2399 *		#
Virginia	1-800-552-3431 or 804-726-7000		
Washington	1-877-501-2233 *		
West Virginia	1-800-642-8589 *		
Wisconsin	1-800-362-3002 *		
Wyoming	307-777-5846		

Notes:

Arkansas, Indiana New Jersey, New Mexico Rhode Island, South Dakota	Client advocate phone number is not toll free.
Delaware	Operates a change report and customer relations center for SNAP customers. The number is 302-571-4900.
District of Columbia	Operates a IMA change center for SNAP customers with questions. The number is 202-724-5506.
Indiana	Client advocate phone number is toll free.
Iowa	Ombudsman handles complaints for all agencies.
Michigan	DHA-ICU-Customer email: DHS-ICU-Customer-Service@michigan.gov
New Hampshire	Client advocate number has both a local and toll free number.
Oklahoma	Customer service and client advocate phone numbers are not toll free.
Pennsylvania	Operates a statewide call center for SNAP customers with questions. The toll-free number is 1-877-395-8930. In addition, Philadelphia operates a Change Center for SNAP customers with questions. The number is 215-560-7226.
Puerto Rico	All numbers are toll free. *Familia en Contacto (Family in Contact): Pre-screening for NAP benefits, questions about the NAP Program, complaints will be received but not handled; they will be routed to the NAP State Agency. **Same services as above, but this line is for the hearing impaired. ***EBT line (Electronic Benefit Transfer): For all calls related to participant's EBT card.

| Texas and Utah | Customer Service numbers are toll free in-state. |
| Virgin Islands | Clients who are not satisfied with information from the customer service phone number contact one of the following office supervisor for assistance with issues. St. Thomas 340-774-0930; Christiansted 340-772-2323; Frederiksted 340-772-0068 |

Emergency Assistance to Needy Families with Children[54]

A federally mandated program called Temporary Assistance to Needy Families (TANF) provides assistance for those families that have one or more minor children. This is a federal program administered through the state family service agency.

A. Kinds of emergencies covered

Situations in which lack of food, clothing, shelter, appliances, or medical supplies may lead to the destitution of a child.

Also covered are situations in which a family is encountering an emergency that could lead, or has led, within the past six months, to removal of a child from the family's home due to child abuse, neglect or dependency.

B. Kinds of assistance provided to meet emergency situations

Emergency assistance payments may not be issued in a warrant payable to the recipient. Emergency Assistance payments may be in the form of a relief supply order or by warrant payable to the provider of the service.

C. Amount of assistance

To qualify the household must have income that does not exceed 200% of the federal poverty level. *The assistance limit is $1,500.00 per household, with a specific limit for clothing of $50.00 per person.* This grant is dependent upon the amount given to the county by the state for this purpose.

D. Kinds of services provided to meet the emergency situations

1. Food - When there is no eligibility for food stamps.

2. Necessary clothing - Replace items lost or destroyed due to a natural disaster such as fire, flood, tornado, blizzard, or chemical disaster or due to a state of civil disorder as declared by the Governor.

3. Household items - Limited to replacement of bedding, linens, and cooking/eating utensils lost or destroyed due to a natural disaster such as fire, flood, tornado, blizzard, or chemical disaster or due to a state of civil disorder as declared by the Governor.

4. Furniture - Limited to the replacement of bed (bed frame, mattress, box spring) and kitchen table and chairs when lost or destroyed due to a natural disaster such as fire, flood, tornado, blizzard, or chemical disaster, or due to a state of civil disorder as declared by the Governor.

5. Appliances - Limited to the repair or replacement of cooking stoves, heating stoves, refrigerators, and, if needed, due to a verified medical disability of a household member, washing machines.

6. Home repairs - Limited to those affecting the basic structures or the home including wall,

---
[54] http://www.acf.hhs.gov/programs/ofa/programs/tanf

roof, flooring, plumbing, water supply, electric, heating, and water/sewage system.

7. Rent - When there is a court-ordered eviction pending or when conditions of the home cause it to be uninhabitable.

8. Interest on principal of mortgage – Must serve to forestall foreclosure.

9. Emergency Family Housing - Used only in extreme situations, when an individual/family is homeless and has no alternative living arrangement available, to provide temporary housing or arrange permanent housing.

10. Security deposits - Issued only when the landlord will not waive it and when the individual/family is homeless due to court-ordered eviction, uninhabitable conditions of the previous home due to natural or chemical disaster, living in temporary shelter, or forced to live in a domestic violence shelter.

11. Heating fuel and utilities - Includes any type of fuel used to provide heating for the home, electricity, water, cooking fuel.

12. Deposit for heating fuel or utilities - Issued only when the provider will not waive it and a deposit is necessary to establish, maintain, or restore service.

13. Telephone installation - Issued only when medically verified as necessary.

14. Medical service - Includes payment for medical supplies (hypodermic needles and syringes for diabetic, oxygen, catheters, etc), laboratory and x-ray services, pharmaceutical supplies (prescription drugs, insulin, no "medicine cabinet" items such as first aid supplies, vitamins, etc), licensed physician care (limited to the minimum appropriate procedure needed to relieve the pain), and dental care (limited to minimum procedure needed to relieve pain or infection.

15. Family preservation/reunification services - Includes diagnostic services, emergency caretaker services, home health aide services, home maker services, parent education services, in-home services, respite care services, special services for alcohol and drug abusers, therapeutic counseling, transportation services, domestic violence services, emergency shelter, post finalization services.

Disaster Dollars

Public Assistance and Disaster Assistance Programs for Disaster Victims

NEED	Families with Children Under 18	Families Without Children Under 18	Seniors or Disabled Individuals (including children)
Food	Disaster Food Stamps Replacement Food Stamps Expedited Food Stamps Apply at County	Disaster Food Stamps Expedited Food Stamps Apply at County	Disaster Food Stamps Possibly Expedited Food Stamps Apply at County
Public Assistance Money for Housing (Temporary)	AFDC Non-Recurring Special Needs (NRSN) AFDC Temporary Homeless Assistance Apply at County	Check with local County General Assistance/ General Relief Apply at County	Possibly if SSI check is lost or delayed (Immediate Payment(IP) Emergency Advance Payments (EAP for SSI Applicants) Apply at Social Security Office
Disaster Assistance Money for Housing (temporary)	FEMA Rental Assistance (RA) FEMA Mortgage and Rental Assistance (MRA) Apply with FEMA	FEMA Rental Assistance (RA) FEMA Mortgage and Rental Assistance (MRA) Apply with FEMA	FEMA Rental Assistance (RA) FEMA Mortgage and Rental Assistance (MRA) Apply with FEMA
Public Assistance Money for Move-In Costs	AFDC Permanent housing Assistance Program Apply at County	Check with local County General Assistance/ General Relief Apply at County	Possibly if SSI check is lost or delayed (Immediate Payment) (IP) Emergency Advance Payments (EAP for SSI Applicants) Apply at Social Security Office
Disaster Assistance Money for Housing Move-In Costs	FEMA Rental Assistance (RA) Apply with FEMA	FEMA Rental Assistance (RA) Apply with FEMA	FEMA Rental Assistance (RA) Apply with FEMA

NEED	Families with Children Under 18	Families Without Children Under 18	Seniors or Disabled Individuals (including children)
Public Assistance Money for Personal Property Lost in Disaster	AFDC Non-Recurring Special Needs (NRSN) AFDC Temporary Homeless Assistance Apply at County	Check with local County General Assistance/ General Relief Apply at County	Possibly if SSI check is lost or delayed (Immediate Payment) (IP) Emergency Advance Payments (EAP for SSI Applicants) SSI Special Circumstances Apply at Social Security Office
Disaster Assistance Money for Personal Property Lost in Disaster	(IHP) Individual and Households Program Personal Property Grant Small Business Administration (SBA) Home Disaster Loan Apply with FEMA and SBA	(IHP) Individual and Households Program Personal Property Grant Small Business Administration (SBA) Home Disaster Loan Apply with FEMA and SBA	(IHP) Individual and Households Program Personal Property Grant Small Business Administration (SBA) Home Disaster Loan Apply with FEMA and SBA

Supplemental Security Income [55]

The Social Security Administration (SSA) administers the Supplemental Security Income (SSI) program. This federal program, provides income to low-income, disabled persons, and persons over age 65. Because they are indigent, SSI recipients automatically qualify for Medicaid, the State's medical program for the poor. *The application process for SSI can take more than a year.*

To apply for Social Security disability benefits or for additional information and brochures about SSDI or SSI, call the Social Security Administration toll-free at 1-800-772-1213 voice or 1-800-325-0778 TTY, or on-line at http://www.ssa.gov

A. Eligibility

1. In General

Individuals must be **aged, blind or disabled** to qualify for SSI. They must also be citizens or legal residents. Persons **over age 65** who are low-income automatically qualify for SSI.

In some states the state in agreement with the Social Security Administration, is responsible for determining medical eligibility for individuals within that state. Social Security Disability Insurance (SSDI) and Supplemental Security Income (SSI) claims. If this is the case, the program is federally regulated and receives 100% of its funding from the Social Security Administration.

---

[55] http://www.ssa.gov/ssi/

2. Definition of Disability

Individuals must be blind or disabled within the meaning of listings which the Social Security Administration issues. A person who claims benefits because of disability must be unable to work at any job for at least 12 months because of a serious impairment.

3. Income and Resources

An individual must be low-income. The individual must also have limited resources. These can include only:

a. A home;
b. A car worth less than $4,500 (unless needed for medical reasons when the value can be more than $4,500);
c. Household goods under $2,000;
d. Burial plot or insurance;
e. Life insurance – maximum $1,500 face value; and
f. Resource maximum of $2,000 for an individual or $3,000 for a couple.

Individuals with greater resources can spend them down until they reach eligible levels.

B. Program Benefit Levels

Program benefits depend on household composition. As of 2015, a single disabled adult may receive as much as $755 per month and a couple may receive as much as $1,100 per month. Individuals sharing expenses with others can expect somewhat lower benefits. SSI benefits include funds to cover food costs.

State Supplement to SSI

Some States supplement the Federal SSI benefit with additional payments. This makes the total SSI benefit levels higher in those States. SSI benefit amounts and State supplemental payment amounts vary based upon your income, living arrangements, and other factors.

The following States or territories **do not** pay a supplement to people who receive SSI:

Arizona	Northern Mariana Islands
North Dakota	West Virginia
Mississippi	

Social Security administers the State supplement for the following States. You may contact Social Security about your total benefit amount.

California	Delaware*	District of Columbia*	Hawaii
Iowa*	Montana	Nevada	New Jersey
New York*	Pennsylvania*	Rhode Island*	Vermont

*Dual administration State. In these States, Social Security administers some categories of State supplement payments, while the State administers other categories of supplemental payments.

SSI Emergency Advance Payments[56]

1. Emergency

SSI applicants who appear to be eligible for SSI and who are having a financial emergency can receive an advance payment to help them through the emergency. This expedited procedure is called Emergency Advance Payments. It is available for applicants who are proven eligible or presumptively eligible.

---

[56] Expedited Payments http://www.ssa.gov/ssi/text-expedite-ussi.htm

2. Application Must be on File with SSA

An individual must file an application at the Social Security office. Documentation must be provided of age over 65, or medical documentation of disability from the treating physician. The applicant should inform SSA of the financial emergency.

3. SSI Immediate Payment Procedure

a. Critical Payments

The Social Security Administration has several procedures for expediting Social Security and SSI checks to people whose applications have already been approved, but who have not received a check. One procedure takes three to five days to complete and is called "critical payment." The U.S. Treasury mails the check to the client. Another procedure is referred to as "A-OTP" or "M-OTP," which takes seven to ten days and also involves mailing the check.

b. Immediate Payment -- Same-Day Payments

If the client has a financial emergency and cannot afford the possibility of computer or mail delays which occur with "A-OTP" and "M-OTP," an "immediate payment" can be made on the same day. Each local SSA office can pay up to $200 via immediate payment checks on hand so there should be no delays due to the computer or mail.

c. During Disasters

The Social Security Administration has procedures in place to expedite applications and to replace checks to disaster survivors.

d. Adverse Public Relations Problem

The management of the local SSA office can decide that the situation is "a potential adverse public relations problem requiring prompt action."

Some local SSA offices consider a phone call from an attorney or a congressional office sufficient to meet this criterion. Complaints made to the Critical Case Unit of the SSA Regional Office, are usually handled as potentially adverse public relations cases. The Critical Case Unit only accepts complaints from advocates, not from clients.

Rural Assistance

The United States Department of Agriculture, Rural Housing Service has two programs to assist rural individuals to purchase and repair dwellings.

NOTE

This program does NOT require a Presidential disaster declaration

"**The section 502 program**[57] offers persons who do not currently own adequate housing, and who cannot obtain other credit, the opportunity to acquire, build, rehabilitate, improve, or relocate dwellings in rural areas." 7 C.F.R. § 3550.2

"**The section 504 program**[58] offers loans to very low-income homeowners who cannot obtain other credit to repair or rehabilitate their properties. The section 504 program also offers grants to homeowners age 62 or older who cannot obtain a loan to correct health and safety hazards or to make the unit accessible to household members with disabilities." 7 C.F.R. § 3550.2

As in any government program, a person may be denied a loan or grant under these USDA programs. If that were to occur, " RHS will provide the participant with written notice of such adverse decision and the participant's rights to a USDA National Appeals Division hearing in accordance with 7 CFR Part 11.

---

[57] http://www.rurdev.usda.gov/HAD-Direct_Housing_Loans.html
[58] http://www.rurdev.usda.gov/had-rr_loans_grants.html

Any adverse decision, whether appealable or non-appealable may be reviewed by the next-level RHS supervisor." 7 C.F.R. § 3550.4

The "Handbook" used by the RHS {HB-1-3550} to administer the 502 and 504 programs is found at: http://www.rurdev.usda.gov/Handbooks.html

To qualify for these programs, the applicant must live in a "Rural Area" which is defined as:

A. Open country which is not part of or associated with an urban area.
B. Any town, village, city, or place, including the immediately adjacent densely settled area, which is not part of or associated with an urban area and which:
   - Has a population not in excess of 10,000 if it is rural in character, or
   - Has a population in excess of 10,000 but not in excess of 20,000 is not contained within a Metropolitan Statistical Area, and has a serious lack of mortgage credit for low- and moderate-income households as determined by the Secretary of Agriculture and the Secretary of HUD.

An area classified as a rural area prior to October 1, 1990, (even if within a Metropolitan Statistical Area), with a population exceeding 10,000, but not in excess of 25,000, which is rural in character, and has a serious lack of mortgage credit for low- and moderate-income families. This is effective through receipt of census data for the year 2010.

Section 502 Loans

The United States Department of Agriculture, Rural Development has a program known as "Section 502 Rural Housing Direct Loan" which allows individuals/families with "established good credit history" to apply for a direct loan to purchase or repair homes. If purchasing a home it must be modest in size, design and cost. The regulations for this program can be found at 7 C.F.R. Part 3550

Section 502 loans can be used to build, repair, renovate or relocate a home, purchase a home, including a manufactured home, or to purchase and prepare sites, including providing water and sewage facilities.

There are actually two Section 502 loan programs; a guaranteed loan program where the lender is a bank or lending institution, and a direct loan program where the lender is the USDA.

Eligibility: Applicants for loans may have an income of up to 115% of the median income for the area for the loan guarantee program, and 80% for the direct USDA loan program. Area income limits for these programs are found at: http://www.rurdev.usda.gov/rhs/sfh/sfh%20guaranteed%20loan%20income%20limits.htm

Approved lenders under the Single Family Housing Guaranteed Loan program include:

Any State housing agency; and Lenders approved by:

HUD for submission of applications for Federal Housing Mortgage Insurance or as an issuer of Ginnie Mae mortgage backed securities;

Terms: The maximum repayment period is 33 years, or under certain conditions, 38 years, except for manufactured homes the limit is 30 years.

And for loans no more than $2,500 the term limit is 10 years. 7 C.F.R. § 3550.67

The promissory note interest rate is set by the lender, but payments may be reduced with a subsidy. The amount of the subsidy is based upon the applicant's adjusted income. 7 C.F.R. § 3550.68(c)(2)

Families whose adjusted income is below the low income limit can be assisted through the Payment Assistance Program. Payment Assistance may have to be repaid, and the amount repaid will be determined at the time the principal and interest are paid in full, but will not exceed 50% of the equity as determined by the USDA. Payment assistance can reduce the interest rate to 1%.

There is no required down payment. The lender must also determine repayment feasibility, using ratios of repayment (gross) income to PITI and to total family debt.

Standards: Under the Section 502 program, housing must be modest in size, design, and cost. Houses constructed, purchased, or rehabilitated must meet the voluntary national model building code adopted by the state and HCFP thermal and site standards. New Manufactured housing must be permanently installed and meet the HUD Manufactured Housing Construction and Safety Standards and HCFP thermal and site standards. Existing manufactured housing will not be guaranteed unless it is already financed with an HCFP direct or guaranteed loan or it is Real Estate Owned (REO) formerly secured by an HCFP direct or guaranteed loan.

Approval: Rural Development officials have the authority to approve most Section 502 loan guarantee requests.

Section 504 Loans and Grants

The United States Department of Agriculture, Rural Development has a program known as "Section 504 Rural Housing Loan/Grant Program" which allows individuals/families with very low income in rural areas to apply for loans and grants to modernize a home {loans} or to remove health and safety hazards {loans and grants}. 7 C.F.R. § 3550.101

Loan funds. Loan funds may be used to make general repairs and improvements to properties or to remove health and safety hazards, as long as the dwelling remains modest in size and design.

7 C.F.R. § 3550.101(b) The sum of all outstanding section 504 loans to 1 borrower or on 1 dwelling may not exceed $20,000. 7 C.F.R. § 3550.112(a) The interest rate for all section 504 loans will be 1 percent. 7 C.F.R. § 3550.113(a)

Grant funds. Grant funds may be used only to pay costs for repairs and improvements that will remove identified health and safety hazards or to repair or remodel dwellings to make them accessible and useable for household members with disabilities. Unused grant funds must be returned to the Rural Housing Service (RHS).

7 C.F.R. § 3550.101 (a) The lifetime total of the grant assistance to any recipient is $7,500. 7 C.F.R. § 3550.112(c)

Grant recipients are required to sign a repayment agreement which specifies that the full amount of the grant must be repaid if the property is sold in less than 3 years from the date the grant agreement was signed. 7 C.F.R. § 3550.114

In addition to construction costs to make necessary repairs and improvements, loan and grant funds may be used for:

1. Reasonable expenses related to obtaining the loan or grant, including legal, architectural and engineering, title clearance, and loan closing fees; and appraisal, surveying, environmental, tax monitoring, and other technical services.

2. The cost of providing special design features or equipment when necessary because of a physical disability of the applicant or a member of the household.

3. Reasonable connection fees, assessments, or the pro rata installation costs for utilities such as water, sewer, electricity, and gas for which the borrower is liable and which are not paid from other funds.

4. Real estate taxes that are due and payable on the property at the time of closing and for the establishment of escrow accounts for real estate taxes, hazard and flood insurance premiums, and related costs.

5. Fees to public and private nonprofit organizations that are tax exempt under the Internal Revenue Code for the development and packaging of applications. 7 C.F.R. § 3550.102 (d)

To be eligible, applicants must meet the following requirements: {7 C.F.R. § 3550.103}

a. Owner-occupant. Applicants must own, as described in § 3550.107, and occupy the dwelling.

b. Age (grant only). To be eligible for grant assistance, an applicant must be 62 years of age or older at the time of application.

c. Income eligibility. At the time of loan or grant approval, the household's adjusted income must not exceed the applicable very low-income limit. Section 3550.54 provides a detailed discussion of the calculation of adjusted income.

d. Citizenship status. The applicant must be a U.S. citizen or a non-citizen who qualifies as a legal alien, as defined in § 3550.10.

e. Need and use of personal resources. Applicants must be unable to obtain financial assistance at reasonable terms and conditions from non-RHS credit or grant sources and lack the personal resources to meet their needs.

In cases where the household is experiencing medical expenses in excess of three percent of the household's income, this requirement may be waived or modified.

Elderly families must use any net family assets in excess of $10,000 to reduce their section 504 request.

Non-elderly families must use any net family assets in excess of $7500 to reduce their section 504 request.

Applicants may contribute assets in excess of the aforementioned amounts to further reduce their request for assistance. The definition of assets for this purpose is net family assets as described in § 3550.54 of subpart B of this part, less the value of the dwelling and a minimum adequate site.

f. Legal capacity. The applicant must have the legal capacity to incur the loan obligation or have a court appointed guardian or conservator who is empowered to obligate the applicant in real estate matters.

g. Suspension or debarment. Applications from applicants who have been suspended or debarred from participation in federal programs will be handled in accordance with FmHA Instruction 1940-M (available in any Rural Development office).

h. Repayment ability (loans only). Applicants must demonstrate adequate repayment ability as supported by a budget.

i. Credit qualifications. Applicants must be unable to secure the necessary credit from other sources under terms and conditions that the applicant could reasonably be expected to fulfill. Loan applicants must have a credit history that indicates reasonable ability and willingness to meet debt obligations.

When the total section 504 loan is $7,500 or more, the property will be secured by a mortgage on the property. 7 CFR § 3550.108

Until the loan is paid in full, any borrower with a secured indebtedness in excess of $15,000 must furnish and continually maintain hazard insurance on the security property, with companies, in amounts, and on terms and conditions acceptable to RHS and include a "loss payable clause" payable to RHS to protect the Government's interest. 7 CFR. § 3550.110(a)

The dwelling and any other essential buildings must be insured in an amount that is the lesser of 100% of the insurable value of the house or the unpaid principal balance. 7 CFR. § 3550.110(b)

Flood insurance must be obtained and maintained for the life of the loan for all property located in Special Flood Hazard Areas (SFHA) as determined by the Federal Emergency Management Agency (FEMA). 7 CFR. § 3550.110(c)

Summary of Differences Between Section 504 Loans and Grants

Note: *This attachment summarizes key requirements to assist the reader in comparing Section 504 loans and grants. It is not a comprehensive description of all requirements.* {HB-1-3550 Attachment 12-A}

Topic	Section 504 Loan	Section 504 Grant
Use of Funds	May be used to: (1) improve or modernize; (2) make dwelling decent, safe, and sanitary; (3) remove hazards. Cannot be used for acquisition or new construction.	May be used only to remove health and safety hazards or to make dwelling accessible to household member with disabilities.
Drug-Free Workplace	N/A	Applicants must certify that they will not engage in the unlawful manufacture, distribution, dispensing, possession, or use of a controlled substance in conducting any activity with the grant.
Credit Reports	Needed if loan > $7,500, but no fee charged.	N/A
Age of Applicant	N/A	62 or older
Leaseholds	The property must be covered by a lease with an unexpired portion of not less than 2 years beyond the term of the promissory note.	The remaining lease period must be at least 5 years.
Appraisals	Fee charged if appraisal completed. Appraisal performed by Agency employee or contractors if loan over $15,000.	N/A
Maximum Assistance	$20,000 outstanding at one time.	$7,500 lifetime limit.

Topic	Section 504 Loan	Section 504 Grant
Security	If Section 504 loan is >or equal to $7,500, a mortgage is required.	No security required.
Insurance	If indebtedness >$15,000, property insurance is required. Flood insurance is required in Special Flood Hazard Areas (SFHA)> $5,000.	Flood insurance is required in SFHA at grant approval for grants of >$5,000.

Farm/Ranch

The United States Department of Agriculture has a number of programs to assist farmers and ranchers after a disaster has occurred.

Overview[59]

On June 18, 2008, the Food, Conservation, and Energy Act of 2008 (2008 Farm Bill) was enacted into Public Law 110-246. This Act amended the Trade Act of 1974 to create new disaster programs, collectively referred to as Supplemental Agriculture Disaster Assistance programs.

To be eligible for disaster assistance programs under the 2014 Farm Bill, producers are no longer required to purchase crop insurance or NAP coverage, which was the risk management purchase mandate under the 2008 Farm Bill.

USDA disaster programs available for farmers and ranchers are:

1. *Livestock Forage Disaster Program (LFP)*
2. *Emergency Assistance Program for Livestock, Honey Bees, and Farm-Raised Fish (ELAP)*
3. *Livestock Indemnity Program (LIP)*
4. *Tree Assistance Program (TAP)*
5. *Non-insured Crop Disaster Assistance (NAP)*
6. *Emergency Conservation Program*
7. *Emergency Loan Program (EM Loans)*
8. *Haying and Grazing of Conservation Reserve Program Acres (CRP) {Case by case for each disaster}*
9. *Emergency Forest Restoration Program (EFRP)*

Types of Assistance

Orchard and Nursery Tree Assistance Program (TAP) (See page 160)

Provides financial assistance to qualifying orchardists to replace eligible trees, bushes, and vines damaged by natural disasters. http://www.fsa.usda.gov/FSA/webapp?area=home&subject=diap&topic=tap

Assistance for Livestock Losses:

Emergency Assistance for Livestock, Honey Bees, and Farm-Raised Fish (ELAP) (See page 153)

Provides Emergency relief to producers of livestock, honey bees, and farm-raised fish. Covers losses from disaster such as adverse weather or other conditions, such as blizzards and wildfires not adequately covered by any other disaster program. http://www.fsa.usda.gov/FSA/webapp?area=home&subject=diap&topic=elap

---

[59] http://www.fsa.usda.gov/FSA/newsReleases?area=newsroom&subject=landing&topic=pfs&newstype=prfactsheet&type=detail&item=pf_20080716_distr_en_buyin.html

Livestock Forage Disaster Program (LFP) (See page 149)

Provides financial assistance to producers who suffered grazing losses due to drought or fire http://www.fsa.usda.gov/FSA/webapp?area=home&subject=diap&topic=lfp

Livestock Indemnity Program (LIP) (See page 143)

Provides assistance to producers for livestock deaths that result from disaster. http://www.fsa.usda.gov/FSA/webapp?area=home&subject=diap&topic=lip

Emergency Haying and Grazing (See page 163)

A voluntary program available to agricultural producers to help them safeguard environmentally sensitive land. Producers enrolled in CRP establish long-term, resource-conserving covers to improve the quality of water, control soil erosion, and enhance wildlife habitat. In return, FSA provides participants with rental payments and cost-share assistance. Contract duration is between 10 and 15 years. http://www.fsa.usda.gov/FSA/webapp?area=home&subject=copr&topic=crp-eg

Assistance to get your farm up and running after a Disaster:

Emergency Farm Loans (See page 142)

Producers can borrow up to 100 percent of actual production or physical losses, to a maximum amount of $500,000. http://www.fsa.usda.gov/FSA/webapp?area=home&subject=fmlp&topic=efl

Emergency Conservation Program (ECP) (See page 164)

Provides emergency funding and technical assistance for farmers and ranchers to rehabilitate farmland damaged by natural disasters and for carrying out emergency water conservation measures in periods of severe drought. http://www.fsa.usda.gov/FSA/webapp?area=home&subject=copr&topic=ecp

Emergency Forest Restoration Program (EFRP) (See page 162)

Provides emergency funding and technical assistance for farmers and ranchers to rehabilitate farmland damaged by natural disasters and for carrying out emergency water conservation measures in periods of severe drought. http://www.fsa.usda.gov/FSA/webapp?area=home&subject=copr&topic=ecp

Prerequisite to Assistance:

Insurance coverage

Insurance coverage through USDA's Risk Management Agency (RMA) http://www.rma.usda.gov/

Or

Noninsured Crop Disaster Assistance Program (NAP) (See page 21)

Provides financial assistance to producers of noninsurable crops when low yields, loss of inventory, or prevented planting occurs due to natural disasters. http://www.fsa.usda.gov/FSA/webapp?area=home&subject=diap&topic=nap

James L. Jaffe, J.D.

Emergency Farm Loans[60]

The USDA Farm Service Agency (FSA) provides emergency loans to help farmers/ranchers recover from production and physical losses due to drought, flooding, other natural disasters, or quarantine.

This program provides direct loans and technical assistance. Loan funds can be used for farm operations and other items necessary to return the disaster victim's farming operations to a financially-sound basis as soon as possible, so that the victim can obtain credit from private sources.

This program requires a Presidential declaration of a major disaster or emergency under the Stafford Act; a designation by the Secretary of Agriculture or by the FSA administrator (physical losses only).

These emergency loan funds may be used to:

- Restore or replace essential property;
- Pay all or part of production costs associated with the disaster year;
- Pay essential family living expenses;
- Reorganize the farming operation; and
- Refinance certain debts.

Emergency loans may be made to farmers and ranchers who:

- Own or operate land located in a county declared by the President as a disaster area or designated by the Secretary of Agriculture as a disaster area or quarantine area (for physical losses only, the FSA Administrator may authorize emergency loan assistance);
- Are established family farm operators and have sufficient farming or ranching experience;
- Are citizens or permanent residents of the United States
- Have suffered at least a 30-percent loss in crop production or a physical loss to livestock, livestock products, real estate, or chattel property;
- Have an acceptable credit history;
- Are unable to receive credit from commercial sources;
- Can provide collateral to secure the loan; and
- Have repayment ability.

FSA loan requirements are different from those of other lenders. Some of the more significant differences are the following:

- Borrowers must keep acceptable farm records;
- Borrowers must operate in accordance with a farm plan they develop and agree to with local FSA staff; and
- Borrowers may be required to participate in a financial management-training program and obtain crop insurance.

All emergency loans must be fully collateralized. The specific type of collateral may vary depending on the loan purpose, repayment ability and the individual circumstances of the applicant. If applicants cannot provide adequate collateral, their repayment ability may be considered as collateral to secure the loan. A first lien is required on property or products acquired, produced, or refinanced with loan funds.

Farmers/ranchers can borrow up to 100 percent of actual production or physical losses, to a maximum amount of $500,000.

Loans for crop, livestock, and non-real estate losses are normally repaid within 1 to 7 years; depending on the loan purpose, repayment ability, and collateral available as loan security.

---

[60] http://www.fsa.usda.gov/FSA/webapp?area=home&subject=fmlp&topic=efl

In special circumstances, terms of up to 20 years may be authorized. Loans for physical losses to real estate are normally repaid within 30 years. In certain circumstances, repayment may be made over a maximum of 40 years.

The current annual interest rate for emergency loans is 3.75 percent.

Applications for emergency loans must be received within 8 months of the county's disaster or quarantine designation date.

Borrowers who receive temporary assistance are expected to return to conventional credit sources. Emergency loans are a temporary source of credit, and borrowers are reviewed periodically to determine whether they can return to commercial credit.

Livestock Indemnity Program (LIP)[61]

Overview

The Agricultural Act of 2014 (2014 Farm Bill) authorized the Livestock Indemnity Program (LIP) to provide benefits to livestock producers for livestock deaths in excess of normal mortality caused by adverse weather. In addition, LIP covers attacks by animals reintroduced into the wild by the federal government or protected by federal law, including wolves and avian predators. LIP payments are equal to 75 percent of the market value of the applicable livestock on the day before the date of death of the livestock as determined by the Secretary.

The 2014 Farm Bill makes LIP a permanent program and provides retroactive authority to cover eligible livestock losses back to Oct. 1, 2011.

---

[61] http://www.fsa.usda.gov/FSA/newsReleases?area=newsroom&subject=landing&topic=pfs&newstype=prfactsheet&type=detail&item=pf_20140415_distr_en_lip.html

LIP is administered by the Farm Service Agency (FSA) of the U.S. Department of Agriculture (USDA).

Eligible Livestock Owners

To be eligible for LIP, a livestock producer must have legally owned the eligible livestock on the day the livestock died.

Owners of the following types of livestock may be eligible for LIP:

Cattle	Poultry	Swine	Other
Adult Beef Bulls	Chickens, Broilers, Pullets (regular size)	Swine, Feeder Pigs (less than 50 pounds)	Alpacas, Deer, Elk,
Adult Beef Cows	Chickens, Chicks	Swine, Sows, Boars, Barrows, Gilts (50 to 150 pounds)	Emus, Equine, Goats, Bucks,
Adult Buffalo, Beefalo Bulls	Chickens, Layers, Pullets/ Cornish Hens (small size)	Swine, Sows, Boars, Barrows, Gilts (151 to 450 pounds)	Goats, Nannies, Goats, Slaughter, Goats/ Kids, Llamas,
Adult Buffalo, Beefalo Cows	Ducks	Swine, Sows, Boars (over 450 Pounds)	Reindeer, Sheep, Ewes, Sheep, Lambs Sheep, Rams
Adult Dairy Bulls	Ducks, Ducklings		
Adult Dairy Cows	Geese, Goose		
Non-Adult Beef Cattle	Geese, Goslings		

Cattle	Poultry	Swine	Other
Non-Adult Buffalo/ Beefalo	Turkeys, Poults		
Non-Adult Dairy Cattle	Turkeys, Toms, Fryers, Roasters		

To be eligible for LIP, an owner's livestock must:

- Have died as a direct result of an eligible adverse weather event or eligible attack by an eligible animal or avian predator occurring:
    o On or after Oct. 1, 2011, and;
    o No later than 60 calendar days from the ending date of the applicable adverse weather event, and;
    o In the calendar year for which benefits are requested.
- Have been maintained for commercial use as part of a farming operation on the day they died, and;
- Not have been produced for reasons other than commercial use as part of a farming operation. Excluded livestock includes wild free roaming animals, pets or animals used for recreational purposes, such as hunting, roping or for show.

Eligible Livestock Contract Growers

To be eligible for LIP, a contract grower must have had the following on the day the livestock died:

- Possession and control of the eligible livestock, and;
- A written agreement with the eligible livestock owner setting the specific terms, conditions and obligations of the parties involved regarding the production of livestock.

In addition to the requirements listed for livestock owners above, the only eligible livestock of contract growers under LIP are poultry and swine.

Payments

LIP payments are calculated by multiplying the national payment rate for each livestock category by the number of eligible livestock in each category. National payment rates are found at the end of this fact sheet.

LIP national payment rate for eligible livestock owners is based on 75 percent of the average fair market value of the livestock.

The LIP national payment rate for eligible livestock contract growers is based on 75 percent of the average income loss sustained by the contract grower with respect to the dead livestock.

A contract grower's LIP payment will be reduced by the amount of monetary compensation received from his/her contractor for the loss of income suffered from the death of livestock under contract.

Payment Limitations and Adjusted Gross Income (AGI)

For 2012 and subsequent program years, no person or legal entity, excluding a joint venture or general partnership, may receive directly or indirectly, more than $125,000 total in payments under LFP, ELAP and LIP combined.

For 2011, no person or legal entity, excluding a joint venture or general partnership, may receive directly or indirectly, more than $125,000 total in the 2011 program year in payments under the LFP, ELAP, LIP and Supplemental Revenue Assistance Payments (SURE) program when at least $25,000 of such total 2011 program payments is from LFP or LIP for losses from Oct. 1, 2011, through Dec. 31, 2011.

In applying the limitation on average adjusted gross income, an individual or entity is ineligible for payment under LIP if the average AGI of the individual or entity exceeds $900,000.

Direct attribution provisions apply to LIP for 2011 and subsequent years. Under direct attribution, any payment to a legal entity also will be considered (for payment limitation purposes) to be a payment to persons or legal entities with an interest in the legal entity or in a sub-entity.

Applying for LIP

Producers may apply to receive LIP benefits at local FSA offices.

Producers who suffer livestock death losses should submit a notice of loss and an application for payment to the local FSA office that maintains their farm records.

To be eligible, the notice of loss must be submitted the earlier of:

- 30 calendar days of when the loss of livestock is apparent to the producer, or;
- 30 calendar days after the end of the calendar year in which the loss of livestock occurred.

The following table provides the final dates to file a notice of loss and application for payments:

Date of Livestock Death	Final Date to File Notice of Loss	Final Date to Submit an Application for Payment
Oct. 1, 2011 to Dec. 31, 2014	Jan. 30, 2015	Jan. 30, 2015
Calendar Years 2015 and all subsequent years	30 days after death is apparent	Jan. 30 of each year

The producer must include a copy of the grower contract if he/she is a contract grower and any other supporting documents required for determining eligibility. Supporting documents must show evidence of loss, current physical location of livestock in inventory and location of the livestock at the time of death.

Payments may be made for eligible losses suffered by an eligible producer who is now deceased or for a dissolved entity if a currently authorized representative signs the application for payment. Proof of authority to sign for a deceased individual or dissolved entity must be provided. If a producer is a dissolved entity, all former members at the time of dissolution or their duly authorized representative(s) must sign the application for payment.

Livestock Death Loss Documentation

Documentation requirements for livestock deaths that occurred after Oct. 1, 2011, through Dec. 31, 2014, have been relaxed from the rules outlined below. Contact a local FSA county office for additional information.

Livestock owners should record all pertinent information of livestock death losses due to adverse weather and attacks by animals reintroduced into the wild by the federal government or protected by federal law.

Documentation of the number and kind of livestock that have died, supplemented if possible by such items as, but not limited to:

- Photographs or video records to document the loss, dated if possible;
- Purchase records, veterinarian records, production records, bank or other loan documents;
- Written contracts, records assembled for tax purposes, private insurance documents and other similar reliable documents.

Applicants must provide adequate proof that the eligible livestock deaths occurred as a direct result of an eligible adverse weather event or eligible attack by an eligible animal or avian predator in the calendar year for which benefits are being requested. The quantity and kind of livestock that died as a direct result of the eligible event may be documented by:

- Purchase records;
- Veterinarian records;
- Bank or other loan documents;
- Rendering truck receipts or certificates;
- Federal Emergency Management Agency records;
- National Guard records;
- Written contracts;
- Production records;
- Records assembled for tax purposes;
- Property tax records;
- Private insurance documents;
- Similar documents.

If adequate verifiable proof of death records documentation is not available, FSA will accept reliable records in conjunction with verifiable beginning and ending inventory records as proof of death. Reliable records may include, but are not limited to:

- Contemporaneous producer records existing at the time of the adverse weather event;
- Picture(s) with a date;
- Brand inspection records;
- Dairy herd improvement records;
- Similar reliable documents.

FSA will accept certifications of livestock deaths by third parties on form CCC-854 along with verifiable beginning and ending inventory documentation if the following conditions are met:

- That there is no other documentation of death available;
- The number of livestock in inventory at the time of the adverse weather event.

The third party provides their telephone number, address and a written statement containing:

- Specific details about their knowledge of the livestock deaths;
- Their affiliation with the livestock owner;
- The accuracy of the deaths claimed by the livestock owner.

FSA will use data furnished by the applicant to determine eligibility for program benefits. Furnishing the data is voluntary; however, without all required data program benefits will not be approved or provided.

Table 1: LIP Payment Rates for Eligible Livestock Owners (rates have been reduced by the required 75%)						
Kind	Type	Weight Range	Payment Rate Per Head			
			2011	2012	2013	2014
Alpacas			$280.53	$262.50	267.87	270.00
Beef	Adult	Bull	$971.03	$1,369.17	$1,381.63	$1,590.49
		Cow	$746.95	$1,053.21	$1,062.79	$1,223.45
	Non-adult	Less than 400 pounds	$336.04	$460.96	$454.46	$553.77
		400 to 799 pounds	$490.68	$669.14	$641.18	$748.34
		800 pounds or more	$766.03	$972.47	$967.99	$1,149.39

Table 1: LIP Payment Rates for Eligible Livestock Owners (rates have been reduced by the required 75%)							
Kind	Type	Weight Range	Payment Rate Per Head			
			2011	2012	2013	2014
Buffalo/ Beefalo	Adult	Bull	$1,232.82	$1,738.30	$1,754.12	$2,019.28
		Cow	$657.50	$927.09	$935.53	$1,076.95
	Non-adult	Less than 400 pounds	$319.24	$437.91	$431.73	$526.08
		400 to 799 pounds	$466.15	$635.68	$609.12	$710.92
		800 pounds or more	$727.73	$923.84	$919.59	$1,091.92
Chickens	Broilers, Pullets (Regular Size)		$2.39	$2.42	$2.60	$2.60
	Chicks		$0.23	$0.21	$0.22	$0.22
	Layers		$11.42	$13.63	$14.49	$15.14
	Pullets, Cornish Hens (Small Size)		$1.72	$1.70	$1.83	$1.83
	Roasters		$2.81	$3.15	$3.41	$3.41
Dairy	Adult	Bull	$997.50	$1,087.50	$1,035.00	$1,080.00
		Cow	$997.50	$1,087.50	$1,035.00	$1,080.00
	Non-adult	Less than 400 pounds	$249.38	$271.88	$258.75	$270.00
		400 to 799 pounds	$498.75	$543.75	$517.50	$540.00
		800 pounds or more	$766.03	$878.37	$835.96	$872.31
Deer			$412.50	$412.50	$420.93	$429.53
Ducks	Ducklings		$0.61	$0.66	$0.66	$0.66
	Ducks		$3.82	$4.15	$4.12	$4.12
Elk			$572.59	$572.59	$584.29	$596.23
Emus			$150.00	$150.00	$153.07	$171.34
Equine			$637.50	$637.50	$650.53	$728.18
Geese	Goose		$19.35	$12.88	$21.31	$21.31
	Gosling		$4.06	$2.70	$4.47	$4.47
Goats	Bucks		$89.91	$121.17	$121.97	$125.58
	Nannies		$68.15	$98.51	$98.54	$105.55
	Slaughter Goats/Kids		$58.89	$66.72	$46.72	$80.25
Llamas			$210.00	$210.00	$214.29	$217.50
Reindeer			$412.50	$412.50	$420.93	$429.53
Sheep	Ewes		$117.39	$175.98	$104.86	$119.83
	Lambs		$126.84	$143.70	$100.63	$172.85
	Rams		$116.04	$173.96	$136.33	$140.19

Table 1: LIP Payment Rates for Eligible Livestock Owners
(rates have been reduced by the required 75%)

Kind	Type	Weight Range	Payment Rate Per Head			
			2011	2012	2013	2014
Swine	Feeder Pigs	Less than 50 pounds	$48.12	$43.90	$42.60	$68.76
	Lightweight Barrows, Gilts	50 to 150 pounds	$67.73	$67.73	$73.93	$88.70
	Sows, Boars, Barrows, Gilts	151 to 450 pounds	$87.33	$104.61	$105.25	$108.64
	Boars, Sows	450 pounds or more	$201.03	$221.80	$234.38	$292.11
Turkeys	Poults		$1.14	$1.10	$1.13	$1.15
	Toms, Fryers, Roasters		$12.20	$14.45	$13.49	$13.68

Table 2: LIP Payment Rates for Eligible Livestock for Livestock Contract Growers
(rates have been reduced by the required 75%)

Kind	Type	Weight Range	Payment Rate Per Head			
			2011	2012	2013	2014
Chickens	Broilers, Pullets (Regular Size)		$0.26	$0.27	$0.29	$0.29
	Layers		$0.69	$0.82	$0.82	$0.91
	Pullets, Cornish Hens (Small Size)		$0.19	$0.19	$0.20	$0.20
	Roasters		$0.31	$0.35	$0.38	$0.38
Ducks			$0.42	$0.46	$0.45	$0.45
Geese			$2.84	$1.89	$3.12	$3.12
Swine	Feeder pigs	Less than 50 pounds	$5.47	$4.99	$4.84	$7.81
Lightweight Barrows, Gilts		50 to 150 pounds	$10.17	$11.15	$11.10	$13.32
Sows, Boars, Barrows, Gilts		151 to 450 pounds	$13.11	$15.71	$15.81	$16.32
Boars, Sows		450 pounds or more	$82.61	$91.15	$96.32	$120.04
Turkeys	Toms, Fryers, Roasters		$0.34	$1.59	$1.48	$1.50

More Information

To find more information about FSA programs, contact your local FSA office or USDA Service Center, or visit the FSA online at http://www.fsa.usda.gov.

Livestock Forage Disaster Program (LFP)[62]

Overview

The Agricultural Act of 2014 (2014 Farm Bill) makes the Livestock Forage Disaster Program (LFP) a permanent program and provides retroactive authority to cover eligible losses back to Oct. 1, 2011. LFP provides compensation to eligible livestock producers that have suffered grazing losses for covered livestock on land that is native or improved pastureland with permanent vegetative cover or is planted specifically for grazing. The grazing losses must be due to a qualifying drought condition during the normal grazing period for the county. LFP also provides compensation to eligible livestock producers that have suffered grazing losses on rangeland managed by a federal agency if the eligible livestock producer is prohibited by the federal agency from grazing the normal permitted livestock on the managed rangeland due to a qualifying fire. The grazing losses must have occurred on or after Oct. 1, 2011.

LFP is administered by the Farm Service Agency (FSA) of the U.S. Department of Agriculture (USDA).

Eligible Counties for Drought

- An eligible livestock producer that owns or leases grazing land or pastureland physically located in a county rated by the U.S. Drought Monitor as having a:

- D2 (severe drought) intensity in any area of the county for at least eight consecutive weeks during the normal grazing period is eligible to receive assistance in an amount equal to one monthly payment;

- D3 (extreme drought) intensity in any area of the county at any time during the normal grazing period is eligible to receive assistance in an amount equal to three monthly payments;

- D3 (extreme drought) intensity in any area of the county for at least four weeks during the normal grazing period or is rated a D4 (exceptional drought) intensity at any time during the normal grazing period is eligible to receive assistance in an amount equal to four monthly payments;

- D4 (exceptional drought) in a county for four weeks (not necessarily four consecutive weeks) during the normal period is eligible to receive assistance in an amount equal to five monthly payments.

A map of eligible counties for LFP drought may be found at http://disaster.fsa.usda.gov.

Eligible Livestock

Eligible livestock types under LFP include alpacas, beef cattle, buffalo, beefalo, dairy cattle, deer, elk, emus, equine, goats, llamas, poultry, reindeer, sheep or swine that have been or would have been grazing the eligible grazing land or pastureland:

- During the normal grazing period for the specific type of grazing land or pastureland for the county, or;

- When the federal agency excluded the livestock producer from grazing the normally permitted livestock on the managed rangeland due to fire.

Eligible livestock must:

- Have been owned, purchased or entered into a contract to purchase during the 60 days

---

[62] http://www.fsa.usda.gov/FSA/newsReleases?area=newsroom&subject=landing&topic=pfs&newstype=prfactsheet&type=detail&item=pf_20140415_distr_en_lfp.html

prior to the beginning date of a qualifying drought or fire condition;

- Have been held by a contract grower or sold or otherwise disposed of due to a qualifying drought condition during the current production year or one or both of the two production years immediately preceding the current production year;

- Have been maintained for commercial use as part of a farming operation on the beginning date of the eligible drought or fire condition;

- Not have been produced and maintained for reasons other than commercial use as part of a farming operation. (Such excluded uses include, but are not limited to, wild free roaming animals or animals used for recreational purposes such as pleasure, hunting, pets, roping or for show);

- Not have been livestock that were or would have been in a feedlot on the beginning date of the qualifying drought or fire as part of the normal business operation of the producer.

Eligible Producers

To be eligible for LFP, producers must:

- Own, cash or share lease, or be a contract grower of covered livestock during the 60 calendar days before the beginning date of a qualifying drought or fire;
  - Provide pastureland or grazing land for covered livestock, including cash-rented pastureland or grazing land that is either:
  - Physically located in a county affected by a qualifying drought during the normal grazing period for the county, or;

- Rangeland managed by a federal agency for which the otherwise eligible livestock producer is prohibited by the federal agency from grazing the normally permitted livestock because of a qualifying fire.

- Certify that they have suffered a grazing loss because of a qualifying drought or fire;

- Timely file an acreage report for all grazing land for which a loss of grazing is being claimed.

Payments

FSA will calculate LFP payments for an eligible livestock producer for grazing losses because of a qualifying drought equal to 1, 3, 4 or 5 times the LFP monthly payment rate. The LFP monthly payment rate for drought is equal to 60 percent of the lesser of the monthly feed cost:

- For all covered livestock owned or leased by the eligible livestock producer;

- Calculated by using the normal carrying capacity of the eligible grazing land of the eligible livestock producer.

Total LFP payments to an eligible livestock producer in a calendar year for grazing losses will not exceed five monthly payments for the same livestock.

In the case of an eligible livestock producer who sold or otherwise disposed of livestock because of drought conditions in one or both of the two previous production years immediately preceding the current production year, the payment rate will equal 80 percent of the monthly payment rate.

FSA will calculate LFP payments for eligible livestock producers for losses suffered because of a qualifying fire on federally managed rangeland for which the producer is prohibited from grazing the normally permitted livestock. The payment begins on the first day the permitted livestock are prohibited from grazing the eligible rangeland and ending on the earlier of the last day of the federal lease of the eligible livestock producer or the day that would make the period a 180 calendar-day period. The payment rate is 50 percent of the monthly feed cost for the number of days the producer is prohibited from grazing the managed rangeland because of a qualifying fire, not to exceed 180 calendar days.

Payment Limitation

For 2012 and subsequent program years, no person or legal entity, excluding a joint venture or general partnership, may receive directly or indirectly, more than $125,000 total in payments under LFP, ELAP and LIP combined.

For 2011, no person or legal entity, excluding a joint venture or general partnership, may receive directly or indirectly more than $125,000 total in the 2011 program year in payments under the LFP, ELAP, LIP and Supplemental Revenue Assistance Payments (SURE) program, when at least $25,000 of such total 2011 program payments is from LFP or LIP for losses from Oct. 1, 2011, through Dec. 31, 2011.

In applying the limitation on average adjusted gross income (AGI), an individual or legal entity is ineligible for payment under LFP if the individual's or legal entity's average AGI exceeds $900,000.

Direct attribution provisions apply to LFP for 2011 and subsequent years. Under direct attribution, any payment to a legal entity also will be considered for payment limitation purposes to be a payment to persons or legal entities with an interest in the legal entity or in a sub-entity.

Sign-Up

For grazing losses that occurred between Oct. 1, 2011 through Dec. 31, 2014, sign-up will begin on April 15, 2014, and end on Jan. 30, 2015. For 2015 and subsequent calendar years, producers must provide a completed application for payment and required supporting documentation to their FSA office within 30 calendar days after the end of the calendar year in which the grazing loss occurred.

The producer should include a copy of the grower contract if the producer is a contract grower and any other supporting documents required for determining eligibility. Supporting documents must show evidence of loss, current physical location of livestock in inventory, evidence that grazing land or pastureland is owned or leased and evidence that if the loss of grazing was due to a fire that the producer was prohibited by the federal agency from grazing the normal permitted livestock on the managed rangeland due to a fire.

Payments on Behalf of Deceased Producers

Payments may be made for eligible losses suffered by an eligible producer who is now deceased or for a dissolved entity if a currently authorized representative signs the application for payment. Proof of authority to sign for a deceased individual or dissolved entity must be provided. If a producer is a dissolved entity, all former members at the time of dissolution or their duly authorized representative(s) must sign the application for payment.

FSA will use data furnished by the applicant to determine eligibility for program benefits. Furnishing the data is voluntary; however, without all required data, program benefits will not be approved or provided.

The following provides the monthly payment rate per head by covered livestock category:

James L. Jaffe, J.D.

Livestock Payment Rates

Kind	Type	Weight Range	Payment Rate Per Head			
			2011	2012	2013	2014
Beef	Adult	Bull, Cow	$34.57	$51.81	$57.27	$52.56
Beef	Non-adult	500 pounds or more	$25.93	$38.86	$42.96	$39.42
Dairy	Adult	Bull, Cow	$89.89	$134.71	$148.90	$136.66
Dairy	Non-adult	500 pounds or more	$25.93	$38.86	$42.96	$39.42
Buffalo/Beefalo	Adult	Bull, Cow	$34.57	$51.81	$57.27	$52.56
Buffalo/Beefalo	Non-adult	500 pounds or more	$25.93	$38.86	$42.96	$39.42
Sheep	All		$8.64	$12.96	$14.32	$13.14
Goats	All		$8.64	$12.96	$14.32	$13.14
Deer	All		$8.64	$12.96	$14.32	$13.14
Equine	All		$25.58	$38.34	$42.38	$38.90
Swine		Less than 45 pounds	$1.03	$1.55	$1.72	$1.56
Swine		45 to 124 pounds	$2.41	$3.63	$4.01	$3.67
Swine		125 to 234 pounds	$4.15	$6.22	$6.87	$6.31
Swine	Sow	235 pounds or more	$14.18	$21.24	$23.48	$21.56
Swine	Boar	235 pounds or more	$8.31	$12.43	$13.74	$12.63
Elk		Less than 400 pounds	$7.61	$11.40	$12.60	$11.58
Elk		400 to 799 pounds	$14.18	$21.24	$23.48	$21.56
Elk		800 pounds or more	$18.67	$27.98	$30.93	$28.39
Poultry		Less than 3 pounds	$0.22	$0.33	$0.36	$0.33
		3 to 7.9 pounds	$0.44	$0.65	$0.72	$0.66
		8 pounds or more	$0.99	$1.48	$1.64	$1.50
Reindeer		All	$7.61	$11.40	$12.60	$11.58
Alpacas		All	$28.48	$42.68	$47.18	$43.30
Emus		All	$17.69	$26.52	$29.31	$26.90
Llamas		All	$12.62	$18.91	$20.90	$19.18

More Information

To find more information about FSA programs, contact your local FSA office or USDA Service Center, or visit the FSA online at www.fsa.usda.gov.

Emergency Assistance Program for Livestock, Honey Bees, and Farm-Raised Fish (ELAP)[63] Overview

The Agricultural Act of 2014 (the 2014 Farm Bill) authorized up to $20 million of Commodity Credit Corporation (CCC) funds in a fiscal year (FY) for the Emergency Assistance for Livestock, Honeybees and Farm-Raised Fish Program (ELAP) to provide emergency assistance to eligible producers of livestock, honeybees and farm-raised fish. ELAP covers losses due to an eligible adverse weather or eligible loss condition, including blizzards, disease (including cattle tick fever), water shortages and wildfires, as determined by the Secretary, that occurs on or after Oct. 1, 2011.

ELAP covers losses that are not covered under other Supplemental Agricultural Disaster Assistance Payment programs established by the 2014 Farm Bill, specifically the Livestock Forage Disaster Program (LFP) and the Livestock Indemnity Program (LIP).

The ELAP program year begins Oct. 1 of the fiscal year and ends Sept. 30 of the fiscal year. (For example, the 2012 ELAP program year began Oct. 1, 2011, and ended Sept. 30, 2012).

There are four categories of livestock losses covered by ELAP:

- Livestock death losses caused by an eligible loss condition;

- Livestock feed and grazing losses that are not due to drought or wildfires on federally managed lands;

- Losses resulting from the additional cost of transporting water to livestock due to an eligible drought;

- Losses resulting from the additional cost associated with gathering livestock for treatment related to cattle tick fever.

Recipients of ELAP payments may receive a pro-rated reduced payment should the total annual national demand for ELAP exceed $20 million in a fiscal year.

ELAP is administered by the Farm Service Agency (FSA) of the United States Department of Agriculture (USDA).

Livestock Death Losses

Eligible Livestock

To be eligible for livestock death losses, livestock must:

- For eligible livestock owners, be alpacas, adult or non-adult dairy cattle, beef cattle, beefalo, buffalo, deer, elk, emus, equine, goats, llamas, poultry, reindeer, sheep or swine;

- For eligible contract growers be poultry or swine;

- Be maintained for commercial use as part of a farming operation on the date of death;

- Have died:

    o As a direct result of an eligible loss condition occurring on or after Oct. 1, 2011;

    o On or after the beginning date of the eligible loss condition;

---

[63] http://www.apfo.usda.gov/FSA/webapp?area=home&subject=diap&topic=elap

o No later than 60 calendar days from the ending date of the eligible loss condition.

Examples of ineligible livestock for livestock death losses include any uses of wild free roaming animals or use of animals for recreational purposes, such as pleasure, hunting, roping, pets or for show.

Eligible Producer

Livestock owners must have legal ownership of the livestock on the day the livestock died. Livestock contract growers must have had:

- A written agreement with the owner of the eligible livestock;

- Control of the eligible livestock on the day the livestock died;

- A risk of loss in the livestock.

Eligible Death Losses

Eligible livestock death losses must be:

- Incurred by an eligible livestock owner or contract grower;

- Due to an eligible loss condition occurring during the program year for which payment is requested and on or after Oct. 1, 2011;

- In excess of normal mortality.

FSA determines the eligible loss conditions for livestock death losses and these loss conditions cannot be covered under LIP.

Death Loss Payments

Payments for eligible livestock death losses will be based on a national payment rate for each livestock category times the number of eligible livestock that died in each category in excess of normal mortality. The national payment rate for eligible livestock owners is based on a minimum of 75 percent of the average fair market value of the livestock. The national payment rate for eligible contract growers is based on a minimum of 75 percent of the average income loss sustained by the contract grower with respect to the dead livestock. USDA will reduce a contract grower's ELAP payment by the amount of monetary compensation they receive from their contractor for the loss of income suffered from the death of livestock under contract.

Livestock Feed And Grazing Losses

Eligible Livestock

For livestock feed and grazing losses, livestock must be:

- Alpacas, adult or non-adult dairy cattle, adult or non-adult beef cattle, adult or non-adult buffalo, adult or non-adult beefalo, deer, elk, emus, equine, goats, llamas, poultry, reindeer, sheep and swine;

- Livestock that would normally have been grazing the eligible grazing land or pastureland during the normal grazing period for the specific pasture type of grazing land or pastureland in the county where the eligible adverse weather or eligible loss condition occurred;

- Owned, cash-leased, purchased, under contract for purchase, or been raised by a contract grower or an eligible livestock producer, during the 60 calendar days prior to the beginning date of the eligible adverse weather or loss condition;

- Maintained for commercial use as part of the producer's farming operation on the beginning date of the eligible adverse weather or loss condition.

Livestock that were or would have been in a feedlot are not eligible for livestock feed and grazing losses under ELAP.

Eligible Producer

For livestock grazing and feed losses, producers must have:

- During the 60 calendar days before the beginning date of the eligible adverse weather or loss condition, owned, cash-leased, purchased, entered into a contract to purchase or been a contract grower of eligible livestock;

- Suffered a loss on land that is either:

  o Native or improved pastureland with a permanent vegatative cover;

  o Planted to a crop specifically for the purpose of providing grazing for covered livestock.

- Provided pastureland or grazing land during the normal grazing period to eligible livestock, including cash-leased pastureland or grazing land for livestock that are physically located in the county where the eligible adverse weather or loss condition occurred during the normal grazing period.

Eligible Adverse Weather or Loss Condition

Eligible adverse weather or loss conditions for livestock feed and grazing losses include, but are not limited to, blizzard, eligible winter storm, flood, hurricane, lightning, tidal surge, tornado, volcanic eruption, or wildfire on non-federal land. Drought and wildfire on federally managed land are not eligible adverse weather or loss conditions for livestock feed and grazing losses under ELAP. These conditions are covered by the LFP.

Eligible Grazing Losses

Eligible grazing losses must be incurred on eligible grazing lands physically located in the county where the eligible adverse weather or loss condition occurred and because of an eligible adverse weather or loss condition.

Eligible Feed Losses

Eligible feed losses under ELAP are losses:

- Of purchased forage or feedstuffs;

- Of mechanically harvested forage or feedstuffs;

- Resulting from the additional costs incurred for transporting feed to eligible livestock because of an eligible adverse weather or loss condition;

- Resulting from the additional costs of purchasing additional feed, above normal quantities, required to maintain eligible livestock during an eligible adverse weather or loss condition, until additional livestock feed becomes available.

Eligible feed losses shall not exceed 150 days of lost feed.

Grazing Loss Payments, Excluding Wildfires on Non-Federal Land

Payments for eligible grazing losses, except grazing losses due to wildfires on non-federal land, will be calculated based on a minimum of 60 percent of the lesser of the total value of:

- The feed cost for all covered livestock owned by the eligible livestock producer based on the number of grazing days lost, not to exceed 150 days of daily feed cost for all covered livestock;

- Grazing lost for eligible livestock based on the normal carrying capacity of the eligible grazing land of the eligible livestock producer for the number of grazing days lost, not to exceed 150 days of lost grazing.

Grazing Loss Payments For Wildfires on Non-Federal Land

Payments for eligible livestock producers for losses suffered because of a wildfire on non-federal land will be calculated based on a minimum of 60 percent of:

- The result of dividing the number of acres of grazing land or pastureland acres affected by the wildfire by the normal carrying capacity of the specific type of eligible grazing land or pasture land, multiplied by

- The daily value of grazing, multiplied by

- The number of days grazing was lost due to the wildfire, not to exceed 180 calendar days.

Livestock Feed Payment Calculations

Payment calculations for feed losses will be based on a minimum of 60 percent of the producer's actual cost for:

- Livestock feed that was purchased or mechanically harvested forage or feedstuffs intended for use as feed for the producer's eligible livestock that was physically damaged or destroyed due to an eligible adverse weather or loss condition;

- The additional costs incurred for transporting livestock feed to eligible livestock due to an eligible adverse weather or loss condition;

- The additional cost of purchasing additional livestock feed above normal to maintain the eligible livestock during an eligible adverse weather or loss condition until additional livestock feed becomes available.

FSA will calculate ELAP payments for an eligible livestock producer for livestock feed and grazing losses for no more than 150 calendar days.

Losses Resulting From Additional Cost Of Transporting Water

Eligible Livestock

For losses resulting from the additional cost of transporting water, eligible livestock must be:

- or non-adult beef cattle, adult or non-adult buffalo, adult or non-adult beefalo, deer, elk, emus, equine, goats, llamas, poultry, reindeer, sheep and swine;

- Owned, cash-leased, purchased, under contract for purchase, or been raised by a contract grower or an eligible livestock producer, during the 60 calendar days prior to the beginning date of the eligible adverse weather or loss condition;

- Livestock that are grazing eligible pastureland or grazing land during the normal grazing period for the specific pasture type of grazing land or pasture land that:

    o Are physically located in the county where the eligible adverse weather or eligible loss condition occurred;

- o Had adequate livestock watering systems or facilities before the eligible adverse weather or eligible loss condition occurred;

- o Do not normally require the transport of water by the producer.

• Livestock that are grazing eligible pastureland or grazing land during the normal grazing period for the specific pasture type of grazing land or pasture land that:

- o Maintained for commercial use as part of the producer's farming operation on the beginning date of the eligible adverse weather or loss condition.

- o Livestock that were or would have been in a feedlot are not eligible for livestock losses resulting from transporting water under ELAP.

Eligible Producer

For losses resulting from transporting water, producers must have during the 60 calendar days before the beginning date of the eligible adverse weather or loss condition, owned, cash-leased, purchased, entered into a contract to purchase or been a contract grower of eligible livestock.

Eligible Adverse Weather or Loss Condition

Eligible adverse weather for losses resuting from the additional cost of transporting water to eligible livestock includes an eligible drought, meaning that any area of the county has been rated by the U.S. Drought Monitor as having a D3 (extreme drought) intensity that directly impacts water availability at any time during the normal grazing period.

Eligible Losses from Transporting Water

Eligible losses due to the additional costs of transporting water under ELAP are losses that:

• Occur on or after Oct. 1, 2013;

• Are due to an eligible drought;

• Are for the additional cost of transporting water to eligible livestock including, but not limited to, costs associated with water transport equipment fees, labor, and contracted water transportation fees;

• Do not include the cost of the water itself.

Payments for Losses from Transporting Water

Payments for losses due to transporting water will be based on a minimum of 60 percent of the lesser of:

The total value of the cost to transport water to eligible livestock for 150 days, based on the daily water requirements for the eligible livestock, or

The total value of the cost to transport water to eligible livestock for the program year, based on the actual number of gallons of water the eligible producer transported to eligible livestock for the program year.

The national average price per gallon to transport water is provided in the following table based on the method the producer uses to transport water for the applicable program year. A state or regional price may be established based on the recommendation and documentation by the FSA State Committee.

Method of Transporting Water	National Average Price per Gallon
Personal/labor Equipment	$0.035
Hired labor/rented equipment	$0.05
Contracted labor equipment	$0.07

Losses Related To Treatment For Cattle Tick Fever

Eligible Livestock

For losses resulting from the additional cost to treat for cattle tick fever, eligible livestock must be:

- Alpacas, adult or non-adult dairy cattle, adult or non-adult beef cattle, adult or non-adult buffalo, adult or non-adult beefalo, deer, elk, emus, equine, goats, llamas, poultry, reindeer,

- Owned, cash-leased, purchased, under contract for purchase, or been raised by a contract grower or an eligible livestock producer, during the 60 calendar days prior to the beginning date of the eligible adverse weather or loss condition;

- Maintained for commercial use as part of the producer's farming operation on the beginning date of the eligible adverse weather or loss condition.

Livestock that were or would have been in a feedlot are not eligible for livestock losses resulting from the additional cost to treat for cattle tick fever under ELAP.

Eligible Losses for Gathering Livestock to Treat for Cattle Tick Fever

Eligible losses include those losses resulting from the additional cost associated with gathering livestock to treat for cattle tick fever. To be considered an eligible loss, acceptable records that provide the number of livestock treated for cattle tick fever and the number of treatments given during the program year must be on file with the USDA Animal and Plant Health Inspection Service (APHIS).

Payments for Losses for Gathering Livestock to Treat for Cattle Tick Fever

Payments for losses resulting from the additional cost associated with gathering livestock to treat for cattle tick fever will be equal to the sum of the following for each treatment:

- A minimum national payment factor of 60 percent, multiplied by

- The number of eligible livestock treated by APHIS for cattle tick fever, multiplied by

- The average cost to gather livestock, per head, as established by FSA.

Socially Disadvantaged, Limited Resource And Beginning Farmers And Ranchers

Starting with the 2012 program year (Oct. 1, 2011), an eligible livestock producer who certifies they are socially disadvantaged, limited resource, or a beginning farmer or rancher, will have their payments for livestock losses under ELAP based on a national payment factor of 90 percent.

Payment Eligibility And Limitations

For 2012 and subsequent program years, no person or legal entity, excluding a joint venture or general partnership, may receive directly or indirectly, more than $125,000 total in payments under ELAP, LFP, and LIP combined.

The average adjusted gross income (AGI) limitation on payments for persons or legal entities, excluding joint ventures and general partnerships, with certain levels of average AGI will apply. Specifically, a person or legal entity with an average adjusted gross income (as defined in 7 CFR Part 1400) that exceeds $900,000 will not be eligible to receive ELAP payments.

Direct attribution provisions also apply to ELAP for 2012 and subsequent program years. Under direct attribution, any payment to a legal entity will also be considered for payment limitation purposes to be a payment to persons or legal entities with an interest in the legal entity or in a sub-entity.

Multiple Benefits

If a producer is eligible to receive a livestock payment under ELAP, then all the following apply:

- The producer cannot receive duplicate payments under LFP or LIP for the same loss;

- Beginning with the 2014 program year, if the producer is eligible to receive assistance for the same loss under Catastrophic Risk Protection or the Noninsured Crop Disaster Assistance Program (NAP), then the producer must elect whether to receive benefits under ELAP or under the other program, but not both.

Sign-Up

Producers can apply to receive ELAP benefits at local FSA service centers beginning April 15, 2014, for eligible livestock losses suffered during 2012, 2013 and 2014 program years (losses occurring on or after Oct. 1, 2011, through Sept. 30, 2014) due to eligible adverse weather or loss conditions.

For 2012 and 2013 program year losses, sign-up ends Aug. 1, 2014, and for 2014 program year losses sign-up ended Nov. 1, 2014.

For 2015 and subsequent program year losses, sign-up will end no later than Nov. 1 after the end of the program year in which the livestock loss occurred.

Applying For ELAP

In addition to submitting an application for payment, producers who suffered livestock losses should submit a notice of loss to the local FSA office that maintains their farm records.

The following table provides the final dates to file a notice of loss and application for payment for livestock losses.

Date of Livestock Loss	Final Date to File Notice of Loss	Final Date to Submit Application for Payment
Program Year 2012 & 2013	Aug. 1, 2014	Aug. 1, 2014
Program Year 2014	Nov. 1, 2014	Nov. 1, 2014
Program Year 2015 and Subsequent Program Years	30 days after livestock loss in apparent	Nov. 1 after the program year in which the loss occurred

The producer must include a copy of the grower contract if they are a contract grower and any other supporting documents required for determining eligibility. Supporting documents must show evidence of loss, current physical location of livestock in inventory, and evidence that grazing land or pastureland is owned or leased.

Payments may be made for eligible losses suffered by an eligible participant who is now a deceased individual or is a dissolved entity if a representative, who currently has authority to act on behalf of the estate of the deceased participant, signs the application for payment.

Proof of authority to sign for a deceased individual or dissolved entity must be provided. If a participant is now a dissolved general partnership or joint venture, all members of the general partnership or joint venture at the time of dissolution or their duly authorized representative(s) must sign the application for payment.

FSA will use data furnished by the applicant to determine eligibility for program benefits. Furnishing the data is voluntary; however, without all required data program benefits will not be approved or provided.

More Information

To find more information about FSA programs, contact your local FSA office or USDA Service Center, or visit FSA online at www.fsa.usda.gov.

Orchard and Nursery Tree Assistance Program (TAP)[64]

Tree Assistance Program Fact Sheet

Overview

The Agricultural Act of 2014 (the 2014 Farm Bill) authorized the Tree Assistance Program (TAP) to provide financial assistance to qualifying orchardists and nursery tree growers to replant or rehabilitate eligible trees, bushes and vines damaged by natural disasters.

---

[64] http://www.fsa.usda.gov/FSA/newsReleases?area=newsroom&subject=landing&topic=pfs&newstype=prfactsheet&type=detail&item=pf_20140415_distr_en_tap14.html

The 2014 Farm Bill makes TAP a permanent disaster program and provides retroactive authority to cover eligible losses back to Oct. 1, 2011.

TAP is administered by the Farm Service Agency (FSA) of the U.S. Department of Agriculture (USDA).

Eligible Tree Types

Eligible trees, bushes and vines are those from which an annual crop is produced for commercial purposes. Nursery trees include ornamental, fruit, nut and Christmas trees produced for commercial sale. Trees used for pulp or timber are ineligible.

Eligible Losses

To be considered an eligible loss: Eligible trees, bushes or vines must have been lost or damaged as a result of natural disaster;

- The individual stand must have sustained a mortality loss or damage loss in excess of 15 percent after adjustment for normal mortality or damage to be determined based on:

- Each eligible disaster event, except for losses due to plant disease;

- For plant disease, the time period as determined by the FSA for which the stand is infected.

- The loss could not have been prevented through reasonable and available measures;

- The damage or loss must be visible and obvious to the FSA representative; if the damage is no longer visible, FSA may accept other loss evidence that the agency determines is reasonable;

FSA may require information from a qualified expert to determine extent of loss in the case of plant disease or insect infestation.

Eligible Producers

To qualify for TAP, orchardists and nursery tree growers must:

- Have suffered qualifying tree, bush or vine losses in excess of 15 percent mortality (adjusted for normal mortality) from an eligible natural disaster for the individual stand;

- Have owned the eligible trees, bushes and vines when the natural disaster occurred, but eligible growers are not required to own the land on which eligible trees, bushes and vines are planted;

- Replace eligible trees, bushes and vines within 12 months from the date the application is approved.

Acreage Limitations

The cumulative total quantity of acres planted to trees, bushes or vines for which a producer can receive TAP payments cannot exceed 500 acres annually.

Payment Limitation and Adjusted Gross Income (AGI)

For 2012 and subsequent program years, no person or legal entity, excluding a joint venture or general partnership, may receive, directly or indirectly, more than $125,000 total in payments under TAP.

For 2011, no person or legal entity, excluding a joint venture or general partnership, may receive, directly or indirectly, more than $125,000 total in the 2011 program year in payments under TAP, when at least $25,000 of such total 2011 program payments is from TAP, for losses from Oct, 1, 2011, through Dec. 31, 2011.

In applying the limitation on average adjusted gross income, an individual or entity is ineligible for payment under TAP if the average AGI of the individual or entity exceeds $900,000.

Direct attribution provisions apply to TAP for 2011 and subsequent years. Under direct attribution, any payment to a legal entity will be considered (for payment limitation purposes) to be a payment to persons or legal entities with an interest in the legal entity or in a sub-entity.

Payment Calculator

For tree, bush or vine replacement, replanting and/or rehabilitation, the payment calculation is the lesser of the following:

- 65 percent of the actual cost of replanting, in excess of 15 percent mortality (adjusted for normal mortality), and/or 50 percent of the actual cost of rehabilitation, in excess of 15 percent damage or mortality (adjusted for normal tree damage and mortality), or

- The maximum eligible amount established for the practice by FSA.

Sign-Up

Orchardists and nursery tree growers may apply to receive TAP benefits with the FSA office that maintains the farm records for their agricultural operation beginning April 15, 2014, for losses suffered on or after Oct. 1, 2011, through the end of the 2014 calendar year.

The following table provides the final dates to submit a TAP application and supporting documentation:

Date of Loss	Final Date to Submit an Application and Supporting Documentation
On or after Oct. 1, 2011, through the end of the 2014 calendar year	Later of Jan. 31, 2015, or: 90 calendar days after the disaster event, or The date the loss is apparent.
Calendar year 2015 and subsequent years	Later of 90 calendar days of: The disaster event, or The date when the loss is apparent.

More Information

To find more information about FSA programs, contact your local FSA office or USDA Service Center, or visit FSA online at www.fsa.usda.gov.

Emergency Forest Restoration Program (EFRP)[65]

Overview

USDA Farm Service Agency's (FSA) Emergency Forest Restoration Program (EFRP) provides payments to eligible owners of nonindustrial private forest (NIPF) land in order to carry out emergency measures to restore land damaged by a natural disaster. Funding for EFRP is appropriated by Congress.

Program Administration

EFRP is administered by FSA's state and county committees and offices. Subject to availability of funds, locally-elected county committees are authorized to implement EFRP for all disasters except drought and insect infestations, which are authorized at the FSA national office.

Land Eligibility

County FSA committees determine land eligibility using on-site damage inspections that assess the type and extent of damage. To be eligible for EFRP, NIPF land must:

- Have existing tree cover (or had tree cover immediately before the natural disaster occurred and is suitable for growing trees); and,
- Be owned by any nonindustrial private individual, group, association, corporation, or other private legal entity, that has definitive decision-making authority over the land.

In addition, the natural disaster must have resulted in damage that if untreated would:

- Impair or endanger the natural resources on the land; and,
- Materially affect future use of the land.

Payments

EFRP program participants may receive financial assistance of up to 75 percent of the cost to implement approved emergency forest restoration practices as determined by county FSA committees.

Individual or cumulative requests for financial assistance of $50,000 or less per person or legal entity, per disaster are approved by the county committee. Financial assistance from $50,001 to $100,000 is approved by the state committee. Financial assistance over $100,000 must be approved at the FSA national office. A payment limitation of $500,000 per person or legal entity applies per disaster.

Emergency Forest Restoration Practices

To restore NIPF, EFRP program participants may implement emergency forest restoration practices, including emergency measures:

---

[65] http://www.apfo.usda.gov/FSA/webapp?area=home&subject=diap&topic=efrp

- Necessary to repair damage caused by a natural disaster to natural resources on nonindustrial private forest land;
- and Restore forest health and forest related resources on the land.

Other emergency measures may be authorized by county FSA committees, with approval from state FSA committees and the FSA national office.

Sign-up Periods

Producers should check with their local county FSA offices regarding EFRP sign-up periods, which are set by county FSA committees.

Emergency Haying and Grazing[66] (This program is authorized on a case by case basis for each disaster.)

The USDA Farm Service Agency (FSA) has a program to help livestock producers in approved counties when the growth and yield of hay and pasture have been substantially reduced because of a widespread natural disaster

This program is triggered by the Secretary of Agriculture to harvest hay or graze cropland or other commercial use of forage devoted to the Conservation Reserve Program (CRP) in response to a drought or other similar emergency.

NOTE

This program does NOT require a Presidential disaster declaration

Emergency haying or grazing is limited to the acreage physically located within the boundary of the eligible county or portion of a county. Under this authority, acreage will only be authorized for a specified time and may end earlier than announced if conditions improve.

All CRP participants in an approved county are eligible to graze eligible CRP acreage regardless of the degree of production loss suffered by the individual producer. CRP participants who do not own or lease livestock may rent or lease the grazing privilege to an eligible livestock producer located in an approved county.

Emergency authorization is provided by either a national FSA office authorization or by a state FSA committee determination utilizing the U.S. Drought Monitor.

After authorized by the national FSA office, county eligibility is based on a county FSA committee request documenting a 40 percent or greater loss in normal hay and pasture production and either:

1. for drought conditions, precipitation levels at an average of 40 percent or greater loss of normal precipitation for the 4 most recent months plus the days in the current month before the date of request; or

2. for excessive moisture conditions, precipitation levels at an average of 140 percent or greater increase in normal precipitation during the 4 most recent consecutive months plus the days in the current month before the date of request.

Acreage available for emergency haying or grazing includes acreage devoted to the following practices:

CP1, CP2, CP4B, CP4D, CP10, CP18B, and CP18C.

Acreage not eligible for this program is acreage devoted to:

---

[66] http://www.apfo.usda.gov/FSA/webapp?area=home&subject=copr&topic=crp-eg

1. Useful life easements;
2. Land within 100 feet of a stream or other permanent water body;
3. The following practices: CP3, CP3A, CP4, CP4A, CP5, CP5A, CP6, CP7, CP8, CP8A, CP9, CP11, CP12, CP13A, CP13B, CP13C, CP13D, CP14, CP15, CP15A, CP16, CP16A, CP17, CP17A, CP18, CP18A, CP19, CP20, CP21, CP22, CP23, CP24, CP25, CP26, CP27, CP28, CP29, and CP30.

The state FSA committee *may approve* emergency haying or grazing on a county-by-county basis if the county is designated as level "D3 Drought-Extreme" or "D4-Exceptional" according to the U.S. Drought Monitor. The U.S. Drought Monitor is available online at: http://droughtmonitor.unl.edu/

Under a state committee determination, emergency *haying* only is authorized for a single period up to *60 days*. Emergency *grazing* is authorized for a single period up to *120 days*.

County FSA committees *may request* emergency haying or grazing for all or part of a county from the state FSA committee using the U.S. Drought Monitor.

Before CRP acreage is declared eligible for haying or grazing a modified conservation plan developed by NRCS or a technical service provider must be obtained.

The modified conservation plan must be site specific, include the authorized duration, and reflect local wildlife needs and concerns. The primary purpose must be to maintain vegetative cover, minimize soil erosion, and protect water quality and wildlife habitat quality.

The CRP-authorizing legislation requires a payment reduction to be assessed. For an area approved for emergency haying or grazing the payment reduction is 10 percent.

CONTACT:

Emergency and Non-insured Assistance Programs, FSA, USDA, P.O. Box 2415, Washington, DC 20013; Telephone: (202) 720-7641.

Emergency Conservation Program (ECP)[67]

Overview

USDA Farm Service Agency's (FSA) Emergency Conservation Program (ECP) provides emergency funding and technical assistance to farmers and ranchers to rehabilitate farmland damaged by natural disasters and for implementing emergency water conservation measures in periods of severe drought. Funding for ECP is appropriated by Congress.

Program Administration

ECP is administered by FSA state and county committees. Subject to availability of funds, locally-elected county committees are authorized to implement ECP for all disasters except drought, which is authorized by the FSA national office.

Land Eligibility

FSA county committees determine land eligibility based on on-site inspections of damaged land and the type and extent of damage. For land to be eligible, the natural disaster must create new conservation problems that, if untreated, would:

- Impair or endanger the land;
- Materially affect the land's productive capacity;
- Represent unusual damage which, except for wind erosion, is not the type likely to recur frequently in the same area; and

---

[67] http://www.fsa.usda.gov/FSA/newsReleases?area=newsroom&subject=landing&topic=pfs&newstype=prfactsheet&type=detail&item=pf_20120103_consv_en_disa.html

- **Be so costly to repair that Federal assistance is or will be required to return the land to productive agricultural use.**

Conservation problems existing before the applicable disaster event are ineligible for ECP assistance.

Payments

As determined by FSA county committees, ECP participants may receive cost-share assistance of up to 75 percent of the cost to implement approved emergency conservation practices. Qualified limited-resource producers receive cost-share assistance of up to 90 percent of the cost to implement approved emergency conservation practices.

Individual or cumulative requests for cost-share assistance of $50,000 or less per person or legal entity, per disaster are approved at the county committee level. Cost-share assistance requests exceeding $50,000 require approval from the state committee or national office level. Cost-share assistance is limited to $200,000 per person or legal entity, per disaster.

Technical assistance may be provided by USDA's Natural Resources Conservation Service.

Emergency Conservation Practices

To rehabilitate farmland, ECP participants may implement emergency conservation practices such as:

- Debris removal from farmland;
- Restoring livestock fences and conservation structures; and
- Providing water for livestock during periods of severe drought.

Other conservation measures may be authorized by FSA county committees, with approval from FSA state committees and the FSA national office.

Sign-up Periods

Producers should inquire with their local FSA county office regarding ECP sign-up periods, which are established by FSA county committees.

For More Information

More information on ECP is available at FSA offices and on FSA's web site at: http://disaster.fsa.usda.gov

The National Emergency or Disaster Grants to Assist Low-Income Migrant and Seasonal Farm Workers[68]

The USDA Rural Housing Service (RHS) has a program of grants to provide emergency services to areas where the Secretary of Agriculture determines that a local, state, or national emergency or disaster has caused low-income migrant or seasonal farmworkers to lose income, be unable to work, or to stay at home or return home in anticipation of work shortages.

Eligibility for grants for emergency services is limited to public agencies or private organizations with tax exempt status under 20 U.S.C. § 501(c)(3) that have experience in providing emergency services to low-income migrant and seasonal farmworkers. These funds are to be administered in areas where the Secretary of Agriculture determines that a local, state, or national emergency or disaster has occurred.

NOTE

This program is not ongoing but rather sporadic in nature, and is dependent upon specific congressional appropriations.

---

[68] http://tgci.com/national-emergency-or-disaster-grants-assist-low-income-migrant-and-seasonal-farmworkers

Emergency services include any service that can be provided under the Robert T. Stafford Disaster Relief and Emergency Assistance Act (Pub. L. 93–288), as amended (Stafford Act), that also meets the requirements of 42 U.S.C. §5177a

The types of services could include, but are not limited to, assistance in meeting rent or mortgage payments, utility bills, child care, transportation, school supplies, food, repair or rehabilitation of farmworker housing, facilities related to farmworker housing such as an infirmary for emergency care of a child care facility, and the rehabilitation of existing farmworker housing units.

The term "low-income migrant or seasonal farmworker" means an individual:

1. who has, during any consecutive 12 month period within the preceding 24 month period, performed farm work for wages,
2. who has received not less than one-half of such individual's total income, or been employed at least one-half of total work time in farm work,
3. whose annual family income within the 12 month period referred to in paragraph (a) does not exceed the higher of the poverty level or 70 percent of the lower living standard income level,
4. is a person lawfully admitted for permanent residence.

The applicant must:

1. Be eligible to receive a grant for the above assistance the applicant must be a broad-based nonprofit organization (which may include faith-based organizations), a nonprofit organization of farmworkers, a community organization, a federally recognized Indian tribe, or an agency or political subdivision of a State or local government, or a public agency (such as housing authorities).
2. Be unable to provide the necessary services from its own resources.
3. Possess the legal and actual capacity, ability, and experience to incur and carry out the undertakings and obligations incurred.
4. Legally obligate itself not to divert income to any other business, enterprise, or purpose.
5. Have experience in providing emergency services to low-income migrant and seasonal farmworkers.
6. Be either a public agency or private organization with tax exempt status under Section 26 U.S.C. §501(c)(3).
7. Not be debarred or suspended.

Summary of Farm/Ranch Disaster Programs

Program	Benefit	Eligibility	Farm Loss Covered	Where Available	Application Deadline	Appeal Rights	Other
Emergency Loans (EM Loans)	Direct Loans & Technical Assistance	Have suffered at least a 30-percent loss in crop production or a physical loss to livestock, livestock products, real estate, or chattel property	Up to 100 percent of actual production or physical losses, to a maximum amount of $500,000.	USDA Farm Service Agency (FSA)	8 months of the county's disaster or quarantine designation date.	No	Contact local FSA Office
Livestock Forage Disaster Program (LFP)	Loss of public grazing land	Grazing losses due to drought or fire on public managed land.	Payment rates are based on monthly feed costs.	USDA Farm Service Agency (FSA)	None Specified	No	Contact local FSA Office
Livestock Indemnity Program (LIP)	Makes payments available to eligible producers for livestock death losses in excess of normal mortality due to adverse weather.	Producers in "disaster counties," and contiguous counties and any farms with losses in normal production of more than 50 percent.	Payment rate is 75 percent of market value of applicable livestock on the day before death	USDA Farm Service Agency (FSA)	None Specified	No	Contact local FSA Office

Program	Benefit	Eligibility	Farm Loss Covered	Where Available	Application Deadline	Appeal Rights	Other
Emergency Assistance Program for Livestock, Honey Bees, and Farm-Raised Fish (ELAP)	Emergency relief to eligible producers of livestock, honey bees, and farm-raised fish	Losses due to disease, adverse weather, or other conditions not covered by the Livestock Indemnity Program or by the Livestock Forage Disaster Program.	Total Program limit is $50 million	USDA Farm Service Agency (FSA)	None Specified	No	Contact local FSA Office
Orchard and Nursery Tree Assistance Program (TAP)	Assistance to eligible orchardists and nursery tree growers for trees lost to natural disasters.	None Specified	Reimbursement of 70 percent of the cost of replanting trees in excess of normal mortality and reimbursement of 50 percent of the cost of salvaging damaged trees and preparing land to replant trees.	USDA Farm Service Agency (FSA)	None Specified	No	Contact local FSA

Program	Benefit	Eligibility	Farm Loss Covered	Where Available	Application Deadline	Appeal Rights	Other
Emergency Conservation Program (ECP) (Presently not funded)	Enable farmers to perform emergency conservation measures to control wind erosion; to rehabilitate farmlands damaged by wind erosion, floods, hurricanes, or other natural disasters; and to carry out emergency water conservation or water-enhancing measures during times of severe drought.	Any person, who, as owner, landlord, tenant, or sharecropper on a farm or ranch, including associated groups, bears a part of the cost of an approved conservation practice in a disaster area	The natural disaster must create new conservation problems	Local county FSA offices.	Check with their local county FSA offices regarding ECP sign-up periods, which are set by county FSA committees.	No	Contact Local FSA Office
Emergency Forest Restoration Program (EFRP)	Up to 75 percent of the cost to implement approved emergency forest restoration practices as determined by county FSA committees.	County FSA committees determine land eligibility using on-site damage inspections that assess the type and extent of damage.	Damage caused by a natural disaster to natural resources on nonindustrial private forest land.	USDA Farm Service Agency (FSA)	Not specified	No	Contact local FSA Office

Program	Benefit	Eligibility	Farm Loss Covered	Where Available	Application Deadline	Appeal Rights	Other
The National Emergency or Disaster Grants To Assist Low-Income Migrant and Seasonal Farmworkers	Provide emergency services to areas where a local, state, or national emergency or disaster has caused low-income migrant or seasonal farm workers to lose income, be unable to work, or to stay at home or return home in anticipation of work shortages.	Eligibility for grants for emergency services is limited to public agencies or private organizations with tax exempt status under 20 U.S.C. § 501(c)(3) that have experience in providing emergency services to low-income migrant and seasonal farm workers.	Services could include, but are not limited to, assistance in rent or mortgage payments, utility bills, child care, transportation, school supplies, food, repair or rehabilitation of farmworker housing, facilities related to farmworker housing such as an infirmary for emergency care of a child care facility, and the rehabilitation of existing farm worker housing units	USDA Rural Housing Service (RHS)	Not Specified	No	Contact local FSA Office

Income Tax Treatment of Crop Insurance and Crop Disaster Payments[69]

You must include in income any crop insurance proceeds you receive as the result of crop damage. You generally include them in the year you receive them. Treat as crop insurance proceeds the crop disaster payments you receive from the federal government as the result of destruction or damage to crops, or the inability to plant crops because of drought, flood, or any other natural disaster.

Note: You can request income tax withholding from crop disaster payments you receive from the federal government. Use Form W-4V, Voluntary Withholding Request (PDF). Refer to How to Get Tax Help in Publication 225 for information about ordering the form.

You May Choose To Postpone Reporting Until The Following Year

If you use the cash method of accounting and receive crop insurance proceeds in the same tax year in which the crops are damaged, you can choose to postpone reporting the proceeds as income until the following tax year. You can make this choice if you can show you would have in-

---

[69] From the IRS website http://www.irs.gov/Businesses/Small-Businesses-&-Self-Employed/Crop-Insurance-and-Crop-Disaster-Payments-Agriculture-Tax-Tips

cluded income from the damaged crops in any tax year following the year the damage occurred.

How To Postpone Reporting Of Crop Insurance Proceeds

To choose to postpone reporting crop insurance proceeds received in the current year, report the amount you received on line 8a of Schedule F, but do not include it as a taxable amount on line 8b. Check the box on line 8c and attach a statement to your tax return. It must include your name and address and contain the following information:

- A statement that you are making a choice under IRC section 451(d) and Treasury Regulation section 1.451-6
- The specific crop or crops destroyed or damaged
- A statement that under your normal business practice you would have included income from the destroyed or damaged crops in gross income for a tax year following the year the crops were destroyed or damaged
- The cause of the destruction or damage and the date or dates it occurred
- The total payments you received from insurance carriers, itemized for each specific crop and the date you received each payment
- The name of each insurance carrier from whom you received payments

Business

U.S. Small Business Administration Disaster Loan Program

Overview

Low-interest loans from the U.S. Small Business Administration (SBA) are the primary form of federal assistance for long-term recovery for **non-profit organizations and non-farm businesses of all sizes**. These SBA loans fund repair of damages to private property not fully covered by insurance.

These loans require a Presidentially or SBA Disaster Declaration.[70]

Business owners may be eligible for the refinancing of existing mortgages or liens on real estate, machinery and equipment, in some cases up to the amount of the loan for the repair or replacement of real estate, machinery, and equipment.

The $2,000,000 statutory limit for business loans applies to the combination of physical and economic injury, and applies to all disaster loans to a business and its affiliates for each disaster.

NOTE

If a business is a major source of employment, SBA has the authority to waive the $2,000,000 statutory limit.

Loans may also include funds for mitigation measures to minimize damage from future disasters of the same kind. Mitigation loan money would be in addition to the amount of the approved loan, but may not exceed *20 percent* of total amount of disaster damage to real estate and/or leasehold improvements, as verified by SBA. It is not necessary for the description of improvements and cost estimates to be submitted with the application. *SBA approval of the mitigating measures will be required before any loan increase.* 15 U.S.C. 636(b), 13 CFR Part 123.

Applicants do not have to wait for their insurance settlement before applying for an SBA loan. SBA can lend them the full amount of their damages (up to the lending limit) even before they receive their insurance recovery. Then SBA can use the insurance funds to reduce the balance of their disaster loan.

Insurance proceeds that are required to be applied against outstanding mortgages may be included in disaster loan eligibility. Insurance proceeds that are voluntarily applied against outstanding mortgages by the owner may not be included in disaster loan eligibility.

---

[70] http://www.sba.gov/content/current-disaster-declarations

Applicants who did not comply with the terms of previous loans or who did not maintain required flood insurance for the insurable value of the property are ineligible for an SBA loan.

Borrowers are required to maintain appropriate insurance coverage for the life of the loan.

SBA personnel are available to assist with completing application forms at no charge. For more information, disaster victims may call the SBA Disaster Assistance information line at (800) 659-2955 from 8AM to 9PM(EST), Mon - Fri, 9AM - 5:30 PM (EST), Sat; or email at disastercustomerservice@sba.gov.

SBA has a web site for disaster assistance, including electronic application for disaster loan. The web site is http://www.sba.gov/services/disaster-assistance/index.html

SBA has two types of loans for businesses:

Business Physical Disaster Loans – Loans to businesses to repair or replace disaster-damaged property owned by the business, including real estate, inventories, supplies, machinery and equipment. Businesses of any size are eligible. Private, non-profit organizations such as charities, churches, private universities, etc., are also eligible.

The limit for business loans is $2,000,000 for the repair or replacement of real estate, inventories, machinery, equipment and all other physical losses. Loan amounts cannot exceed the verified uninsured disaster loss.

Economic Injury Disaster Loans (EIDLs) – Working capital loans to help small businesses, small agricultural cooperatives and most private, non-profit organizations of all sizes meet their ordinary and necessary financial obligations that cannot be met as a direct result of the disaster.

EIDL assistance is available only to entities and their owners who cannot provide for their own recovery from non government sources, as determined by the SBA

These loans are intended to assist through the disaster recovery period. These working capital loans are available to businesses financially impacted by the disaster, even if they had no property damage. EIDLs are also available to small businesses located in counties contiguous to the declared counties.

The limit for EIDL(s) is $2,000,000 for alleviating economic injury caused by the disaster. The actual amount of each loan is limited to the economic injury determined by SBA, less business interruption insurance and other recoveries up to the administrative lending limit. SBA also considers potential contributions that are available from the business and/or its owner(s) or affiliates. (The definition of a "small" business is provided in the Standard Industrial Classification manual.)

Loan Modifications

Loans can be modified if the borrower can substantiate in writing a change of circumstances which affects ability to repay, or justify a change in the purpose of the loan.

Reconsiderations and Appeals of Declined Applicants

Applicants who are denied an SBA loan can request reconsideration in writing **within six months** of the decision denying the loan. The request must explain why the decision is wrong and include any new information which supports the request (i.e.:. increased ability to repay the loan due to increased income, or the applicant refinanced his/her home). The notification letter will provide instructions on who to send the request to and where to send it.

If the request for reconsideration is denied, a written appeal may be filed *within 30 days*. The appeal should address the reasons for denial, listed in the denial letter. After the appeal is submitted, it may be amended with further information. The appeal should be sent to:

U.S. Small Business Administration Disaster Office
Disaster Assistance Processing & Disbursement Center
14925 Kingsport Road
Fort Worth, Texas 76155
(Toll Free) (800) 366-6303
(Phone) (817) 868-2300
(TTY) (817) 267-4688
(Fax) (817) 684-5616

The decision on the appeal is final.

Business Physical Disaster Loans[71]

The application deadline for Business Physical Disaster Loans is 60 days from the disaster declaration date.

Businesses of all sizes and non-profit organizations may apply for low-interest SBA disaster loans to fund repairs or replacement of damaged or destroyed real estate, machinery and equipment, inventory and other business assets. These loans are available up to **$2.0 million** for losses not fully covered by insurance.

1. Eligibility

a. Applicant must have been the owner of the damaged property, or was a commercial tenant or a non-profit organization responsible for the damage at the time of the disaster;
b. All physical losses or damage to real property must have been caused by the disaster; and
c. Applicant must have the ability to repay the loan.

2. Verification and Documentation

The following information must be provided with the loan application, or after the loan application has been approved:

a. Deed of trust, mortgage, lease or rental agreement;
b. Brief history of the business;
c. Personal and business financial statements;
d. Internal Revenue Service Form 8821 (authorization for SBA to obtain Federal Tax Returns);
e. Itemized list of losses with estimates of repair or replacement costs; and
f. Copy of insurance settlement, adjuster's proof of loss or schedule of coverage if claim has not been settled.

3. Credit Requirements

a. SBA's disaster assistance is in the form of low-interest loans. Applicants must show a reasonable assurance of their ability to repay all loans and must demonstrate a reasonable assurance that they will comply with the terms of a loan agreement, based upon their credit history (as reported by a credit bureau).
b. Applicants must not be delinquent on a federal debt obligation or child support payments.

4. Collateral Requirement

Collateral is required for all physical loss loans over $14,000. SBA takes real estate as collateral where it is available. Applicants do not need to have full collateral; SBA will take what is available to secure each loan. However, if a borrower refuses to pledge collateral, SBA may decline a disas-

---

[71] http://www.sba.gov/content/business-physical-disaster-loans

ter loan for that reason. For businesses, personal guarantees of the principals may be required.

5. Term of Loan

For businesses that are unable to obtain credit elsewhere, the maximum term is 30 years. Maturity dates and installment terms are determined by the borrower's needs and ability to repay. *However, for businesses with credit available elsewhere, the law limits the loan term to a maximum of three years.*

Economic Injury Disaster Loans[72]

The application deadline for Economic Injury Disaster Loans is nine months from the disaster declaration date.

For small businesses only, SBA also makes Economic Injury Disaster Loans (EIDLs) of *up to $2.0 million* to provide working capital to pay necessary obligations until operations return to normal after the disaster. These working capital loans are available to businesses financially impacted by the disaster, even if they had no property damage, and are also available to small businesses located in counties contiguous to the declared counties. EIDL assistance is available only to applicants with no credit available elsewhere; this means that the business owners cannot provide for their own recovery from non-government sources as determined by SBA.

1. Eligibility

a. Applicant was owner of the property or the commercial tenant responsible for damage at the time of the disaster;

b. Applicant has the ability to repay the loan; and

c. A change in the financial condition of the business due to the disaster renders the business unable to pay its debts and ordinary and necessary operating expenses (a lack of profit or loss of anticipated sales are not enough).

2. Verification and Documentation

The following information must be provided with the loan application, or after the loan application has been approved:

a. Deed of trust, mortgage, lease or rental agreement;
b. Brief history of the business;
c. Personal and business financial statements;
d. Internal Revenue Service form 8821 (authorization for SBA to obtain Federal Tax Returns);
e. Itemized list of losses with estimates of repair or replacement costs;
f. Copy of insurance settlement, adjuster's proof of loss or schedule of coverage if claim has not been settled; and
g. Balance sheets and operating statements for comparative periods of time.

3. Credit Requirements

a. SBA's disaster assistance is in the form of low-interest loans. Applicants must show a reasonable assurance of their ability to repay all loans and must demonstrate a reasonable assurance that they will comply with the terms of a loan agreement, based upon their credit history (as reported by a credit bureau).

b. Applicants must not be delinquent on a federal debt obligation or child support payments.

4. Collateral Requirement

Collateral is required for all EIDL loans over $5,000. SBA takes real estate as collateral where

---

[72] http://www.sba.gov/content/economic-injury-disaster-loans

it is available. Applicants do not need to have full collateral; SBA will take what is available to secure each loan. If a borrower refuses to pledge collateral, SBA may decline a disaster loan.

5. Interest Rates

Interest rates are determined by formulas set by law, and may vary over time with market conditions. The laws that govern the disaster loan program require the SBA to determine whether credit is available elsewhere to all disaster loan recipients from non-government sources in the amount needed to effect full repairs, without creating an undue financial hardship. Accordingly, the availability of sufficient credit (based on cash flow and available assets of the applicant) from non government sources on reasonable terms and conditions is determined through a comprehensive analysis of all the financial information submitted for consideration. This test is uniformly applied to all disaster loan recipients.

Generally, more than 90% of disaster loan applicants do not have credit available elsewhere.

6. Immigration Status

SBA does not require proof of immigration status. Please note, however, that *Social Security numbers are required for SBA disaster loans.*

7. Refinancing

SBA can refinance all or part of prior mortgages, evidenced by a recorded lien, when the applicant:

1. Does not have credit available elsewhere;
2. Has suffered substantial damage (40% or more of the value of the predisaster fair market value of the property); and
3. Intends to repair the damage.

Refinancing of prior debts improves the victim's ability to afford the SBA disaster loan.

Personal guarantees of the principal may be required

See the next page for current interest rates.

Current Interest Rates

As of April 18, 2014, the applicable interest rates are:

	No Credit Available	Credit Available
Home Loans	2.188%	4.375%
Business Loans	4.000%	6.000%
Non-Profits	2.625%	2.625%
Economic Injury Loan	4.000%	n/a
Economic Injury Loan	2.625	n/a

Call SBA at 1-800-695-2955 to inquire about current interest rates.

Military Reservist Economic Injury Disaster Loans[73]

Small Businesses may apply for economic injury loans if an essential employee who is a Reservist is called to active duty whose absence will cause the small businesses to meet its ordinary and necessary operating expenses that it could have met, but is unable to meet, because an essential employee was "called-up" to active duty in their role as a military reservist.

These loans are intended only to provide the amount of working capital needed by a small business to pay its necessary obligations as they mature until operations return to normal after the essential employee is released from active military duty.

---

[73] Application forms and instructions are found at http://www.sbaonline.sba.gov/services/disasterassistance/militaryreservistsloans/index.html

The purpose of these loans is not to cover lost income or lost profits. MREIDL funds cannot be used to take the place of regular commercial debt, to refinance long-term debt or to expand the business.

The *Filing Period* for small businesses to apply for economic injury loan assistance begins on the date the *essential employee* receives a notice of expected call-up and ends 1 year after the essential employee is discharged or released from active duty.

Disbursement of Funds: Loan funds will be disbursed only after the essential employee has been officially called to active duty.

Essential Employee: An individual (whether or not an owner of the small business) whose managerial or technical expertise is critical to the successful day-to-day operations of the small business.

Substantial Economic Injury: This means that your business either has been or will be adversely impacted by the deployment of the military reservist and that the business is:

1. unable to meet its financial obligations as they mature, and/or
2. unable to pay its ordinary and necessary operating expenses, and/or
3. the small business is unable to market, produce or provide a service ordinarily marketed, produced or provided.

Small Business: SBA has established a Table of Small Business Size Standards, which is matched to the North American Industry Classification System (NAICS) industries. A size standard, which is usually stated in number of employees or average annual receipts, represents the largest size that a business (including its subsidiaries and affiliates) may be to remain classified as a small business for SBA and Federal contracting programs. The table of size standards is found at: http://www.sba.gov/content/small-business-size-standards

Federal law requires SBA to determine whether credit in an amount needed to accomplish full recovery is available from non-government sources without creating an undue financial hardship to the applicant. The law calls this credit available elsewhere. Generally, SBA determines that over 90% of disaster loan applicants do not have sufficient financial resources to recover without the assistance of the Federal government. Because the Military Reservist economic injury loans are taxpayer subsidized, Congress intended that applicants with the financial capacity to fund their own recovery should do so and therefore are not eligible for MREIDL assistance.

Credit Requirements: SBA's assistance is in the form of loans, as such SBA must have a reasonable assurance that such loans can and will be repaid.

Collateral Requirements: Collateral is required for all MREIDLs over $50,000. SBA takes real estate as collateral when it is available. SBA will not decline a loan for lack of collateral, but SBA will require the borrower to pledge collateral that is available.

Interest Rate: The interest rate is 4.000%

Loan Term: The law authorizes loan terms up to a maximum of 30 years. SBA determines the term of each loan in accordance with the borrower's ability to repay. Based on the financial circumstances of each borrower, SBA determines an appropriate installment payment amount, which in turn determines the actual term.

Loan Amount Limit - $2,000,000: The actual amount of each loan, up to this maximum, is limited to the actual economic injury as calculated by SBA, not compensated by business interruption insurance or otherwise, and beyond the ability of the business and/or its owners to provide. If a business is a major source of employment, SBA has authority to waive the $2,000,000 statutory limit.

Insurance Requirements: To protect each borrower and the Agency, SBA requires borrowers to obtain and maintain appropriate insurance. Borrowers of all secured loans (over $50,000) must purchase and maintain hazard insurance for the life of the loan on the collateral property. By law, borrowers whose collateral property is located in a special flood hazard area must also purchase and maintain flood insurance for the full insurable value of the property for the life of the loan.

Filing Requirements: These are listed at the beginning of the application. In addition to the financial information required you would normally submit for any loan, your application package must also include the following:

1. A copy of the essential employee's notice of expected call-up to active duty, official call-up orders, or discharge or release papers from active duty status.

2. A statement from the small business owner that the reservist is essential to the day-to-day operations of the business along with a written concurrence by the essential employee.

3. A written explanation and estimate of how the essential employee's activation to military service has or will result in the small business experiencing substantial economic injury.

4. A description of the steps the business is taking to alleviate the substantial economic injury a certification from the small business owner that the essential employee will be offered the same job or similar job upon the employee's return from active duty.

Contact

Contact the Disaster Assistance Customer Service Center at (800) 659-2955 or e-mail at disastercustomerservice@sba.gov for an application.

Completed SBA disaster loan applications may be submitted to:

U. S. Small Business Administration
Processing and Disbursement Center
14925 Kingsport Road
Ft. Worth, TX 76155-2243

If you have questions, contact SBA at 1-800-659-2955 or (TTY) (800) 877-8339

Fisheries Disaster Relief

The Department of Commerce can provide disaster assistance under either Sections 312(a) or 315 of the Magnuson-Stevens Fishery Conservation and Management Act (MSA) (16 U.S.C. § 1861), as amended, or Sections 308(b) or 308(d) of the Interjurisdictional Fisheries Act (IFA) (16 U.S.C. § 4107).

Money

Monies for fisheries disaster relief is appropriated on a case by case basis by the Congress based upon a recommendation of the Department of Commerce. So the better the application and underlying information, the greater the likelihood of getting money from Congress. And the key to this is the "Documented Spending Plan" that says how much money is needed and for what purposes.

Objectives

To deal with commercial fishery failures due to fishery resource disasters. Disaster causes may be (a) natural; (b) man-made (if they are "beyond the control of fisheries managers to mitigate through conservation and management measures"); or (c) undetermined.

The Assistant Administrator for Fisheries, NOAA, must first make the relevant determination. See National Marine Fisheries Service Instruction [31-108-01] May 8, 2007 for the procedures used in making this determination.

This Instruction is located at: http://www.nmfs.noaa.gov/sfa/sf3/disaster_policy2011.pdf

NOTE

Overfishing by itself is not an acceptable cause of a fishery resource disaster under either MSA 312(a) or IFA 308(b), because overfishing is not considered to be beyond the control of fishery managers to mitigate.

Uses and Use Restrictions

Funds can be used for assessing the effects of commercial fishery failures, or restoring fisheries or preventing future failures, and assisting fishing communities affected by the failures. However, the Secretary of Commerce must first determine that the activity will not expand the commercial fishery failure in that fishery or into other fisheries or other geographical regions.

How the Process Begins

This process typically begins when the governor of the affected state or a representative of the affected fishing community (i.e. mayor, city manager, county executive, etc.) makes a request to the Secretary of Commerce. The Secretary or Assistant Administrator may also initiate a review at their own discretion.

Applicant Eligibility

Eligible applicants are agencies of State governments or fishing communities for programs to provide assistance to fishing communities (including fishing vessel owners, operators, and crew and United States fish processors that are based in such community).

Beneficiary Eligibility

This program directly benefits fishing communities (including fishing vessel owners, operators, crew, and U.S. fish processors based in such communities) that are adversely affected by commercial fishery failures due to a fishery resource disaster.

Credentials/Documentation

Applicants are required to satisfy all Department of Commerce, National Oceanic and Atmospheric Administration (DOC/NOAA) standards and regulations, including routine and special terms and conditions, for financial assistance programs application and conduct. Costs will be determined in accordance with OMB Circular No. A-87 for State and local governments.

Application Procedure

Submission of an application on Standard Form 424, including all required certifications, to the appropriate National Marine Fisheries Service (NMFS) regional administrator, science and research director, or office director. This program is subject to the provisions of 15 CFR Part 24 (Uniform Administrative Requirements for Grants and Cooperative Agreements to State and Local Governments). Other programs may be developed to provide assistance to universities, nonprofit, or individuals and are subject to the provisions of 15 CFR Part 14, Institutions of Higher Education and

Other Nonprofit Organizations. NOAA reserves the right to withhold the awarding of a grant or cooperative agreement to any individual or organization delinquent on a debt to the Federal government until payment is made or satisfactory arrangements are made with the agency to whom the debt is owed.

Criteria for Selecting Proposals

Proposals may be selected from several sources, e.g., unsolicited and solicited proposals, Congressionally-mandated projects, and applications received as a result of notices published in the Federal Register. All proposals must undergo rigorous technical and merit review. Recipients, subrecipients and their proposals are subject to all applicable Federal laws and Federal and departmental policies, regulations, and procedures applicable to Federal financial assistance awards.

Only One Positive Determination per Disaster

Once a positive determination of a fisheries disaster has been made no other determination may be made in any subsequent year based on the same fishery resource disaster. In order to make a new determination in a fishery for which an earlier positive determination was made, there must be a new triggering event based on a fishery resource disaster arising from new data that evidences an appreciable change in the fishery resource. Additionally, there must be a showing of new disaster incurred based on the average revenues during the immediately preceding 5-year period.

Award Procedure

Proposals are initially evaluated by the pertinent National Marine Fisheries Service (NMFS) office, region science center, or their component laboratories, and are subject to review for technical merit, soundness of design, competency of the applicant to perform the proposed work, potential contribution of the project to national or regional goals, and appropriateness and reasonableness of proposed costs. Projects recommended for funding will be submitted to the NOAA Grants Management Division for review and approval.

Deadlines

Project applications must be received by the receiving NMFS office at least 120 days before the requested start date of the project.

NOTE

Approval time is expected to range from 90 to 120 days, which includes processing of the award through the NMFS and DOC financial assistance procedures.

Formula and Matching Requirements

The Federal share of any activity under this program must not exceed 75 percent of the total costs of the activity. The minimum 25 percent contribution from the recipient may be as cash or in-kind contributions.

Length and Time Phasing of Assistance

Varies. Award funds must be spent in the indicated budget period and are expended in accordance with OMB Cost Principles and DOC financial and reporting procedures. Funds are released in advance or by reimbursement, as agreed to in the Standard Terms and Conditions document required for each grant.

Reports

Reports are due in accordance with the terms and conditions of the award. The Department's financial assistance standard terms and conditions generally require that financial and performance reports be submitted on a semi-annual basis.

Audits

Audits are required at lease biennially by DOC Office of the Inspector General auditors, or an independent public accountant, and are subject to the Audit Act of 1984, 312 U.S.C. 7501-7507. Recipients that are subject to the provisions of OMB Circular No. A-133

Records

All financial and programmatic records, supporting documents, statistical reports, and other records of grantees or subgrantees are required to be maintained by the terms of the agreement. The grantee must retain records for 3 years from the date when the final financial status report is submitted unless otherwise directed by DOC/NOAA pursuant to the exception or 15 CFR Part 24, as applicable.

Regulations, Guidelines and Literature

Grants administration will be in accordance with provisions of 15 CFR Part 24 for State and Local Governments. For other projects developed to provide assistance to universities, nonprofits, and individuals, grants administration will be in accordance with 15 CFR Part 14 and costs will be determined in accordance with OMB Circular No. A-21 for Institutions of Higher Education, Circular No. A-122 for Nonprofit Organizations, and for Commercial Organizations 48 CFR Part 31.

Range and Average of Financial Assistance

$343,500 to $7,000,000. Average: $2,781,167.

NOAA Regional or Local Office Contacts

Alaska: Alaska Regional Office, NMFS, P.O. Box 21668, Juneau, AK 99802-1668. Telephone: (907) 586-7280, Fax: (907) 586-7255. Use the same numbers for FTS. Email: peter.d.jones@noaa.gov.

Northeast: Director, State, Federal, and Constituent Programs Office, National Marine Fisheries Service; Northeast Regional Office, One Blackburn Drive, Gloucester, MA 01930-2298. Telephone: (978)281-9243. Fax: (978) 281-9117. Email: Grants.Information@noaa.gov.

Northwest: Northwest Regional Office, NMFS, Sustainable Fisheries Division, 7600 Sand Point Way NE, Seattle, WA 98115. Telephone: (206) 526-6113. Fax: (206) 526- 4461.

Southeast: State/Federal Liaison Staff, Southeast Regional Office, 9721 Executive Center Drive, North, St. Petersburg, FL 33702-2432. Telephone: (727) 570-5324. Fax: (727) 570-5364..

Southwest: Federal Program Officer, Southwest Regional Office, 501 W. Ocean Blvd., Long Beach, CA 90802-4213. Telephone: (562) 980- 4033. Fax: (562) 980-4047.

NOAA Headquarters Office Contacts

Financial Services Division (F/SF2), National Marine Fisheries Service, 1315 East-West Highway, Silver Spring, MD 20910. Telephone: (301) 713-2358. Fax: (301) 713- 1939.

How It all Really Works

Initiating a request for a fishery resource disaster

The Secretary of Commerce (actually the National Marine Fisheries Service [NMFS]) accepts requests for fisheries disaster assistance under from the Governor of an affected state, or an elected or politically appointed representative of the affected fishing community (i.e., mayor, city manager, or county executive).

Generally speaking, these requests are usually only several pages in length. Once a request is received it is forwarded to the National Marine Fisheries Service Regional Office that has responsibility for that geographic area.

The Regional Office then works with the state agency that has jurisdiction over the fishery of concern and Regional Fishery Management Council or interstate fishery commission to gather all the necessary data. The requester is encouraged to contact the appropriate NMFS regional office informally for assistance in identifying materials that would assist in the evaluation before submitting the initiation letter.

Necessary Information

The information that is necessary for the NMFS to make a determination and request to Congress for an appropriation to cover the disaster is:

1. A clear definition of the fishery, **including identification of all fish stocks** and whether it includes non-Federal fisheries as well as Federal fisheries, and the geographical boundaries of the fishery for which the request is being made;

2. The rationale and supporting documentation, including:

    i. Characteristics of the fishery which is the subject of the request and other related fisheries that participants also fish in (size and value; number of participants; seasonal and other environmental limitations; socio-economic data; landings data; and market conditions);

    ii. Decline in landings, economic impact, revenues, or net revenues by vessel category, port, etc. (this should represent the proportion of the affected fishery resource compared to the commercial fishery as a whole, not just for the affected fishery resource);

    iii. Number of participants involved by vessel category, port, etc.;

    iv. Length of time the resource (or access to it) has been or will be restricted;

    v. Documented decline in the stock(s);

    vi. In the case of a fishery disaster request for a fishery that has been subject to overfishing during the 5-year period immediately preceding the claimed disaster, it will be presumed that overfishing or inadequate harvest controls was the cause of the claimed disaster unless the requester provides:

    A. Information that demonstrates that overfishing did not cause the disaster if the stock(s) was subject to overfishing during the 5-year period immediately preceding the claimed disaster; and

    B. Information that demonstrates that adequate harvest controls were in place during the 5-year period immediately preceding the claimed disaster if the disaster was claimed to be caused by undetermined causes.

    vii. Documented spending plan which describes the activities that could be used to mitigate adverse impacts if a commercial fishery failure due to a fishery resource disaster were determined; and

    viii. A comprehensive economic and socio-economic evaluation of the affected region's fisheries, including economic losses to coastal and fishing communities, if the request is for a catastrophic regional fishery disaster.

3. The amount of financial assistance needed to alleviate the claimed commercial fishery failure or the serious disruption affecting future production, or harm incurred, including which groups of fishery participants would be eligible to receive assistance.

4. Overfishing or inadequate harvest controls will be presumed to be the cause of the claimed disaster unless the requester demonstrates otherwise.

5. The requester may submit any additional information he or she believes relevant to an evaluation of the request.

6. *If the request fails to meet any one of the appropriate three prongs required to make a determination, the request will be denied.*

The Three Prong Test

1. *There was a fishery resource disaster within the meaning of the law;*

2. *The cause for the disaster must have been (a) natural; (b) man-made (if they are "beyond the control of fisheries managers to mitigate through conservation and management measures"); or (c) undetermined, and*

3. *The harm incurred was a direct result of the fishery resource disaster*

4. Any new request from the applicant for disaster assistance in the same fishery for which a positive determination has previously been made must include an explanation of a new triggering event based on new data that evidences an appreciable change in the fishery resource, and the economic conditions of the commercial fishery showing new harm.

5. Any vessel-specific fishery information submitted to the Secretary with a request for a Magnuson-Stevens section 312(a) or 315 determination would be subject to the confidentiality provisions and limitations of section 402(b) of the Magnuson-Stevens Act and regulations in 50 CFR 600 subpart E. Information submitted with a request for an Interjurisdictional Fisheries Act section 308(b) or 308(d) determination will be protected to the extent permitted by statute.

Local Government

Government

"After any major disaster strikes, you should expect to be dealing with FEMA for anywhere from five to seven years before the incident is closed. FEMA staff that you will be working with will change. FEMA rules will change. Items that have been approved at one level will be denied at another level. The only protection you have is to document everything that is humanly possible to document."[74]

Cash

The tendency is to spend whatever it takes to protect your community and respond to a disaster. This generally means that a municipality obligates itself for response costs and then attempts to pay them out of general funds, or with loans, and seek FEMA reimbursement. Obtaining FEMA reimbursement is an art in itself. Experience has shown that the initial FEMA response is very positive "yes do it, it is a covered expense". Then later when the auditors show up the statement becomes "nope, not covered". Where to turn to find out what is, and is not, reimbursed by FEMA becomes a critical activity.

First Thing to Do

The first thing is to take care of the municipality's own assets because you have to take care of your municipality, and you can't do that without structures, equipment, manpower and money.

The key federal statute governing FEMA's requirements is known as the STAFFORD ACT. If you do not know the Stafford Act and its regulations intimately, the your municipality will lose eligible reimbursements. The key to reimbursement is to have a staff member, or someone you can hire, who has the requisite degree of knowledge regarding the Stafford Act.

FEMA

Basically, FEMA requires that a municipal or non-profit applicant apply with *30 days* of the Presidential declaration of a disaster by filing a *FEMA Form 90-49* with their State Public Assistance Officer. This filing gets the process started and allows, in certain cases, for immediate funds to be distributed to the impacted municipality or non-profit. FEMA has an "Applicant Handbook" for Municipalities and non-profit organizations which can be found at: http://www.fema.gov/pdf/government/grant/pa/apphndbk.pdf

After a presidential declaration has been made, FEMA will designate the area eligible for assistance and announce the types of assistance avail-

---

[74] Harrington, Ed; 01 December 2007; Government Finance Review 28; ISSN: 0883-7856; Volume 23; Issue 6; Copyright 2007 Gale Group Inc.

able. FEMA provides supplemental assistance for State and local government recovery expenses, and the Federal share will always be *at least 75 percent of the eligible costs*. Please don't forget that little phrase, "eligible costs" which means that not all costs will be reimbursed.

A FEMA/State team will usually visit local applicants and view their damage first hand to assess the scope of damage and estimate repair costs. A Preliminary Damage Assessment (PDA) is the process used to determine the magnitude and impact of the State's damage.

During the PDA, *immediate needs are noted* for each area surveyed. During this PDA the municipality or non-profit officials should point out the immediate needs for disaster response. state may institute Immediate Needs Funding (INF) on the municipality's or non-profit's behalf. Up to 50% of the Federal share estimate of emergency monies will then be placed in the State's account.

If the State thinks damage costs warrant the need for immediate cash flow, this money can be made available in advance of normal procedures once a disaster has been declared.

Immediate Needs Funding (INF) is money earmarked for the most urgent work in the initial aftermath of a disaster that must be performed immediately, and paid for within the first 60 days following declaration. Eligible work typically includes debris removal, emergency protective measures, and removal of health and safety hazards. Immediate needs funds can be used for expenses resulting from this eligible work, such as temporary labor costs, overtime payroll, equipment, and material fees.

INF is usually based on a percentage of the emergency work identified during the PDA for eligible emergency work that requires payment within the first 60 days following declaration. Any INF funds will be offset against the costs of actual emergency work projects as they are received.

A. Public Assistance: Local, State, Tribal and Non-Profit[75]

Through the PA Program, FEMA provides supplemental Federal disaster grant assistance for debris removal, emergency protective measures, and the repair, replacement, or restoration of disaster-damaged, publicly owned facilities and the facilities of certain Private Non-Profit (PNP) organizations.

The PA Program also encourages protection of these damaged facilities from future events by providing assistance for hazard mitigation measures during the recovery process.

The Federal share of assistance is not less than 75% of the eligible cost for emergency measures and permanent restoration. The grantee (usually the State) determines how the non-Federal share (up to 25%) is split with the subgrantees (eligible applicants).

The funding process consists of the following steps:

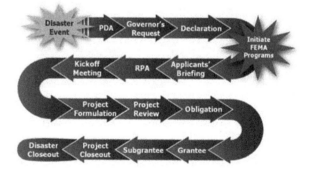

---

[75] https://www.fema.gov/public-assistance-local-state-tribal-and-non-profit

Eligibility

The Public Assistance (PA) Program is based on statutes, regulations and policies. The Robert T. Stafford Disaster Relief and Emergency Assistance Act (Stafford Act) is the underlying document that authorizes the program. Regulations published in Title 44 of the Code of Federal Regulations (44 CFR) Part 206 implement the statute. Policies are written to apply the statute and regulations to specific situations and provide clarification on a range of issues. These authorities govern the eligibility criteria through which FEMA provides funds for public assistance.

These criteria have the following four components:

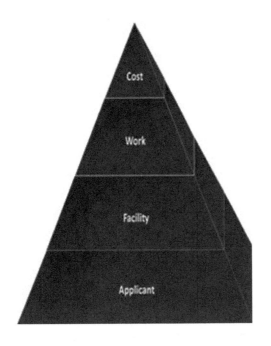

The diagram above refers to the four building blocks of eligibility. Using guidelines, FEMA determines if the various components are eligible for disaster assistance. The applicant is the basis for eligibility. The applicant must be eligible for the facility to be eligible. The facility must be eligible for the work to be eligible. The work must be eligible for the cost to be eligible.

Eligible Applicants

There are four types of eligible applicants for public assistance. If an entity meets the requirements of one of the types, the Applicant may be eligible to receive Federal disaster assistance.

1. **State Government Agencies**

2. **Local Governments and Special Districts**
   Any county, city, village, town, district, or other political subdivision of any State and includes any rural community, unincorporated town or village, or other public entity for which an application for assistance is made by a State or political subdivision thereof.

   Other State and local political subdivisions may be eligible if they are formed in accordance with State law as a separate entity and have taxing authority. These include, but are not limited to, school districts, irrigation districts, fire districts, and utility districts.

3. **Private Non-Profit Organizations**
   Private Nonprofit organizations or institutions that own or operate facilities that are open to the general public and that provide certain services otherwise performed by a government agency. These services include:

   - *Education*
     Colleges and universities
     Parochial and other private schools

   - *Utility*
     Systems of energy, communication, water supply, sewage collection and treatment, or other similar public service facilities.

   - *Emergency*
     Fire protection, ambulance, rescue, and similar emergency services.

- *Medical*
  Hospital, outpatient facility, rehabilitation facility, or facility for long-term care for mental or physical injury or disease.

- *Custodial Care*
  Homes for the elderly and similar facilities that provide institutional care for persons who require close supervision, but do not require day-to-day medical care.

- *Other Essential Governmental Services*
  Museums, zoos, community centers, libraries, homeless shelters, senior citizen centers, rehabilitation facilities, shelter workshops and facilities that provide health and safety services of a governmental nature. Health and safety services are essential services that are commonly provided by all local governments and directly affect the health and safety of individuals. Low-income housing, alcohol and drug rehabilitation, programs for battered spouses, transportation to medical facilities, and food programs are examples of health services.

4. **Federally recognized Native American Indian Tribes, Alaskan Native Tribal Governments, Alaskan Native village organizations or authorized tribal organizations and Alaskan Native village organizations.** This *does not* include Alaska Native Corporations, which are owned by private individuals.

Eligible Facilities

An eligible facility is any building, works, system, or equipment that is built or manufactured, or any improved and maintained natural feature that is owned by an eligible public or private nonprofit (PNP) applicant with certain exceptions.

To be eligible a facility must:

- Be the responsibility of an eligible applicant.
- Be located in a designated disaster area.
- Not be under the specific authority of another Federal agency.
- Be in active use at the time of the disaster.

Examples of eligible public facilities include:

- Roads (non-Federal aid)
- Sewage Treatment Plants
- Airports
- Irrigation Channels
- Schools
- Buildings
- Bridges and Culverts
- Utilities

Eligible private non-profit facilities include:

- Educational facilities (classrooms, supplies, and equipment)
- Gas, Water, and Power systems
- Emergency facilities (fire stations and rescue squads)
- Medical facilities (hospitals and outpatient centers)
- Custodial care facilities
- Other Essential government services (to be eligible these PNP facilities must be open to the general public)

Restrictions

1. *Alternative use facilities*
   If a facility was being used for purposes other than those for which it was designed, restoration will only be eligible to the extent necessary to restore the immediate pre-disaster alternative purpose.

2. *Inactive facilities*

Facilities that were not in active use at the time of the disaster are not eligible except in those instances where the facilities were only temporarily inoperative for repairs or remodeling, or where active use by the applicant was firmly established in an approved budget, or where the owner can demonstrate to FEMA's satisfaction an intent to begin use within a reasonable time.

Eligible Work

To be eligible for funding, disaster recovery work performed on an eligible facility must:

- Be required as the result of a major disaster event,
- Be located within a designated disaster area, and
- Be the legal responsibility of an eligible applicant.

Other federal agency (OFA) programs

FEMA will not provide assistance when another Federal agency has specific authority to restore or repair facilities damaged by a major disaster.

Negligence

No assistance will be provided to an applicant for damages caused by its own negligence through failure to take reasonable protective measures. If negligence by another party results in damages, assistance may be provided on the condition that the applicant agrees to cooperate with FEMA in all efforts to recover the cost of such assistance from the negligent party.

Special considerations requirements

Necessary assurances shall be provided to document compliance with special requirements including, but not limited to, floodplain management, environmental assessments, hazard mitigation, protection of wetlands, and insurance.

Categories of Work

Emergency Work

Category A: Debris Removal

Clearance of trees and woody debris; certain building wreckage; damaged/ destroyed building contents; sand, mud, silt, and gravel; vehicles; and other disaster-related material deposited on public and, in very limited cases, private property.

Category B: Emergency Protective Measures

Measures taken before, during, and after a disaster to eliminate/reduce an immediate threat to life, public health, or safety, or to eliminate/reduce an immediate threat of significant damage to improved public and private property through cost-effective measures.

Permanent Work

Category C: Roads and Bridges

Repair of roads, bridges, and associated features, such as shoulders, ditches, culverts, lighting, and signs.

Category D: Water Control Facilities

Repair of drainage channels, pumping facilities, and some irrigation facilities. Repair of levees, dams, and flood control channels fall under Category D, but the eligibility of these facilities is restricted.

Category E: Buildings and Equipment

Repair or replacement of buildings, including their contents and systems; heavy equipment; and vehicles.

Category F: Utilities

Repair of water treatment and delivery systems; power generation facilities and distribution facilities; sewage collection and treatment facilities; and communications.

Category G: Parks, Recreational Facilities, and Other Facilities

Repair and restoration of parks, playgrounds, pools, cemeteries, mass transit facilities, and beaches. This category also is used for any work or facility that cannot be characterized adequately by Categories A-F.

Eligible Costs

Generally, costs that can be directly tied to the performance of eligible work are eligible. Such costs must be reasonable and necessary to accomplish the work; Compliant with Federal, State, and local requirements for procurement; and Reduced by all applicable credits, such as insurance proceeds and salvage values.

A cost is reasonable if, in its nature and amount, it does not exceed that which would be incurred by a prudent person under the circumstances prevailing at the time the decision was made to incur the cost. In other words, a reasonable cost is a cost that is both fair and equitable for the type of work being performed.

For example: If the going rental rate for a backhoe is $25/hour, it would not be reasonable to charge $75/hour for a backhoe. Determining reasonableness is particularly important when Federal funds are involved. Considerations should be given to whether the cost is of a type generally recognized as ordinary and necessary for the subject facility and type of work and whether the individuals concerned acted with prudence in conducting work. In addition, normal procedures must not be altered because of the potential for reimbursement from Federal funds.

Reasonable costs can be established through

- The use of historical documentation for similar work;
- Average costs for similar work in the area;
- Published unit costs from national cost estimating databases; and
- FEMA cost codes. In performing work, applicants must adhere to Federal, State, and local procurement requirements. An applicant may not receive funding from two Federal sources to repair disaster damage this is considered a duplication of benefits. Such a duplication of benefits is prohibited by the Stafford Act. A State disaster assistance program is not considered a duplication of Federal funding. Insurance proceeds, donated grants from banks, private organizations, trust funds, and contingency funds must be evaluated individually to determine whether they constitute a duplication of benefits.

The eligible cost criteria referenced above apply to all direct costs, including labor, materials, equipment, and contracts awarded for the performance of eligible work.

Debris Removal

Debris removal is the clearance, removal, and/or disposal of items such as trees, sand, gravel, building components, wreckage, vehicles, and personal property.

James L. Jaffe, J.D.

Debris removal can be as much as 15%-50% of the total disaster response costs. To get federal reimbursement for you must follow a lengthy, complex and sometimes convoluted set of rules.

The FEMA Debris Management Guide, FEMA P-325, covers all the major aspects of debris removal that must be followed. The guide is 149 pages long plus 92 pages of appendices and can be downloaded from the FEMA web site at: http://www.fema.gov/pdf/government/grant/pa/demagde.pdf

FEMA also has a Debris Contracting Guide Fact Sheet to assist in the contracting portion of debris removal. This Fact Sheet can be downloaded from the FEMA web site at: http://www.fema.gov/pdf/government/grant/pa/9580_201.pdf

The Department of Homeland Security (DHS) Office of Inspector General (OIG) prepared a report on debris removal after auditing FEMA's Oversight and management of Debris Removal Operations[76]. This report, which is an easy read, is a "must read" for any community confronted with debris removal as the result of a presidentially declared disaster.

Decisions made in the first few days after a disaster are critical in determining the success of a debris removal operation. FEMA regulations allow for reimbursement of less restrictive time and materials procedures during the first 70 working hours after a disaster after which some other method must be used.

For debris removal to be eligible for federal reimbursement, the work must be necessary to:

Eliminate an immediate threat to lives, public health and safety.

Eliminate immediate threats of significant damage to improved public or Private property.

Ensure the economic recovery of the affected community to the benefit of the community-at large.

Mitigate the risk to life and property by removing substantially damaged structures and associated appurtenances as needed to convert property acquired through a FEMA hazard mitigation program to uses compatible with open space, recreation, or wetlands management practices.

Examples of *eligible debris removal* activities include:

- Debris removal from a street or highway to allow the safe passage of emergency vehicles; and

- Debris removal from public property to eliminate health and safety hazards.

Examples of *ineligible debris removal* activities include:

- Removal of debris, such as tree limbs and trunks, from natural (unimproved) wilderness areas.

- Removal of pre-disaster sediment from engineered channels.

- Removal of debris from a natural channel unless the debris poses an immediate threat of flooding to improved property.

---

[76] Department of Homeland Security Office of Inspector General FEMA's Oversight and Management of Debris Removal Operations. OIG-11-40, February 2011. http://www.oig.dhs.gov/assets/Mgmt/OIG_11-40_Feb11.pdf

Private Property Debris Removal

Debris removal from private property is generally not eligible because it is the responsibility of the individual property owner.

If property owners move the disaster-related debris to a public right-of-way, the local government may be reimbursed for curb side pickup and disposal for a limited period of time.

If the debris on private business and residential property is so widespread that public health, safety, or the economic recovery of the community is threatened, FEMA may fund debris removal from private property, *but it must be approved in advance by FEMA.*

FEMA Public Assistance Grant Funding for Debris Removal

Public Assistance applicants can use force account resources or contractors to monitor debris removal operations, or a combination of both.

Regardless of the method, the applicant is responsible for ensuring that applicant-managed debris removal work (either force account or contract) being funded through Public Assistance grants is eligible in accordance with Public Assistance guidelines.

Costs Must Be Reasonable

To be eligible for reimbursement, a cost incurred must be reasonable in amount.

A reasonable cost is defined by the Office of Management and Budget (OMB) Circular A-87, *Cost Principles for State, Local, and Indian Tribal Governments* and Circular A-122, *Cost Principles for Non-Profit Organizations,* as a cost which in its nature and amount does not exceed that which would be incurred by a prudent person under the circumstance prevailing at the time the decision was made to incur the cost.

Considerations include evaluating historical costs for similar work, analyzing costs for similar work in the region, reviewing published unit cost data for the work, or comparing costs with the FEMA Schedule of Equipment Rates and Cost Codes.

The source of costs may include: the applicant's force account labor, equipment, and materials; contracted services; and mutual aid agreements.

Applicant Resources

Eligible work accomplished with an applicant's own labor, equipment, and materials may be funded under the Public Assistance Program. An applicant's employees' labor and an applicant's equipment are called force account labor and force account equipment, respectively.

Reimbursement for the use of force account equipment is limited to the time the equipment is actually in use. Standby and idle time are not eligible for Public Assistance grant funding.

Reimbursement is based either on the local rates or the FEMA Schedule of Equipment Rates, whichever is less. If the local rate is lower and the applicant certifies that the local rate does not reflect the actual cost, the FEMA Schedule of Equipment Rates may be used.

It is important for the applicant's staff to document hours worked and equipment used to complete the eligible work.

Mutual Aid Agreements

FEMA will reimburse mutual aid costs provided that:

- The assistance is requested by the receiving applicant;

- The work performed is directly related to the disaster and is otherwise eligible for FEMA assistance;

- The entity that received the aid incurred a cost for that aid, i.e. the providing jurisdiction or agency bills the receiving applicant for the service;

- Provision of services under the agreement are not contingent upon declaration of a major disaster or emergency by FEMA; and

- The requesting and providing entities can provide documentation of rates and payment for services.

Documentation

Appendix C, *FEMA Forms* are frequently used to document work completed with force account labor and equipment. The FEMA summary record forms provide the minimum information required for Public Assistance grant reimbursement consideration.

These summary record forms are not required forms; the applicant may use its own forms or accounting summary, or alter the FEMA forms to fit its needs, as long as the minimum information required is provided.

Duplication of Benefits

In accordance with Section 312 of the Stafford Act, no applicant will receive assistance for any loss for which financial assistance has been received under any other program or from insurance or from any other source.

Therefore, the use of Federal or State funds, insurance settlements, and other grants or cash donations granted for the same purpose constitutes a duplication of benefits.

If another Federal agency has the authority to provide an applicant with assistance for debris removal operations, FEMA cannot provide funds for that project. Applicants should pursue funding assistance offered through those agencies.

The following agencies may provide assistance to applicants for certain debris removal activities.

- Federal Highway Administration (FHWA),
- United States Army Corps of Engineers (USACE),
- National Resources Conservation Service (NRCS),
- Environmental Protection Agency (EPA),
- Department of Housing and Urban Development (HUD), and
- United States Coast Guard (USCG)

Applicants must become aware of the agencies' roles, responsibilities, and jurisdictions to ensure a duplication of benefits does not occur between other Federal agencies and FEMA.

Descriptions of other Federal agencies and their programs are found in Appendix G, *FEMA RP9580.202, Fact Sheet: Debris Removal - Authorities of Federal Agencies*.

Insurance Settlements

Insurance policies that include coverage for debris removal activities are potentially a duplication of benefits.

The applicant should contact its insurance provider for a statement of loss to determine the amount of insurance settlement related to debris removal.

The insurance settlement is reflected in the Public Assistance grant as a line-item credit against the eligible cost for the project.

Similarly, applicants should be aware that some residents within a declared disaster area may obtain funds for removing debris from their property through their homeowner insurance or under the FEMA Individual Assistance (IA) Program.

If residents receive funds under the IA Program or insurance proceeds for the removal and disposal of debris from their properties, but also place debris at the curbside rights-of-way, the applicant should *make a concerted effort to collect the proportionate cost of the curbside removal from those residents in an effort to comply with Section 312 of the Stafford Act.*

While FEMA understands that this could become an arduous task, applicants can put in place protocols to inform residents that receiving a benefit for the same purpose from the Federal government or any other source is in violation of Federal law.

When applicants receive reimbursements from residents for the cost of curbside collection applicants are required to report the total amount of proceeds collected from those residents to FEMA. The Federal share of the Public Assistance grant is calculated after the reimbursement proceeds are reduced from the total cost of the curbside collection.

Salvage Value

Applicants may choose to recover materials from disaster debris for beneficial uses.

Applicants may sell materials such as metals, woody debris, concrete, masonry, or other types of debris to recyclers, to the construction or agricultural industry, or to energy generators.

Applicants that sell disaster debris for a salvage value must offset the cost of the eligible debris removal work by the revenues received from the sale of the debris.

Applicants must document and report to FEMA the revenues obtained through the sale of debris materials.

Public Assistance grant funding is limited to the Federal share of the difference between the amount of revenue received and the cost of the debris removal.

Applicants that contract for debris removal may allow the contractor to take possession of the recoverable debris materials. This type of agreement must take into account the salvage value, and the applicant should negotiate a credit to reflect this value within the terms of the contract.

The sale of the recoverable disaster debris materials should offset the cost of the contracted services.

Debris Monitoring Roles and Responsibilities

Monitoring debris removal operations requires comprehensive observation and documentation by the Public Assistance applicant of debris removal work performed from the point of debris collection to final disposal.

Monitoring debris removal work involves constant observation of crews to ensure that workers are performing eligible work in accordance with Public Assistance guidelines, and helps to verify compliance with all applicable Federal, State, and local regulations.

A number of different entities play a role in monitoring debris removal operations to ensure that they are efficient, effective and eligible for FEMA Public Assistance funding. It is important that these entities work together to communicate and resolve issues in the field so that reimbursement funding for debris removal operations is not jeopardized.

Below is a table which addresses the general monitoring responsibilities and tasks of different partners in the debris removal operation. The table is followed by specific monitoring responsibilities and duties for both force account and contractor debris monitors in the field.

Entity	Responsibilities	Tasks
Debris Removal Contractor	Conduct debris removal operations per the terms of the contract.	Monitor its own day-to-day operations to ensure its contractual obligations are being met.
Public Assistance Applicant Monitoring Contractor	Works for Applicant to monitor debris contractor's day-to-day operations to ensure the applicants expectations and contractual requirements are being met.	• Provide debris monitoring personnel who are trained in eligibility. • Monitor operations in accordance with the contract requirements. • Provide all monitoring documents as required in the monitoring contract.
Public Assistance Applicant (subgrantee)	Provide oversight and quality assurance of both the debris removal contract and the monitoring contract (if applicable). Request PA funds for eligible work. Ensure performance measures are met and eligible work is documented. Understand eligibility requirements and ensure work performed under the contract meets these requirements.	• Designate project manager. *If debris removal is performed by force account labor:* • Provide documentation to substantiate eligible debris quantities. • Ensure compliance with subgrant requirements. *If debris removal is performed under contract:* • Ensure that debris removal contractors and monitoring contractors (if applicable) understand eligibility requirements for the debris removal operations. • Ensure that only eligible debris quantities are being claimed for Public Assistance. • Resolve issues or discrepancies associated with the contract.

Entity	Responsibilities	Tasks
State (Grantee)	Ensure grant requirements outlined in the 44 CFR are being met and that PA applicants are receiving funds for eligible costs. Responsible for monitoring the grant and subgrant to ensure compliance with Federal, State and local laws and regulations.	• Monitor the grant and subgrant requirements. • Ensure that the applicant is sufficiently monitoring the debris removal operation (FEMA\Grantee effort). • Conduct random monitoring at load sites and disposal sites to ensure compliance with grant requirements (FEMA\Grantee effort). • Notify subgrantee of compliance issues and outline corrective actions (FEMA\Grantee effort).
FEMA	Ensure grant requirements outlined in 44 CFR are being met. Fund eligible work. Responsible for the preparation of large project worksheets, development of the scope of work and the obligation of funds. Responsible for monitoring the grant to ensure compliance with Federal, State and local laws and regulations.	• Develop large project worksheets in coordination with the Grantee and subgrantee. • Utilize monitors to ensure that the applicant is sufficiently monitoring the debris removal operation. (FEMA\Grantee effort) • Conduct random monitoring at load sites and disposal sites to ensure compliance with grant requirements. (FEMA\Grantee effort). • Notify Grantee/subgrantee of compliance issues and outline corrective actions (FEMA\Grantee effort). • Increase or decrease monitoring efforts as necessary to ensure corrective actions are in place and operations are being effectively monitored.

The specific responsibilities and duties of individual debris monitors in the field are the same for both force account and contracted debris monitoring operations. They are:

1. Report issues to their direct supervisor which require action (such as safety concerns, contractor non-compliance and equipment use)
2. Accurately measure and certify truck capacities (recertify on a regular basis)
3. Properly and accurately complete and physically control load tickets (in tower and field)
4. Ensure that trucks are accurately credited for their load
5. Ensure that trucks are not artificially loaded (ex: debris is wetted, debris is fluffed-not compacted)

6. Validate hazardous trees, including hangers, leaners, and stumps
7. Ensure that hazardous wastes are not mixed in loads
8. Ensure that all debris is removed from trucks at Debris Management Sites (DMS)
9. Report if improper equipment is mobilized and used
10. Report if contractor personnel safety standards are not followed
11. Report if general public safety standards are not followed
12. Report if completion schedules are not on target
13. Ensure that only debris specified in the contract is collected (and is identified as eligible or ineligible)
14. Assure that force account labor and/or debris contractor work is within the assigned scope of work
15. Monitor site development and restoration of DMSs
16. Report to supervisor if debris removal work does not comply with all local ordinances as well as State and Federal regulations (i.e., proper disposal of hazardous wastes)
17. Record the types of equipment used (Time & Materials contract)
18. Record the hours equipment was used, include downtime of each piece of equipment by day (Time & Materials contract)

Applicants may request FEMA/State assistance with debris monitoring or monitor training.

Only FEMA has the authority to make eligibility decisions; contractors cannot make eligibility determinations.

Information on eligibility can be found in the Public Assistance Debris Management Guide FEMA 325, the Public Assistance Policy Digest FEMA 321, the Public Assistance Applicant Handbook FEMA 323, and the Public Assistance Guide FEMA 322.

Monitoring Requirements by Type of Contract

Unlike other categories of work eligible or Public Assistance grants, initial debris removal project worksheets typically do not have a defined scope of work, since precise quantities of debris are difficult to attain.

Therefore, unit price contracts which pay by debris volume or weight removed are typically implemented. Unit price contracts require extensive monitoring to determine accurate quantities of eligible debris removed and disposed. As load tickets are compiled and accurate quantities are determined through monitoring, the scope of work for the project worksheet, or version, is established. In some cases, time and materials contracts may be more cost effective and appropriate for the amount and type of eligible work to be performed. For both time and materials and lump sum contracts, debris monitors must still document and quantify eligible debris amounts in order to determine reasonableness of costs.

The table below includes a breakdown of monitoring requirements by contract type.

Type of Contract	Project Worksheet Scope of Work	Subgrantee Monitoring Required Crew Efficiency	Subgrantee Monitoring Required Load site	Subgrantee Monitoring Required DMSs	Subgrantee Monitoring Required Disposal sites	Subgrantee Monitoring Required Fraud	Comments
Lump Sum	Defined debris quantities and reasonable costs. Estimate is basis for contract costs.		√		√		Quantities are still required to determine reasonable costs.
Unit Price - CYs	Based on eligible debris listed on load tickets	√	√	√	√		
Unit Price - Ton	Based on actual weight measurements of eligible debris listed on load tickets.		√		√	√	
Time and Materials	Based on labor, equipment and materials records. Reasonable costs evaluated by determining costs per unit.	√	√		√	√	Typically used for road clearance. If used for debris removal, quantities are still required to determine reasonable costs. Eligible costs are restricted to up to 70 hrs.

Monitoring Contracts

The request for proposal (RFP) for debris monitoring contracts should outline the qualification of debris monitors. The qualifications should be appropriate for the individual responsibilities and duties listed above, and debris monitors should have experience working on construction sites and be familiar with safety regulations.

It is not necessary to have professional engineers and other certified professionals perform these duties.

Debris monitors primarily should have the ability to estimate debris quantities, differentiate between debris types, properly fill out load tickets, and follow all site safety procedures.

The RFP should also outline possible locations to be monitored and reporting requirements to document eligible debris quantities.

Monitoring contracts are typically time and materials and must contain a *not-to exceed* clause per the requirements of Part 13 of 44 CFR.

The subgrantee should ensure the level of monitoring and overhead claimed is commensurate with the level of effort required to effectively monitor the debris removal and monitoring operation.

In addition to the costs for the monitors, the subgrantee can claim as part of its monitoring project worksheet reasonable costs for the debris monitoring contractor to provide training, oversight, and data compilation as required by the terms of the contract. Architectural and engineering service overhead should not be claimed. Additional information on costs that are eligible can be found in the *Public Assistance Debris Management Guide FEMA 325*.

The monitoring contractor costs associated with compiling data to verify costs invoiced by the debris removal contractor can be an eligible expense. Costs associated with attending meetings with FEMA and/or the Grantee and compiling documentation for the production of project worksheets are funded through the administrative allowance as stated in 44 CFR, Part 206.228 and cannot be a direct charge to a Public Assistance grant.

Reporting Requirements & Performance Measures

If FEMA is providing grant assistance for the applicant's monitoring contract, a sample of the reporting requirements outlined in the contract will be required to substantiate the eligible costs.

This sample must be adequate to demonstrate that sufficient measures were taken to ensure eligibility and accurate quantities are being reported as part of the grant.

Applicants should require debris monitors to submit daily reports on load quantities, debris management site operations, and operational and safety issues in the field. Regular reporting helps to promote quality assurance and provides the applicant with a consistent accounting of operations in the field.

If a time and materials monitoring contract is used, the contractor will have to supply labor, equipment and material records to the subgrantee in order to substantiate the actual costs in the project worksheet.

Continuous monitoring of all activities of a debris contractor can help promote efficiency and effectiveness in the debris removal operation. In evaluating a contractor's performance, primary interest is in the progress toward completion of the services called for and the financial status of the contract. It is important that the contract provide for submission of reports and payment estimates to aid in evaluating the contractor's progress.

Applicant debris monitoring responsibilities may include tracking performance measures used to assess the progress of debris removal operations in the field. Specific debris contract performance measures may include:

- Percentage completion tracking
- Adherence to contract time schedules
- Adherence to contract cost schedules

Contract Procurement Requirements

To be eligible for reimbursement under the Public Assistance Program, contracts for debris monitoring must meet rules for Federal grants, as provided for in 44 CFR Part 13.36 Procurement (http://www.access.gpo.gov/nara/cfr/waisidx_04/44cfr13_04.html).

Public Assistance applicants should comply with their own procurement procedures in accordance with applicable State and local laws and regulations, provided that they conform to applicable Federal laws and standards identified in Part 13.

Local Governments Reimbursement Program for Hazardous Substance Releases[77]

In the event of a release (or threatened release) of hazardous substances, EPA may reimburse local governments for expenses related to the release and associated emergency response measures. The Local Governments Reimbursement (LGR) Program provides a "safety net" of up to $25,000 per incident to local governments that do not have funds available to pay for response actions.

To be eligible for the Local Governments Reimbursement (LGR) program, your local government must meet the following requirements:

Determining Your Eligibility

The applicant must be a general purpose unit of local government

Local governments that are eligible to receive reimbursement under the LGR program include any general purpose unit of local government, such as a county, parish, city, town, township, and municipality. Federally-recognized Indian Tribes are also eligible for reimbursement under the LGR program.

States are not eligible for reimbursement under the Local Governments Reimbursement program

States may not request reimbursement on the behalf of a local government or a federally-recognized Indian Tribe within the state.

The applicant must have legal jurisdiction over the site where the incident occurred

Only one request for reimbursement will be accepted for each eligible incident. When more than one local government has participated in such a response, the local government that has legal jurisdiction over the site where the incident occurred must submit the application. The application can be made on behalf of all participating local governments. If multiple local governments or agencies have jurisdiction over the site, then the respondents must decide which single government or agency will submit the reimbursement request.

Reimbursement cannot be made to a responsible party

If the local government applying for reimbursement is also the responsible party, the application will be denied. Responsible parties are liable for response cost regardless of whether or not they are a local government.

Substances released or threatened to be released must be designated as hazardous under the Comprehensive Environmental Response, Compensation, and Liability Act (CERCLA)

Incidents involving petroleum products including petroleum, natural gas, crude oil, or any other specified fractions thereof that are not specifically designated as CERCLA hazardous substances do

---
[77] http://www.epa.gov/oem/content/lgr/

not qualify under this program. Some mixed waste may be allowable. Under CERCLA, potentially responsible parties are liable for cleanup costs. Under the LGR program, if a local government is the responsible party, they would not be eligible for reimbursement.

Requirements for Reimbursement

Once a local government has decided to apply for reimbursement, there are a number of basic requirements that must be met to comply with the regulations of the Local Governments Reimbursement (LGR) program. When completing the LGR application, local governments should pay special attention to the following requirements to facilitate the reimbursement process:

Reimbursement cannot supplant local funds normally provided for a response.

In other words, if a local government budgets for emergency response activities, it must draw from this budget to pay for the cost of a response. However, if a local government's funds have been depleted, then it may be eligible for reimbursement under EPA's LGR program. In addition, other items that may not be budgeted for (e.g., overtime pay, unanticipated materials and supplies) may also be reimbursable under the LGR program.

Cost recovery must be pursued prior to applying for reimbursement.

The applicant must complete the Cost Recovery Summary Table, included in the application, to document the background and current status of cost recovery efforts. It should be clear that all available sources of cost recovery (i.e., responsible parties and their insurance, the state, and local government insurance) have been pursued. Although not required, it is recommended that a copy of all related correspondence also be included in the application to document the applicant's cost recovery efforts. Potential cost recovery sources should be given a minimum of 60 days to respond before an LGR application is filed. By signing on the last page of the application, a local government is certifying that cost recovery was pursued.

Detailed cost documentation must be submitted with the application.

The applicant must complete the detailed Cost Breakdown Table, included in the application. All costs for which reimbursement is being requested must be listed and supporting documentation (e.g., invoices, sales receipts, time sheets, or rental agreements) must be attached. (Please note: Costs incurred for long-term remedial measures do not qualify under the LGR program. Reimbursement is made only for temporary emergency measures conducted in response to hazardous substance releases, or threatened releases).

The application must be signed by the local government's highest ranking official.

Examples of the highest ranking official include: Mayor, City Manager, Board of Commissioners Chair, County Judge, or head of a federally recognized Indian Tribe. In instances where the highest ranking local official is unable to sign the application form, a letter of delegation along with the application that authorizes a delegate to sign the application on his or her behalf, must be submitted.

Applications must be submitted to EPA within one year of the "date of response completion" of the response.

For the LGR program, the date of completion is the date when all field work has been completed and all project deliverables (e.g., lab results, technical expert reports, or invoices) have been received by the local government. (The date of completion is not determined by cost recovery efforts, which can continue after an application for reimbursement is submitted.) In general, a local government should allow at least 60 days for each potential source of reimbursement to respond to a request for repayment before submitting an application to LGR. EPA will consider late applications on a case-by-case basis.

The Application Package (with forms and line-by-line instructions) for Reimbursement to Local Governments can be found at:

http://www2.epa.gov/sites/production/files/documents/application_package_for_local_government_reimbursement.pdf

USDA Emergency Watershed Protection Program[78]

Through the Emergency Watershed Protection (EWP) program, the U.S. Department of Agriculture's Natural Resources Conservation Service (NRCS) can help communities address watershed impairments that pose imminent threats to lives and property. If your land has suffered damage due to flood, fire, drought, windstorm, or other natural occurrence, please contact your local authorities and/or your local NRCS office to find out if you qualify for the EWP program.

City and county governments, flood and water control districts, and soil and water conservation districts are the most common sponsors of EWP projects. Contact them directly to see if they are aware of the program or have contacted NRCS for help. More information is available from NRCS offices throughout the United States and the Caribbean and Pacific Basin Areas.

The Facts – The Emergency Watershed Protection Program

Congress established the EWP program and provides funding for it. Please know that eligibility for the program does not depend upon the declaration of a national emergency. All projects undertaken through EWP, with the exception of the purchase of floodplain easements, must have a project sponsor. Sponsors must be a legal subdivision of the State, such as a city, county, general improvement district, or conservation district, or an Indian Tribe or Tribal organization as defined in Section 4 of the Self-Determination and Education Assistance Act. Sponsors are responsible for:

- Providing land rights to do repair work;
- Securing necessary permits;
- Furnishing the local cost share;
- Accomplishing the installation of work; and
- Performing any necessary operation and maintenance.

Through EWP, the NRCS may pay up to 75 percent of the construction costs of emergency measures. Ninety percent may be paid for projects within limited-resource areas as identified by U.S. Census data. The remaining costs must come from local sources and can be made in cash or in-kind services.

All EWP projects must reduce threats to lives and property; be economically, environmentally, and socially defensible; be designed and implemented according to sound technical standards; and conserve natural resources.

Type of Work Authorized

As mentioned above, the EWP program addresses watershed impairments, which include, but are not limited to:

---

[78] http://www.nrcs.usda.gov/Internet/FSE_DOCUMENTS/stelprdb1045263.pdf

- Debris-clogged stream channels;
- Undermined and unstable stream banks;
- Jeopardized water control structures and public infrastructures;
- Wind-borne debris removal; and

• Damaged upland sites stripped of protective vegetation by fire or drought. Floodplain easements for restoring, protecting, maintaining, and enhancing the functions and values of floodplains, including associated wetlands and riparian areas, are available through EWP. These easements also help conserve fish and wildlife habitat, water quality, flood water retention, and ground water recharge, as well as safeguard lives and property from floods, drought, and erosion. EWP work is not limited to any one set of measures.

NRCS completes a Damage Survey Report that provides a case-by-case investigation of the work necessary to repair or protect a site. NRCS will only provide funding for work that is necessary to reduce applicable threats.

Sponsors that want to increase the level of protection in a particular project are responsible for paying 100 percent of the costs of the desired upgrade and additional work.

Emergency Watershed Protection Program - Floodplain Easement Option (EWP-FPE)[79]

The Emergency Watershed Protection - Floodplain Easement Program (EWP-FPE) provides an alternative measure to traditional EWP recovery, where it is determined that acquiring an easement in lieu of recovery measures is the more economical and prudent approach to reducing a threat to life or property.

The easement area will be restored to the maximum extent practicable to its natural condition. Restoration utilizes structural and nonstructural practices to restore the flood storage and flow, erosion control, and improve the practical management of the easement.

Floodplain easements restore, protect, maintain and enhance the functions of floodplains while conserving their natural values such as fish and wildlife habitat, water quality, flood water retention and ground water recharge. Structures, including buildings, within the floodplain easement must be demolished and removed, or relocated outside the 100-year floodplain or dam breach inundation area.

Background

Section 382 of the Federal Agriculture Improvement and Reform Act of 1996 (Public Law 104-127) amended the Emergency Watershed Protection Program (EWP), which was established under the Agricultural Credit Act of 1978, to provide for the purchase of floodplain easements as an emergency response to natural disasters or other circumstances. Since 1996, the USDA Natural Resources Conservation Service (NRCS) has purchased permanent floodplain easements on 1,418 properties, totaling 184,254 acres located in 36 states.

Land Eligibility

NRCS may purchase EWP-FPE permanent easements on floodplain lands that:

The floodplain lands were damaged by flooding at least once within the previous calendar year or have been subject to flood damage at least twice within the previous 10 years 1.

Other lands within the floodplain are eligible, provided the lands would contribute to the res-

---

[79] http://www.nrcs.usda.gov/wps/portal/nrcs/detail/national/programs/financial/ewp/?cid=nrcs143_008225

toration of the flood storage and flow, provide for control of erosion, or that would improve the practical management of the floodplain easement.

Lands would be inundated or adversely impacted as a result of a dam breach.

1If FPE is being offered as recovery for a specific natural disaster, at least one of the instances of flooding must have been a result of that natural disaster.

Enrollment Option

A permanent easement is the only enrollment option available for EWP-FPE floodplain easements. Permanent FPE easements are available on the following types of land:

Agricultural or open lands. In these cases, NRCS will pay up to 100% of the easement value and up to 100% of the costs for easement restoration.

Lands primarily used for residential housing. In these cases, NRCS will pay up to 100% of the easement value and up to 100% of the structure's value if the landowner chooses to have it demolished. If the landowner wished to relocate their residence instead of demolishing it, the NRCS will pay 100% of the costs associated with relocating it to a location outside of the floodplain. A project sponsor is required for these projects and is required to purchase the remaining lot after structures are removed.

Easement Payments

Although participation in EWP-FPE is voluntary, landowners selected for enrollment are required to sign a permanent conservation easement for the property included in their application. Through the signing of the easement, the NRCS purchases a series of rights from the landowner including the authority to restore and enhance the floodplain's functions and values. Once an easement has closed, the boundary configuration and terms of the agreement cannot be modified under any circumstances.

As compensation for the rights purchased by the NRCS, the landowner will receive the lowest of three values:

The fair market value (FMV) of the land. The fair market value may be determined through either of two methods: an area-wide market analysis or survey (AWMA) or an individual Uniform Standards for Professional Appraisal Practice (USPAP) appraisal. (See NEWPPM, Section 515.60(B)(D)).

The geographic area rate cap (GARC). The GARC reflects the value the State Conservationist, with the advice of the State Technical Committee, determines to be fair compensation for the value of the easement.

A voluntary written offer by the landowner. At the time of application, the landowner may voluntarily offer to accept less compensation than would be offered by NRCS. This may enhance the probability of enrollment. An offer to accept a lower compensation amount will be documented in writing on the ranking factors worksheet.

Easement compensation for projects that include residences or other structures will be determined by an appraisal.

Easement Restoration

The easement provides NRCS with the authority to restore and enhance the floodplain's functions and values. NRCS may pay up to 100% of the restoration costs. To the extent practicable, NRCS actively restores the natural features and characteristics of the floodplain through re-creating the topographic diversity, increasing the duration of inundation and saturation, and providing for the re-establishment of native vegetation. The landowner is provided the opportunity to participate in the restoration efforts. NRCS may pay 75 percent of the cost of removing buildings when appropriate.

Landowner Use

After the sale of the permanent EWP-FPE easement, landowners still retain several property rights, including:

- The right to quiet enjoyment
- The right to control public access and
- The right to undeveloped recreational use such as hunting and fishing

At any time, a landowner may request authorization from NRCS to engage in other activities, provided that NRCS determines it will further the protection and enhancement of the easement's floodplain functions and values. These compatible uses may include managed timber harvest, periodic haying, or grazing. NRCS determines the amount, method, timing, intensity, and duration of any compatible use that might be authorized. While a landowner can realize economic returns from an activity allowed on the easement area, a landowner is not assured of any specific level or frequency of such use, and the authorization does not vest any rights outside of those specified in the easement to the landowner.

How to Apply

If you are interested in applying for EWP-FPE, please review the documents listed below as they will need to be completed when you apply. More information about the EWP-FPE can be obtained from your local USDA NRCS Field Office.

Program Signup Forms Available Online

Form AD-1153, Application for Long-Term Contracted Assistance
Form AD-1157, Option Agreement to Purchase
Form AD-1161, Application for Payment

Additional Program Information

7 C.F.R. Part 624
Federal Agriculture Improvement and Reform Act of 1996
Emergency Watersheds Protection Program Floodplain Warranty Easement Deed, NRCS-LTP-20

Environmental and Historic Preservation Special Considerations

State and local regulations, laws, and ordinances need to be addressed and followed for all environmental and historic preservation issues.

National Environmental Policy Act (NEPA)

FEMA is provided with statutory exclusions under Section 316 of the Stafford Act. These exclusions exempt certain actions from the NEPA review process and generally include debris removal, clearance of roads, and demolition of unsafe structures.

Clean Water Act

Debris removal projects such as dredging, demolition, and construction and operation of sites used for debris management must comply with the requirements of CWA as administered by the Federal, State, or local regulatory agency.

Clean Air Act

Projects that are funded under the Public Assistance Program such as debris clearance, removal, disposal, recycling, reduction, and demolition, must comply with the air quality standards required by the Federal, State, or local regulatory agencies.

Coastal Barrier Resources Act

Costs for debris removal and emergency protective measures in designated CBRS units may be eligible for reimbursement under the Public Assistance Program provided the actions eliminate an immediate threat to lives, public health and safety, or protect improved property.

Resource Conservation and Recovery Act

It applies to disposal of disaster-generated debris and is of particular concern when hazardous materials may be present.

Endangered Species Act

If a project involves the known habitat of a threatened or endangered species, FEMA must consult with the United States Fish and Wildlife Service and the National Marine Fisheries Service before approving funding for that project.

National Historic Preservation Act

FEMA complies with NHPA and its implementing regulations in 36 CFR Part 800, either by executing Statewide programmatic agreements or by following standard regulatory procedures, commonly referred to as the Section 106 Process.

Coastal Zone Management Act

Requires that Federal agencies, such as FEMA, be consistent in enforcing the policies of State coastal zone management programs when conducting or supporting activities that affect a coastal zone.

Fish and Wildlife Coordination Act

If a proposed project would destroy wildlife habitat or modify a natural stream or body of water, it requires an evaluation of that action's impact on fish and wildlife.

Wild and Scenic Rivers Act

If a proposed project is located on a river designated as wild and scenic, FEMA must review it for compliance with WSRA.

Executive Orders

EO 11988 requires Federal agencies to undertake certain responsibilities for floodplain management. FEMA's procedures for complying with this EO are outlined in 44 CFR Part 9.

EO 11990 outlines the protection of wetlands and requires a planning process that considers alternatives and evaluates impacts to wetlands. The process for complying with this EO is similar to that for complying with EO 11988 and is outlined in 44 CFR Part 9.

EO 12898 requires Federal agencies to evaluate actions for disproportionately high and adverse effects on minority or low-income populations and to find ways to avoid or minimize these impacts where possible. Field personnel should identify any neighborhoods or communities with minority or low-income populations.

Record Keeping

The key to getting reimbursed for disaster costs is record keeping. Two organizations have spelled out, as recommendations, what proper record keeping entails, they are, Department of Homeland Security, Office of Inspector General Recom-

Government Officers Finance Association Recommendations

The Government Officers Finance Association has made a recommendation regarding the documentation of disaster response and recovery costs. The Government Officers Finance Association Recommended Practice approved by the GFOA's Executive Board, February 22, 2008, for documentation is as follows[80]:

Ensuring Adequate Documentation of Costs to Support Claims For Disaster Recovery Assistance (2008) (CAAFR)

<u>Background</u>. Many governments each year must face the challenge of disasters. Financial assistance frequently is available from one or more levels of government (e.g., Federal Emergency Management Agency – FEMA, state). Accountants in the public sector must ensure that the governments they serve collect and maintain adequate documentation on reimbursable costs to take full advantage of this assistance.

<u>Recommendation.</u> The Government Finance Officers Association (GFOA) urges state and local government financial managers to take all necessary steps to ensure that they will be able to collect and maintain adequate documentation on disaster-related costs to support maximum reimbursement from all levels of government that offer such assistance, including the following:

1. Establish Formal Policies and Procedures for the documentation of disaster-related costs

a. Every government should establish written policies and procedures on how to account for disaster-related reimbursable costs. These policies and procedures should be:

   i. included within the government's overall disaster recovery plan,
   ii. reviewed *and tested* annually,
   iii. updated at least once every three years;

b. Both financial and nonfinancial staff should receive training on these policies and procedures;

c. Financial and nonfinancial staff also should receive training on FEMA requirements and guidelines, as well as those of other assistance providers;[81]

d. Finance staff should review and approve all costs submitted by program staff before those costs are assigned to an emergency account;

e. An "emergency disaster" clause should be incorporated into all contracts for goods and services that might be needed in the event of a disaster to ensure that those goods and services will be available on a timely basis at a reasonable price. Also, vendors should be required to supply the necessary level of detail in their billing to support reimbursement (e.g., detailed breakdown of labor v. materials);

---

[80] Copyright 2008 by the Government finance Officers Association. Used with Permission. http://www.gfoa.org/index.php?option=com_content&task=view&id=1456

[81] Federal assistance may come from more than one agency (e.g., both the Federal Highway Administration and FEMA). In such cases, it is important to determine from the start which agency's rules apply to a given project.

f. Bids and contracts should be reviewed in advance for compliance with relevant reimbursement requirements;

g. Adequate controls should be set in place for inventories of emergency supplies;

h. Any provision for changes in compensation levels for salaried staff who work long hours in the event of a disaster should be properly approved and documented before a disaster occurs;

i. Audit(s) from those providing reimbursement should be sought as soon as possible (e.g., request a separate audit of immediate response costs) to minimize the possibility of disallowance because additional requested documentation is no longer available; and

j. If a government plans to use nonprofit organizations to provide certain types of assistance in the event of an emergency, it may wish to consider obligating itself by contract to using the services of selected nonprofit organizations so those costs can be eligible for reimbursement.

2. Ensure Adequate Detail to Support Claims

a. To ensure sufficiently detailed documentation to support reimbursement of disaster-related costs, governments should:

 i. Establish a supplemental chart of accounts specifically designed to collect data on disaster-related costs, including payroll, at a level of detail sufficient to meet grantor documentation requirements. The supplemental chart of accounts should, for example:

   a. classify projects based on categories used by the government offering reimbursement (e.g., large projects v. small projects; emergency repairs v. permanent repairs)

   b. track costs, at a minimum, at the project worksheet level

   c. for staff hours, specify name, title, dates, times, and rates;

 ii. Educate program staff in the various departments on the level of detail on costs required to substantiate claims for reimbursement;

 iii. Collect and maintain appropriate non-financial data to support claims for reimbursement, such as the following:

   a. "before and after" photographs of each repair, labeled by location (with map, as needed) and date

   b. relevant correspondence

   c. precise information on materials used (e.g., number of bricks v. square footage);

b. Track volunteer hours (applicable to local share, even if not reimbursable); and

c. Track local equipment usage (by hours actually used)

Since these forms will have to be used to request disaster relief from FEMA, it is suggested that the forms, and how an agency or department would fill them out, be determined in advance of a disaster.

Department of Homeland Security, Office of Inspector General Recommendations

The Department of Homeland Security [the agency where FEMA lives] Office of Inspector

General [the outfit responsible for making sure that grant monies are properly spent] has spelled out points[82] to remember when administering FEMA grants:

1. Designate a person to coordinate the accumulation of records.

2. Establish a separate and distinct account for recording revenue and expenditures, and a separate subsidy account for each distinct project awarded funds by FEMA.

3. Ensure that the final claim made for each project is supported by amounts recorded in the accounting system.

4. Ensure that each expenditure is recorded in the accounting books and references supporting source documentation (checks, invoices, etc.) that can be readily retrieved.

5. Research insurance coverage and seek reimbursement for the maximum amount. Credit the appropriate FEMA project with that amount.

6. Check with your Federal Grant Program Coordinator about the availability of funding under other Federal programs (i.e., Federal Highway, Housing and Urban Development, etc.) and ensure that the final project claim does not include costs that were funded or should be funded by another Federal agency.

7. Ensure that inventory withdrawal and usage records document materials taken from existing inventories for use under FEMA projects.

8. Do not charge the regular salary of permanent employees or seasonal employees (whose salaries are contained in annual appropriations) to FEMA debris removal and emergency service projects.

9. Do not claim costs for items or activities for which you did not have a cash outlay.

10. Ensure that claims for overtime fringe benefits are based on cost items (i.e., F.I.C.A., worker's compensation, etc.) that accrue as a result of overtime. Items such as health benefits and leave are not eligible as overtime fringe benefits.

11. Ensure that expenditures claimed under the FEMA project are reasonable and necessary, are authorized under the scope of work, and directly benefit the project.

12. Ensure that you document pertinent actions for contracts let under FEMA projects, including the rationale for the method of procurement, the basis for contractor selection, and the basis for the contract price. Remember that Federal regulations prohibit "cost plus a percentage of cost" contracts.

---

[82] AUDIT TIPS FOR MANAGING DISASTER-RELATED PROJECT COSTS
Department of Homeland Security
Office of Inspector General
September 2012
http://www.oig.dhs.gov/assets/Audit_Tips.pdf

FEMA Forms Governmental Agencies and Non-Profits must utilize

Document Number	Form Name
FF90-49	Request for Public Assistance
FF90-91	Project Worksheet
FF90-91A	PW-Damage Description and Scope of Work Continuation Sheet

Disaster Dollars

Document Number	Form Name
FF90-91B	PW-Cost Estimate Continuation sheet
FF90-91C	PW-Maps and Sketches Sheet
FF90-91D	PW-Photo Sheet
FF90-118	Validation Worksheet
FF90-119	Project Validation Form
FF90-120	Special Considerations Questionnaire
FF90-121	PNP Facility Questionnaire
FF90-122	Historic Review For Determination of Adverse Effect
FF90-123	Force Account Labor Summary Record
FF90-124	Materials Summary Record
FF90-125	Rented Equipment Summary Record
FF90-126	Contract Work Summary Record
FF90-127	Force Account Equipment Summary Record
FF90-128	Applicant's Benefit Calculation

Additional FEMA documents that may be of use are:

- FEMA 321, *Public Assistance Digest* (October 2001)
- FEMA 322, *Public Assistance: Public Assistance Guide* (June 2007)
- FEMA 323, *Public Assistance: Applicant Handbook* (September 1999)
- FEMA 325, *Public Assistance: Debris Management Guide* (June 2007)
- FEMA Disaster Assistance Policy (9500 series policy statements)

http://www.fema.gov/government/grant/pa/policy.shtm.

In addition to the requirements of the Robert T. Stafford Disaster Relief and Emergency Assistance Act, and FEMA regulations, the following accounting/auditing requirements apply to disaster grants and loans.

	State and Local Governments	Public and Private Institutions of Higher Learning	Hospitals Affiliated with Institutions of Higher Learning	Quasi-Public and Private Nonprofits	Public and Private Hospitals
Administration of Grants	44 CFR 13 OMB Circular A-102	OMB Circular A-110	OMB Circular A-110	OMB Circular A-110	OMB Circular A-110
Cost Principles	OMB Circular A-87	OMB Circular A-21	OMB Circular A-21	OMB Circular A-87	OMB Circular A-87
Audits	OMB Circular A-133	OMB Circular A-133	OMB Circular A-133	OMB Circular A-133	OMB Circular A-133

OMB Circulars are available online at the following website: www.whitehouse.gov/omb/circulars/index.html.

Government Audits After the Grant Has Been Received (and most likely spent)

If you receive $500,000.00 or more in federal grants for disaster relief or disaster mitigation you will be subject to an audit. The purpose of the audit is to insure that the disaster monies were spent as intended, and as required by law. Additionally, the audit will determine if you have met the proper accounting and record keeping requirements. If not, then you may be required to repay all or part of your grants. While the federal government is entitled to conduct this audit, most states have agreed to undertake these audits on behalf of the federal government. So, sooner or later, you can expect an auditor to knock on your door.

The Department of Homeland Security [the agency where FEMA lives] Office of Inspector General [the outfit responsible for making sure that grant monies are properly spent] has prepared a list of the most likely problems with spending, and accounting for, grant monies[83]. The problems you are most likely to have are:

A. Poor Project Accounting

Federal regulations (44 CFR 13.20 and 206.205) require each subgrantee to maintain a system that accounts for FEMA funds on a project-by-project basis. The system must disclose the financial results for all FEMA-funded activities accurately, currently, and completely. It must identify funds received and disbursed and reference source documentation (i.e., cancelled checks, invoices, payroll, time and attendance records, contracts, etc.).

B. Unsupported Costs

Federal regulations (OMB Circular A-87 and 44 CFR 13.20) require that costs claimed under Federal programs must be adequately supported by source documentation such as cancelled checks, payrolls, contracts, etc.

C. Duplication of Benefits

Government policy (Stafford Act and 44 CFR 206.191) prohibits duplication of benefits. In other words, a subgrantee cannot receive disaster funding for activities covered by insurance benefits, other Federal programs, or any other source.

D. Excessive Equipment Charges

Federal regulations (44 CFR 206.228) require that subgrantees use the FEMA schedule of equipment rates or their local rates -- whichever are lower. Applicants that do not have local established rates must use the FEMA equipment rates when claiming costs under a FEMA project.

E. Excessive Labor and Fringe Benefit Charges

According to OMB Circular A-87, allowable costs must be consistent with policies, regulations, and procedures that apply uniformly to both Federal awards and other activities of the governmental unit. According to 44 CFR 206.228, straight or regular-time salaries and benefits of permanent employees engaged in emergency service work are not eligible for FEMA assistance.

---

[83] AUDIT TIPS FOR MANAGING DISASTER-RELATED PROJECT COSTS
Department of Homeland Security
Office of Inspector General
September 2012
http://www.oig.dhs.gov/assets/Audit_Tips.pdf

F. Unrelated Project Charges

According to OMB Circular A-87, charges to Federal grants must be necessary and reasonable to fulfill the objective of the grant program.

G. Unapplied Credits

According to OMB Circular A-87, grants must be reduced by credits that offset or reduce expenses allocable to Federal awards.

H. Excessive Administrative Charges

Under the Stafford Act, the subgrantee is entitled to an administrative allowance based on a statutory formula to cover the costs associated with requesting, obtaining, and administering FEMA awards. Federal regulation (44 CFR 206.228) limits funding for administrative costs to that allowance.

I. Poor Contracting Practices

Federal regulations contain procurement standards with which a subgrantee must comply under FEMA-sponsored projects. According to 44 CFR 13.36:

The subgrantee must maintain records in sufficient detail to reflect the significant history of the procurement, including the rationale for the method of procurement, the basis for the contractor selection, and the basis for the contract price;

The subgrantee is prohibited from using time-and-material-type contracts unless a determination is made that no other contract is suitable, and provided that the contract includes a ceiling price that the contractor exceeds at its own risk; and

The subgrantee is prohibited from using a "cost plus a percentage of cost" contract arrangement.

Record Keeping, Audits & Income Tax Issues

Rules to live by

VERIFY IN ADVANCE WHAT KIND OF DATA FEMA WANTS FROM YOU SO YOU CAN GET REIMBURSEMENT. GET EVERY KIND OF DATA YOU CAN FROM A COST ACCOUNTING POINT OF VIEW. BE SPECIFIC AND DETAILED.

IF YOU DO NOT INTIMATELY UNDERSTAND THE STAFFORD ACT YOU WILL NOT GET ALL THE REIMBURSEMENT YOU MAY BE ELIGIBLE FOR. REMEMBER, <u>AFTER THE DISASTER IS OVER, YOU WILL BE AUDITED</u>.

Stafford Act Requirements

The "Stafford Act" (Robert T. Stafford Disaster Relief and Emergency Assistance Act, Public Law 93-288, as amended, 42 U.S.C. 5121-5207) is the primary authorization for the United States to respond to disasters, and to assist state and local governments in disaster response. It is the basis for FEMA's jurisdiction. It tells us what is, and is not eligible for reimbursement.

Among other things, the regulations under the Stafford Act regulate how the states, and individual recipients, manage the financial aspects or grants and awards made under this law.

The Stafford Act and the Single Audit Act spell out how a recipient is to keep sufficient records to substantiate eligible costs, and how an audit will be conducted. One way to look at this is that it is akin to a cost accounting analysis with very detailed record keeping requirements. For example, a municipality engaged in flood debris removal, normally an eligible cost, had a written contract with a private company to haul the debris to the local landfill. The landfill provided a written ticket/receipt with the date, time, cost and material dumped. So far so good, however FEMA staff, after the fact, then asked for a written record of exactly where the debris came from street by street, a record no one thought to compile. Detail is the key to record keeping.

NOTE

If you have to go back after the fact and recreate or add to financial records it delays payments.

Stafford Act regulations relating to financial records

44 C.F.R. 206.4 State emergency plans

The State shall set forth in its emergency plan all responsibilities and actions specified in the Stafford Act and these regulations that are required of the State and its political subdivisions to prepare for and respond to major disasters and emergencies and to facilitate the delivery of Federal disaster assistance.

Sec. 13.1 Purpose and scope of this part

This part establishes uniform administrative rules for Federal grants and cooperative agreements and subawards to State, local and Indian tribal governments.

Sec. 13.20 Standards for financial management systems

a. A State must expand and account for grant funds in accordance with State laws and procedures for expending and accounting for its own funds. Fiscal control and accounting procedures of the State, as well as its subgrantees and cost-type contractors, must be sufficient to--

1. Permit preparation of reports required by this part and the statutes authorizing the grant, and (2) Permit the tracing of funds to a level of expenditures adequate to establish that such funds have not been used in violation of the restrictions and prohibitions of applicable statutes.

b. The financial management systems of other grantees and subgrantees must meet the following standards:

1. Financial reporting. Accurate, current, and complete disclosure of the financial results of financially assisted activities must be made in accordance with the financial reporting requirements of the grant or subgrant.

2. Accounting records. Grantees and subgrantees must maintain records which adequately identify the source and application of funds provided for financially-assisted activities. These records must contain information pertaining to grant or subgrant awards and authorizations, obligations, unobligated balances, assets, liabilities, outlays or expenditures, and income.

3. Internal control. Effective control and accountability must be maintained for all grant and subgrant cash, real and personal property, and other assets. Grantees and subgrantees must adequately safeguard all such property and must assure that it is used solely for authorized purposes.

4. Budget control. Actual expenditures or outlays must be compared with budgeted amounts for each grant or subgrant. Financial information must be related to performance or productivity data, including the development of unit cost information whenever appropriate or specifically required in the grant or subgrant agreement. If unit cost data are required, estimates based on available documentation will be accepted whenever possible.

5. Allowable cost. Applicable OMB cost principles, agency program regulations, and the terms of grant and subgrant agreements will be followed in determining the reasonableness, allowability, and allocability of costs.

6. Source documentation. Accounting records must be supported by such source documentation as cancelled checks, paid bills, payrolls, time and attendance records, contract and subgrant award documents, etc.

7. Cash management. Procedures for minimizing the time elapsing between the transfer of funds from the U.S. Treasury and disbursement by grantees and subgrantees must be followed whenever advance payment procedures are used. Grantees must establish reasonable procedures to ensure the receipt of reports on subgrantees' cash balances and cash disbursements in sufficient time to enable them to prepare complete and accurate cash transactions reports to the awarding agency. When advances are made by letter-of-credit or electronic transfer of funds methods, the grantee must make drawdowns as close as possible to the time of making disbursements. Grantees must monitor cash drawdowns by their subgrantees to assure that they conform substantially to the same standards of timing and amount as apply to advances to the grantees.

c. An awarding agency may review the adequacy of the financial management system of any applicant for financial assistance as part of a preaward review or at any time subsequent to award.

Sec. 13.41 Financial reporting

a. General.

1. Except as provided in paragraphs (a) (2) and (5) of this section, grantees will use only the forms specified in paragraphs (a) through (e) of this section, and such supplementary or other forms as may from time to time be authorized by OMB, for:

    i. Submitting financial reports to Federal agencies, or
    ii. Requesting advances or reimbursements when letters of credit are not used.

2. Grantees need not apply the forms prescribed in this section in dealing with their subgrantees. However, grantees shall not impose more burdensome requirements on subgrantees.

3. Grantees shall follow all applicable standard and supplemental Federal agency instructions approved by OMB to the extend required Under the Paperwork Reduction Act of 1980 for use in connection with forms specified in paragraphs (b) through (e) of this section. Federal agencies may issue substantive supplementary instructions only with the approval of OMB. Federal agencies may shade out or instruct the grantee to disregard any line item that the Federal agency finds unnecessary for its decisionmaking purposes.

4. Grantees will not be required to submit more than the original and two copies of forms required under this part.

5. Federal agencies may provide computer outputs to grantees to expedite or contribute to the accuracy of reporting. Federal agencies may accept the required information from grantees in machine usable format or computer printouts instead of prescribed forms.

6. Federal agencies may waive any report required by this section if not needed.

7. Federal agencies may extend the due date of any financial report upon receiving a justified request from a grantee.

b. Financial Status Report

1. Form. Grantees will use Standard Form 269 or 269A, Financial Status Report, to report the status of Funds for all non-

construction grants and for construction grants when required in accordance with paragraph (e)(2)(iii) of this section.

2. Accounting basis. Each grantee will report program outlays and program income on a cash or accrual basis as prescribed by the awarding agency. If the Federal agency requires accrual information and the grantee's accounting records are not normally kept on the accural basis, the grantee shall not be required to convert its accounting system but shall develop such accrual information through and analysis of the documentation on hand.

3. Frequency. The Federal agency may prescribe the frequency of the report for each project or program. However, the report will not be required more frequently than quarterly. If the Federal agency does not specify the frequency of the report, it will be submitted annually. A final report will be required upon expiration or termination of grant support.

4. Due date. When reports are required on a quarterly or semiannual basis, they will be due 30 days after the reporting period. When required on an annual basis, they will be due 90 days after the grant year. Final reports will be due 90 days after the expiration or termination of grant support.

c. Federal Cash Transactions Report

1. Form.

    i. For grants paid by letter or credit, Treasury check advances or electronic transfer of funds, the grantee will submit the Standard Form 272, Federal Cash Transactions Report, and when necessary, its continuation sheet, Standard Form 272a, unless the terms of the award exempt the grantee from this requirement.

    ii. These reports will be used by the Federal agency to monitor cash advanced to grantees and to obtain disbursement or outlay information for each grant from grantees. The format of the report may be adapted as appropriate when reporting is to be accomplished with the assistance of automatic data processing equipment provided that the information to be submitted is not changed in substance.

2. Forecasts of Federal cash requirements. Forecasts of Federal cash requirements may be required in the ``Remarks'' section of the report.

3. Cash in hands of subgrantees. When considered necessary and feasible by the Federal agency, grantees may be required to report the amount of cash advances in excess of three days' needs in the hands of their subgrantees or contractors and to provide short narrative explanations of actions taken by the grantee to reduce the excess balances.

4. Frequency and due date. Grantees must submit the report no later than 15 working days following the end of each quarter. However, where an advance either by letter of credit or electronic transfer of funds is authorized at an annualized rate of one million dollars or ore, the Federal agency may require the report to be submitted within 15 working days following the end of each month.

d. Request for advance or reimbursement

1. Advance payments. Requests for Treasury check advance payments will be submitted on Standard Form 270, Request for Advance or Reimbursement. (This form will not be used for drawdowns under a letter of credit, electronic funds transfer or when Treasury check advance payments are made to the grantee automatically on a predetermined basis.)

2. Reimbursements. Requests for reimbursement under nonconstruction grants will also be submitted on Standard Form 270. (For reimbursement requests under construction grants, see paragraph (e)(1) of this section.)

3. The frequency for submitting payment requests is treated in paragraph (b)(3) of this section.

e. Outlay report and request for reimbursement for construction programs.

1. Grants that support construction activities paid by reimbursement method.

    i. Requests for reimbursement under construction grants will be submitted on Standard Form 271, Outlay Report and Request for Reimbursement for Construction Programs. Federal agencies may, however, prescribe the Request for Advance or Reimbursement form, specified in paragraph (d) of this section, instead of this form.

    ii. The frequency for submitting reimbursement requests is treated in paragraph (b)(3) of this section.

2. Grants that support construction activities paid by letter of credit, electronic funds transfer or Treasury check advance.

    i. When a construction grant is paid by letter of credit, electronic funds transfer or Treasury check advances, the grantee will report its outlays to the Federal agency using Standard Form 271, Outlay Report and Request for Reimbursement for Construction Programs. The Federal agency will provide any necessary special instruction. However, frequency and due date shall be governed by paragraphs (b) (3) and (4) of this section.

    ii. When a construction grant is paid by Treasury check advances based on periodic requests from the grantee, the advances will be requested on the form specified in paragraph (d) of this section.

    iii. The Federal agency may substitute the Financial Status Report specified in paragraph (b) of this section for the Outlay Report and Request for Reimbursement for Construction Programs.

3. Accounting basis. The accounting basis for the Outlay Report and Request for Reimbursement for Construction Programs shall be governed by paragraph (b)(2) of this section.

Sec. 13.42 Retention and access requirements for records

a. Applicability.

1. This section applies to all financial and programmatic records, supporting doc-

uments, statistical records, and other records of grantees or subgrantees which are:

   i. Required to be maintained by the terms of this part, program regulations or the grant agreement, or

   ii. Otherwise reasonably considered as pertinent to program regulations or the grant agreement.

   2. This section does not apply to records maintained by contractors or subcontractors. For a requirement to place a provision concerning records in certain kinds of contracts, see Sec. 13.36(i)(10).

b. Length of retention period.

   1. Except as otherwise provided, records must be retained for three years from the starting date specified in paragraph (c) of this section.

   2. If any litigation, claim, negotiation, audit or other action involving the records has been started before the expiration of the 3-year period, the records must be retained until completion of the action and resolution of all issues which arise from it, or until the end of the regular 3-year period, whichever is later.

   3. To avoid duplicate recordkeeping, awarding agencies may make special arrangements with grantees and subgrantees to retain any records which are continuously needed for joint use. The awarding agency will request transfer of records to its custody when it determines that the records possess long-term retention value. When the records are transferred to or maintained by the Federal agency, the 3-year retention requirement is not applicable to the grantee or subgrantee.

c. Starting date of retention period--

   1. General. When grant support is continued or renewed at annual or other intervals, the retention period for the records of each funding period starts on the day the grantee or subgrantee submits to the awarding agency its single or last expenditure report for that period. However, if grant support is continued or renewed quarterly, the retention period for each year's records starts on the day the grantee submits its expenditure report for the last quarter of the Federal fiscal year. In all other cases, the retention period starts on the day the grantee submits its final expenditure report. If an expenditure report has been waived, the retention period starts on the day the report would have been due.

   2. Real property and equipment records. The retention period for real property and equipment records starts from the date of the disposition or replacement or transfer at the direction of the awarding agency.

   3. Records for income transactions after grant or subgrant support. In some cases grantees must report income after the period of grant support. Where there is such a requirement, the retention period for the records pertaining to the earning of the income starts from the end of the grantee's fiscal year in which the income is earned.

   4. Indirect cost rate proposals, cost allocations plans, etc. This paragraph applies to the following types of documents, and

their supporting records: indirect cost rate computations or proposals, cost allocation plans, and any similar accounting computations of the rate at which a particular group of costs is chargeable (such as computer usage chargeback rates or composite fringe benefit rates).

    i. If submitted for negotiation. If the proposal, plan, or other computation is required to be submitted to the Federal Government (or to the grantee) to form the basis for negotiation of the rate, then the 3-year retention period for its supporting records starts from the date of such submission.

    ii. If not submitted for negotiation. If the proposal, plan, or other computation is not required to be submitted to the Federal Government (or to the grantee) for negotiation purposes, then the 3-year retention period for the proposal plan, or computation and its supporting records starts from end of the fiscal year (or other accounting period) covered by the proposal, plan, or other computation.

d. Substitution of microfilm. Copies made by microfilming, photocopying, or similar methods may be substituted for the original records.

e. Access to records--

    1. Records of grantees and subgrantees. The awarding agency and the Comptroller General of the United States, or any of their authorized representatives, shall have the right of access to any pertinent books, documents, papers, or other records of grantees and subgrantees which are pertinent to the grant, in order to make audits, examinations, excerpts, and transcripts.

    2. Expiration of right of access. The rights of access in this section must not be limited to the required retention period but shall last as long as the records are retained.

f. Restrictions on public access. The Federal Freedom of Information Act (5 U.S.C. 552) does not apply to records Unless required by Federal, State, or local law, grantees and subgrantees are not required to permit public access to their records.

Sec. 13.21 Payment

a. Scope. This section prescribes the basic standard and the methods under which a Federal agency will make payments to grantees, and grantees will make payments to subgrantees and contractors.

b. Basic standard. Methods and procedures for payment shall minimize the time elapsing between the transfer of funds and disbursement by the grantee or subgrantee, in accordance with Treasury regulations at 31 CFR part 205.

c. Advances. Grantees and subgrantees shall be paid in advance, provided they maintain or demonstrate the willingness and ability to maintain procedures to minimize the time elapsing between the transfer of the funds and their disbursement by the grantee or subgrantee.

d. Reimbursement. Reimbursement shall be the preferred method when the requirements in paragraph (c) of this section are not met. Grantees and subgrantees may also be paid by reimbursement for any construction grant. Except as otherwise specified in regulation, Federal agencies shall not use the percentage of completion method to pay construction grants. The grantee or subgrantee may use that method to pay its construction contractor, and if it does, the awarding agency's payments to the grantee or subgrantee will be based on the grantee's or subgrantee's actual rate of disbursement.

e. Working capital advances. If a grantee cannot meet the criteria for advance payments described in paragraph (c) of this section, and the Federal agency has determined that reimbursement is not feasible because the grantee lacks sufficient working capital, the awarding agency may provide cash or a working capital advance basis. Under this procedure the awarding agency shall advance cash to the grantee to cover its estimated disbursement needs for an initial period generally geared to the grantee's disbursing cycle. Thereafter, the awarding agency shall reimburse the grantee for its actual cash disbursements. The working capital advance method of payment shall not be used by grantees or subgrantees if the reason for using such method is the unwillingness or inability of the grantee to provide timely advances to the subgrantee to meet the subgrantee's actual cash disbursements.

f. Effect of program income, refunds, and audit recoveries on payment.

1. Grantees and subgrantees shall disburse repayments to and interest earned on a revolving fund before requesting additional cash payments for the same activity.

2. Except as provided in paragraph (f)(1) of this section, grantees and subgrantees shall disburse program income, rebates, refunds, contract settlements, audit recoveries and interest earned on such funds before requesting additional cash payments.

g. Withholding payments.

1. Unless otherwise required by Federal statute, awarding agencies shall not withhold payments for proper charges incurred by grantees or subgrantees unless--

    i. The grantee or subgrantee has failed to comply with grant award conditions or

    ii. The grantee or subgrantee is indebted to the United States.

2. Cash withheld for failure to comply with grant award condition, but without suspension of the grant, shall be released to the grantee upon subsequent compliance. When a grant is suspended, payment adjustments will be made in accordance with Sec. 13.43(c).

3. A Federal agency shall not make payment to grantees for amounts that are withheld by grantees or subgrantees from payment to contractors to assure satisfactory completion of work. Payments shall be made by the Federal agency when the grantees or subgrantees actually disburse the withheld funds to the contractors or to escrow accounts established to assure satisfactory completion of work.

h. Cash depositories.

1. Consistent with the national goal of expanding the opportunities for minority business enterprises, grantees and subgrantees are encouraged to use minority banks (a bank which is owned at least 50 percent by minority group members). A list of minority owned banks can be obtained from the Minority Business De-

velopment Agency, Department of Commerce, Washington, DC 20230.

2. A grantee or subgrantee shall maintain a separate bank account only when required by Federal-State agreement.

   i. Interest earned on advances. Except for interest earned on advances of funds exempt under the Intergovernmental Cooperation Act (31 U.S.C. 6501 et seq.) and the Indian Self-Determination Act (23 U.S.C. 450), grantees and subgrantees shall promptly, but at least quarterly, remit interest earned on advances to the Federal agency. The grantee or subgrantee may keep interest amounts up to $100 per year for administrative expenses.

Sec. 13.22 Allowable costs

a. Limitation on use of funds. Grant funds may be used only for:

   1. The allowable costs of the grantees, subgrantees and cost-type contractors, including allowable costs in the form of payments to fixed-price contractors; and

   2. Reasonable fees or profit to cost-type contractors but not any fee or profit (or other increment above allowable costs) to the grantee or subgrantee.

b. Applicable cost principles. For each kind of organization, there is a set of Federal principles for determining allowable costs. Allowable costs will be determined in accordance with the cost principles applicable to the organization incurring the costs.

The following lists the kinds of organizations and the applicable cost principles.

For the costs of a--	Use the principles in--
State, local or Indian tribal government.	OMB Circular A-87.
Private nonprofit organization other than an (1) institution of higher education, (2) hospital, or (3) organization namedin OMB Circular A-122 as not subject to that circular.	OBM Circular A-122.
Educational institutions	OMB Circular A-21.
For-profit organization other than a hospital and an organization named in OBM Circular A-122 as not subject to that costcircular.	48 CFR part 31. Contract Cost Principles and Procedures, or uniform accounting standards that accounting standards that comply with cost principles acceptable to the Federal agency.

Sec. 13.23 Period of availability of funds

a. General. Where a funding period is specified, a grantee may charge to the award only costs resulting from obligations of the funding period unless carryover of unobligated balances is permitted, in which case the carryover balances may be charged for costs resulting from obligations of the subsequent funding period.

b. Liquidation of obligations. A grantee must liquidate all obligations incurred under the award not later than 90 days after the end of the funding period (or as specified in a program regulation) to coincide with the submission of the annual Financial Status Report (SF-269). The Federal agency may extend this deadline at the request of the grantee.

Sec. 13.24 Matching or cost sharing

a. Basic rule: Costs and contributions acceptable. With the qualifications and exceptions listed in paragraph (b) of this section, a matching or cost sharing requirement may be satisfied by either or both of the following:

   1. Allowable costs incurred by the grantee, subgrantee or a cost-type contractor under the assistance agreement. This includes allowable costs borne by non-Federal grants or by others cash donations from non-Federal third parties.

   2. The value of third party in-kind contributions applicable to the period to which the cost sharing or matching requirements applies.

b. Qualifications and exceptions—

   1. Costs borne by other Federal grant agreements. Except as provided by Federal statute, a cost sharing or matching requirement may not be met by costs borne by another Federal grant. This prohibition does not apply to income earned by a grantee or subgrantee from a contract awarded under another Federal grant.

   2. General revenue sharing. For the purpose of this section, general revenue sharing funds distributed under 31 U.S.C. 6702 are not considered Federal grant funds.

   3. Cost or contributions counted towards other Federal costs-sharing requirements. Neither costs nor the values of third party in-kind contributions may count towards satisfying a cost sharing or matching requirement of a grant agreement if they have been or will be counted towards satisfying a cost sharing or matching requirement of another Federal grant agreement, a Federal procurement contract, or any other award of Federal funds.

   4. Costs financed by program income. Costs financed by program income, as defined in Sec. 13.25, shall not count towards satisfying a cost sharing or matching requirement unless they are expressly permitted in the terms of the assistance agreement. (This use of general program income is described in Sec. 13.25(g).)

   5. Services or property financed by income earned by contractors. Contractors under a grant may earn income from the activities carried out under the contract in addition to the amounts earned from the party awarding the contract. No costs of services or property supported by this income may count toward satisfying a cost sharing or matching requirement unless other provisions of the grant agreement expressly permit this kind of income to be used to meet the requirement.

   6. Records. Costs and third party in-kind contributions counting towards satisfying a cost sharing or matching requirement must be verifiable from the records of grantees and subgrantee or cost-type contractors. These records must show how the value placed on third party in-kind contributions was derived. To the extent feasible, volunteer services will be supported by the same methods that the organization uses to support the allocability of regular personnel costs.

7. Special standards for third party in-kind contributions.

   i. Third party in-kind contributions count towards satisfying a cost sharing or matching requirement only where, if the party receiving the contributions were to pay for them, the payments would be allowable costs.

   ii. Some third party in-kind contributions are goods and services that, if the grantee, subgrantee, or contractor receiving the contribution had to pay for them, the payments would have been an indirect costs. Costs sharing or matching credit for such contributions shall be given only if the grantee, subgrantee, or contractor has established, along with its regular indirect cost rate, a special rate for allocating to individual projects or programs the value of the contributions.

   iii. A third party in-kind contribution to a fixed-price contract may count towards satisfying a cost sharing or matching requirement only if it results in:

      A. An increase in the services or property provided under the contract (without additional cost to the grantee or subgrantee) or

      B. A cost savings to the grantee or subgrantee.

   iv. The values placed on third party in-kind contributions for cost sharing or matching purposes will conform to the rules in the succeeding sections of this part. If a third party in-kind contribution is a type not treated in those sections, the value placed upon it shall be fair and reasonable.

c. Valuation of donated services—

   1. Volunteer services. Unpaid services provided to a grantee or subgrantee by individuals will be valued at rates consistent with those ordinarily paid for similar work in the grantee's or subgrantee's organization. If the grantee or subgrantee does not have employees performing similar work, the rates will be consistent with those ordinarily paid by other employers for similar work in the same labor market. In either case, a reasonable amount for fringe benefits may be included in the valuation.

   2. Employees of other organizations. When an employer other than a grantee, subgrantee, or cost-type contractor furnishes free of charge the services of an employee in the employee's normal line of work, the services will be valued at the employee's regular rate of pay exclusive of the employee's fringe benefits and overhead costs. If the services are in a different line of work, paragraph (c)(1) of this section applies.

d. Valuation of third party donated supplies and loaned equipment or space.

   1. If a third party donates supplies, the contribution will be valued at the market value of the supplies at the time of donation.

   2. If a third party donates the use of equipment or space in a building but retains title, the contribution will be valued at the fair rental rate of the equipment or space.

e. Valuation of third party donated equipment, buildings, and land. If a third party donates equipment, buildings, or land, and title passes to a grantee or subgrantee, the treatment of the donated property will depend upon the purpose of the grant or subgrant, as follows:

1. Awards for capital expenditures. If the purpose of the grant or subgrant is to assist the grantee or subgrantee in the acquisition of property, the market value of that property at the time of donation may be counted as cost sharing or matching,

2. Other awards. If assisting in the acquisition of property is not the purpose of the grant or subgrant, paragraphs (e)(2) (i) and (ii) of this section apply:

    i. If approval is obtained from the awarding agency, the market value at the time of donation of the donated equipment or buildings and the fair rental rate of the donated land may be counted as cost sharing or matching. In the case of a subgrant, the terms of the grant agreement may require that the approval be obtained from the Federal agency as well as the grantee. In all cases, the approval may be given only if a purchase of the equipment or rental of the land would be approved as an allowable direct cost. If any part of the donated property was acquired with Federal funds, only the non-Federal share of the property may be counted as cost-sharing or matching.

    ii. If approval is not obtained under paragraph (e)(2)(i) of this section, no amount may be counted for donated land, and only depreciation or use allowances may be counted for donated equipment and buildings. The depreciation or use allowances for this property are not treated as third party in-kind contributions. Instead, they are treated as costs incurred by the grantee or subgrantee. They are computed and allocated (usually as indirect costs) in accordance with the cost principles specified in Sec. 13.22, in the same way as depreciation or use allowances for purchased equipment and buildings. The amount of depreciation or use allowances for donated equipment and buildings is based on the property's market value at the time it was donated.

f. Valuation of grantee or subgrantee donated real property for construction/acquisition. If a grantee or subgrantee donates real property for a construction or facilities acquisition project, the current market value of that property may be counted as cost sharing or matching. If any part of the donated property was acquired with Federal funds, only the non-Federal share of the property may be counted as cost sharing or matching.

g. Appraisal of real property. In some cases under paragraphs (d), (e) and (f) of this section, it will be necessary to establish the market value of land or a building or the fair rental rate of land or of space in a building. In these cases, the Federal agency may require the market value or fair rental value be set by an independent appraiser, and that the value or rate be certified by the grantee. This requirement will also be imposed by the grantee on subgrantees.

Sec. 13.25 Program Income

a. General. Grantees are encouraged to earn income to defray program costs. Program income includes income from fees for services performed, from the use or rental of real or personal property acquired with grant funds, from the sale of commodities or items fabricated under a grant agreement, and from payments of principal and interest on loans made with grant funds. Except as otherwise provided in regulations of the Federal agency, program income does not include interest on grant funds, rebates, credits, discounts, refunds, etc. and interest earned on any of them.

b. Definition of program income. Program income means gross income received by the grantee or subgrantee directly generated by a grant supported activity, or earned only as a result of the grant agreement during the grant period. During the grant period is the time between the effective date of the award and the ending date of the award reflected in the final financial report.

c. Cost of generating program income. If authorized by Federal regulations or the grant agreement, costs incident to the generation of program income may be deducted from gross income to determine program income.

d. Governmental revenues. Taxes, special assessments, levies, fines, and other such revenues raised by a grantee or subgrantee are not program income unless the revenues are specifically identified in the grant agreement or Federal agency regulations as program income.

e. Royalties. Income from royalties and license fees for copyrighted material, patents, and inventions developed by a grantee or subgrantee is program income only if the revenues are specifically identified in the grant agreement or Federal agency regulations as program income. (See Sec. 13.34.)

f. Property. Proceeds from the sale of real property or equipment will be handled in accordance with the requirements of Sec. Sec. 13.31 and 13.32.

g. Use of program income. Program income shall be deducted from outlays which may be both Federal and non-Federal as described below, unless the Federal agency regulations or the grant agreement specify another alternative (or a combination of the alternatives). In specifying alternatives, the Federal agency may distinguish between income earned by the grantee and income earned by subgrantees and between the sources, kinds, or amounts of income. When Federal agencies authorize the alternatives in paragraphs (g) (2) and (3) of this section, program income in excess of any limits stipulated shall also be deducted from outlays.

   1. Deduction. Ordinarily program income shall be deducted from total allowable costs to determine the net allowable costs. Program income shall be used for current costs unless the Federal agency authorizes otherwise. Program income which the grantee did not anticipate at the time of the award shall be used to reduce the Federal agency and grantee contributions rather than to increase the funds committed to the project.

   2. Addition. When authorized, program income may be added to the funds committed to the grant agreement by the Federal agency and the grantee. The program income shall be used for the purposes and under the conditions of the grant agreement.

   3. Cost sharing or matching. When authorized, program income may be used to meet the cost sharing or matching re-

quirement of the grant agreement. The amount of the Federal grant award remains the same.

h. Income after the award period. There are no Federal requirements governing the disposition of program income earned after the end of the award period (i.e., until the ending date of the final financial report, see paragraph (a) of this section), unless the terms of the agreement or the Federal agency regulations provide otherwise.

Sec. 13.26 Non-Federal audit

a. Basic rule. Grantees and subgrantees are responsible for obtaining audits in accordance with the Single Audit Act Amendments of 1996 (31 U.S.C. 7501-7507) and revised OMB Circular A-133, ``Audits of States, Local Governments, and Non-Profit Organizations.'' The audits shall be made by an independent auditor in accordance with generally accepted government auditing standards covering financial audits.

b. Subgrantees. State or local governments, as those terms are defined for purposes of the Single Audit Act Amendments of 1996, that provide Federal awards to a subgrantee, which expends $500,000 or more (or other amount as specified by OMB) in Federal awards in a fiscal year, shall:

　1. Determine whether State or local subgrantees have met the audit requirements of the Act and whether subgrantees covered by OMB Circular A-110, ``Uniform Administrative Requirements for Grants and Agreements with Institutions of Higher Education, Hospitals, and Other Non-Profit Organizations,'' have met the audit requirements of the Act. Commercial contractors (private for-profit and private and governmental organizations) providing goods and services to State and local governments are not required to have a single audit performed. State and local governments should use their own procedures to ensure that the contractor has complied with laws and regulations affecting the expenditure of Federal funds;

　2. Determine whether the subgrantee spent Federal assistance funds provided in accordance with applicable laws and regulations. This may be accomplished by reviewing an audit of the subgrantee made in accordance with the Act, Circular A-110, or through other means (e.g., program reviews) if the subgrantee has not had such an audit;

　3. Ensure that appropriate corrective action is taken within six months after receipt of the audit report in instance of noncompliance with Federal laws and regulations;

　4. Consider whether subgrantee audits necessitate adjustment of the grantee's own records; and

　5. Require each subgrantee to permit independent auditors to have access to the records and financial statements.

c. Auditor selection. In arranging for audit services, Sec. 13.36 shall be followed.

Sec. 13.30 Changes

a. General. Grantees and subgrantees are permitted to rebudget within the approved direct cost budget to meet unanticipated requirements and may make limited program changes to the approved project. However, unless waived by the awarding agency, certain types of post-award changes in budgets and projects shall require the prior written approval of the awarding agency.

b. Relation to cost principles. The applicable cost principles (see Sec. 13.22) contain requirements for prior approval of certain types of costs. Except where waived, those requirements apply to all grants and subgrants even if paragraphs (c) through (f) of this section do not.

c. Budget changes--

1. Nonconstruction projects. Except as stated in other regulations or an award document, grantees or subgrantees shall obtain the prior approval of the awarding agency whenever any of the following changes is anticipated under a nonconstruction award:

    i. Any revision which would result in the need for additional funding.

    ii. Unless waived by the awarding agency, cumulative transfers among direct cost categories, or, if applicable, among separately budgeted programs, projects, functions, or activities which exceed or are expected to exceed ten percent of the current total approved budget, whenever the awarding agency's share exceeds $100,000.

    iii. Transfer of funds allotted for training allowances (i.e., from direct payments to trainees to other expense categories).

2. Construction projects. Grantees and subgrantees shall obtain prior written approval for any budget revision which would result in the need for additional funds.

3. Combined construction and nonconstruction projects. When a grant or subgrant provides funding for both construction and nonconstruction activities, the grantee or subgrantee must obtain prior written approval from the awarding agency before making any fund or budget transfer from nonconstruction to construction or vice versa.

d. Programmatic changes. Grantees or subgrantees must obtain the prior approval of the awarding agency whenever any of the following actions is anticipated:

1. Any revision of the scope or objectives of the project (regardless of whether there is an associated budget revision requiring prior approval).

2. Need to extend the period of availability of funds.

3. Changes in key persons in cases where specified in an application or a grant award. In research projects, a change in the project director or principal investigator shall always require approval unless waived by the awarding agency.

4. Under nonconstruction projects, contracting out, subgranting (if authorized by law) or otherwise obtaining the services of a third party to perform activities which are central to the purposes of the award. This approval requirement is in addition to the approval requirements of Sec. 13.36 but does not apply to the procurement of equipment, supplies, and general support services.

e. Additional prior approval requirements. The awarding agency may not require prior approval for any budget revision which is not described in paragraph (c) of this section.

f. Requesting prior approval.

   1. A request for prior approval of any budget revision will be in the same budget formal the grantee used in its application and shall be accompanied by a narrative justification for the proposed revision.

   2. A request for a prior approval under the applicable Federal cost principles (see Sec. 13.22) may be made by letter.

   3. A request by a subgrantee for prior approval will be addressed in writing to the grantee. The grantee will promptly review such request and shall approve or disapprove the request in writing. A grantee will not approve any budget or project revision which is inconsistent with the purpose or terms and conditions of the Federal grant to the grantee. If the revision, requested by the subgrantee would result in a change to the grantee's approved project which requires Federal prior approval, the grantee will obtain the Federal agency's approval before approving the subgrantee's request.

Sec. 13.35 Subawards to debarred and suspended parties

Grantees and subgrantees must not make any award or permit any award (subgrant or contract) at any tier to any party which is debarred or suspended or is otherwise excluded from or ineligible for participation in Federal assistance programs under Executive Order 12549, ``Debarment and Suspension.''

Sec. 13.36 Procurement

a. States. When procuring property and services under a grant, a State will follow the same policies and procedures it uses for procurements from its non-Federal funds. The State will ensure that every purchase order or other contract includes any clauses required by Federal statutes and executive orders and their implementing regulations. Other grantees and subgrantees will follow paragraphs (b) through (i) in this section.

b. Procurement standards.

   1. Grantees and subgrantees will use their own procurement procedures which reflect applicable State and local laws and regulations, provided that the procurements conform to applicable Federal law and the standards identified in this section.

   2. Grantees and subgrantees will maintain a contract administration system which ensures that contractors perform in accordance with the terms, conditions, and specifications of their contracts or purchase orders.

   3. Grantees and subgrantees will maintain a written code of standards of conduct governing the performance of their employees engaged in the award and administration of contracts. No employee, officer or agent of the grantee or subgrantee shall participate in selection, or in the award or administration of a contract supported by Federal funds if a conflict of interest, real or apparent, would be involved. Such a conflict would arise when:

i. The employee, officer or agent,

ii. Any member of his immediate family,

iii. His or her partner, or

iv. An organization which employs, or is about to employ, any of the above, has a financial or other interest in the firm selected for award. The grantee's or subgrantee's officers, employees or agents will neither solicit nor accept gratuities, favors or anything of monetary value from contractors, potential contractors, or parties to subagreements. Grantee and subgrantees may set minimum rules where the financial interest is not substantial or the gift is an unsolicited item of nominal intrinsic value. To the extent permitted by State or local law or regulations, such standards or conduct will provide for penalties, sanctions, or other disciplinary actions for violations of such standards by the grantee's and subgrantee's officers, employees, or agents, or by contractors or their agents. The awarding agency may in regulation provide additional prohibitions relative to real, apparent, or potential conflicts of interest.

4. Grantee and subgrantee procedures will provide for a review of proposed procurements to avoid purchase of unnecessary or duplicative items. Consideration should be given to consolidating or breaking out procurements to obtain a more economical purchase. Where appropriate, an analysis will be made of lease versus purchase alternatives, and any other appropriate analysis to determine the most economical approach.

5. To foster greater economy and efficiency, grantees and subgrantees are encouraged to enter into State and local intergovernmental agreements for procurement or use of common goods and services.

6. Grantees and subgrantees are encouraged to use Federal excess and surplus property in lieu of purchasing new equipment and property whenever such use is feasible and reduces project costs.

7. Grantees and subgrantees are encouraged to use value engineering clauses in contracts for construction projects of sufficient size to offer reasonable opportunities for cost reductions. Value engineering is a systematic and creative analysis of each contract item or task to ensure that its essential function is provided at the overall lower cost.

8. Grantees and subgrantees will make awards only to responsible contractors possessing the ability to perform successfully under the terms and conditions of a proposed procurement. Consideration will be given to such matters as contractor integrity, compliance with public policy, record of past performance, and financial and technical resources.

9. Grantees and subgrantees will maintain records sufficient to detail the significant history of a procurement. These records will include, but are not necessarily limited to the following: rationale for the method of procurement, selection of contract type, contractor selection or rejection, and the basis for the contract price.

10. Grantees and subgrantees will use time and material type contracts only--

i. After a determination that no other contract is suitable, and

ii. If the contract includes a ceiling price that the contractor exceeds at its own risk.

11. Grantees and subgrantees alone will be responsible, in accordance with good administrative practice and sound business judgment, for the settlement of all contractual and administrative issues arising out of procurements. These issues include, but are not limited to source evaluation, protests, disputes, and claims. These standards do not relieve the grantee or subgrantee of any contractual responsibilities under its contracts. Federal agencies will not substitute their judgment for that of the grantee or subgrantee unless the matter is primarily a Federal concern. Violations of law will be referred to the local, State, or Federal authority having proper jurisdiction.

12. Grantees and subgrantees will have protest procedures to handle and resolve disputes relating to their procurements and shall in all instances disclose information regarding the protest to the awarding agency. A protestor must exhaust all administrative remedies with the grantee and subgrantee before pursuing a protest with the Federal agency. Reviews of protests by the Federal agency will be limited to:

   i. Violations of Federal law or regulations and the standards of this section (violations of State or local law will be under the jurisdiction of State or local authorities) and

   ii. Violations of the grantee's or subgrantee's protest procedures for failure to review a complaint or protest. Protests received by the Federal agency other than those specified above will be referred to the grantee or subgrantee.

c. Competition.

1. All procurement transactions will be conducted in a manner providing full and open competition consistent with the standards of section 13.36. Some of the situations considered to be restrictive of competition include but are not limited to:

   i. Placing unreasonable requirements on firms in order for them to qualify to do business,

   ii. Requiring unnecessary experience and excessive bonding,

   iii. Noncompetitive pricing practices between firms or between affiliated companies,

   iv. Noncompetitive awards to consultants that are on retainer contracts,

   v. Organizational conflicts of interest,

   vi. Specifying only a ``brand name'' product instead of allowing ``an equal'' product to be offered and describing the performance of other relevant requirements of the procurement, and

   vii. Any arbitrary action in the procurement process.

2. Grantees and subgrantees will conduct procurements in a manner that prohibits the use of statutorily or administratively imposed in-State or local geographical preferences in the evaluation of bids or proposals, except in those cases where applicable Federal statutes expressly mandate or encourage geographic preference. Nothing in this section preempts State licensing laws. When contracting for architectural and engineering (A/E) services, geographic location may be a selection criteria provided its application leaves an appropriate number of qualified firms, given the nature and size of the project, to compete for the contract.

3. Grantees will have written selection procedures for procurement transactions. These procedures will ensure that all solicitations:

    i. Incorporate a clear and accurate description of the technical requirements for the material, product, or service to be procured. Such description shall not, in competitive procurements, contain features which unduly restrict competition. The description may include a statement of the qualitative nature of the material, product or service to be procured, and when necessary, shall set forth those minimum essential characteristics and standards to which it must conform if it is to satisfy its intended use. Detailed product specifications should be avoided if at all possible. When it is impractical or uneconomical to make a clear and accurate description of the technical requirements, a ``brand name or equal'' description may be used as a means to define the performance or other salient requirements of a procurement. The specific features of the named brand which must be met by offerors shall be clearly stated; and

    ii. Identify all requirements which the offerors must fulfill and all other factors to be used in evaluating bids or proposals.

4. Grantees and subgrantees will ensure that all prequalified lists of persons, firms, or products which are used in acquiring goods and services are current and include enough qualified sources to ensure maximum open and free competition. Also, grantees and subgrantees will not preclude potential bidders from qualifying during the solicitation period.

d. Methods of procurement to be followed—

1. Procurement by small purchase procedures. Small purchase procedures are those relatively simple and informal procurement methods for securing services, supplies, or other property that do not cost more than the simplified acquisition threshold fixed at 41 U.S.C. 403(11) (currently set at $100,000). If small purchase procedures are used, price or rate quotations shall be obtained from an adequate number of qualified sources.

2. Procurement by sealed bids (formal advertising). Bids are publicly solicited and a firm-fixed-price contract (lump sum or unit price) is awarded to the responsible bidder whose bid, conforming with all the material terms and conditions of the invitation for bids, is the lowest in price. The sealed bid method is the preferred method for procuring construction, if the conditions in Sec. 13.36(d)(2)(i) apply.

i. In order for sealed bidding to be feasible, the following conditions should be present:

   A. A complete, adequate, and realistic specification or purchase description is available;

   B. Two or more responsible bidders are willing and able to compete effectively and for the business; and

   C. The procurement lends itself to a firm fixed price contract and the selection of the successful bidder can be made principally on the basis of price.

ii. If sealed bids are used, the following requirements apply:

   A. The invitation for bids will be publicly advertised and bids shall be solicited from an adequate number of known suppliers, providing them sufficient time prior to the date set for opening the bids;

   B. The invitation for bids, which will include any specifications and pertinent attachments, shall define the items or services in order for the bidder to properly respond;

   C. All bids will be publicly opened at the time and place prescribed in the invitation for bids;

   D. A firm fixed-price contract award will be made in writing to the lowest responsive and responsible bidder. Where specified in bidding documents, factors such as discounts, transportation cost, and life cycle costs shall be considered in determining which bid is lowest. Payment discounts will only be used to determine the low bid when prior experience indicates that such discounts are usually taken advantage of; and

   E. Any or all bids may be rejected if there is a sound documented reason.

3. Procurement by competitive proposals. The technique of competitive proposals is normally conducted with more than one source submitting an offer, and either a fixed-price or cost-reimbursement type contract is awarded. It is generally used when conditions are not appropriate for the use of sealed bids. If this method is used, the following requirements apply:

   i. Requests for proposals will be publicized and identify all evaluation factors and their relative importance. Any response to publicized requests for proposals shall be honored to the maximum extent practical;

   ii. Proposals will be solicited from an adequate number of qualified sources;

   iii. Grantees and subgrantees will have a method for conducting technical evaluations of the proposals received and for selecting awardees;

   iv. Awards will be made to the responsible firm whose proposal is most advantageous to the program, with price and other factors considered; and

v. Grantees and subgrantees may use competitive proposal procedures for qualifications-based procurement of architectural/engineering (A/E) professional services whereby competitors' qualifications are evaluated and the most qualified competitor is selected, subject to negotiation of fair and reasonable compensation. The method, where price is not used as a selection factor, can only be used in procurement of A/E professional services. It cannot be used to purchase other types of services though A/E firms are a potential source to perform the proposed effort.

4. Procurement by noncompetitive proposals is procurement through solicitation of a proposal from only one source, or after solicitation of a number of sources, competition is determined inadequate.

   i. Procurement by noncompetitive proposals may be used only when the award of a contract is infeasible under small purchase procedures, sealed bids or competitive proposals and one of the following circumstances applies:

      A. The item is available only from a single source;

      B. The public exigency or emergency for the requirement will not permit a delay resulting from competitive solicitation;

      C. The awarding agency authorizes noncompetitive proposals; or

      D. After solicitation of a number of sources, competition is determined inadequate.

   ii. Cost analysis, i.e., verifying the proposed cost data, the projections of the data, and the evaluation of the specific elements of costs and profits, is required.

   iii. Grantees and subgrantees may be required to submit the proposed procurement to the awarding agency for pre-award review in accordance with paragraph (g) of this section.

e. Contracting with small and minority firms, women's business enterprise and labor surplus area firms.

   1. The grantee and subgrantee will take all necessary affirmative steps to assure that minority firms, women's business enterprises, and labor surplus area firms are used when possible.

   2. Affirmative steps shall include:

      i. Placing qualified small and minority businesses and women's business enterprises on solicitation lists;

      ii. Assuring that small and minority businesses, and women's business enterprises are solicited whenever they are potential sources;

      iii. Dividing total requirements, when economically feasible, into smaller tasks or quantities to permit maximum participation by small and minority business, and women's business enterprises;

      iv. Establishing delivery schedules, where the requirement permits, which encourage participation by small and minority business, and women's business enterprises;

v. Using the services and assistance of the Small Business Administration, and the Minority Business Development Agency of the Department of Commerce; and

vi. Requiring the prime contractor, if subcontracts are to be let, to take the affirmative steps listed in paragraphs (e)(2) (i) through (v) of this section.

f. Contract cost and price.

1. Grantees and subgrantees must perform a cost or price analysis in connection with every procurement action including contract modifications. The method and degree of analysis is dependent on the facts surrounding the particular procurement situation, but as a starting point, grantees must make independent estimates before receiving bids or proposals. A cost analysis must be performed when the offeror is required to submit the elements of his estimated cost, e.g., under professional, consulting, and architectural engineering services contracts. A cost analysis will be necessary when adequate price competition is lacking, and for sole source procurements, including contract modifications or change orders, unless price resonableness can be established on the basis of a catalog or market price of a commercial product sold in substantial quantities to the general public or based on prices set by law or regulation. A price analysis will be used in all other instances to determine the reasonableness of the proposed contract price.

2. Grantees and subgrantees will negotiate profit as a separate element of the price for each contract in which there is no price competition and in all cases where cost analysis is performed. To establish a fair and reasonable profit, consideration will be given to the complexity of the work to be performed, the risk borne by the contractor, the contractor's investment, the amount of subcontracting, the quality of its record of past performance, and industry profit rates in the surrounding geographical area for similar work.

3. Costs or prices based on estimated costs for contracts under grants will be allowable only to the extent that costs incurred or cost estimates included in negotiated prices are consistent with Federal cost principles (see Sec. 13.22). Grantees may reference their own cost principles that comply with the applicable Federal cost principles.

4. The cost plus a percentage of cost and percentage of construction cost methods of contracting shall not be used.

g. Awarding agency review.

1. Grantees and subgrantees must make available, upon request of the awarding agency, technical specifications on proposed procurements where the awarding agency believes such review is needed to ensure that the item and/or service specified is the one being proposed for purchase. This review generally will take place prior to the time the specification is incorporated into a solicitation document. However, if the grantee or subgrantee desires to have the review accomplished after a solicitation has been developed, the awarding agency may still re-

view the specifications, with such review usually limited to the technical aspects of the proposed purchase.

2. Grantees and subgrantees must on request make available for awarding agency pre-award review procurement documents, such as requests for proposals or invitations for bids, independent cost estimates, etc. when:

   i. A grantee's or subgrantee's procurement procedures or operation fails to comply with the procurement standards in this section; or

   ii. The procurement is expected to exceed the simplified acquisition threshold and is to be awarded without competition or only one bid or offer is received in response to a solicitation; or

   iii. The procurement, which is expected to exceed the simplified acquisition threshold, specifies a "brand name" product; or

   iv. The proposed award is more than the simplified acquisition threshold and is to be awarded to other than the apparent low bidder under a sealed bid procurement; or

   v. A proposed contract modification changes the scope of a contract or increases the contract amount by more than the simplified acquisition threshold.

3. A grantee or subgrantee will be exempt from the pre-award review in paragraph (g)(2) of this section if the awarding agency determines that its procurement systems comply with the standards of this section.

   i. A grantee or subgrantee may request that its procurement system be reviewed by the awarding agency to determine whether its system meets these standards in order for its system to be certified. Generally, these reviews shall occur where there is a continuous high-Dollar funding, and third-party contracts are awarded on a regular basis.

   ii. A grantee or subgrantee may self-certify its procurement system. Such self-certification shall not limit the awarding agency's right to survey the system. Under a self-certification procedure, awarding agencies may wish to rely on written assurances from the grantee or subgrantee that it is complying with these standards. A grantee or subgrantee will cite specific procedures, regulations, standards, etc., as being in compliance with these requirements and have its system available for review.

h. Bonding requirements. For construction or facility improvement contracts or subcontracts exceeding the simplified acquisition threshold, the awarding agency may accept the bonding policy and requirements of the grantee or subgrantee provided the awarding agency has made a determination that the awarding agency's interest is adequately protected. If such a determination has not been made, the minimum requirements shall be as follows:

1. A bid guarantee from each bidder equivalent to five percent of the bid price. The "bid guarantee" shall consist of a firm

commitment such as a bid bond, certified check, or other negotiable instrument accompanying a bid as assurance that the bidder will, upon acceptance of his bid, execute such contractual documents as may be required within the time specified.

2. A performance bond on the part of the contractor for 100 percent of the contract price. A ``performance bond'' is one executed in connection with a contract to secure fulfillment of all the contractor's obligations under such contract.

3. A payment bond on the part of the contractor for 100 percent of the contract price. A ``payment bond'' is one executed in connection with a contract to assure payment as required by law of all persons supplying labor and material in the execution of the work provided for in the contract.

i. Contract provisions. A grantee's and subgrantee's contracts must contain provisions in paragraph (i) of this section. Federal agencies are permitted to require changes, remedies, changed conditions, access and records retention, suspension of work, and other clauses approved by the Office of Federal Procurement Policy.

1. Administrative, contractual, or legal remedies in instances where contractors violate or breach contract terms, and provide for such sanctions and penalties as may be appropriate. (Contracts more than the simplified acquisition threshold)

2. Termination for cause and for convenience by the grantee or subgrantee including the manner by which it will be effected and the basis for settlement. (All contracts in excess of $10,000)

3. Compliance with Executive Order 11246 of September 24, 1965, entitled ``Equal Employment Opportunity,'' as amended by Executive Order 11375 of October 13, 1967, and as supplemented in Department of Labor regulations (41 CFR chapter 60). (All construction contracts awarded in excess of $10,000 by grantees and their contractors or subgrantees)

4. Compliance with the Copeland ``Anti-Kickback'' Act (18 U.S.C. 874) as supplemented in Department of Labor regulations (29 CFR Part 3). (All contracts and subgrants for construction or repair)

5. Compliance with the Davis-Bacon Act (40 U.S.C. 276a to 276a-7) as supplemented by Department of Labor regulations (29 CFR part 5). (Construction contracts in excess of $2000 awarded by grantees and subgrantees when required by Federal grant program legislation)

6. Compliance with Sections 103 and 107 of the Contract Work Hours and Safety Standards Act (40 U.S.C. 327-330) as supplemented by Department of Labor regulations (29 CFR Part 5). (Construction contracts awarded by grantees and subgrantees in excess of $2000, and in excess of $2500 for other contracts which involve the employment of mechanics or laborers)

7. Notice of awarding agency requirements and regulations pertaining to reporting.

8. Notice of awarding agency requirements and regulations pertaining to patent rights with respect to any discovery or

invention which arises or is developed in the course of or under such contract.

9. Awarding agency requirements and regulations pertaining to copyrights and rights in data.

10. Access by the grantee, the subgrantee, the Federal grantor agency, the Comptroller General of the United States, or any of their duly authorized representatives to any books, documents, papers, and records of the contractor which are directly pertinent to that specific contract for the purpose of making audit, examination, excerpts, and transcriptions.

11. Retention of all required records for three years after grantees or subgrantees make final payments and all other pending matters are closed.

12. Compliance with all applicable standards, orders, or requirements issued under section 306 of the Clean Air Act (42 U.S.C. 1857(h)), section 508 of the Clean Water Act (33 U.S.C. 1368), Executive Order 11738, and Environmental Protection Agency regulations (40 CFR part 15). (Contracts, subcontracts, and subgrants of amounts in excess of $100,000)

13. Mandatory standards and policies relating to energy efficiency which are contained in the state energy conservation plan issued in compliance with the Energy Policy and Conservation Act (Pub. L. 94-163, 89 Stat. 871).

Sec. 13.37 Subgrants

a. States. States shall follow state law and procedures when awarding and administering subgrants (whether on a cost reimbursement or fixed amount basis) of financial assistance to local and Indian tribal governments. States shall:

1. Ensure that every subgrant includes any clauses required by Federal statute and executive orders and their implementing regulations;

2. Ensure that subgrantees are aware of requirements imposed upon them by Federal statute and regulation;

3. Ensure that a provision for compliance with Sec. 13.42 is placed in every cost reimbursement subgrant; and

4. Conform any advances of grant funds to subgrantees substantially to the same standards of timing and amount that apply to cash advances by Federal agencies.

b. All other grantees. All other grantees shall follow the provisions of this part which are applicable to awarding agencies when awarding and administering subgrants (whether on a cost reimbursement or fixed amount basis) of financial assistance to local and Indian tribal governments. Grantees shall:

1. Ensure that every subgrant includes a provision for compliance with this part;

2. Ensure that every subgrant includes any clauses required by Federal statute and executive orders and their implementing regulations; and

3. Ensure that subgrantees are aware of requirements imposed upon them by Federal statutes and regulations.

c. Exceptions. By their own terms, certain provisions of this part do not apply to the award and administration of subgrants:

1. Section 13.10;
2. Section 13.11;
3. The letter-of-credit procedures specified in Treasury Regulations at 31 CFR part 205, cited in Sec. 13.21; and
4. Section 13.50.

Sec. 13.40 Monitoring and reporting program performance

a. Monitoring by grantees. Grantees are responsible for managing the day-to-day operations of grant and subgrant supported activities. Grantees must monitor grant and subgrant supported activities to assure compliance with applicable Federal requirements and that performance goals are being achieved. Grantee monitoring must cover each program, function or activity.

Sec. 13.50 Closeout

a. General. The Federal agency will close out the award when it determines that all applicable administrative actions and all required work of the grant has been completed.

b. Reports. **Within 90 days** after the expiration or termination of the grant, the grantee must submit all financial, performance, and other reports required as a condition of the grant. Upon request by the grantee, Federal agencies may extend this timeframe. These may include but are not limited to:

1. Final performance or progress report.
2. Financial Status Report (SF 269) or Outlay Report and Request for Reimbursement for Construction Programs (SF-271) (as applicable.)
3. Final request for payment (SF-270) (if applicable).
4. Invention disclosure (if applicable).
5. Federally-owned property report: In accordance with Sec. 3.32(f), a grantee must submit an inventory of all federally owned property (as distinct from property acquired with grant funds) for which it is accountable and request disposition instructions from the Federal agency of property no longer needed.

c. Cost adjustment. The Federal agency will, within 90 days after receipt of reports in paragraph (b) of this section, make upward or downward adjustments to the allowable costs.

d. Cash adjustments.

1. The Federal agency will make prompt payment to the grantee for allowable reimbursable costs.
2. The grantee must immediately refund to the Federal agency any balance of unobligated (unencumbered) cash advanced that is not authorized to be retained for use on other grants.

44 C.F.R. § 206.14 Criminal and civil penalties

a. Misuse of funds. Any person who knowingly misapplies the proceeds of a loan or other cash benefit obtained under this Act [*The Robert T. Stafford Disaster Relief and Emergency Assistance Act, 42 U.S.C. 5121 et seq.*] shall be fined an amount equal to one and one-half times the misapplied amount of the proceeds or cash benefit.

b. Civil enforcement. Whenever it appears that any person has violated or is about to violate any provision of this Act, including any civil penalty imposed under this Act, the Attorney General may bring a civil action for such relief as may be appropriate. Such action may be brought in an appropriate United States district court.

c. Referral to Attorney General. The Associate Director shall expeditiously refer to the Attorney General for appropriate action any evidence developed in the performance of functions under this Act that may warrant consideration for criminal prosecution.

d. Civil penalty. Any individual who knowingly violates any order or regulation issued under this Act shall be subject to a civil penalty of not more than $5,000 for each violation.

Single Audit Act [31 U.S.C. § 7502]

When, as the result of a disaster or mitigation for disasters, the federal government makes a grant of $500,000.00 or more the requirement for an audit attaches. The audit must be in conformance with the federal Single Audit Act. The audit may be performed by a government auditor or a private auditor hired by the government. Most audits will be performed by the state, or a private auditor hired by the state.

Audit requirements

(a)(1)(A) Each non-Federal entity that expends a total amount of Federal awards equal to or in excess of $500,000 or such other amount specified by the Director {Note: Director means the Director of the Office of Management} under subsection (a)(3) in any fiscal year of such non-Federal entity shall have either a single audit or a program-specific audit made for such fiscal year in accordance with the requirements of this chapter.

(a)(1)(B) Each such non-Federal entity that expends Federal awards under more than one Federal program shall undergo a single audit in accordance with the requirements of subsections (b) through (i) of this section and guidance issued by the Director under section 7505

"(c) Each audit conducted pursuant to subsection (a) shall be conducted by an independent auditor in accordance with generally accepted government auditing standards, except that, for the purposes of this chapter, performance audits shall not be required except as authorized by the Director.

"(d) Each single audit conducted pursuant to subsection (a) for any fiscal year shall—

"(1) cover the operations of the entire non-Federal entity; or

"(2) at the option of such non-Federal entity such audit shall include a series of audits that cover departments, agencies, and other organizational units which expended or otherwise administered Federal awards during such fiscal year provided that each such audit shall encompass the financial statements and schedule of expenditures of Federal awards for each such department, agency, and organizational unit, which shall be considered to be a non-Federal entity.

"(e) The auditor shall—

"(1) determine whether the financial statements are presented fairly in all material respects in conformity with generally accepted accounting principles;

"(2) determine whether the schedule of expenditures of Federal awards is presented fairly in all material respects in relation to the financial statements taken as a whole;

"(3) with respect to internal controls pertaining to the compliance requirements for each major program—

"(A) obtain an understanding of such internal controls;

"(B) assess control risk; and

"(C) perform tests of controls unless the controls are deemed to be ineffective; and

"(4) determine whether the non-Federal entity has complied with the provisions of laws, regulations, and contracts or grants pertaining to Federal awards that have a direct and material effect on each major program.

"(g)(1) The auditor shall report on the results of any audit conducted pursuant to this section, in accordance with guidance issued by the Director.

"(2) When reporting on any single audit, the auditor shall include a summary of the auditor's results regarding the non-Federal entity's financial statements, internal controls, and compliance with laws and regulations.

"(h) The non-Federal entity shall transmit the reporting package, ...to a Federal clearinghouse designated by the Director, and make it available for public inspection.

"(i) If an audit conducted pursuant to this section discloses any audit findings, ... including material noncompliance with individual compliance requirements for a major program by, or reportable conditions in the internal controls of, the non-Federal entity with respect to the matters described in subsection (e), the non-Federal entity shall submit to Federal officials designated by the Director, a plan for corrective action... Such plan shall be consistent with the audit resolution standard promulgated by the Comptroller General.

Single Audit Act Regulations and Requirements imposed by the Director of OMB

OMB Circulars:

A-21, Cost Principles for Educational Institutions (August 8, 2000)

A-87, Cost Principles for State, Local and Indian Tribal Governments (May 4, 1995)

A-122, Cost Principles for Non-Profit Organizations (June 1, 1998)

A-102, Grants and Cooperative Agreements With State and Local Governments (October 7, 1994) (further amended August 29, 1997)

A-110, Uniform Administrative Requirements for Grants and Agreements With Institutions of Higher Education, Hospitals, and Other Non-Profit Organizations (November 19, 1993) (further amended September 30, 1999)

A-133, Audits of States, Non-Profits, and Local Organizations (June 24, 1997, includes revisions published in the *Federal Register* June 27, 2003)

Circular A-133, 2008 Compliance Supplement

Circular A-133, 2007 Compliance Supplement

Circular A-133, 2006 Compliance Supplement

The diagram on the next page spells out the ingle Audit Process. It is from Highlights of the Single Audit Process; Chief Financial Officers Council, Grants Management Committee, October 2001.

James L. Jaffe, J.D.

Overview of the Single Audit Process[84]

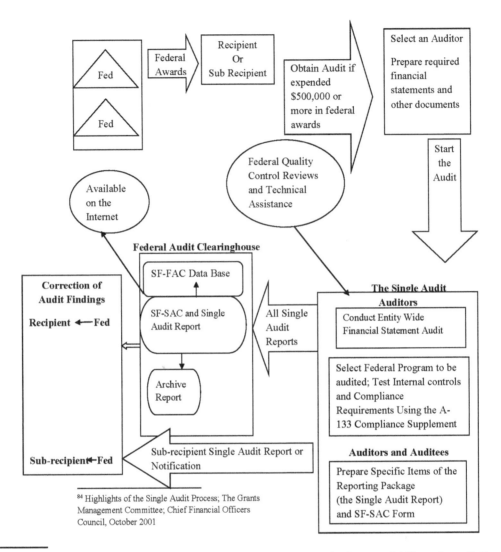

[84] Highlights of the Single Audit Process; The Grants Management Committee; Chief Financial Officers Council, October 2001

Income Tax Issues

Obviously any disaster loss to a for profit entity, be it a business or individual will have income tax implications. Since each state that has a state income tax will have its own rules regarding disaster losses, we will only discuss the federal income tax implications of a disaster loss.

Obtaining Copies of Income Tax Returns

Immediately after a casualty, you can request a copy of your return and all attachments (including Form W-2) by using Form 4506, Request for Copy of Tax Return.

An information return or transcript can be ordered by calling 1-800-829-1040 or using Form 4506-T, Request for Transcript of Tax Return. There is no fee for a transcript. Transcripts are available for the current year and returns processed in the three prior years.

IRS publications and web sites regarding disasters

For Individuals and Businesses

Publication 2194, Disaster Resource Guide for Individuals and Businesses

This resource guide provides information to individuals and businesses affected by a federally declared disaster and the assistance available to disaster victims. This Disaster Relief Resource

Guide can help you claim unreimbursed casualty losses on property that was damaged or destroyed.

This guide can be found at http://www.irs.gov/pub/irs-pdf/p2194.pdf

For Tax Professionals

Disaster Relief Resource Center for Tax Professionals

Through this resource center the IRS addresses many of the questions received from tax professionals. Included is information published by the IRS, along with links to IRS partners who may offer additional assistance. Many of the IRS partners have developed Web pages that highlight the efforts they've made to help their fellow practitioners to recover and get re-established. http://www.irs.gov/Tax-Professionals/Disaster-Relief-Resource-Center-for-Tax-Professionals

Disaster Assistance Self-Study

The Disaster Assistance Self-Study provides the basic information needed to assist taxpayers in a disaster. It provides the volunteer practitioner disaster representative member with information on distributing Disaster Kits, computing gains/losses as the result of a disaster, information about administrative tax relief and information about the psychological effects of a disaster on its victims. http://www.irs.gov/Businesses/Small-Businesses-&-Self-Employed/Disaster-Assistance-Self-Study

For Charitable Organizations

Disaster Relief - Resources for Charities and Contributors

After a disaster or in another emergency hardship situation, people may be interested in using a charitable organization to help victims. The IRS provides a number of resources to help them accomplish this goal. http://www.irs.gov/Charities-&-Non-Profits/Charitable-Organizations/Disaster-Relief-Resources-for-Charities-and-Contributors

Publication 3833, Disaster Relief, Providing Assistance Through Charitable Organizations (PDF)

This publication describes how members of the public can use charitable organizations to provide assistance to victims of disasters or other emergency hardship situations. http://www.irs.gov/pub/irs-pdf/p3833.pdf

For assistance and additional information, use these resources

- For Recent Grants of Relief, see Tax Relief in Disaster Situations
- Reconstructing Your Records

IRS Disaster Assistance Hotline at 1-866-562-5227 (Monday through Friday from 7 a.m. to 10 p.m. local time).

James L. Jaffe, J.D.

Income Tax Aspects of the Emergency Economic Stabilization Act of 2008

National Disaster Relief - (Sec. 706) Waives the 10% adjusted gross income limitation on personal casualty losses for losses sustained from a federally declared disaster occurring before January 1, 2010. Defines "federally declared disaster" as any disaster determined by the President to warrant federal assistance under the Robert T. Stafford Relief and Emergency Assistance Act.

Increases the standard tax deduction by a taxpayer's net disaster loss (i.e., personal casualty losses in a disaster area over personal casualty gains).

Increases until December 31, 2009, the threshold for deductible casualty losses (from $100 to $500).

(Sec. 707) Allows the expensing of business-related costs incurred due to a federally declared disaster for: (1) the abatement or control of hazardous substances; (2) removal of debris or demolition of damaged structures; or (3) repair of damaged property.

(Sec. 708) Provides for a five-year carryback period for net operating losses attributable to a federally declared disaster. Allows such losses as a deduction in computing alternative minimum taxable income.

(Sec. 709) Modifies certain mortgage revenue bond requirements for principal residences damaged or destroyed in a federally declared disaster occurring before January 1, 2010.

(Sec. 710) Allows accelerated depreciation and increases the expensing allowance for qualified disaster assistance property. Defines "qualified disaster assistance property" to include nonresidential real or residential rental property in a federally declared disaster area.

IRS answers to disaster income tax questions [85]

Are mitigation payments under Code Section 139 tax free?

A: Qualified disaster relief payments are excludable from the recipient's income. Qualified disaster payments include taxpayers who receive qualified disaster mitigation payments before, on or after April 15, 2005. Such payments are amounts paid under the Robert T. Stafford Disaster Relief and Emergency Assistance Act or the National Flood Insurance Act to or for the benefit of the owner of any property for hazard mitigation. There is no resulting increase in the basis or adjusted basis of the property for which the payments are made.

Also, no person for whose benefit a qualified disaster relief or mitigation payment is made is allowed to take a deduction or credit due to an expenditure for which exclusion for a payment is granted. The exclusion does not apply to amounts received for the sale or disposition of property.

Do you have to subtract FEMA payments, such as the $10,000 and $5,200 payments, in arriving at the calculation for your net casualty loss?

A: According to Publication 547 on page 6, food, medical supplies, and other forms of assistance you receive do not reduce your casualty loss, unless they are replacements for lost or destroyed property. In calculating your casualty loss, if the payment is for replacement of lost or destroyed property, then you would subtract the amount in figuring your casualty loss.

---

[85] http://www.irs.gov/Businesses/Small-Businesses-&-Self-Employed/FAQs-for-Disaster-Victims-Mitigation-Payments

How are FEMA "Individuals and Households Program" payments treated for income tax purposes?

A: Under the Individuals and Households Program (IHP), FEMA provides grant payments to individuals for critical expenses and losses, not covered by insurance or in other ways that are incurred as a result of a presidentially declared disaster. FEMA makes the following types of payments under the program:

- Temporary Housing Assistance: To rent a different place to live or a government provided housing unit when rental properties are not available.

- Repair Assistance: For homeowners to repair damage from the disaster to their primary residence that is not covered by insurance. The goal is to make the damaged home safe, sanitary, and functional.

- Replacement Assistance: For homeowners to replace their primary residence destroyed in the disaster that is not covered by insurance.

- Other Needs Assistance: For necessary expenses and serious needs caused by the disaster, such as medical, dental, funeral, personal property, transportation, moving, and storage.

In general, FEMA IHP payments received by eligible individuals for any of the above purposes are excluded from his or her gross income for federal income tax purposes to the extent that the expenses compensated for by the IHP payments are not compensated for by insurance or otherwise. The recipient of a FEMA IHP repair assistance payment or replacement assistance payment must reduce the amount of any casualty loss attributable to the damaged or destroyed residence by the amount of the FEMA IHP payment. In addition, the recipient must reduce his or her tax basis in the damaged or destroyed residence by the amount of the FEMA IHP repair assistance payment or replacement assistance payment, as well as by the amount of the allowable casualty loss deduction attributable to the damaged or destroyed residence. If the recipient repairs a damaged residence, the cost of repairs ordinarily is capitalized and added to the recipient's tax basis in the damaged residence. For more information on determining your adjusted basis, see Publication 530, Tax information for First-Time Homeowners, and Publication 551, Basis of Assets. Also, in general, the recipient of a FEMA IHP payment for reimbursement of a medical (including dental) expense must reduce the amount of his or her medical expenses by the amount of that FEMA IHP payment to determine the amount of any medical expense deduction. However, if the individual receives the FEMA IHP payment in a later year for reimbursement of medical expenses deducted in an earlier year, the individual generally must report the reimbursement as income up to the amount previously deducted as medical expenses. For more information, see Publication 502, Medical and Dental Expenses.

An individual whose principal residence is damaged or destroyed by a disaster receives a FEMA IHP repair assistance or replacement assistance payment and/or insurance proceeds that exceed his or her adjusted tax basis in the damaged or destroyed principal residence. How is this treated for federal income tax purposes?

A: If the FEMA IHP repair assistance or replacement assistance payment and/or insurance proceeds (and any other form of compensation for the damaged or destroyed residence) exceed the recipient's adjusted tax basis in the damaged or destroyed residence, the recipient has realized gain for federal income tax purposes. However, because the damage or destruction is considered an "involuntary conversion" of the residence for federal income tax purposes, the recipient may ordinarily defer reporting any gain if the cost of the repairs or the replacement residence is at least as much as the compensation received for the damage (including any FEMA IHP repair assistance or replacement assistance payment and/or insurance proceeds), and if certain other conditions are met. For more information, see Publication 547, Casualties, Disasters, and Thefts and Form 4684, Casualties and Thefts, and Instructions. If the principal residence is destroyed, the destruction may be treated as a sale for purposes of the tax provisions governing the exclusion of gain from the sale of a principal residence, and gain may be excluded up to $250,000 ($500,000 for certain situations involving joint returns), if certain conditions are met. Additionally, because the destruction is considered an involuntary conversion of the residence, any gain in excess of the $250,000/$500,000 limitation may also be deferred by buying similar or related replacement property, if certain conditions are met. For more information, see Publications 547 and 4492, and Form 4684, Casualties and Thefts and Instructions. The recipient of a FEMA IHP repair assistance payment or replacement assistance payment (and any other compensation for the damaged or destroyed residence) must reduce his or her "cost" basis in any replacement residence by the amount of any deferred gain from the damaged or destroyed residence.

Record Reconstruction

In the aftermath of a disaster there is a need to reconstruct lost or destroyed records for many reasons, not the least of which is for obtaining assistance, income tax and insurance purposes. The IRS has an excellent web site for that purpose which is reproduced here. http://www.irs.gov/uac/Reconstructing-Your-Records

- Tax purposes – You may need to reconstruct your records to prove you have a casualty loss and the amount of the loss. To compute your casualty loss, you need to determine: 1) the decrease in value of the property as a result of the casualty and 2) the adjusted basis of the property (usually the cost of the property and improvements). You may deduct the smaller of these two amounts, minus insurance or other reimbursement. See Publication 547 for further information on figuring your casualty loss deduction.

If you repair damage caused by the casualty, or spend money for cleaning up, keep the repair bills and any other records of what was done and how much it cost. You cannot deduct these costs, but you can use them as a measure of the decrease in fair market value caused by the casualty if the repairs are actually made, are not excessive, are necessary to bring the property back to its condition before the casualty, take care of the damage only, and do not cause the property to be worth more than before the casualty.

- Insurance reimbursement.

- Federal Emergency Management Agency (FEMA) and Small Business Administration aid – The more accurately you estimate your loss, the more loan and grant money there may be available to you.

The following tips may help to reconstruct your records to prove loss of personal-use or business property:

Personal Residence/Real Property

- Be sure to take photographs as quickly as possible after the casualty to establish the extent of the damage.

- Contact the title company, escrow company or bank that handled the purchase to obtain copies of escrow papers. Your real estate broker may also be able to help.

- Use the current property tax statement for land vs. building ratios, if available; if not available, get copies from the county assessor's office.

- Check with appraisal companies to locate a library of old multiple listing books. These can be used for "comps" to establish a basis or fair market value. "Comps" are comparable sales within the same neighborhood.

- Check with your mortgage company for copies of any appraisals or other information they may have about cost or fair market value.

    o Tax records – Immediately after the casualty, file Form 4506, Request for Copy of Tax Return, to request copies of the previous four years of income tax returns. To obtain copies of the previous four years of transcripts you may file a Form 4506-T, Request for Transcripts of a Tax Return. Write the appropriate disaster designation, such as "HURRICANE KATRINA," in red letters across the top of the forms to expedite processing and to waive the normal user fee.

    o Form 4506, Request for Copy of Tax Return

    o Form 4506-T, Request for Transcript of Tax Return

- Insurance Policy – Most policies list the value of the building to establish a base figure for replacement value insurance.

    o If you are unsure how to reach your insurance company, check with your state insurance department. http://www.naic.org/state_web_map.htm

Improvements – Call the contractor(s) to see if records are available. If possible get

- statements from the contractors verifying their work and cost.

    o Get written accounts from friends and relatives who saw your house before and after any improvements. See if any of them have photos taken at get-togethers.

    o If a home improvement loan was obtained, obtain paperwork from the institution issuing the loan. The amount of the loan may help establish the cost of the improvements.

- Inherited Property – Check court records for probate values. If a trust or estate existed, contact the attorney who handled the estate or trust.

- No other records are available – Check at the county assessor's office for old records about the property. Look for assessed valued and ask for the percentage of assessment to value at the time of purchase. This is a rough guess, but better than no records at all.

Vehicles

Kelley's Blue Book [http://www.kbb.com/], NADA [http://www.nada.com/] and Edmunds [http://www.edmunds.com/] are available online and at most libraries. They are good sources for the current fair market value of most vehicles on the road.

- Call the dealer and ask for a copy of the contract. If not available, give the dealer all the facts and details and ask for a comparable price figure.

- Use newspaper ads for the period in which the vehicle was purchased to determine cost basis. Use ads for the period when it was destroyed for fair market value. Be sure to keep copies of the ads.

- If you're still making payments, check with your lien holder.

Personal Property

The number and types of personal property may make it difficult to reconstruct records. One of the best methods is to draw pictures of each room. Draw a floor plan showing where each piece of furniture was placed. Then show pictures of the room looking toward any shelves or tables. These do not have to be professionally drawn, just functional. Take time to draw shelves with memorabilia on them. Do the same with kitchens and bedrooms. Reconstruct what was there, especially furniture that would have held items — drawers, dressers, shelves. Be sure to include garages, attics and basements.

- Get old catalogs. These catalogs are a great way to establish cost basis and fair market value.

- Check the prices on similar items in your local thrift stores to establish fair market value. Walk through the stores and look at comparable items, especially items such as kitchen gadgets. Look for odds and ends you may have had but forgotten because of infrequent use.

- Use your local "advertiser" as a source for fair market value. Keep copies of the issues handy and copy pages used for specific items to put with your tax records file on the disaster.

- Check local newspaper want ads for similar items. Again keep a copy of any you use for comparison with the tax file.

- If you bought items using a credit card, contact your credit card company.

- Check with your local library for back issues of newspapers. Most libraries keep old issues on microfilm. The sale sections of these back issues may help establish original costs on items such as appliances.

- Go to a used bookstore with a tape measure and the diagram of the destroyed property. Measure several rows of used books and count the number of books per shelf. Add up the prices of those books and determine an average cost per shelf. Then count the number of shelves you had in your home and multiply by the average cost per shelf. This will help determine the value of your books before the loss.

Business Records

- Inventories – Get copies of invoices from suppliers. Whenever possible, the invoices should date back at least one calendar year.

- Income – Get copies of bank statements. The deposits should closely reflect what the sales were for any given time period.

  o Obtain copies of last year's federal, state and local tax returns including sales tax reports, payroll tax returns and business licenses (from city or county). These will reflect gross sales for a given time period.

- Furniture and fixtures – Sketch an outline of the inside and outside of the business location. Then start to fill in the details of the sketches. (Inside the building — what equipment was where; if a store, where were the products/inventory located. Outside the building — shrubs, parking, signs, awnings, etc.)

- If you purchased an existing business, go back to the broker for a copy of the purchase agreement. This should detail what was acquired.

- If the building was constructed for you, contact the contractor for building plans or the county/city planning commissions for copies of any plans.

Locate Unknown Insurance Policies

To find out if an individual has, or had, life, health, disability income, long-term care or critical illness insurance

MIB Group, Inc. ("MIB") is a membership corporation owned by approximately 470 member insurance companies in the US and Canada. MIB maintains a database for insurance companies to exchange confidential information of underwriting significance when an individual applies for **life, health, disability income, long-term care or critical illness insurance.**

Living Individual's Insurance

An individual can obtain their MIB consumer file annually without charge. MIB will not have a consumer file (consumer report information) on a person if they have not applied for **individually underwritten** life, health, or disability income insurance during the preceding seven year period.

To obtain free copy of their consumer file, an individual must call MIB's toll-free phone number for disclosure, which is 866-692-6901 (TTY 866-346-3642 for hearing impaired)

Deceased Person's Life Insurance

An executor, or administrator, or in cases where there have been no probate proceedings, a surviving spouse or other relative eligible for appointment may be entitled to order the MIB report to determine if the decedent had life insurance. The cost of this search is $75.00.

The decedent's name is searched against inquiries submitted on individually underwritten life insurance applications processed since January 1, 1996.

To order a search for a deceased person's life insurance:

1. Download the search request form[86] and fill in the required information. Or order online.[87]

2. Search applicants must provide documentation of their appointments as executors or administrators of the decedent's estate. In cases where there have been no probate proceedings, a surviving spouse or other relative eligible for appointment may be entitled to order the report.

3. Include an original death certificate with official seal must accompany all search applications.

4. Include a $75.00 check (payable to MIB Solutions, Inc.) or money order in U.S. currency.

5. Mail the above four items to MIB Solutions at the address listed below, or supplied on the form. Mailing address: MIB Solutions, Inc., P.O. Box 105, Essex Station, Boston, MA 02110

---

[86] http://www.mib.com/lost_life_insurance.html
[87] http://www.mib.com/lost_life_insurance_howto.html

James L. Jaffe, J.D.

Credit Reports

In the United States there are three main consumer credit reporting companies; Experian, Equifax and TransUnion.

a. Legal Authority

The Federal Fair Credit Reporting Act, 15 U.S.C.A. § 1681, is enforced by the Federal Trade Commission.

To file a complaint or to get free information, visit ftc.gov or call toll-free, (877) FTC-HELP (877-382-4357); TTY: 866-653-4261.

Federal Fair Credit Reporting Act requires credit reporting agencies to:

1. furnish a free copy of a consumer's credit report upon request within 30 days after the consumer is notified of an adverse action.
2. provide you with a free copy of your credit report, at your request, once every 12 months.
3. to investigate consumers' claims.

Only one website is authorized to fill orders for the free annual credit report you are entitled to under law – annualcreditreport.com.

You need to provide your name, address, Social Security number, and date of birth. If you have moved in the last two years, you may have to provide your previous address. To maintain the security of your file, each nationwide consumer reporting company may ask you for some information that only you would know, like the amount of your monthly mortgage payment. Each company may ask you for different information because the information each has in your file may come from different sources.

If you request your report online at annualcreditreport.com you should be able to access it immediately. If you order your report by calling toll-free 1-877-322-8228, your report will be processed and mailed to you within 15 days. If you order your report by mail using the Annual Credit Report Request Form, your request will be processed and mailed to you within 15 days of receipt.

b. Incomplete or Inaccurate Information

Under the FCRA, both the consumer reporting company and the information provider (that is, the person, company, or organization that provides information about you to a consumer reporting company) are responsible for correcting inaccurate or incomplete information in your report. To take full advantage of your rights under this law, contact the consumer reporting company and the information provider.

1. Tell the consumer reporting company, in writing, what information you think is inaccurate.

2. Consumer reporting companies must investigate the items in question – usually within 30 days – unless they consider your dispute frivolous. They also must forward all the relevant data you provide about the inaccuracy to the organization that provided the information. After the information provider receives notice of a dispute from the consumer reporting company, it must investigate, review the relevant information, and report the results back to the consumer reporting company. If the information provider finds the disputed information is inaccurate, it must notify all three nationwide consumer reporting companies so they can correct the information in your file. When the investigation is complete, the consumer reporting company must give you the written results and a free copy of your report if the dispute results in a change. (This free report does not count as your annual free report under the FACT Act.) If an item is changed

or deleted, the consumer reporting company cannot put the disputed information back in your file unless the information provider verifies that it is accurate and complete. The consumer reporting company also must send you written notice that includes the name, address, and phone number of the information provider.

3. Tell the creditor or other information provider in writing that you dispute an item. Many providers specify an address for disputes. If the provider reports the item to a consumer reporting company, it must include a notice of your dispute. And if you are correct – that is, if the information is found to be inaccurate – the information provider may not report it again.

If an investigation doesn't resolve your dispute with the consumer reporting company, you can ask that a statement of the dispute be included in your file and in future reports. You also can ask the consumer reporting company to provide your statement to anyone who received a copy of your report in the recent past. You can expect to pay a fee for this service.

If you tell the information provider that you dispute an item, a notice of your dispute must be included any time the information provider reports the item to a consumer reporting company.

A consumer reporting company can report most accurate negative information for seven years and bankruptcy information for 10 years. There is no time limit on reporting information about criminal convictions; information reported in response to your application for a job that pays more than $75,000 a year; and information reported because you've applied for more than $150,000 worth of credit or life insurance. Information about a lawsuit or an unpaid judgment against you can be reported for seven years or until the statute of limitations runs out, whichever is longer.

c. Obtaining a Credit Report

The FCRA specifies who can access your credit report. Creditors, insurers, employers, and other businesses that use the information in your report to evaluate your applications for credit, insurance, employment, or renting a home are among those that have a legal right to access your report.

Your employer can get a copy of your credit report only if you agree. A consumer reporting company may not provide information about you to your employer, or to a prospective employer, without your written consent.

d. Fraud Alert Messages

NOTE

Consumers can add a fraud alert message to their credit report to protect credit information. Fraud alert messages notify potential credit grantors to verify the consumers' identification before extending credit in their names in case someone is using their information without their consent.

If consumers suspect that their identification information has been or could be used fraudulently, they can add an Initial Security Alert to their credit report. An Initial Security Alert remains on their report for 90 days.

Consumers can add an Extended Fraud Victim Alert to their credit report by submitting a copy of a valid identity theft report filed with a Federal, State, or Local law enforcement agency. An Extended Alert will remain on the credit report for seven years.

Active duty military consumers can add an Active Duty Alert to their credit report. An Active Duty Alert will remain on the credit report for one year.

Consumer Credit Reporting Agencies[88]

Experian

To obtain a credit report, call Experian at (800) 682-7654 or log on at: http://www.experian.com/.

To dispute credit information:

First, determine the right option to file a dispute online. Disputing information online is FREE, and all options offer step-by-step instructions on how to complete your request online.

Experian credit reports include a report number on top of the report (near the name), log on to: http://www.experian.com/disputes2/index.html and follow the directions to file the dispute.

The FTC enters Internet, telemarketing, identity theft, and other fraud-related complaints into Consumer Sentinel, a secure online database available to hundreds of civil and criminal law enforcement agencies in the U.S. and abroad.

Step 1: Start with a current copy of the Experian credit report. If the consumer doesn't have one, order online for immediate access. If reviewing a credit report online, access the dispute process while viewing the report. If the consumer has a paper copy of the report, access the online dispute process and enter the report number.

Step 2: Once online, view the report section by section. Click on a particular item to see more details about the item. If something is inaccurate, click on the blue 'Dispute this item' button that appears beside each item.

Step 3: Select a specific reason why the information is inaccurate, and enter any additional information that further explains the reason and click on Submit. Be sure to read the "Tell me more about dispute reasons" for tips on how to dispute particular information. *Accurate information, or information verified as accurate, cannot be removed from your report.*

Step 4: A notice is immediately sent to the source of the information requesting that they verify the account information. Within 30 days, the source must respond and we'll notify the consumer that the results of the dispute investigation are ready to be viewed, and we'll provide a link to the results. Make sure to provide an email address.

Consumers who have a dispute with a creditor over an item on an Experian report should send a letter to the address listed on the credit report.

The procedure for disputing an item should also be provided on the credit report.

Equifax

To obtain a credit report from Equifax, call 1-800-685-1111 or log on at: https://aa.econsumer.equifax.com/aad/landing.ehtml

Consumers who dispute items on an Equifax report should complete a research request form, included with the consumer's copy of the credit report, and send it to:

Equifax Information Services LLC
P.O. Box 740256
Atlanta, GA 30374

---

[88] The following information is quoted from the web sites of Experian, Equifax, TransUnion, TeleCheck, and Cetergy, Inc.

Or, consumers can go on-line to https://help.equifax.com/app/answers/detail/a_id/16/noIntercept/1/kw/dispute/session/L3RpbWUvMTQxMjI3NDQ3MS9zaWQvUHpOYXFUM20%3D and dispute their credit report.

TransUnion

To obtain a credit report from TransUnion Corporation, call (877) 322-8228.

Trans Union Corporation
111 West Jackson, 16th Floor
Chicago, Ill 60604.

If a consumer has a dispute regarding a TransUnion credit report, the consumer can:

a. call Trans Union at 1-800-916-8800.
b. download and fill out the form found on-line at: http://www.transunion.com/personal-credit/credit-disputes/credit-disputes.page
c. and mail it to:

TransUnion Consumer Solutions
P.O. Box 2000
Chester, PA 19022-2000

d. file the dispute on-line at: https://annualcreditreport.transunion.com/entry/disputeonline

Stolen Checks and Checks Using Your Identity

If your checks are stolen, or you are the victim of identity theft, stopping checks made out to your account by someone posing as you is critical. In addition to immediately contacting your bank, you can also contact the companies that clear checks presented to merchants at the point of sale. Merchants use the service of one of several companies to clear checks when they are presented at a retail store for payment. The major point of sale check clearing companies are: TeleCheck, Cetergy, Inc. and SCAN. Contact these companies and request that they authorize merchants to decline your checks.

TeleCheck

(Reporting Forgery or Identity Theft, call 1-800-710-9898) http://www.firstdata.com/telecheck/telecheck-forgery-identity-theft.htm

The TeleCheck web site posts the following information:

If you wish to report a forged, counterfeit, lost or stolen check, or identity theft to TeleCheck or TRS Recovery Services, please fax or mail ONE of the documents below to these companies' shared services Forgery Department:

- A notarized Affidavit of Forgery
- A notarized Identity Theft Affidavit
- A police report, filed, with assigned case/incident number.

The document should include the bank routing and account number, check number or check series and dollar amount of all check (s) reported.

NOTE: Insufficiently identified or unreported checks will not be updated to fraud status.

In your correspondence, include your personal information that was compromised (such as your name, address, state ID, driver's license, and/or your Social Security number) and copies of collection notices you may have received. Please include a phone number where you may be reached during business hours.

You may FAX this information to:

TeleCheck Services, Inc. Or TRS Recovery Services, Inc.
Attention: Forgery Department
Fax: (402) 916-8180

You may MAIL this information to:

TeleCheck Services Inc. Or TRS Recovery Services, Inc.
Attention: Forgery Department
P.O. Box 4451
Houston, TX 77210-4451

Cetergy, Inc

If you wish to report a lost or stolen check, forged, counterfeit, or identity theft to Certegy, please mail or fax the appropriate document(s) as described below to our Correspondence Department:

Download Affidavit Form https://www.askcertegy.com/download/Affidavit.pdf

Checks were stolen or forged

Send a signed and notarized Affidavit of Forgery and a police report to Certegy. If the Drivers License * was used, also send a copy of the Drivers License * it can be cleared in our system.

Checks Counterfeited (with consumer's name and account)

Send a signed and notarized Affidavit of Forgery and a police report to Certegy. If the Drivers License * was used, also send a copy of the Drivers License * it can be cleared in our system.

Checks Counterfeited (used consumers name and address only)

Send a signed letter stating that your name and address was used on counterfeit checks, and you have no knowledge of the account.

Checks Counterfeited (used consumers name and Drivers License *)

Send a signed and notarized Affidavit of Forgery and a police report to Certegy. If the Drivers License * was used, also send a copy of the Drivers License ** it can be cleared in our system.

Company Checks

If the check is counterfeit, send a signed letter stating the check is counterfeit. If the check was forged, send a signed and notarized Affidavit of Forgery and a police report to Certegy.

Mail your Affidavit documents to:

Certegy Check Services, Inc.
P.O. Box 30296
Tampa, FL 33630-3296

Fax your Affidavit documents to:
Fax: 727-570-4936

* A State Issued ID Card is only acceptable if you do not have a Drivers License.

** If the account is a joint account, all parties must sign the affidavit. Affidavits are processed within thirty days of receipt. Once the affidavit is processed you will receive a confirmation letter.

Documents

During a disaster, people often must abandon their homes on short notice. Lost documents are a serious consequence of almost every disaster. Many persons cannot qualify for insurance, disaster assistance or public benefits without documentation. Individuals must replace lost documents as soon as possible to avoid interrupting essential services or benefits. Thus, it is beneficial to keep copies of all important documents in a "grab and go" box.

Locating Important Documents:

First, check safe deposit boxes and other safekeeping places which may contain an original or copy of important documents.

Second, appropriate agencies should be contacted for current information or replacement of documents.

Third, a fee to process requests or to obtain certified copies may be required.

Fourth, determine whether it is faster to go to the office that has the document or to request the information by mail or FAX. In many cases, agencies take several weeks to process requests by mail.

Federal Documents

A. Federal Information Center

For general information about how to get information or documents from any federal agency call (800)333-4636 or TDD (800) 462-7585 or visit www.info.gov. Check the Government Listings of the White Pages of the phonebook to get addresses and local phone numbers. Many agencies have toll-free (800) lines which provide information on various services available including how to replace lost documents.

B. Social Security Cards

The Social Security Administration will replace a lost Social Security card. Individuals can go to their local district office, go to www.ssa.gov or call 1-800-772-1213 for forms and information. Social Security requires individuals to fill out a lost card form (Form SS-5) and provide one type of identification. The identification must be an original or certified copy. An excellent web site for Social Security information is http://www.ssa.gov/OP_Home/handbook/handbook.01/handbook-0101.html

C. Medicare Cards

The Social Security Administration will also replace lost Medicare cards. Call 1-800-772-1213 or go to the local district office for information regarding a free replacement. You can also go to https://secure.ssa.gov/apps6z/IMRC/main.html and replace your Medicare card online.

D. Veterans Administration

Each county has an office of Veteran's Assistance. Call 1-800-827-1000 to get information on document replacement and veteran's benefits during a disaster. The TDD number is 1-800-829-4833. Look in the Federal listings of the Government Pages of the Telephone Book's White Pages.

E. Citizenship and Immigration Services (USCIS)

Immigrants and naturalized citizens face great difficulties if they do not have documentation of their status. They cannot work and they may be subject to deportation. The INS has different forms to replace different documents. There are frequently significant time delays in obtaining replacement documents. To order forms, log on to http://www.uscis.gov/portal/site/uscis. Local offices also have forms. To call the nearest USCIS office, look in the Government Listings of the White Pages under Federal Government, Department Homeland Security.

To replace a work registration or "green" card, an individual must fill out a Form I-90

(Application by Lawful Permanent Resident for new Alien Registration Receipt Card).

Individuals must submit a completed I-90 in person at the nearest office of the Immigration & Naturalization Service. Applicants for replacement cards must also submit two color photographs taken within the last 30 days. They must bring a check or money order to cover the processing fee. INS will fingerprint each individual.

Note on Replacing a "Green Card"

This web link shows how to replace a green card. http://www.uscis.gov/green-card/after-green-card-granted

F. Passports and Department of State Documents

Individuals with lost visas or passports may get replacement documents from the Department of State. In Ohio, the County Clerk of the Court will have the forms for passports. Check the Federal Government Listings of the White Pages of the phonebook for the number of the Passport Agency.

A useful link for visa or passport replacement is: http://travel.state.gov/content/passports/english/passports/lost-stolen.html

Other Records

A. Bank Accounts/ATM Cards

Appropriate financial institutions must be contacted to replace bank passbooks, checkbooks, ATM and/or credit cards, and safe deposit box keys. Most banks have (800) numbers to report lost or stolen cards, which should be called immediately to make a report. Individuals must go to the branch where they opened their account, which has their original signature in order to obtain replacement cards, check books, and other bank books if they have no identification. For a bank's contact information or information on how to gain access to funds, call the Federal Deposit Insurance Corporation's (FDIC) 24-hour hotline: (877) ASK-FDIC or (877) 275-3342.

B. Credit Cards

Banks and other institutions have (800) numbers to report lost or stolen credit cards.

Once the losses are reported the cards will usually be sent only to the original address. This may pose a problem if the home is destroyed and the family is living in temporary shelter. Some credit card programs have local offices or banking institutions where replacement cards can be obtained.

C. Birth, Marriage and Death Certificates

Go to http://www.cdc.gov/nchs/w2w.htm for the contact information for each state.

D. Driver's License

Go to http://www.usa.gov/Topics/Motor-Vehicles.shtml for the contact information for each state.

E. Wills

To obtain a copy of a will, trust or other testamentary instrument, the attorney who prepared the document should be contacted. If the attorney does not have a copy, individuals should prepare a new will or other document. If a will has already been probated with the county Probate Court, then the Court will have a copy of the will.

F. Deeds

Certified copies of deeds to real property are available at the County Recorder's Office in the county where the property is located. The following information is needed:

1. Current owner's name(s)
2. Property address
3. Seller's name
4. Date of the recording
5. Document number

If a person does not have detailed information, the Recorder's Office may charge a fee to search the records for the correct document.

G. Court Records

Contact the Clerk's Office of the appropriate Court where the documents are on file. Call the clerk of the court or the executive office of the courts to find the correct courthouse. Many counties have different physical locations for different court files. In some instances, an individual must locate the record on microfiche and must return to check the file and obtain a copy. Have the year, the names of plaintiff and defendant and, if possible, the case number.

H. Food Stamp Identification, Medicaid Cards/Stickers

The County will replace documents, checks and stickers for recipients of public benefits. There is an expedited emergency procedure for all individuals. *Individuals must ask for the expedited procedure.*

I. Unemployment Insurance or State Disability

Check with the local unemployment insurance office for replacement information or documents.

Handy Dandy FEMA, SBA & Farm Service Agency Disaster Forms

FEMA Disaster Assistance Forms

FEMA requires an applicant to apply in person at a FEMA staffed disaster recovery center, on-line at http://www.fema.gov/assistance/index.shtm or by phone at 1-800-621-FEMA (3362)/ TTY 1-800-462-7585 for people with speech or hearing disabilities.

Farm Services Agency Disaster Assistance Forms

FSA forms can be found at http://forms.sc.egov.usda.gov/eForms/searchAction.do

Form Number	Description
CCC 452	NAP Actual Production History and Approved Yield Record
CCC 471 NAP BP	Noninsured Crop Disaster Assistance 2015 and Subsequent Years Basic Provisions
CCC 576-1	Appraisal/Production Report Noninsured Crop Disaster Assistance Program
CCC 576-1 Spanish	Appraisal/Production Report Noninsured Crop Disaster Assistance Program
CCC 577 Spanish	Transfer of NAP Coverage
CCC 851-851A	Emergency Loss Assistance for Livestock Application
CC 851-851A Spanish	Emergency Loss Assistance for Livestock Application
CCC 852	Livestock Indemnity Program Application
CCC 853	Livestock Forage Disaster Program Application
CCC 854	Livestock Indemnity Program-third party Certification
CCC 934-934A	Emergency Loss Assistance for Honeybees/Farm Raised Fish Application
CCC 934-934A Spanish	Emergency Loss Assistance for Honeybees/Farm Raised Fish Application
FSA 409	Measurement Service Record
FSA 755	Supplemental Agricultural Disaster Assistance Relief for Noninsurable Crops

SBA Disaster Assistance Forms

SBA Electronic Disaster Loan Application Forms can be found at: **https://disasterloan.sba.gov/ela/**

SBA disaster assistance forms can be found at:
http://www.sba.gov/category/type-form/small-business-forms/disaster-assistance-forms

These forms include:

SBA Form ▲	Form Name	Version	Size	Updated Date
	REQUIREMENTS FOR DISASTER LOAN SERVICING ACTIONS - BIRMINGHAM DLSC			08/20/2014 - 11:05
	REQUIREMENTS FOR DISASTER LOAN SERVICING ACTIONS - SANTA ANA NDLRC			08/20/2014 - 11:15
	REQUIREMENTS FOR DISASTER LOAN SERVICING ACTIONS - EL PASO DLSC			08/20/2014 - 11:07
	BIRMINGHAM DLSC REQUIREMENTS FOR DISASTER LOAN SERVICING ACTIONS			06/14/2014 - 00:50
1086	Secondary Participation Guaranty Agreement	2-14	381.53 KB	07/30/2014 - 15:34
1088	Loan Pool or Guaranteed Certificate	5-11		05/13/2014 - 08:16
1366	SBA Disaster Assistance Program SBA Form 1366 Borrower's Progress Certification	12-09	365.69 KB	06/14/2014 - 00:50
1368	Additional Filing Requirements Economic Injury Disaster Loan (EIDL), and Military Reservist Economic Injury Disaster Loan (MREIDL)	1-12	476.55 KB	06/14/2014 - 00:50
159D	Fee Disclosure Form and Compensation Agreement	7-05	161.9 KB	06/14/2014 - 00:50
1919	BORROWER INFORMATION FORM	(Revised 4/14)	174.75 KB	07/17/2014 - 14:55
1920	LENDER'S APPLICATION FOR GUARANTY FOR ALL 7(a) PROGRAMS	(Revised 4/14)	527.01 KB	08/20/2014 - 11:27

SBA Form	Form Name	Version	Size	Updated Date
2202	Schedule of Liabilities	11-01	131.29 KB	06/14/2014 - 00:50
2310	Preferred Lenders Program (PLP) for Export Working Capital Program (EWCP) Loans	06-2010	926.99 KB	06/14/2014 - 00:50
2416	Lender Certification for Refinanced Loan	4-11	952.46 KB	06/14/2014 - 00:50
5	Disaster Business Loan Application	1-12	265.29 KB	06/14/2014 - 00:50
5C	Disaster Home Loan Application	03-09	289.65 KB	06/14/2014 - 00:50
601	Agreement of Compliance	10-85	57.39 KB	06/14/2014 - 00:50
652	SBA Form 652	11-91	78.17 KB	09/16/2014 - 15:04
81-93	FEMA Form 81-93: Standard Flood Hazard Determination	DEC 05	147.6 KB	06/14/2014 - 00:50
8821	Tax Information Authorization	10-2011	60.72 KB	06/14/2014 - 00:50
8821	Instructions for Completing the IRS Tax Authorization Form 8821	10-11		06/14/2014 - 00:50
SF 5510	Authorization Agreement for Preauthorized Payments	2/2005	305.62 KB	06/14/2014 - 00:50

Publications Regarding the Economic Aspects Of Disaster Planning, Response & Mitigation

Farmer/Rancher

An excellent manual:

Farmers' Guide to Disaster Assistance (Sixth Edition, 2008)
Farmers' Legal Action Group, Inc.
360 North Robert Street, Suite 500
Saint Paul, Minnesota 55101-1589
Phone: 651-223-5400
Fax: 651-223-5335

http://www.flaginc.org/publication/farmers-guide-to-disaster-assistance-sixth-edition/

USDA Farm Service Agency Emergency Conservation Program Manual

Emergency Conservation Program Handbook 1-ECP (Revision)
http://www.fsa.usda.gov/Internet/FSA_File/1-ecp_r04_a06.pdf

Emergency Forest Restoration Handbook
http://www.fsa.usda.gov/Internet/FSA_File/1-efrp_r00_a01.pdf

Livestock Disaster Assistance Programs Handbook
http://www.fsa.usda.gov/Internet/FSA_File/1-ldap_r00_a27.pdf

Tree Assistance Program Handbook
http://www.fsa.usda.gov/Internet/FSA_File/1-tap_r04_a04.pdf

James L. Jaffe, J.D.

Disaster Designations Handbook
http://www.fsa.usda.gov/Internet/FSA_File/1-dis_r00_a01.pdf

Program Appeals, Mediation, and Litigation Handbook
http://www.fsa.usda.gov/Internet/FSA_File/1-app_r02_a14.pdf

USDA Food & Nutrition Service

Food Distribution Disaster Assistance
http://www.fns.usda.gov/fdd/about-fd-food-disaster-assistance
Note the list of resources on the left hand column of this web site.

EBT Disaster Plan Guide
Food & Nutrition Service has developed this *EBT Disaster Plan Guide* to help States to plan for the electronic issuance of food stamp benefits during a disaster.
http://www.fns.usda.gov/disaster/disaster-snap-guidance

USDA Rural Housing Service

The "Handbook" {HB-1-3550) (called "The Field Office handbook") used by the RHS to administer the 502 and 504 programs is found at: http://www.rurdev.usda.gov/Handbooks.html

FEMA

Are You Ready; A guide for individuals and families on how to prepare for emergencies. http://www.fema.gov/areyouready/

Emergency Management Guide for Business and Industry; FEMA's 67 page step-by-step advice to organizations on how to create and maintain a comprehensive emergency management program. FEMA 141/ October 1993 http://www.fema.gov/library/viewRecord.do?id=1689

FEMA 321 Public Assistance Policy Digest - January 2008 - Easy-to-read, brief summary of Public Assistance program policies. For States, local governments, and Non-Profit organizations. http://www.fema.gov/pdf/government/grant/pa/pdigest08.pdf

FEMA 322 Public Assistance Guide - June 2007 - Describes provisions and application procedures for Public Assistance program grants. For States, local governments, and Non-Profit organizations. http://www.fema.gov/media-library-data/20130726-1826-25045-1802/fema_publication_322_public_assistance_guide_6_1_07.pdf

FEMA 323 Applicant Handbook - March 2010 - Questions and answers on how to apply for Public Assistance program grants. For States, local governments, and Non-Profit organizations. http://www.fema.gov/pdf/government/grant/pa/fema323_app_handbk.pdf

FEMA 325 Debris Management Guide - July 2007 - Comprehensive guidance for community leaders in planning, mobilizing, organizing, and controlling large-scale debris clearance and disposal operations. http://www.fema.gov/pdf/government/grant/pa/demagde.pdf

Hazard Mitigation Assistance Program Guidance Pre-Disaster Mitigation, Flood Mitigation Assistance, Repetitive Flood Claims, Severe Repetitive Loss; dated June 19, 2008, http://www.fema.gov/library/viewRecord.do?id=3309 (This is an excellent manual)

Local Multi-Hazard Mitigation Planning Guidance, July 1, 2008 http://emergencymanagement.wi.gov/mitigation/docs/FEMA_HQ_Local_Mitigation_Plan_Guidance_FINAL_Release07_01_08_(2).pdf

Sample Local Mitigation Plan Scope of Work for Mitigation Grant Application www.fema.gov/library/viewRecord.do?id=1858

National Flood Insurance Program Community Rating System Coordinator's Manual FIA-15/2006 http://www.fema.gov/library/viewRecord.do?id=2434

Applicant's Guide to the Individuals & Households Program; FEMA 545 / July 2008 http://www.fema.gov/pdf/assistance/process/help_after_disaster_english.pdf

FEMA 9500 Policy Publication

The FEMA Public Assistance (PA) Program is administered through a coordinated effort between the Federal Emergency Management Agency (FEMA), the State (grantee), and the applicants (subgrantees).

While all three entities must work together to meet the overall objective of quick, efficient, effective program delivery, each has a different role.

FEMA's primary responsibilities are to determine the amount of funding, participate in educating the applicant on specific program issues and procedures, assist the applicant with the development of projects, and review the projects for compliance.

FEMA 9500 Series Policy Publications
Complete Public Assistance Policy Reference Manual (PDF 2.58MB)
Contains all Public Assistance policies formatted for printing.
http://www.fema.gov/9500-series-policy-publications

Table of Contents

9500 Infrastructure

- Table of Contents
- Index

- 9510 Public Assistance Program Administration and Appeals
- 9510.1 Coordination Requirements for Public Assistance and Fire Management Assistance Program Documentation (1/9/01) and Appendix (4/17/01)

9520 Public Assistance Eligibility

- 9521 Applicant Eligibility
- 9521.1 Community Center Eligibility (6/19/08), (PDF 3.6MB)
- 9521.2 Private Nonprofit Museum Eligibility (1/14/09), (PDF 490KB)
- 9521.3 Private Nonprofit Facility (PNP) Eligibility (7/18/07), (PDF 3.8MB)
- 9521.4 Administering American Indian and Alaska Native Tribal Government Funding 4/30/07), (PDF 395KB)
- 9521.5 Eligibility of Charter Schools (6/16/06), (PDF 76KB)
- 9522 General Work Eligibility

9523 Emergency Work

- 9523.1 Snow Assistance Policy (11/02/09), (PDF 2MB, TXT 17KB)
- 9523.2 Eligibility of Building Inspections in a Post-Disaster Environment (1/28/08), (PDF 845KB)
- 9523.3 Provision of Temporary Relocation Facilities (7/16/98) Provision of Temporary Relocation Facilities - Waiver Request (11/13/06), (PDF 395KB)
- 9523.4 Demolition of Private Structures (7/18/07), (PDF 1.76MB)
- 9523.5 Debris Removal from Waterways (3/29/10), (PDF 2MB)
- 9523.6 Mutual Aid Agreements for Public Assistance and Fire Management Assistance (8/13/07), (PDF 381KB)
- 9523.7 Public Assistance Funding for Public Housing Facilities (8/13/09), (PDF 422KB)
- 9523.8 Mission Assignments for ESF #10 (6/4/01)
- 9523.9 100% Funding for Direct Federal Assistance and Grant Assistance (6/9/06), (PDF 1.5MB)
- 9523.10 Eligibility of Vector Control (Mosquito Abatement) (9/12/06), (PDF 325KB)
- 9523.11 Hazardous Stump Extraction and Removal Eligibility (5/15/07), (PDF 722KB)
- 9523.12 Debris Operations – Hand-Loaded Trucks and Trailers (5/1/06)
- 9523.13 Debris Removal from Private Property (7/18/07), (PDF 4.4MB)
- 9523.15 Eligible Costs Related to Evacuations and Sheltering (4/6/07), (PDF 374KB)
- 9523.17 Emergency Assistance for Human Influenza Pandemic (11/25/09), (PDF 313KB)
  - En Español (PDF 313KB)
- 9523.18 Host-State Evacuation and Sheltering Reimbursement (7/18/07), (PDF 760KB)
- Host State Policy Clarification Memorandum (8/30/08), (PDF 131KB)
- 9523.19 Eligible Costs Related to Pet Evacuations and Sheltering (10/24/07), (PDF 1.49MB)
- 9523.20 Purchase and Distribution of Ice (8/26/09), (PDF 519KB)

9524 Restoration of Damaged Facilities

- 9524.1 Welded Steel Moment Frame Inspections (11/05/07), (PDF 1.61MB)
- 9524.2 Landslides and Slope Failures (5/23/06), (PDF 249KB)

- 9524.3 Rehabilitation Assistance for Levees and Other Flood Control Works (2/25/09), (PDF 1.15MB) Memo updating Policy 9524.3 - August 5, 2009 (PDF 220 KB, TXT 2.21 KB)
- 9524.4 Repair vs. Replacement of a Facility under 44 CFR §206.226(f) (The 50% Rule) (3/25/09), (PDF 1.42MB)
- 9524.5 Trees, Shrubs and Other Plantings Associated with Facilities (7/18/07), (PDF 660KB)
- 9524.6 Collections and Individual Object Eligibility (6/30/08), (PDF 1.98MB)
- 9524.7 Interim Welded Steel Moment Frame Policy for the Nisqually Earthquake Disaster (6/8/01)
- 9524.8 Eligibility for Permanent Repair and Replacement of Roads on Tribal Lands (7/24/07), (PDF 813KB)
- 9524.9 Replacement of Animals Associated with Eligible Facilities (8/18/08), (PDF 1.05MB)
- 9524.10 Replacement of Equipment, Supplies and Vehicles (PDF 753KB, TXT 4KB)

9525 Allowable Costs

- 9525.1 Post Disaster Property Tax Assessment (12/12/07), (PDF 535KB)
- 9525.2 Donated Resources (4/9/07), (PDF 314KB)
- 9525.3 Duplication of Benefits - Non-Government Funds (7/24/07), (PDF 989KB)
- 9525.4 Emergency Medical Care and Medical Evacuations (7/16/08), (PDF 1.53MB)
- 9525.5 Americans with Disabilities Act (ADA) Access Requirements (10/26/00)
- 9525.6 Project Supervision and Management Costs of Subgrantees (4/22/01)
- 9525.7 Labor Costs - Emergency Work (11/16/06), (PDF 1.1MB)
- 9525.8 Damage to Applicant Owned Equipment (12/17/08), (PDF 892KB)
- 9525.9 Section 324 Management Costs and Direct Administrative Costs (3/12/08), (PDF 2.6MB)
- 9525.11 Payment of Contractors for Grant Management Tasks (4/22/01)
- 9525.12 Disposition of Equipment, Supplies and Salvageable Materials (7/14/08), (PDF 1.13MB)
- 9525.13 Alternate Projects (8/22/08), (PDF 1.90MB)
- 9525.14 Public Assistance Grantee Administrative Costs (11/7/06), (PDF 101KB)
- 9525.15 Telecommunications Support Lines for States (7/11/00)
- 9525.16 Research-related Equipment and Furnishings (5/4/07), (PDF 433KB)

9526 Mitigation

- 9526.1 Hazard Mitigation Funding Under Section 406 (Stafford Act) (3/30/10), (PDF 3.3MB)
- 9527 Codes and Standards
- 9527.1 Seismic Safety - New Construction (11/21/07), (PDF 897KB)
- 9527.4 Construction Codes and Standards (2/5/08), (PDF 3.74MKB)

- 9528 (Reserved)
- 9529 (Reserved)

9530 Public Assistance Insurance Requirements

- 9530.1 Retroactive Application of a Letter of Map Amendment (LOMA) or a Letter of Map Revision (LOMR) to Infrastructure Grants (1/2/09), (PDF 1.19MB)

- 9540 (Reserved)
- 9550 Fire Suppression Assistance

9560 Historic Preservation, Cultural Initiatives, Other Related Laws

- 9560.1 Environmental Policy Memoranda (8/17/99)
- 9560.3 Programmatic Agreement - Historic Review (5/29/02)
- 9570 Standard Operating Procedures (limited distribution of hard copy - separate filing)
- 9580 Job Aids and Fact Sheets (limited distribution of hard copy - separate filing)
- 9580.2 Fact Sheet: Insurance Responsibilities For Field Personnel (6/4/07), (PDF 1.39MB)
- 9580.3 Fact Sheet: Insurance Considerations For Applicants (5/29/08), (PDF 1.52MB, TXT 11KB)
- 9580.4 Fact Sheet: Debris Operations - Clarification (10/23/08)
- 9580.5 Fact Sheet: Elements of a Project Worksheet (12/17/08), (PDF 1.42MB)
- 9580.6 Electric Utility Repair (9/22/09), (PDF 2MB, TXT 21KB)
- 9580.8 Eligible Sand Replacement on Public Beaches (10/1/09), (PDF 954KB, TXT 9KB)
- 9580.100 Fact Sheet: Mold Remediation (11/7/06), (PDF 1.4MB)
- 9580.101 2006 Special Community Disaster Loan Program (8/21/06), (PDF 136KB)
- 9580.102 Fact Sheet: Permanent Relocation (11/2/06), (PDF 1.0MB) Permanent Relocation Fact Sheet Clarification Memorandum (5/29/07), (PDF 318KB)
- 9580.103 Fact Sheet: GSA Disaster Recovery Purchasing Program (7/7/08), (PDF 1.19MB)
- 9580.104 Fact Sheet: Public Assistance for Ambulance Services (1/2/09), (PDF 1.03MB)
- 9580.105 H1N1 Influenza Frequently Asked Questions (FAQs) (11/25/09), (PDF 1.2MB)
  - En Español (PDF 1.2MB)
- 9580.106 Fact Sheet: Pandemic Influenza Fact Sheet (11/25/09), (PDF 1MB)
  - En Español (PDF 1MB)
- 9580.107 Child Care Services (PDF 1MB, TXT 4KB)
- 9580.201 Fact Sheet: Debris Removal - Applicant's Contracting Checklist (4/10/06), (PDF 40KB)
- 9580.202 Fact Sheet: Debris Removal - Authorities of Federal Agencies (1/27/07), (PDF 333KB)
- 9580.203 Fact Sheet: Debris Monitoring (5/3/07), (PDF 370KB)
- 9580.204 Documenting and Validating Hazardous Trees, Limbs and Stumps (08/02/09), (PDF 2MB, TXT 21KB)
- 9580.205 Fact Sheet: Public Assistance Funding for Public Housing Facilities (06/15/10), (PDF 473KB, TXT 3KB)

HAZUS-MH[89] [FEMA's Software Program for Estimating Potential Losses from Disasters]

The **Hazards U.S. Multi-Hazard (HAZUS-MH)** is a nationally applicable standardized methodology that estimates potential losses from earthquakes, hurricane winds, and floods. HAZUS-MH was developed by the Federal Emergency Management Agency (FEMA) under contract with the National Institute of Building Sciences (NIBS).

---

[89] http://www.fema.gov/hazus#1

HAZUS-MH uses state-of-the-art Geographic Information Systems (GIS) software to map and display hazard data and the results of damage and economic loss estimates for buildings and infrastructure. It also allows users to estimate the impacts of earthquakes, hurricane winds, and floods on populations.

Estimating losses is essential to decision-making at all levels of government, providing a basis for developing mitigation plans and policies, emergency preparedness, and response and n HAZUS-MH, current scientific and engineering knowledge is coupled with the latest geographic information systems (GIS) technology to produce estimates of hazard-related damage before, or after, a disaster occurs.

Potential loss estimates analyzed in HAZUS-MH include:

- **Physical damage** to residential and commercial buildings, schools, critical facilities, and infrastructure;
- **Economic loss**, including lost jobs, business interruptions, repair and reconstruction costs; and
- **Social impacts**, including estimates of shelter requirements, displaced households, and population exposed to scenario floods, earthquakes and hurricanes.

Federal, state and local government agencies and the private sector can download the latest version of Hazus free-of-charge online by visiting the FEMA Flood Map Service Center (MSC).

Hazus software is available to download online. Users may visit the MSC to download Hazus software and state datasets. The online download option is only available to US users. International users will continue to order a Hazus DVD by contacting the FEMA Map Information eXchange (FMIX) at 1-877-336-2627 or FEMAMapSpecialist@riskmapcds.com.)

Small Business Administration

Disaster Recovery Plan, 2012

http://www.sba.gov/sites/default/files/Disaster%20Recovery%20Plan%202012.pdf

This Handbook sets forth the SBA's disaster response plan to aid individuals and businesses.

SBA's Disaster Preparedness and Recovery Plan (DPRP) supports the following outcomes:

> Processes coordinated with federal guidance and protocols for preparedness (e.g., the National Response Framework (NRF) and the National Disaster Recovery Framework (NDRF)).

> A customer-focused, transparent, outcome-driven model of performance. Timely decision-making and available resources (human capital, facilities, technology, and partnerships) throughout the Disaster Loan Making (DLM) process.

> Support of long-term economic recovery by providing access to capital, counseling, and contracting services for disaster victims to rebuild and withstand economic injury.

James L. Jaffe, J.D.

Social Media sites that can be used before during and after a disaster

Facebook

- FEMA: http://www.facebook.com/FEMA
- NOAA: http://www.facebook.com/usnoaagov
- U.S. National Hurricane Center http://www.facebook.com/US.NOAA.NationalHurricaneCenter.gov
- The Salvation Army: http://www.facebook.com/SalvationArmyUSA
- American Red Cross: http://www.facebook.com/redcross

Twitter

- FEMA: www.twitter.com/fema
- NEMA: www.twitter.com/nema_web
- NOAA: www.twitter.com/usnoaagov
- U.S. National Hurricane Center (Atlantic): www.twitter.com/nhc_atlantic
- U.S. National Hurricane Center (Pacific): www.twitter.com/NHC_Pacific
- The Salvation Army: www.twitter.com/salvationarmy
- American Red Cross: www.twitter.com/redcross

An internet recruiting tool for more than 90,000 nonprofit organizations.... http://www.volunteermatch.org/about/

Miscellaneous

A good general website for homeowners and small businesses on how to plan for disasters that are most likely to occur in a specific area (by zip code): http://www.disastersafety.org/

The National Association of States United for Aging and Disabilities (NASUAD) has an excellent web site containing a list of links for Disaster Planning and recovery. The web site is http://www.nasuad.org/I_R/disaster_preparedness_guide/anticipating.html

The United States government has a new web portal for disaster information and disaster relief applications. http://www.disasterassistance.gov/daip_en.portal

To volunteer to help in disaster recovery go to: http://www.nvoad.org/
It is the web site of the National Voluntary Organizations Active in Disasters (VOAD).

National Weather Service National hurricane Center.................................... http://www.nhc.noaa.gov/
About Storm Surges......................http://www.nws.noaa.gov/os/hurricane/resources/surge_intro.pdf
Make a Plan..http://www.ready.gov/make-a-plan
FEMA Family Emergency Plan Form........http://www.ready.gov/sites/default/files/FamEmePlan_2012.pdf
Federal Government Data of all sorts... http://www.data.gov/

FEMA Hurricane Response web site:
http://www.fema.gov/hazard/hurricane/

The web site contains a list of FEMA resources to assist with recovery as well as mitigation efforts. This is an excellent site has links to information on what to do before, during and after a hurricane.

Before a Hurricane

To prepare for a hurricane, you should take the following measures:

- To begin preparing, you should build an emergency kit and make a family communications plan.
- Know your surroundings.
- Learn the elevation level of your property and whether the land is flood-prone. This will help you know how your property will be affected when storm surge or tidal flooding are forecasted.
- Identify levees and dams in your area and determine whether they pose a hazard to you.
- Learn community hurricane evacuation routes and how to find higher ground. Determine where you would go and how you would get there if you needed to evacuate.
- Make plans to secure your property:
- Cover all of your home's windows. Permanent storm shutters offer the best protection for windows. A second option is to board up windows with 5/8" marine plywood, cut to fit and ready to install. Tape does not prevent windows from breaking.
- Install straps or additional clips to securely fasten your roof to the frame structure. This will reduce roof damage.
- Be sure trees and shrubs around your home are well trimmed so they are more wind resistant.
- Clear loose and clogged rain gutters and downspouts.
- Reinforce your garage doors; if wind enters a garage it can cause dangerous and expensive structural damage.
- Plan to bring in all outdoor furniture, decorations, garbage cans and anything else that is not tied down.
- Determine how and where to secure your boat.
- Install a generator for emergencies.
- If in a high-rise building, be prepared to take shelter on or below the 10th floor.
- Consider building a safe room.

Hurricanes cause heavy rains that can cause extensive flood damage in coastal and inland areas. Everyone is at risk and should consider flood insurance protection. Flood insurance is the only way to financially protect your property or business from flood damage.

To learn more about your flooding risk and how to protect yourself and your business, visit the Federal Insurance and Mitigation Administration (NFIP) Web site, www.floodsmart.gov or call 1-800-427-2419.

During a Hurricane

If a hurricane is likely in your area, you should:

- Listen to the radio or TV for information.
- Secure your home, close storm shutters and secure outdoor objects or bring them indoors.
- Turn off utilities if instructed to do so. Otherwise, turn the refrigerator thermostat to its coldest setting and keep its doors closed.
- Turn off propane tanks
- Avoid using the phone, except for serious emergencies.
- Moor your boat if time permits.
- Ensure a supply of water for sanitary purpose such as cleaning and flushing toilets. Fill the bathtub and other larger containers with water.
- Find out how to keep food safe during and after and emergency.

You should evacuate under the following conditions:

- If you are directed by local authorities to do so. Be sure to follow their instructions.
- If you live in a mobile home or temporary structure – such shelter are particularly hazardous during hurricane no matter how well fastened to the ground.
- If you live in a high-rise building – hurricane winds are stronger at higher elevations.
- If you live on the coast, on a floodplain, near a river, or on an island waterway.

Read more about evacuating yourself and your family. If you are unable to evacuate, go to your wind-safe room. If you do not have one, follow these guidelines:

- Stay indoors during the hurricane and away from windows and glass doors.
- Close all interior doors – secure and brace external doors.
- Keep curtains and blinds closed. Do not be fooled if there is a lull; it could be the eye of the storm – winds will pick up again.
- Take refuge in a small interior room, closet or hallway on the lowest level.
- Lie on the floor under a table or another sturdy object.
- Avoid elevators.

After a Hurricane

- Continue listening to a NOAA Weather Radio or the local news for the latest updates.
- Stay alert for extended rainfall and subsequent flooding even after the hurricane or tropical storm has ended.
- If you have become separated from your family, use your family communications plan or contact the American Red Cross at 1-800-RED-CROSS/1-800-733-2767 or visit the American Red Cross Safe and Well site:www.safeandwell.org
  o The American Red Cross also maintains a database to help you find family. Contact the local American Red Cross chapter where you are staying for information. Do not contact the chapter in the disaster area.
- If you evacuated, return home only when officials say it is safe.
- If you cannot return home and have immediate housing needs. Text **SHELTER** + your ZIP code to **43362** (4FEMA) to find the nearest shelter in your area (example: *shelter 12345*).
- For those who have longer-term housing needs, FEMA offers several types of assistance, including services and grants to help people repair their homes and find replacement housing. Apply for assistance or search for information about housing rental resources
- Drive only if necessary and avoid flooded roads and washed¬ out bridges. Stay off the streets. If you must go out watch for fallen objects; downed electrical wires; and weakened walls, bridges, roads, and sidewalks.
- Keep away from loose or dangling power lines and report them immediately to the power company.
- Walk carefully around the outside your home and check for loose power lines, gas leaks and structural damage before entering.
- Stay out of any building if you smell gas, floodwaters remain around the building or your home was damaged by fire and the authorities have not declared it safe.
- Inspect your home for damage. Take pictures of damage, both of the building and its contents, for insurance purposes. If you have any doubts about safety, have your residence inspected by a qualified building inspector or structural engineer before entering.
- Use battery-powered flashlights in the dark. Do NOT use candles. Note: The flashlight

should be turned on outside before entering - the battery may produce a spark that could ignite leaking gas, if present.
- Watch your pets closely and keep them under your direct control. Watch out for wild animals, especially poisonous snakes. Use a stick to poke through debris.
- Avoid drinking or preparing food with tap water until you are sure it's not contaminated.
- Check refrigerated food for spoilage. If in doubt, throw it out.
- Wear protective clothing and be cautious when cleaning up to avoid injury.
- Use the telephone only for emergency calls.
- **NEVER** use a generator inside homes, garages, crawlspaces, sheds, or similar areas, even when using fans or opening doors and windows for ventilation. Deadly levels of carbon monoxide can quickly build up in these areas and can linger for hours, even after the generator has shut off.

<u>FEMA Tornado Response and Recovery web site</u>: http://www.ready.gov/tornadoes

The web site contains a list of FEMA resources to assist with recovery as well as mitigation efforts. This is an excellent site has links to information on what to do before, during and after a tornado.

Before a Tornado

Preparing for a Tornado

- To begin preparing, you should build an emergency kit and make a family communications plan.
- Learn about the emergency plans that have been established in your area by your state and local government. In any emergency, always listen to the instructions given by local emergency management officials.
- Listen to NOAA Weather Radio or to commercial radio or television newscasts for the latest information. In any emergency, always listen to the instructions given by local emergency management officials.
- Be alert to changing weather conditions. Look for approaching storms.
- Look for the following danger signs:
  o Dark, often greenish sky
  o Large hail
  o A large, dark, low-lying cloud (particularly if rotating)
  o Loud roar, similar to a freight train.
  o If you see approaching storms or any of the danger signs, be prepared to take shelter immediately.

Build a Safe Room

Extreme windstorms in many parts of the country pose a serious threat to buildings and their occupants. Your residence may be built "to code" but that does not mean it can withstand winds from extreme events such as tornadoes and major hurricanes. The purpose of a safe room or a wind shelter is to provide a space where you and your family can seek refuge that provides a high level of protection. You can build a safe room in one of several places in your home.

- Your basement
- Atop a concrete slab-on-grade foundation or garage floor.
- An interior room on the first floor.

Safe rooms built below ground level provide the greatest protection, but a safe room built in a first-floor interior room also can provide the necessary protection. Below-ground safe rooms must be designed to avoid accumulating water during the heavy rains that often accompany severe windstorms.

To protect its occupants, a safe room must be built to withstand high winds and flying debris, even if the rest of the residence is severely damaged or destroyed. Consider the following when building a safe room:

- The safe room must be adequately anchored to resist overturning and uplift.
- The walls, ceiling and door of the shelter must withstand wind pressure and resist penetration by windborne objects and falling debris.
- The connections between all parts of the safe room must be strong enough to resist the wind.
- Sections of either interior or exterior residence walls that are used as walls of the safe room must be separated from the structure of the residence so that damage to the residence will not cause damage to the safe room.

Additional information about Safe Rooms available from FEMA:

- *Taking Shelter from the Storm: Building a Safe Room Inside Your House.* FEMA L-233. Brochure providing details about obtaining information about how to build a wind-safe room to withstand tornado, hurricane and other high winds.
- *Taking Shelter from the Storm: Building a Safe Room Inside Your House.* FEMA L-320. Manual with detailed information about how to build a wind-safe room to withstand tornado, hurricane and other high winds.

Monitoring Tornadoes

The National Oceanic and Atmospheric Administration (NOAA) National Weather Service (NWS) provides weather, hydrologic, and climate forecasts and warnings to the United States.

- Storm Prediction Center
  http://www.spc.noaa.gov/
- StormReady
  http://www.stormready.noaa.gov/
- NOAA Weather Radio
  http://www.nws.noaa.gov/nwr/
- Emergency Alert System
  http://transition.fcc.gov/pshs/services/eas/

During a Tornado

If you are under a tornado warning, seek shelter immediately! Most injuries associated with high winds are from flying debris, so remember to protect your head.

IF YOU ARE IN:	THEN:
A structure (e.g. residence, small building, school, nursing home, hospital, factory, shopping center, high-rise building)	• Go to a pre-designated shelter area such as a safe room, basement, storm cellar, or the lowest building level. If there is no basement, go to the center of an interior room on the lowest level (closet, interior hallway) away from corners, windows, doors, and outside walls. Put as many walls as possible between you and the outside. Get under a sturdy table and use your arms to protect your head and neck. • In a high-rise building, go to a small interior room or hallway on the lowest floor possible. • Put on sturdy shoes. • Do not open windows.
A trailer or mobile home	• Get out immediately and go to the lowest floor of a sturdy, nearby building or a storm shelter. Mobile homes, even if tied down, offer little protection from tornadoes.

IF YOU ARE IN:	THEN:
The outside with no shelter	• Immediately get into a vehicle, buckle your seat belt and try to drive to the closest sturdy shelter. If your vehicle is hit by flying debris while you are driving, pull over and park. • Stay in the car with the seat belt on. Put your head down below the windows; cover your head with your hands and a blanket, coat or other cushion if possible. • If you can safely get noticeably lower than the level of the roadway, leave your car and lie in that area, covering your head with your hands. Do not get under an overpass or bridge. You are safer in a low, flat location. • Never try to outrun a tornado in urban or congested areas in a car or truck. Instead, leave the vehicle immediately for safe shelter. • Watch out for flying debris. Flying debris from tornadoes causes most fatalities and injuries.

After a Tornado

Injury may result from the direct impact of a tornado or it may occur afterward when people walk among debris and enter damaged buildings. A study of injuries after a tornado in Marion, Illinois, showed that 50 percent of the tornado-related injuries were suffered during rescue attempts, cleanup and other post-tornado activities. Nearly a third of the injuries resulted from stepping on nails. Because tornadoes often damage power lines, gas lines or electrical systems, there is a risk of fire, electrocution or an explosion. Protecting yourself and your family requires promptly treating any injuries suffered during the storm and using extreme care to avoid further hazards.

Injuries

Check for injuries. Do not attempt to move seriously injured people unless they are in immediate danger of further injury. Get medical assistance immediately. If someone has stopped breathing, begin CPR if you are trained to do so. Stop a bleeding injury by applying direct pressure to the wound. Have any puncture wound evaluated by a physician. If you are trapped, try to attract attention to your location.

General Safety Precautions

- Here are some safety precautions that could help you avoid injury after a tornado:
- Continue to monitor your battery-powered radio or television for emergency information.
- Be careful when entering any structure that has been damaged.
- Wear sturdy shoes or boots, long sleeves and gloves when handling or walking on or near debris.
- Be aware of hazards from exposed nails and broken glass.
- Do not touch downed power lines or objects in contact with downed lines. Report electrical hazards to the police and the utility company.
- Use battery-powered lanterns, if possible, rather than candles to light homes without electrical power. If you use candles, make sure they are in safe holders away from curtains, paper, wood or other flammable items. Never leave a candle burning when you are out of the room.

- Never use generators, pressure washers, grills, camp stoves or other gasoline, propane, natural gas or charcoal-burning devices inside your home, basement, garage or camper - or even outside near an open window, door or vent. Carbon monoxide (CO) - an odorless, colorless gas that can cause sudden illness and death if you breathe it - from these sources can build up in your home, garage or camper and poison the people and animals inside. Seek prompt medical attention if you suspect CO poisoning and are feeling dizzy, light-headed or nauseated.
- Hang up displaced telephone receivers that may have been knocked off by the tornado, but stay off the telephone, except to report an emergency.
- Cooperate fully with public safety officials.
- Respond to requests for volunteer assistance by police, fire fighters, emergency management and relief organizations, but do not go into damaged areas unless assistance has been requested. Your presence could hamper relief efforts and you could endanger yourself.

Inspecting The Damage

- After a tornado, be aware of possible structural, electrical or gas-leak hazards in your home. Contact your local city or county building inspectors for information on structural safety codes and standards. They may also offer suggestions on finding a qualified contractor to do work for you.
- In general, if you suspect any damage to your home, shut off electrical power, natural gas and propane tanks to avoid fire, electrocution or explosions.
- If it is dark when you are inspecting your home, use a flashlight rather than a candle or torch to avoid the risk of fire or explosion in a damaged home.
- If you see frayed wiring or sparks, or if there is an odor of something burning, you should immediately shut off the electrical system at the main circuit breaker if you have not done so already.
- If you smell gas or suspect a leak, turn off the main gas valve, open all windows and leave the house immediately. Notify the gas company, the police or fire departments, or State Fire Marshal's office and do not turn on the lights, light matches, smoke or do anything that could cause a spark. Do not return to your house until you are told it is safe to do so.

Safety During Clean Up

- Wear sturdy shoes or boots, long sleeves and gloves.
- Learn proper safety procedures and operating instructions before operating any gas-powered or electric-powered saws or tools.

Clean up spilled medicines, drugs, flammable liquids and other potentially hazardous materials.

FEMA Earthquake Response and Recovery web site: http://www.fema.gov/earthquake

The web site contains a list of FEMA resources to assist with recovery as well as mitigation efforts. This is an excellent site has links to information on what to do before, during and after an earthquake

Before an Earthquake

- The following are things you can do to protect yourself, your family and your property in the event of an earthquake.
- To begin preparing, you should build an emergency kit and make a family communications plan.
- Fasten shelves securely to walls.
- Place large or heavy objects on lower shelves.
- Store breakable items such as bottled foods, glass, and china in low, closed cabinets with latches.

- Fasten heavy items such as pictures and mirrors securely to walls and away from beds, couches and anywhere people sit.
- Brace overhead light fixtures and top heavy objects.
- Repair defective electrical wiring and leaky gas connections. These are potential fire risks. Get appropriate professional help. Do not work with gas or electrical lines yourself.
- Install flexible pipe fittings to avoid gas or water leaks. Flexible fittings are more resistant to breakage.
- Secure your water heater, refrigerator, furnace and gas appliances by strapping them to the wall studs and bolting to the floor. If recommended by your gas company, have an automatic gas shut-off valve installed that is triggered by strong vibrations.
- Repair any deep cracks in ceilings or foundations. Get expert advice if there are signs of structural defects.
- Be sure the residence is firmly anchored to its foundation.
- Store weed killers, pesticides, and flammable products securely in closed cabinets with latches and on bottom shelves.
- Locate safe spots in each room under a sturdy table or against an inside wall. Reinforce this information by moving to these places during each drill.

Hold earthquake drills with your family members: Drop, cover and hold on.

During an Earthquake

Drop, cover and Hold On. Minimize your movements to a few steps to a nearby safe place and if you are indoors, stay there until the shaking has stopped and you are sure exiting is safe.

If Indoors

- DROP to the ground; take COVER by getting under a sturdy table or other piece of furniture; and HOLD ON until the shaking stops. If there isn't a table or desk near you, cover your face and head with your arms and crouch in an inside corner of the building.
- Stay away from glass, windows, outside doors and walls, and anything that could fall, such as lighting fixtures or furniture.
- Stay in bed if you are there when the earthquake strikes. Hold on and protect your head with a pillow, unless you are under a heavy light fixture that could fall. In that case, move to the nearest safe place.
- Do not use a doorway except if you know it is a strongly supported, load-bearing doorway and it is close to you. Many inside doorways are lightly constructed and do not offer protection..
- Stay inside until the shaking stops and it is safe to go outside. Do not exit a building during the shaking. Research has shown that most injuries occur when people inside buildings attempt to move to a different location inside the building or try to leave.
- DO NOT use the elevators.

Be aware that the electricity may go out or the sprinkler systems or fire alarms may turn on.

If Outdoors

- Stay there.
- Move away from buildings, streetlights, and utility wires.

Once in the open, stay there until the shaking stops. The greatest danger exists directly outside buildings, at exits and alongside exterior walls. Many of the 120 fatalities from the 1933 Long Beach earthquake occurred when people ran outside of buildings only to be killed by falling debris from collapsing walls. Ground movement during an earthquake is seldom the direct cause of death or injury. Most earthquake-related casualties result from collapsing walls, flying glass, and falling objects.

If in a Moving Vehicle

- Stop as quickly as safety permits and stay in the vehicle. Avoid stopping near or under buildings, trees, overpasses, and utility wires.
- Proceed cautiously once the earthquake has stopped. Avoid roads, bridges, or ramps that might have been damaged by the earthquake.

If Trapped Under Debris

- Do not light a match.
- Do not move about or kick up dust.
- Cover your mouth with a handkerchief or clothing.

Tap on a pipe or wall so rescuers can locate you. Use a whistle if one is available. Shout only as a last resort. Shouting can cause you to inhale dangerous amounts of dust.

After an Earthquake

- When the shaking stops, look around to make sure it is safe to move. Then exit the building.
- Expect aftershocks. These secondary shockwaves are usually less violent than the main quake but can be strong enough to do additional damage to weakened structures and can occur in the first hours, days, weeks, or even months after the quake.
- Help injured or trapped persons. Remember to help your neighbors who may require special assistance such as infants, the elderly and people with access and functional needs. Give first aid where appropriate. Do not move seriously injured persons unless they are in immediate danger of further injury. Call for help.
- Look for and extinguish small fires. Fire is the most common hazard after an earthquake.
- Listen to a battery-operated radio or television for the latest emergency information.
- Be aware of possible tsunamis if you live in coastal areas. These are also known as seismic sea waves (mistakenly called "tidal waves"). When local authorities issue a tsunami warning, assume that a series of dangerous waves is on the way. Stay away from the beach.
- Use the telephone only for emergency calls.
- Go to a designated public shelter if your home had been damaged and is no longer safe. Text **SHELTER** + your ZIP code to **43362** (4FEMA) to find the nearest shelter in your area (example: *shelter 12345*).
- Stay away from damaged areas. Stay away unless your assistance has been specifically requested by police, fire, or relief organizations. Return home only when authorities say it is safe.
- Be careful when driving after an earthquake and anticipate traffic light outages.
- After it is determined that its' safe to return, your safety should be your primary priority as you begin clean up and recovery.
- Open cabinets cautiously. Beware of objects that can fall off shelves.
- Find out how to keep food safe during and after and emergency by visiting :http://www.foodsafety.gov/keep/emergency/index.html
- Put on long pants, a long-sleeved shirt, sturdy shoes and work gloves to protect against injury from broken objects.
- Clean up spilled medicines, bleaches, gasoline or other flammable liquids immediately. Leave the area if you smell gas or fumes from other chemicals.
- Inspect the entire length of chimneys for damage. Unnoticed damage could lead to a fire.
    - Inspect utilities.
    - Check for gas leaks. If you smell gas or hear blowing or hissing noise, open a window and quickly leave the building. Turn

off the gas at the outside main valve if you can and call the gas company from a neighbor's home. If you turn off the gas for any reason, it must be turned back on by a professional.
- ○ Look for electrical system damage. If you see sparks or broken or frayed wires, or if you smell hot insulation, turn off the electricity at the main fuse box or circuit breaker. If you have to step in water to get to the fuse box or circuit breaker, call an electrician first for advice.
- ○ Check for sewage and water lines damage. If you suspect sewage lines are damaged, avoid using the toilets and call a plumber. If water pipes are damaged, contact the water company and avoid using water from the tap. You can obtain safe water by melting ice cubes.

For additional information

- *Avoiding Earthquake Damage: A Checklist for Homeowners.* Safety tips for before, during and after an earthquake.

- How to Guides to Protect Your Property or Business from Earthquakes. Available online athttp://www.fema.gov/library/viewRecord.do?id=3260

FEMA Wildfire Response and Recovery web site: http://www.ready.gov/wildfires

The web site contains a list of FEMA resources to assist with recovery as well as mitigation efforts. This is an excellent site has links to information on what to do before, during and after an earthquake

An excellent publication on wildfire safety is a FEMA publication *Wildfires: Are You Prepared*. L-203. Wildfire safety tips, preparedness and mitigation techniques. http://www.usfa.fema.gov/downloads/pdf/publications/fa-287-508.pdf

Before a Wildfire

- The following are things you can do to protect yourself, your family and your property in the event of a fire.
- To begin preparing, you should build an emergency kit and make a family communications plan.
- Design and landscape your home with wildfire safety in mind. Select materials and plants that can help contain fire rather than fuel it.
- Use fire-resistant or noncombustible materials on the roof and exterior structure of the dwelling, or treat wood or combustible material used in roofs, siding, decking or trim with fire-retardant chemicals evaluated by a nationally recognized laboratory, such as Underwriters Laboratories (UL).
- Plant fire-resistant shrubs and trees. For example, hardwood trees are less flammable than pine, evergreen, eucalyptus or fir trees.
- Regularly clean roof and gutters.
- Inspect chimneys at least twice a year. Clean them at least once a year. Keep the dampers in good working order. Equip chimneys and stovepipes with a spark arrester that meets the requirements of National Fire Protection Association Standard 211. (Contact your local fire department for exact specifications.)
- Use 1/8-inch mesh screen beneath porches, decks, floor areas, and the home itself. Also, screen openings to floors, roof and attic.
- Install a dual-sensor smoke alarm on each level of your home, especially near bedrooms; test monthly and change the batteries at least once each year.
- Teach each family member how to use a fire extinguisher (ABC type) and show them where it's kept.

- Keep handy household items that can be used as fire tools: a rake, axe, handsaw or chain saw, bucket and shovel.
- Keep a ladder that will reach the roof.
- Consider installing protective shutters or heavy fire-resistant drapes.
- Clear items that will burn from around the house, including wood piles, lawn furniture, barbecue grills, tarp coverings, etc. Move them outside of your defensible space.

Plan Your Water Needs

- Identify and maintain an adequate outside water source such as a small pond, cistern, well, swimming pool, or hydrant.
- Have a garden hose that is long enough to reach any area of the home and other structures on the property.
- Install freeze-proof exterior water outlets on at least two sides of the home and near other structures on the property. Install additional outlets at least 50 feet from the home.
- Consider obtaining a portable gasoline powered pump in case electrical power is cut off.

Your best resource for proper planning is www.firewise.org which has outstanding information used daily by residents, property owners, fire departments, community planners, builders, public policy officials, water authorities, architects and others to assure safety from fire - it really works. Firewise workshops are offered for free all across the nation in communities large and small and free Firewise materials can be obtained easily by anyone interested.

During a Wildfire

If advised to evacuate, do so immediately. Take your disaster supply kit, lock your home and choose a route away from the fire hazard. Watch for changes in the speed and direction of the fire and smoke. Tell someone when you left and where you are going.

If you see a wildfire and haven't received evacuation orders yet, call 9-1-1. Don't assume that someone else has already called. Describe the location of the fire, speak slowly and clearly, and answer any questions asked by the dispatcher.

- If you are not ordered to evacuate, and have time to prepare your home, FEMA recommends you take the following actions:
- Arrange temporary housing at a friend or relative's home outside the threatened area in case you need to evacuate.
- Wear protective clothing when outside – sturdy shoes, cotton or woolen clothes, long pants, a long-sleeved shirt, gloves and a handkerchief to protect your face.
- Gather fire tools such as a rake, axe, handsaw or chainsaw, bucket and shovel.
- Close outside attic, eaves and basement vents, windows, doors, pet doors, etc. Remove flammable drapes and curtains. Close all shutters, blinds or heavy non-combustible window coverings to reduce radiant heat.
- Close all doors inside the house to prevent draft. Open the damper on your fireplace, but close the fireplace screen.
- Shut off any natural gas, propane or fuel oil supplies at the source.
- Connect garden hoses to outdoor water faucet and fill any pools, hot tubs, garbage cans, tubs or other large containers with water.
- Place lawn sprinklers on the roof and near above-ground fuel tanks. Leave sprinklers on and dowsing these structures as long as possible.
- If you have gas-powered pumps for water, make sure they are fueled and ready.
- Place a ladder against the house in clear view.
- Disconnect any automatic garage door openers so that doors can still be opened by hand if the power goes out. Close all garage doors.
- Place valuable papers, mementos and anything "you can't live without" inside the car in the garage, ready for quick departure. Any pets still with you should also be put in the car.

- Place valuables that will not be damaged by water in a pool or pond.
- Move flammable furniture into the center of the residence away from the windows and sliding-glass doors.
- Turn on outside lights and leave a light on in every room to make the house more visible in heavy smoke.

Surviving a Wildfire

Survival in a Vehicle

- This is dangerous and should only be done in an emergency, but you can survive the firestorm if you stay in your car. It is much less dangerous than trying to run from a fire on foot.
- Roll up windows and close air vents. Drive slowly with headlights on. Watch for other vehicles and pedestrians. Do not drive through heavy smoke.
- If you have to stop, park away from the heaviest trees and brush. Turn headlights on and ignition off. Roll up windows and close air vents.
- Get on the floor and cover up with a blanket or coat.
- Stay in the vehicle until the main fire passes.
- Stay in the car. Do not run! Engine may stall and not restart. Air currents may rock the car. Some smoke and sparks may enter the vehicle. Temperature inside will increase. Metal gas tanks and containers rarely explode.

If You Are Trapped at Home

If you do find yourself trapped by wildfire inside your home, stay inside and away from outside walls. Close doors, but leave them unlocked. Keep your entire family together and remain calm.

If Caught in the Open

- The best temporary shelter is in a sparse fuel area. On a steep mountainside, the back side is safer. Avoid canyons, natural "chimneys" and saddles.
- If a road is nearby, lie face down along the road cut or in the ditch on the uphill side. Cover yourself with anything that will shield you from the fire's heat.
- If hiking in the back country, seek a depression with sparse fuel. Clear fuel away from the area while the fire is approaching and then lie face down in the depression and cover yourself. Stay down until after the fire passes!

After a Wildfire

- The following are guidelines for different circumstances in the period following a fire:
- Go to a designated public shelter if you have been told to evacuate or you feel it is unsafe to remain in your home. Text **SHELTER** + your ZIP code to **43362** (4FEMA) to find the nearest shelter in your area (example: *shelter 12345*).
- If you are with burn victims, or are a burn victim yourself, call 9-1-1 or seek help immediately; cool and cover burns to reduce chance of further injury or infection.
- If you remained at home, check the roof immediately after the fire danger has passed. Put out any roof fires, sparks or embers. Check the attic for hidden burning sparks.
- For several hours after the fire, maintain a "fire watch." Re-check for smoke and sparks throughout the house.
- If you have evacuated, do not enter your home until fire officials say it is safe.
- If a building inspector has placed a color-coded sign on the home, do not enter it until you get more information, advice and instructions about what the sign means and whether it is safe to enter your home.
- If you must leave your home because a building inspector says the building is unsafe, ask someone you trust to watch the property during your absence.

- Use caution when entering burned areas as hazards may still exist, including hot spots, which can flare up without warning.
- If you detect heat or smoke when entering a damaged building, evacuate immediately.
- If you have a safe or strong box, do not try to open it. It can hold intense heat for several hours. If the door is opened before the box has cooled, the contents could burst into flames.
- Avoid damaged or fallen power lines, poles and downed wires.
- Watch for ash pits and mark them for safety—warn family and neighbors to keep clear of the pits also.
- Watch animals closely and keep them under your direct control. Hidden embers and hot spots could burn your pets' paws or hooves.
- Follow public health guidance on safe cleanup of fire ash and safe use of masks.
- Wet debris down to minimize breathing dust particles.
- Wear leather gloves and heavy soled shoes to protect hands and feet.
- Cleaning products, paint, batteries and damaged fuel containers need to be disposed of properly to avoid risk.
- Discard any food that has been exposed to heat, smoke or soot.
- Do **NOT** use water that you think may be contaminated to wash dishes, brush teeth, prepare food, wash hands, make ice or make baby formula.
- Remain calm. Pace yourself. You may find yourself in the position of taking charge of other people. Listen carefully to what people are telling you, and deal patiently with urgent situations first.

Hazards after Wildfires; Floods and Landslides

You may be at an even greater risk of flooding due to recent wildfires that have burned across the region. Large-scale wildfires dramatically alter the terrain and ground conditions. Normally, vegetation absorbs rainfall, reducing runoff. However, wildfires leave the ground charred, barren, and unable to absorb water, creating conditions ripe for flash flooding and mudflow. Flood risk remains significantly higher until vegetation is restored—up to 5 years after a wildfire.

Flooding after fire is often more severe, as debris and ash left from the fire can form mudflows. As rainwater moves across charred and denuded ground, it can also pick up soil and sediment and carry it in a stream of floodwaters. These mudflows can cause significant damage.